# John Hicks

Sir John R. Hicks

with a foreword by **Paul A. Samuelson**

# *K. Puttaswamaiah*
### *editor*

# John
# Hicks

## His Contributions to
## Economic Theory & Application

**Routledge**
Taylor & Francis Group

LONDON AND NEW YORK

First published 2001 by Transaction Publishers

Published 2017 by Routledge
2 Park Square, Milton Park, Abingdon, Oxon OX14 4RN
711 Third Avenue, New York, NY 10017

*Routledge is an imprint of the Taylor and Francis Group, an informa business*

Library of Congress Catalog Number: 00-064785

Library of Congress Cataloging-in-Publication Data

John Hicks: his contributions to economic theory and application / edited by K. Puttaswamaiah ; foreword by Paul A. Samuelson.
    p. cm.
Includes bibliographical references and index.
ISBN 0-7658-0703-3 (pbk : alk. paper)
1. Hicks, John Richard, Sir, 1940- 2. Economists—Great Britain.
3. Consumption (Economics) 4. Capital. 5. Economics
I. Puttaswamaiah, K. II. Samuelson, Paul Anthony, 1915-

HB103.H47 J64 2000
330'.092—dc21

00-064785

ISBN 13: 978-0-7658-0703-8 (pbk)

# CONTENTS

# FOREWORD

J.R. Hicks - - Sir John Hicks - - was the first British economist to receive the Nobel Prize. This was a wise and informed choice, a richly deserved honor. He was one of the great economists of the twentieth century. For more than fifty years numerous important contributions bubbled out from his pen.

Hicks was one of the last of an almost extinct species of scholars: a generalist who covered microeconomics and macroeconomics, mathematical economics and literary economics, pure theory and policy applications. He was part of no school; John Hicks was his own school. Blooming late after taking his Oxford degree, Hicks achieved world notice as part of the early 1930s LSE renaissance under Lionel Robbins: Abba Lerner was his tutee; he married Ursala Webb, one of the young founders of *The Review of Economic Studies*, along with Nicholas Kaldor. Hicks learned much from the mathematically talented R.G.D. Allen and together they made beautiful *avant garde* music. A temperament of no small aspiration, he thought of himself as a rival of Keynes in creating a new less-than-full-employment equilibrium paradigm. And in point of objective fact, with an important assist from Roy Harrod, Hicks did provide the IS-LM graphical diagram of *The General Theory*, which still best serves the realistic macro analysts at century's end. Axel Leijonhufvud, in his 1966 *On Keynesian Economics and the Economics of Keynes,* put forward the thesis that Keynes himself was different from and much greater than his *General Theory* disciples who formalized the 1936 system-Reddaway, Meade, Harrod, Hicks, Lange,.... I believe he got things $180^0$ wrong: what counts in a serious discipline is its formulateable and testable hypotheses and not the elusive intuitions of even the subtlest genius; what economists can and do do with a paradigm is what, in the end, constitutes its pragmatic cash value, plus or minus.

From Hicks' strategic posts at LSE, Cambridge, Manchester and finally at Oxford he influenced three generations of students, drawn from the Empire, America and Asia. Lionel McKenzie, Ian Little, Charles Kennedy and Michio Morishima are only a few of the many names in his seminar circles. At a time when the U.K. was losing its 1900-1930 dominance in economics, Sir John as a lone-wolf researcher kept the flag flying near to the frontier of evolving political economy.

Am I strident in my claims for Hicks, as so to speak the Hayden of political economy? (Hayden wrote more than 100 symphonies, no one of them unworthy of his genius.) Yes, I am. For, as I have written before, Hicks in his own country was not sufficiently appreciated. At LSE where the Marshallian tradition was *not* all dominant, the young Hicks was early much influenced by Knut Wicksell, who at that time had to be read in German or Swedish. It was a happy happenstance to abjure the fading tradition in favor of the rising suns.

A final element of luck enhanced Hicks' total impact on the field. He was privileged to be able to write well and knew how to blow his own horn. His books, ranging from pure theory to a theory of economic history and a beginners' textbook exposition of national income accounting, sold well over a long period of years. It would be unfair to compare Hicks' total impact on the evolution of our subject with that of Harry Johnson who wrote hundreds more papers than Hicks did. A better contrast would be to compare William Fellner, a deep and fertile migrant from Hungary who taught at Yale and Berkeley. Fellner wrote on a number of important topics and with considerable subtlety and novelty, swimming sometimes against the tides of politically-correct post-Keynesian fashion. But he lacked Sir John's facile pen and easy prolific flow. And in consequence the scales of history understandably curtsy down in Hicks' direction.

Readers stand to learn much from the many facets of this important scholar's work as collected together here.

January 5,2000.

Paul A. Samuelson
Institute Professor Emeritus
Department of Economics,
Massachusetts Institute of Technology,
Cambridge, U.S.A.

# PREFACE

The development of economic ideas from ancient to the medieval period, then, ideas during the period of classical economists like Adam Smith, Thomas Robert Malthus, David Ricardo and their critics were a good beginning to thinkers in economics. During the period when capitalism and socialism were the main themes for writers and their critics, it was yet a better period for economists to ponder over new ideas. The *Das Capital* and the Ricardian theories swept all paths and led to the modern period. The works of Ricardo and Marx are the starting milestones and laid the foundation to the present day thoughts, to a large extent. It was during the modern period predominated by the development of the new economic ideas, neoclassical economics and, as an offshoot of that, the recent economic thought, which we may term as *new economics* came to stay. Starting from *Principles of Economics* by Alfred Marshall and *Economic Welfare* by A. C. Pigou, it was J. M. Keynes who through his *General Theory* (1939) tried to influence economics through his various ideas including areas concerning *micro* and *macro* economics, the *Theory of Employment, consumption and investment* and the concept of *marginal efficiency of capital* and many more concepts including *Theory of Price and Trade Cycles*. John Maynard Keynes is, in fact, the important stand point in the annals of modern economic theory.

Later, R. G. Hawtrey, D. H. Robertson and Lord Lionel Robbins tried to develop their own ideas based on the *General Theory*. The *General Equilibrium Theory* was well set by J. M. Keynes and the strength of the English economists lie under the writings of Keynes and his predecessors. *Sir John Hicks was one economist who was considered as the eminent economist in England after J.M.Keynes.* He was undoubtedly the greatest economist after Marshall and Keynes. It is Hicks who gave further orientation to the *General Theory* of Keynes by his wide ranging contributions. He is the first British Economist to win the Nobel Prize in Economic Science (1972) for his wide ranging contributions in general and *Value and Capital* in particular. Hicks shared this Nobel Prize with Prof. Kenneth J. Arrow for his pioneering contributions in the *General Equilibrium Theory and Welfare Theory*. Sir John Hicks has contributed to this fundamental areas in no less a measure.

Prof. Paul A. Samuelson has aptly put it in his paper: *'My John Hicks'* and has said, referring to *Value and Capital* that it "was a major

[xi]

intellectual stimulus for me. I went over his contributions with a powerful microscope, a much more intensive analysis than he ever gave either to my own work or to that of any other economist. That was the way Hicks was. Always he preferred to do things his way. And that was the source both of his creative originality and prolific scientific productivity". He has further said that *"Value and Capital* is a scientific epic saga and a jewel among his works". Prof. Samuelson has further rightly mentioned that: "if J.M. Keynes was the *greatest economist of the World (1936), J.R.Hicks was the greatest young economist of the time"*. Hicks later became one of the greatest economist, in fact, a World economist by his contributions which are listed at the end of this Volume (the list is reprinted from Puttaswamaiah, K. *Nobel Economists – Lives and Contributions*, Vol. I, Ch. VII, pp 333-343). Prof. Samuelson has done much research work on Keynes and his praise on Hicks in his paper and quoted from the *New Palgrave Dictionary of Economics* (1997) – is the real description which one has to keep in mind while recognising Hicks as a British pioneer in new ideas in economics which made him great.

While Prof. Paul A. Samuelson has quoted from Christopher Bliss about *Value and Capital* as above, I am tempted to quote a few more lines from the same source. It is stated that *"Value and Capital* is a work so rich in ideas that a short account of it cannot hope to do it justice. It showed that the basic results of consumer theory could be obtained from ordinal utility; it expounded what became known as the *'Hicksian substitution effect'*, obtained by varying income as relative prices changed so as to maintain an index of utility constant; it developed the parallel results for production theory; and it popularized among English speaking economists the notion of a general equilibrium of markets" (1939, p.60).

The *Value and Capital* (1939, 46) was written when the author was 35 and is described by Prof. Samuelson *"as a scientific epic saga – full of new and beautiful things and a springboard toward future advances"*. The appreciation of the works of Hicks, the first British Nobel Laureate, by Prof. Paul A. Samuelson, the first American Nobel Laureate, has established more credibility in the hard work of Hicks, which, one is afraid, even the British economists have rarely done. It is noteworthy that Prof. Samuelson himself has said "no single misprint mars its mathematical text; and the one major omission in its first edition, he was able to repair by altering a few pages only".

The *Value and Capital* which is undoubtedly the monumental work of Hicks came out as it did just after three years of the publication of the *General Theory* of Keynes which, in fact, revolutionized the entire fabric of economic science and became a starting point for the subsequent micro and macro economic theories in Britain and United States too, thanks to the pioneering efforts by Prof. Paul A. Samuelson, who revolutionized economics and led to further research on the *General Theory* and many others followed. Prof. Samuelson's abiding interest in *General Theory* may be amplified by the fact that when the copies of it were not available, when published, he managed to borrow one from his teacher and summarised it in a few days. The summary prepared in short duration, will certainly have covered the crest areas of Keynes's *'General Theory'* and would be an invaluable piece if that could be traced and printed. He is the first American economist who has evinced such great interest in the works of Keynes and created himself and scope for others a World of research pieces which might be called *"Keynes ramified World created by Professor Samuelson"* and he himself became popular among economists as the *'American Keynes'*. It is with this background that Professor Samuelson took interest in the works of John Hicks and studied them 'microscopically' and appreciated his works and became so intimate that he has aptly given the title *My John Hicks* to his paper.

The idea of bringing out this volume on 'John Hicks' occurred to me because of the following reasons: -

i.    Prof. Hicks, Prof. Ursula Hicks and their family friends and colleagues were known to me eversince 1975 when I started translating *Value and Capital* into an Indian language, and since then, they have been very affectionate;

ii.   Hicks, as a great thinker, by his varied contributions including *Value and Capital* which is termed by one and all as the 'Jewel' of his works was translated by me, published by the University of Mysore and released by Hicks himself in 1979 at the campus of University of Mysore, India;

iii.  Hicks by nature is a brilliant British economist without whose effort the present day economist would not have grown in such dimension by now and the *Value and Capital* is a work which revolutionised the science of economics and, probably, such of these works prompted the Royal Swedish Academy to institute the Nobel Prize to *'Economics'* recognising it as a *'Science'* in 1969;

iv.    Prof. Samuelson has taken very keen interest in the works of Keynes and Hicks and there is no part of Hicks' works which is not touched by him by one way or the other and he has presented his frank and fair views. He has so much of admiration to Hicks that he has titled his paper: '*My John Hicks*';

v.     There was an overwhelming enthusiasm when I requested the Keynesian economists and those who were friends of Hicks, colleagues and students, and they agreed to contribute papers in the areas of Hicks in which they were very familiar and they informed me of the title even before they started writing;

vi.    When I thought of a work on 'John Hicks' and contacted the right men who could contribute, about 25 in number, all of them happily contributed and lent their support to bring out this volume. The authors are very eminent in areas of '*Hicksian Economics*', each one of them specialised in some aspect or the other in the contributions of Hicks;

vii.   Personally, I had become part of Hicks' family and we were in good correspondence till the Hicks Couple passed away; and

viii.  The works of Hicks after Keynes have definitely created land marks which became the basis for further research for economists later and, therefore, the current thinking was felt necessary.

Keeping the above points in view, it was felt necessary to bring out this volume in memory of Hicks, and contrary to expectations, the overwhelming enthusiasm among authors resulted in receiving about 25 papers (all authors requested sent their papers) -depicting various aspects of Hicks's works and personality. Some of the facts contained in the articles, probably may throw new light to economists on the works of Hicks.

Before we go into the details of this '*Contents*' in this book, based on Chapter 7 of Volume 1 of *Nobel Economists – Lives and Contributions* authored by Puttaswamaiah,K., pp.309-343, and '*Foreword*' by *Jan Tinbergen*, the first Nobel Laureate in Economics, I would like to briefly summarise Hicks and his works.

The chief characteristic of Hicks's works was that he moved away from the partial equilibrium approach of Alfred Marshall back towards the older continental Walrasian *General Equilibrium* approach. He also introduced a dynamic dimension with his work on period analysis and his theory of elasticity of expectations. His book *Value and Capital* in which his approach to *general equilibrium theory* really is one of the rarest books in economic science which marked a definite stage in the advance of a science. It may be pertinent to quote that "Everything Prof. Hicks writes bears the hallmark of quality and connoisseures will pick up his book on *Value and Capital* expecting authentic, desiccated thrill which can be got only from the contemplation of abstract reasoning. They will not be disappointed". His work in developing concepts in the theory of value is built on the writings of Edgeworth, Pareto and Slutsky. This led to an original exposition of the roles of income elasticity of the elasticity of substitution in determining the elasticity of demand. He later drew heavily on the great Swedish School, led by Myrdal and Lindhal in working out his ideas on income and the role of expectations. Further, modern and demand theory substitutes indifference curves for marginal utility. More than any other economist, he rehabilitated and extended the indifference curve apparatus. The book contains, in its first 52 pages, the best exposition of contemporary theory.

Before the *General Theory* of Keynes appeared in 1936, Hicks had already acquired the necessary background through his well-known papers. Hicks's reaction to *General Theory* of Keynes was therefore valuable. Hicks in his paper *The General Theory: A First Impression* has approached Keynes's work in a typically Hicksian style. He has said: "The reviewer of this book is best by two contrary temptations. On the one hand, he can accept Mr.Keynes' elaborate disquisition about his own theory, and its place in the development of economics; praising or blaming the alleged more than Jevonian revolution. Or, on the other hand, he can concentrate upon investigating these disquisition, and tracing (perhaps) a pleasing degree of continuity and tradition, surviving the revolution from the *ancient regime.* But it seems better to avoid such questions, and try to consider the new theory on its merits .... The new theory is a theory of employment, in so far as the problem of employment and unemployment is the most urgent practical problem to which this sort of theoretical improvement is relevant". [1]

With the *General Theory* behind him, Hicks completed *Value and Capital*, which may be regarded as his greatest work, perhaps which was

---

[1]Hicks, John, The Economics of John Hicks, Selected and with an Introduction by Dieter Helm, Basil Blackwell, 1984, P. 6.

more successful intellectually.

Harrod wrote in 1939: "Prof. Hicks, his place in the first rank of economic theorists long since secure, establishes by this volume his claim to admission to a narrow circle-the economists with a distinctive and distinguished style of writing. Take up any page of Pigou, Macgregor, Keynes, Robertson; you do not need to be told the author. And, henceforth, I think the Hicks' manner will be unmistakable". [2]

"*Value and Capital* is sometimes misrepresented as an attempt to bridge the gap between micro and macro propositions, in a comparison between it and the *General Theory*. However, a much more reasonable interpretation would be as an attempt to bridge the gap between statics and dynamics, and in particular to extend static methods to dynamic cases. Just as consumer theory had been unrealistic in employing cardinality assumptions, so economic theory was in general unrealistic in being 'out of time'. *Value and Capital* should be perceived more as an attempt to drop the latter assumption".[3]

To quote Dieter Helm, "What did Hicks make of the new theory in his first attempts at reviewing it? Analytically he broke down its components in a fashion that would enable the Keynesian theory to be compared and contrasted with the position that it purported to attack, the Classic view".[4]

F.A.Hayek, has evaluated Hicks *Value and Capital* in the following words: "absolutely first-class work in his time. So far as there is a theory of value proper, which does not extend beyond this and which doesn't really analyze it in terms of directing production, I think it's the final formulation of the theory of value". [5]

Ordinal utility in terms of indifference curves and budget lines could derive the same conclusions as cardinal utility in terms of justifiable marginal utilities. However, the former achieved the ends with greater precision.

Hicks appears to have tacitly accepted Marshall's neglect of the

---

[2] Economic Journal, p.294, Review. Quoted in Hicks, John., *The Economics of John Hicks*, Selected and with an Introduction by Dieter Helm, Basil Blackwell, 1984, p.8.

[3] Hicks, John, *The Economics of John Hicks*, Selected and with an Introduction by Dieter Helm, Basil Blackwell, 1984, p.9.

[4]*Ibid.*, p.6

[5]*Kresge, Stephen and Wenar, Leif, Edited, Hayek on Hayek*-An Autobiographical Dialogue, Routledge, 1994, p.87

income effect so long as the commodity in question forms a small part of the consumer's budget.

The other pioneering works are *The Social Framework* and *A Revision of Demand Theory*. Pigou writing about 'The Social Framework' has said that "beginner coming to this book will find concepts with which he has long been familiar in a vague way clarified and given a more significant meaning and he will also acquire a good deal of actual knowledge. Hicks's experiment is an enterprising and ingenious one'. While praising this book, Harrod has observed that 'it is an introduction to economics written by an economist of the highest calibre. His style is easy and popular.... the presentation is straight forward and dignified'. Hicks explains that the ideas with which economics is concerned are chiefly those which arise, not in connection with one industry only, but with most of all industries, such ideas as capital, income, cost, arise in all business problems-these are the sort of ideas we have particularly to study. Economic theory tends to shape itself into a system of thought, for the questions we want to ask turn out to be inter-related."

His contribution to the *Theory of Trade Cycle* has been regarded as one of the major contributions to trade cycle theory. It is apt to quote. "A beautiful theory of the cycle is here built up with an admirable economy of means.... Undoubtedly a *tour de force*."

His book on *A Revision of Demand Theory* has received academic acclamation, being "A superb exercise to exposition" and "Probably the last word there is to be said on this aspect of demand theory". He explains that the law of demand does apply, with full force, to the behaviour of groups as much as to the behaviour of individuals. The theory of the demand for a single commodity is only the beginning of demand theory. The general theory of demand is a theory of the relation between the set of prices, at which purchases are made, and the set of quantities which are purchased. The foundations of demand theory have deserved careful definition, mainly because we are thereby enabled to get significant results in this wider field also.

The generalised law of demand, when properly stated, is a symmetrical relation between price changes and quantity changes. It can accordingly be interpreted into a "price into quantity" or in a "quantity into price" manner.

In his book on *Essays in World Economics*, the problems of the under-developed countries are discussed. The problem of inflation has also been discussed. The problem is severe in most of the underdeveloped countries. One of the most crucial difficulties of monetary theory is to distinguish between temporary changes in conditions and permanent conditions and to make adjustments that are appropriate to each.

The countries have been classified into two groups viz., manufacturing countries and primary producing countries. The first depending mainly on manufactured exports and the second upon the export of raw materials and foodstuffs. Though the under-developed countries are primary producers, but there are primary producers which are not under-developed. There are countries which have natural resources that are so abundant, relatively to their population, that they can do better by exploiting those resources than they could do if they turned to manufacturing. The under-developed countries are primary producers which are not in this happy position, their natural resources are insufficient for them to be able to achieve a full prosperity by the exploitation of those resources alone. It is futile to tell such countries to rely for development on the further exploitation of their natural resources. Of course they will only harm themselves if they neglect to do what they can in that direction, but they are right in thinking that the only way in which they can break out of their impasse is by industrialising.

In *Capital and growth*, Hicks assumes that prices are determined exogenously. The flex price/fix price bifurcation of markets is adopted. The former refers to the price flexibility of competitive markets; the later to the 'stickness' of prices in some types of markets. This distinction has vital and different implications for stocks and flows. In his analysis of the bond market, Keynes, according to Hicks, realised the essentiality of this distinction. The multiplier process is dependent on supply adjustments in fix price markets.

*Critical Essays in Monetary Theory* is a collection of papers published in journals right from 1935. Though not a monetary economist, the book is the result of his original thinking on the subject. Two of the papers viz., *A Suggestion for Simplifying the Theory of Money* and *Mr.Keynes and the Classics* are well known in the World of economists and monetary thinkers. The book contains gist of the contributions to monetary theory of three economists-Henry Thornton (Paper and Credit), Keynes (Treatise), and Hayek (Prices and Production). The equilibrium is determined by subjective factors like prices, when we are looking for policies which make for economic stability, we must not be led aside by a feeling that monetary troubles are due to bad economic policy. He emphasises that money is a human institution. A fully developed monetary system is very sensitive and is therefore unstable. The famous 'Hicks-Hansen' effect in interest theory is an acknowledged improvement in the Keynesian framework.

A *Theory of Economic History* (1969), in this, he introduces the concept of an impulse, a shock which can be traced through a sequence of consequences flowing from the potential of a major new invention. It is the same impulse which *Capital and Time* attempts of model.

In his *Theory of Economic History* Hicks delves into the past to analyze the effects of operations of merchants in the flex price market-merchants were the price sellers depending on the stock positions of goods. He emphasises the transformation of the economy through different stages. The poorer a country, the narrower will be its range of technological opportunities, the more likely, therefore, it is that it will suffer long-lasting damage, now and then, from a backwash of improvements that have occurred elsewhere. Even in already industrialised countries, mobility of labour is not perfect. It is a motive for protectionism. But it is an obstacle. Temporary use of such measures is defensible. The symptoms are inflation, balance of payments deficits, a variety of monetary and exchange disorders. These will change their forms by technical adjustments, purely monetary adjustments and changes in monetary policy. So long as the resources of the richer countries are kept under strain, what they have to spare for furthering the growth of the world economy is bound to be restricted.

The book *Capital and Time-A Neo Austrian Theory* was published after he secured the coveted award in 1972. This is the third book that Hicks has written about Capital, the first two being *Value and Capital*, and *Capital and Growth*. *Value and Capital* was a product of the Keynesian thirties. It is deeply influenced by Keynes. The second book *Capital and Growth* is critical and expository, rather than constructive. The concept of full employment is emphasised in this volume. With the given techniques and given employment of labour, production and distribution are entirely separated. The movement of productivity will fairly reflect the movement of wages.

The *Crisis in Keynesian Economics* elaborates on the 'fix price' and 'flex price' market systems described earlier. In the context of high transaction costs, prices are geared to absorb 'permanent' market conditions. *Transaction-dominating assets* emerge the highest being money which substitutes for all, at the margin. There is a lucid plea for a wider portfolio composition than the narrow choice of money versus bonds. In the last chapter, the lack of a coherent wage theory in the Keynesian tradition is pinpointed.

The *Theory of Wages* was originally published in 1932 and revised in 1963. While the first edition was an extension of the thinking of Marshall in his principles, Clark in his *Distribution of Wealth* and Pigou in his *Economics of Welfare*, the second edition contains his revised views on the subject. Section 3 contained in the book entitled 'Commentary' is a piece written exclusively for the new edition. Hicks pays highest recognition to all the critical reviews of his book published in 1932 and says that "I am very anxious that my readers who ever now are tempted to take the 1932 volume literally should read Shove's criticism." Thus Section 3 of this book contains "pre-natal as well as the post-natal vicissitudes" of his earlier edition of this book. The book is a valuable contribution in the theory of wages.

The concept of elasticity of substitution was introduced to demonstrate its usefulness in highlighting relative factor shares. Inventions are autonomous and induced and can be neutral, labour-saving or capital saving. With a given capital-labour ratio, a labour-saving change reduces labour's share of national income. Autonomous inventions are likely to be neutral; induced inventions, are in developed countries, likely to labour saving with upward shifts in the supply price of labour. These concepts saw the rise of prolonged debate with Harrod, Samuelson and other savants on the nature of inventions. The way relative factor prices change, determines the isoquant chosen by the firm.

He emphasises that despite high interest rates inflation is not contro-lled and there is a real threat to recession and unemployment. The supply of commodities is concentrated in a small group of countries for this he has given the example of the recent oil crises. There is a major shift in distribution of international income, without it leading to corresponding changes in consumption since the oil consuming countries have failed to reduce their consumption or to generate savings for the required transfer of income and the oil producing countries have failed to reduce their consumption or investment in keeping with their higher income. In this context, he has made an important contribution to the study of Keynesian economics.

*Economic Perspectives* contains several refreshing ideas. His concept of long-term growth approximates to that of Kuznets. The Ricardo-Wicksell effects in monetary theory are examined. The quantity approach of Friedman is decried. He favours a credit squeese to control inflation.

*Causality in Economics* is developed from his stock flow analysis. Three relationships are identified-static, contemporaneous and sequential. It is difficult to trace out causal relationships when stock and flow relationships have to be dovetailed. Relations must be deduced in sequential form. There is an intermediate stage between cause and effect where decisions are made. Prior and posterior lags should be understood as also reactions to signals. An integrated general theory of the multiplier process and liquidity spectrum is attempted.

Regarding *Causality in Economics* (1979), it may be quoted that: "It was a brave book to write; it strays on to others' territory, and it contains a particular view as to the nature of economics as distinct from science, history, and other areas of social concern, yet requiring all three types of consideration. But its importance for the student of Hicks' work lies with the critique which it provides of the possibility of economic theory. In particular it provides careful reasons as to why prediction is not a strong possibility, and thus it explains Hicks' dislike of econometric practice. The book provides careful categorisation of different kinds of 'cause' from two dimensions; first with regard to time in terms of contemporaneous sequential and static causality, and second in terms strength of influence. This later division is between 'strong' and 'weak' causality, where to claim that A strongly causes B is to say that A is the only cause of B. If A is a weak cause, then it is one of potentially many, and in explanation must be protected by a series of *ceteris paribus clauses*. Now it is only in cases of strong causality that prediction is possible, and it is unlikely, Hicks points out, that there are many cases of strong causality in economics. Economists are doomed to deal with weak causality, and are thus limited in their ability to predict. Falsification, at least in its naïve form, is inapplicable, as the *ceteris paribus clauses* cannot be tested for. And the evolution of economic theory is not to be perceived as the rationalistic programme encapsulated by the philosophers of science such as Lakatos and Popper."[6]

*Wealth and Welfare* (Vol.I) is a collection of earlier pieces having a penetrating one on social income. The other two of his collected works are *Money, Interest and Wages* (Vol. II) and *Classics and Moderns* (Vol.III). *The Wealth and Welfare* (Vol. I) brings together into a coherent

---

[6] Hicks, John, The Economics of John Hicks, Selected and with an Introduction by Dieter Helm, Basil Blackwell, 1984, pp. 19–20.

whole certain essays which are already justly celebrated and others, often of no less importance, which have been relatively neglected, perhaps because till then, they were not readily accessible. These essays on *welfare economics* are not represented in any previous collections of the author's works, although it was for some of them that Sir John received the Nobel Prize for Economics in 1972.

Again in volume *Wealth and Welfare*, the economist has observed that: "...much of what is taken for granted in the subject has its point of departure in Sir John's writings. Moreover, a good deal which seems obvious to commonsense turns out to be extremely problematic when subject to the critical scrutiny of a Hicks. In this connection, it is very much to his credit that so much of what he has had to say on the theory of value and welfare is incorporated into the main body of the economics and is now taken for granted with scarcely a reference to its origin....Sir John is an extremely careful and rigorous thinker."

The *Money, Interest and Wages*, the second volume of the collection, has centered upon the monetary discussions and shows that the author is not merely an *interpreter of Keynes* but has views of his own, which owe as much to other of Keynes' contemporaries as to Keynes himself. This second volume of Hicks's Collected Essays traces the evolution of his thinking over five decades. Five highly original papers, published before he saw Keynes's *General Theory*, show that he anticipated certain aspects of the Keynesian revolution. The story of this early work is set out in an introductory paper written especially for this book. The essays which follow show how subsequently his thinking was modified and expanded.

Robert M. Solow, who became a Nobel Laureate later, has said as follows about this volume: "Here are both the classic paper of 1937 and after thoughts of 1980, together with Hicks's review of the *General Theory* on its appearance. These, and other references reprinted in this fascinating collection, will help the contemporary reader to understand both the depth of the Keynesian revolution and the importance of John Hicks as an economic theorist."

In the third volume, *Classics and Moderns*, John Hicks discusses the various classical traditions, the nature of revolutions in economics, and, indeed, the nature of economics itself. He has also presented his contributions to our understanding of competition, monopoly and international trade. All the essays are distinguished by the clarity and elegance which is characteristic of his approach to economic problems. Talking about *Classics and Moderns*, Milton Friedman, the other Nobel Laureate has said thus: "There can be no doubt that Sir John Hicks is one of the most distinguished theorists of the twentieth century. He has had a tremendous influence on economic thought......".

Besides, the above books, Hicks has contributed countless numbers of articles to the various journals of repute in the world like Econometrics, Review of Economic Studies Economica, Economic Journal, etc. His article on *A Suggestion for simplifying the theory of money* is a masterpiece. Three decades after his eloquent call for a marginal revolution in monetary theory, our students still detect that their mastery of the presumed fundamental theoretical apparatus of economics is put to very little test in their studies of monetary and aggregative models.

As Hicks complained, anything seems to go in a subject where propositions do not have to be grounded in some one's optimising behaviour. Mechanics or thermo-dynamics take the place of inferences from utility and profit maximisation. From the other side of the chasm, the student of monetary phenomena can complain that pure economic theory has never delivered the tools to build a structure of his brilliant design. The utility maximising individual and the profit maximising firm know everything relevant about the present and future and about the consequences of their decisions. His prescription for monetary theory in 1935 was in much the same spirit as the approach of Lavington and Pigou. His strictures were nonetheless timely. The spirit of the original Cambridge theory had become obscured by the mechanical constant-velocity tradition.

Macro-economics texts have immortalised Hicks' decomposition of the Keynesian system into sub-models. One of these tells what asset stock equilibrium corresponds to any tentative assumption about aggregate real income and the commodity price level. In this conditional equilibrium, the interest rate equates the demand and supply of money and clears the markets for other assets.

Two of his articles viz., *Preface and a manifesto* and *The Rehabilitation of Consumer's Surplus* have been included in one of the books edited by Arrow and Scitovsky entitled *Readings in Welfare Economics*. These two papers stress the narrowness of traditional welfare economics and warn against the aridity into which it might too easily fall. Hicks has eminently argued that the increasing affluence renders wealth relatively unimportant. These papers are quite in tune with the present policies of the Government of India where equal opportunities for all and equalisation of wealth among the different people of the society are emphasised. The most well-known contribution by Hicks to welfare theory are his analysis of criteria for comparisons between different economic situations and his revision of the concept of consumer's surplus. Pigou had correlated economic and general welfare and he had made freely inter-personal comparisons. He had identified the sum of consumer surpluses with the real value of the national dividend. Hicks has advocated certain steps to rectify these measures. To mention a few, he suggested changes in tax structure and alternations in tariff schedules. Later, he felt that there could be gains to some when tariff schedules are altered and he felt vital to identify the gains and losses. Modern welfare economics thus became the process in the precise identification of the conditions of maximum welfare.

Some other imporatnt articles of Hicks are: *Mr.Keynes and the Classics, Public Finance in the National Income, Distribution and economic progress: a revised version, Marginal productivity and the principle of variation, Wages and interest-the dynamic problem, Marshall and the indeterminates of wages, Maintaining capital intact: a further suggestion, Mr.Hautrey on bank rate and the long term rate of interest*, and *Theory of uncertainties and profits*.

Hicks has contributed abundantly on various aspects of economic theory. However, his major contributions are in the field of equilibrium theory which culminated in his book *Value and Capital*. This immortal book has been translated into a number of other languages in the world and the author of this present volume has had the fortune of translating it into Kannada, one of the important languages in India, at the instance of the University of Mysore which has published it.

By his brilliant contributions in the field of economic theory, Hicks has joined the rank of immortals like the earlier economists like Alfred Marshall and Keynes. He has a language of his own and his style and diction are uncommon among other economists. His language is full of profundity of sense and the real meaning could be available at times at a farther distance. He has been outstanding as a clear and tireless thinker, a widely read scholar and a lucid expositor. He is the pioneer who has laid theoretical ground-work for the renewal of the equilibrium theory. His books on *Value and Capital* and *The Theory of Wages* are the masterly works in the field of economic science. For the most part, he has worked with labour and capital only. He correctly perceived that capitalism has shown greater growth of capital than of labour. Even more important is his analysis of how technical invention affects progress. Hicks' *Causality in Economics* published in 1979 examines the heart of the problem. Questions like why economics? Is it a science? Kinds of causality and its theory of application are the subject matters of contemporaneous causality in Keynes as well described. Hicks says that as a youngster he started reading history and went into philosophy which provided him thinking the causality in Economics. Certain other questions like *macro* and *micro* economics are discussed. Although it is over five or six decades that the author started dositing, in this treatise, he has examined *Causality in Economics* as one case of causality in general. The book contains an unconventional approach which sheds new light on some of the old basic concepts of economics. The role of statistics and economics is examined. Hicks has rightly observed that "the economist is concerned with the future as well as with the past; but it is with the past that he has to begin. It is the past that provides him with the facts, the facts which he uses to make his generalisations; he then uses his generalisations as bases for predictions and for advice on planning."[7]

According to Schumpeter (1954), "Economics does not possess scientific status, nor can this be attained ..... Economics is for Hicks's discipline, not a science, and it might be added, a pluralistic one. It is the discipline of which Hicks has become a master."[8]

The last book of Hicks is *The Status of Economics*. It is said that, at the time of his death, the manuscript of this title was still to be published and was published in September 1991. This volume brings together the selection of work spanning the late Sir John Hicks' entire career, highlighting his concern with the status of economics as a science and the controversies between economists. This concern with the validity of the discipline led Hicks to consider subjects traditionally outside the boundaries of economics, in particular political theory and cultural history. In the concluding, previously unpublished, essay, Hicks reflects on his own role as an economist. The volume as a whole stands as a magnificent testament to a remarkable career.

According to Hicks, "theory should be the servant of the applied economics, but I have also been aware that theory gives one no right to pronounce on practical problems unless one has been through the labour, so

---

[7] Hicks, John, *Causality in Economics*, Basil Blackwell, Oxford, 1979.

[8] Hicks, John, *The Economics of John Hicks*, Selected and with an Introduction by Dieter Helm, Basil Blackwell, 1984, p.20.

often the formidable labour, of mastering the relevant facts."[9] This observations of Keynes shows that he was aware that theories alone would not help, unless they are applied to the practical problems with formidable labour.

Royal Swedish Academy in its official announcement has said that General equilibrium theory had earlier essentially the character of formal analysis which was brought to light in his celebrated work *Value and Capital*. The construction of the model relating to the general equilibrium theory included a number of innovations, i.e., a further development of older theories of consumption and of production, the formulation of conditions for multimarket stability, an extension of the applicability of the static method of analysis to include multiperiod analysis and the introduction of a capital theory based on profit maximization assumptions. By being deeply anchored in theories of the behaviour of consumers and of entrepreneurs Hicks' model offered far better possibilities to study the consequence of changes in externally given variables than earlier models in this field and Hicks succeeded in formulating a number of economically interesting theorems. Hicks model became of great importance also as a connecting link between general equilibrium theory and current theories of business cycles... As his mathematical tool Hicks used traditional differential analysis. When later on more modern mathematical methods were introduced in economic sciences, Arrow applied these methods in his studies of general equilibrium systems. In a series of papers, which preferentially treated the properties of solubility and stability of such systems, he provided the basis for a radical reformulation of the traditional equilibrium theory. Though this reformulation, which was based on the mathematical theory of convex sets, the general equilibrium theory gained both in generality and in simplicity. The pioneering work, a paper from 1954, was written together with Gerard Debreu. The model presented in this paper became the starting point for the major part of further research in this field. Among Arrow's many important contributions should also be mentioned his development of the theory of uncertainty and its incorporation within the frame of general equilibrium theory and, furthermore, his analysis of the possibilities for decentralized decisions in a society where the price system is fixed by the central authority. This analysis was made in collabo-

---

[9] Hicks, John, *The Formation of an Economist*, in Kregel, J.A., Edited *Recollections of Eminent Economists*, Vol.I, Macmillan Press, 1988, p.6.

ration with Leonid Hurwicz."[10]

Ragnar Bentzel of the Royal Academy of Sciences, in his speech on the occasion of prize awarding function has said about Hicks thus: "When in 1939 John Hicks published his book *Value and Capital*, he breathed fresh life into general equilibrium theory. He constructed a complete equilibrium model, which was systematically built up, to a much greater extent than previous efforts in this field, on assumptions about the behaviour of consumers and producers. This gave greater concreteness to the equations included in the system and made it possible to study the effects produced within the system by impulses coming from outside it. For example, the model could show how changes in phenomena such as the harvest yield, the consumers' taste and the price expectations of business enterprises had consequences which spread throughout the whole economic system and affected prices, production, employment, interest rates, etc. However, Hicks could not have got as far as this if he had not, on several points, himself created the necessary foundations for his model construction, amongst other things, by developing earlier theories of consumption and production and by constructing a theory of capital on the basis of assumptions about profit maximization."[11]

Hayek has expressed in *Economics and Knowledge* about Hicks thus: "Maximising behaviour is a characteristic of Hicks of the making of choices; in that sense it is a *priori* true, but its truth is also argued to derive from intuitive appeal. There can be no micro/macro distinction for Hicks; macro propositions cannot be allowed to float without foundation. He is never to be found picking out observations, in the manner of Keynes, such as 'a man's habitual habits having first claim on his income' or, in the long run, 'as a rule, a greater proportion of income (will be) saved as real income increases', without first deriving the result from simple principles. These have to be explained within the framework of rational behaviour. *Value and*

---

[10] *The Nobel Memorial Prize in Economics* 1972, The Official Announcement of the Royal Academy of Sciences, The Swedish Journal of Economics, Vol.74, No.4, December 1972, pp.486-487.

[11] *The Prize for Economic Science, in Memory of Alfred Nobel*, speech by Prof. Ragnar Bentzel of the Royal Academy of Sciences on the occasion of the Prize awarding function. In Lindbeck, Assar., Edited, *Economics Sciences* 1969-1980: Nobel Lectures, World Scientific, published for the Nobel Foundation, 1992, p.203.

*Capital* is completed by a mathematical appendix in which the amenability of the arguments in the book to this type of reasoning is demonstrated. But it is more than that; mathematical arguments are used to prove the generality of the propositions to *n* commodities. It is in the appendix where Hicks demonstrates the general equilibrium method to its full potential."[12]

While I got in touch with Prof. Jan Tinbergen in 1977, I had the fortune of establishing intimate contacts with Sir John Hicks and Prof. Ursula Hicks in 1975 itself. Though I was very familiar with his works as an economist and a researcher, I was fortunate that the University of Mysore in Karnataka, India, through a resolution of the Syndicate requested me through the Institute of Kannada studies of the University to take up translation of one of the two books under the Government of India funded textbooks series in the local language. *A History of Economic Thought* by Eric Roll (1938) and *Value and Capital* of John R. Hicks were suggested to me to take up one of them. I chose the latter as *Value and Capital* is a landmark text in the history of economic thought. *It is* very terse in its presentation of the fundamental ideas of Hicks, making it difficult to find equivalent words. I thought I should try out *Value and Capital* only. I came in touch with Hicks and Ursula Hicks by writing to them to ensure that the Oxford University Press released the copyright so that my work would not be delayed. Though the letter from Oxford University Press came later, there was already a letter from Hicks to go-ahead. At that time, I was working in the *United Nation's Asian Institute* at Bangkok and in afternoons, I used to devote to identifying equivalent words for tough technical words in economics contained in *Value and Capital* and also used my leisure hours in developing parameters for identifying or demarketing backward and forward areas with particular reference to Karnataka, a major state in South India, which work, of course, was later used by the Indian Planning Commission for identifying backward areas in India. Sri.B.Shivaraman, a well-known planner and a Member of the Planning Commission at that time mentioned this book and its utility in several meetings and in all parts of India. After completing my tenure with the *United Nation's Asian Institute*, I concentrated, in addition to my official work which was abundant, on Hicks's *Value*

---

[12] Hicks, John, *The Economics of John Hicks*, Selected and with an Introduction by Dieter Helm, Basil Blackwell, 1984, pp.9-10. *Economica*, 1937, pp.33-54; reprinted in his *Individualism and Economic Order*, 1948[1212]

*and Capital.* The experience of translating this work was thrilling. The Kannada version of *Value and Capital* was released at the University of Mysore on February 7, 1979 in a function organised by the University. Prof. Hicks and Ursula Hicks came to India at that time. It was our fortune that he received in a public function organised by the University of Mysore his own *Value and Capital* translated into Kannada. This function was very largely attended from all economists who could afford to reach Mysore and of course by the Mysore citizens. It was one of the grandest function, that I have ever seen. I was given the task of introducing Hicks to the audience – it was a task to talk about Hicks and his contributions in his own presence. Prof. John Hicks in his reply said that he wrote *Value and Capital* and as days passed, he went on changing his ideas and now many of the concepts mentioned in that work have undergone some changes in his mind which could be seen in his later books. He was surprised to hear from me that my translation was the eleventh language to which *Value and Capital* was going. He said that he was not himself aware that it had gone to so many languages. Prof. Ursula Hicks mentioned on this occasion that it was the first instance that she and her husband were found on the same platform in a public function of that kind.

Prof. V.K.R.V. Rao, my well-wisher, who was the first professor to estimate national income of India in the 1940's said that "*Value and Capital* does not make easy reading, especially Parts I and II and the reader has to keep alert all the time lest he miss a step in the intricate but continuous logic that characterises this work and Dr. Puttaswamaiah has done an excellent job. It is now possible for Kannada students to obtain in their own language access to a key book in economic theory, and in turn this should enable production in Kannada of books and articles on practical problems of both macro-economic and micro-economic policy by using the logical apparatus and the lucid analysis of economic inter-relations and economic causes and consequences that Prof. Hicks has contributed in this pioneering treatise. I count it as a piece of good fortune and should mark the beginning of a new era of Kannada literature in economics".

I have described some of the outstanding works of Hicks. There are many books and research articles and right from his early days, each one of them created a landmark. *Value and Capital – A Inquiry into Some Fundamental Principles of Economic Theory* (1939, 1946), *Capital and Growth* (1965) and *Capital and Time* (1973), which may be called 'Hicks's Triology of Capital', are the most important of his contributions which have created landmarks after the *General Theory* and provided opportunity to several economists to do further research on these works. These three works of Hicks relating to 'Capital' are the three 'Avataras' of 'Capital' of which I consider *Value and Capital* as the *Jewel* among them and even among his works.

This Volume in Memory of John Hicks consists of 24 papers. Prof. Paul A. Samuelson's paper identifies the land marks in Hicks's life. He considers "*Value and Capital* as a scientific epic saga - full of new and beautiful ideas and a springboard toward future advances, as said earlier. He goes on saying that even before the *General Theory*, if Keynes was considered as the *greatest economist of the world*, J.R.Hicks was the *greatest young economist at that time. - Hicks's works are immortal*". Thus, Samuelson has briefly but aptly described Hicks's works and I am extremely grateful to him for his immediate response in sending this paper under the title: *My John Hicks*. The title itself shows what an amount of affection Prof. Samuleson has had for Hicks and how his works were held in esteem.

Prof. Colin Simkin who describes vividly his close association with Prof. Hicks and his wife gives a vivid account of their inner life which makes the reader want to read it more than once. Prof. Colin Simkin tells that he had the good fortune of knowing two men who are something of genius, both of whom became lifelong friends. He derived intellectual benefits from them and feels that he cannot forget them and also their two exceptionally friendly wives. These two exceptional friends are Sir John Hicks and Karl Popper. Simkin has given a separate paper on Karl Popper also, since these three had a close association in academic work discussions and even in travels.

Prof. O.F.Hamouda in his paper: *Hicks, a World Economist* has tried with great difficulty to condense as best he can all he has to say about Hicks and his works. The paper presents a scholarly and comprehensive analysis of Hicks's economics. The paper is an offshoot of his ambitious work: *John R. Hicks – The Economists' Economist* (Basil Blackwell, 1993). Prof. Michio Morishima, Sir John Hicks Professor of Economics in London School of Economics and Political Science writing under the title "*Mr.Keynes in Hicks's Value and Capital*" deals with the *theory of firm* and ideas of *Hicks's IS and LM curves* and his views on it. He gives a vivid account of Keynes and *Value and Capital* – how they are related and in the process identifies some inconsistencies. Syed Ahmad, McMaster University, Canada, while, writing about *Hicks on Capital* briefly writes about Hicks and classifies capital into three ways: (i) exactly like any other factor, (ii) as a produced means of production and (iii) as representing the role of time in the production process and Hicks contributed to theories in all these frameworks. After describing under these three main heads, he comes out with the significance of the *Theory of Capital*.

Prof. Frank Hahn in his paper: *Hicks and Economic Theory* vividly and with brevity writes about his views on major works of Hicks and he has been a balanced critic without loss of appreciation whereever necessary in the paper. Harald Hagemann has chosen the area of *Monetary Causes of the Business Cycles and Technological Changes: Hicks vs. Hayek* tries to distinguish between the works of Hicks and Hayek. While Hicks was a pure economist, Hayek was not only an economist but a social thinker. Harald Hagemann has brought out very well in his paper a critical analysis of the works of these two great thinkers, both Nobel Laureates. The rest of the authors like Professors Michael Emmett Brady, Joseph Halevi, J.W.Nevile, B.B.Price, John Lodewijks, Carlo Benetti, Kunibert Raffer, Mauro Baranzini, Michael Rosier and Christian Tutin, John Luc Gaffard with other authors, Keith Griffin, Surajit Sinha, R.S.Dhananjayan with N.Sasikaladevi have chosen different areas of Hicks's works - sometimes confining themselves to a single work of Hicks and have given a vivid account of their own thoughts on selected Hicks's works. These papers are invaluable to any economist and to all those senior professors and students who are concerned with Hicks's works in relation to his earlier thinkers and the present day thinking. Since each paper contains the summary of one work or the other of Hicks and their views, I do not wish to elaborate further as the papers speak for themselves.

Sir John Hicks started the Sienna Workshop and he attended the first two workshops during 1987 and 1988 and he was to attend the third in 1989 but could not do so as he had by then passed away. Proceedings of the first two workshops have been published. We are fortunate in getting a small piece in the form of a "memoriam" of John Hicks by Axel Leijonhufvud. He goes to Sienna to attend the Third Summer Workshop. He was earlier anticipating that he would listen to the presentation of Hicks; instead he had to present a memoriam containing the life and works of Hicks and, to some extent, the main events of Hicks' life and works in economics. Though the memoriam provides the necessary material which gives more and more of Hicks inner life, yet, I am tempted to, draw attention to a few points. He was dedicated and determined in his life when he thinks of a academic life. Axel Leijonhufvud checklists three important points as reflections on the achievement of Hicks:

(i) He has, of course, been enormously, amazingly influential. His ideas have seeped into the ways economists think and work to the point where the very familiarity of many Hicksian ideas make it difficult for us rightly to assess the contribution.

Yet, it is parts of his work that has had this influence – and some of it has not had quite the influence that he originally intended or would later have wished. Hicks, more than most authors, had to experience in his lifetime how the readers wrest control of the text from the author. So, it was part of the *Suggestion for Simplifying Monetary Theory'*, most of *'Mr.Keynes and the Classics*, only the first eight chapters of *'Value and Capital'*, and so on – that went into the foundations on which post-World War II economic theory was built.

(ii) Economic theory to John Hicks was always more an exercise in judgment than in deduction. The economist constantly makes choices – among methods or approaches, among assumptions, and among 'facts'. Hicks, even 55 years ago, always discussed his choices with the reader. You always know the reasons for all his choices and, if you disbelieve his conclusions, it is possible to track back and find where you differ with his judgment.

(iii) Over the years he developed a style of writing that is really quite remarkable. It is clean, spare, direct with a simple conversational tone that is quite engaging – but can be in equal measure misleading, if the apparent simplicity lulls you into overlooking the depth at which he is penetrating very complex problems.

It is clear that whatever Hicks has said is not final and he would go on thinking time after time and change his views. Ex: At the Mysore Function on the occasion of the release of the translated *Value and Capital,* he said that he had changed his views on several concepts contained in it. His nature was one of churning, meaning he would go on brooding over something till he saw the ultimate reality. In this connection, I will not be wrong if I quote: "John Hicks was a Ulysses among economists; his life is a journey in economics of a striver, seeker, a finder and a non-yielder. The paths are hewed by him; and the tools designed by him. The strange and fascinating aspect of his journey is that he is always going forward and back, back and forward. The greatest critic of Hicks is Hicks himself. And he has left a complete record of these introspections and forward thrusts. He is thus both a contributor and a commentator, a player and a sports critic, the latter of himself".

The other qualities of Hicks are those which relate to his nature as an economist and a man. He gave away the entire Nobel Prize money to the Library of London School of Economics. He phrased it as a gift of gratitude to that institution but it was also a declaration of his dedication to a life of strictly limited material ambitions. He was always thoughtful and thought provoking. He would profess on his own some ideal and not allow himself to be detracted from it. In Sienna Workshop II, Hicks with his few friends including Axel Leijonhufvud was eating in a grape arbor at a restaurant outside town, Axel asked Hicks whether he still did a number theory which was a pet for him, "No" he said, "I stopped doing that a couple of years ago. Now, I have this game I play with myself to go to sleep. I try to remember at least one stanza of poetry from each century from about 500 BC to the present." And he started to tell about what centuries were the most difficult and so on. Before they left that place, they had heard John Hicks quote poetry from memory for at least a couple of hours. Hicks on the occasion of the function at Mysore for releasing the Kannada version of *Value and Capital* said that "I have changed my emphasis of ideas quite a good deal. My book *Theory of Economic History* was of quite of different kind from *Value and Capital;* but there is change to make a sort of statement from our point of view and of a much less formal kind.... I should perhaps say that in my very last published book of essays called *Economic Perspectives-Further Essays on Money and Growth* (1977), there is a process which is what is called a survey and it is from my own point of view on the development on my ideas. I tried to stress there what things seem to be important where my emphasis is drastically changed. All, I can say is on this happy occasion that I am glad to receive the Kannada version of *Value and Capital*. My blessings to the Translator".

Finally to end with the words of Prof. Paul A. Samuelson "Sir John Hicks was as he had been throughout his life: a loner scholar, for whom the sun rose in the morning when first he opened his eyes. His works constitute his immortality".

Coming to the acknowledgement, I cannot express in mere words the blessings of Prof. Paul A. Samuelson, the Nobel Laureate who has given an excellent piece under the title: *My John Hicks* spontaneously which shows the utmost affection to the Editor of this book. I wish to place on record my affectionate and highest regards to him. I am extremely grateful to him for writing his 'Foreword' also to this work. It is again a brief piece of literature on economic history and his views on Hicks is true and remarkable which runs thus: "He was part of no school, John Hicks was his own school." Prof. Samuelson has thus said that Prof. Hicks did not belong to any school of thought and he had his own independent thinking in his works.

The other Professors who are also members of the Editorial Advisory Board of the Internationational Journal of Applied Economics and Econometrics (formerly Indian Journal of Applied Economics) have supported me in large measure by writing papers, like Profs. Nevile, Keith Griffin, and many others also refereed the articles. I was happy to have received the articles from many others including Prof. Frank Hahn and Prof. Michio Morishima. It is really fortunate to have received two papers from Prof. Colin Simkin who has given us the real insight into Hicks' way of working and life style. It is good that Prof. Axel Leijonhufvud has given a brief memoriam in which he has pointed out Hicks as a great traveller and has appreciated him which throws lot of light about Hicks to the readers. Prof. O.F.Hamouda, the author of book entitled: *John R. Hicks – The Economist's Economist* has summarised Hicks's works and called him a *World Economist*. The paper from Prof. B.B.Price, is also an excellent contribution of Hicks's works. Many British economists including Prof. G.C.Harcourt have supported and encouraged me to great extent.

The status of economics today would have been something far behind what it is. It is the work of earlier economists which has really prompted the Royal Swedish Academy to recognize *Economics* as a *Science* and institute the Nobel Prize Award.

In a work of this nature it is always likely that we miss somebody or the other who should have been mentioned. If I have erred in any way, I hope I will be forgiven; but I wish that the readers will take all the good contained in this work. I am happy that most of the authors are eminent professors from all parts of the World and some of them are students of Hicks and many of them are intimate colleagues and friends. I am glad that this book, which is based on the special issue published in three parts in the *Indian Economic Journal*, which is now retitled as *International Journal of Applied Economics and Econometris,* has now come out.

I lack words to express my gratitude to Dr. Irving Louis Horowitz, Chairman and Editorial Director, and Ms. Mary E. Curtis, President and

Publisher, Transaction Publishers, RUTGERS, The State of University of New Jersey, for all the support and co-operation in bringing out this publication in such a short time and so well. I wish to record my appreciation in this context. I also thank Ms. Anne Schneider, Associate Editor and other staff connected with this publication.

January 20, 2000                                            K.Puttaswamaiah

CHAPTER - 1

# MY JOHN HICKS

## Paul A. Samuelson

**ABSTRACT**

In this paper, contributions of J.R. Hicks have been evaluated briefly. The landmarks in Hick" working life is described. Among the major works of Hicks, "*Value and Capital*" written at his age of 35, is a scientific epic saga – full of new and beautiful things and a springboard towards future advances. Even before the '*General Theory*' if Keynes was considered as the greatest economist of the world', J.R. Hicks was the greatest young economist at that time. Hick's works are immortal.

I was lucky in my teachers at Chicago and Harvard. But being in love with the subject of economics and possessed of boundless youthful energy and a ferocious power to read and focus on everything that interested me, most of what I learned was not by word of mouth in lecturers and conversations with economists at those two great universities in the 1932–1940 period. The wide world was my school. It was from books and journal articles that I learned what were the important scientific questions to ponder over; and many of the best answers that could be then given to those questions came from those away-from-home sources, from the great "invisible college" of economic and other sciences. With two great libraries at hand, I read essentially *all* the journals when they were, so to speak, still hot, and I was excessively eclectic in sampling almost all of their contents.

It was a wonder that I had time to do independent thinking! And if the brain has only so much room in it (as Sherlock Holmes insisted to Dr. Watson), then my excellent memory could have endangered my own

[1]

originality. But there was little danger of that, for as Chicago's Professor Paul Douglas wrote to Professor Jacob Viner in recommending that as an undergraduate I be admitted to Viner's celebrated Chicago graduate seminar in economic theory: "Young Samuelson is able if cantankerous and argumentative".

All this is by way of saying that John Hicks (born 1904), early and late, was a major intellectual stimulus for me. I went over his contributions with a powerful microscope, a much more intensive analysis than he ever gave either to my own work or to that of any other economist. That was the way Hicks was. Always he preferred to do things *his* way. And that was the source both of his creative originality and prolific scientific productivity. Of course such a scientific style can lead to blind spots even in the best of scholars, and to the rediscovery of a certain number of round wheels. But the completed record shows that, if this was a Faustian bargain with the Devil, it was one with high net payoff.

More than once I have recorded the autobiographical fact that, as a teenager at Chicago, I was told by an early tutor that John Maynard Keynes was then – 1932 or 1933, well before *The General Theory* (1936) – "the greatest economist in the world" and told also, that at Harvard around 1935 by an Assistant Professor friend J.R. Hicks was the greatest *young* economist at that time. Both evaluations squared with my own early impressions. I spent a lot of time dissecting Hicks's (1932) *Theory of Wages*; and, incidentally, I later disagreed with Hick's own damning-with-faint-praise that early first book. By then I had learned to accept only with guarded reservations John's claims and disclaimers about his own contributions. Expressions of modesty can sometimes be veiled signs both of vanity and Napoleonic ambition.

I wish present readers to understand that I always regarded Hicks as having been somewhat undervalued, particularly in Britain his own country. As he learned during his brief and not happy sojourn at Cambridge University – in between his nine golden years at the LSE and his decade of loner productivity at Manchester – Hicks was not "politically correct" and therefore not popular with the leftish elite at Oxbridge. Dennis Robertson engineered Hicks' Cambridge appointment to keep down Joan Robinson; but subsequently Robertson kept somewhat at a distance. Moreover, in England an early failure to earn a First leaves scars on the ego that will not fade. If I ran the world I would heap every honor early on whomever was later to shine in the scientific barnyard; that might get out of the way some of the pathology of unbridled ambition, which can never be satiated even by the greatest of accomplishments. (I think of Joseph Schumpeter and of the mathematician Norbert Wiener as examples in point.)

John Hicks had another fault. He wrote well. This is not a common crime among economists. And it meant that his was a wide audience among readers, some of whom were not very expert in mathematical jargon and techniques. The good fairies balance their gifts. Hicks was not a terribly good lecturer. He did not stammer but his flow of words was not smooth, and in a personal dialogue with a Nicholas Kaldor or Milton Friedman he did not excel in quick repartee.

At Oxford over the years Hicks had some very good students. To name just two, these included the American Lionel McKenzie and the Japanese Michio Morishima. On their travels all over the world, John and Ursula Hicks would be met by admiring former pupils. But the master was not a warm, outgoing personality. He wrote few joint papers and tended to concentrate most on his own research puzzles. It was not a rash decision for him to retire early from his Drummond Professorship: that kept him in step with his older wife; and it in no way inhibited twenty more years of prolific and provocative innovative contributions.

In *The New Palgrave A Dictionary of Economics* (1987, pp. 641–646), Christopher Blisst gives an admirable selective description of J.R. Hicks's many and fine contributions to varied fields of economic theory. I shall not duplicate that here. Let me merely sing the praises of *Value and Capital* (1939, 1946). Written when the author was 35, this is a scientific epic saga – full of new and beautiful things and a springboard toward future advances. No single misprint mars its mathematical text; and the one major omission in its first edition he was able to repair by altering a few pages only.

To summarize my superlative evaluation of John Hicks, I believe it would have been as well for the Royal Swedish Academy of Science to have named Hicks *alone* for the second Nobel Prize in 1970, following immediately after Ragner Frisch and Jan Tinbergen in 1969. That would have left Kenneth Arrow to receive later an unshared award: the Hicks and Arrow coupling was not particularly optimal; and it came about, I suspect, from the happenstance that some of the judging committee resented Hicks's cavalier citings of contemporary work by other scholars – a non-Scandinavian practise not uncommon in the British senior com-

4

mon rooms of that time. (I should add that Kenneth Arrow, in my book, deserves at least two Nobel Prizes).

I remember Sir John the last time I saw him in person, toward the end of his life, at the Saltzesbaden 1987 conference near Stockholm in honor of Erik Lundberg. He was in good form for an octogenarian. "Fortunately I am dying from my feet up rather than from my brain down", he quipped.[1] Years before John Hicks had confided to me, "When one of us – Ursula or I – dies, the other will be left lonely". And so it was for this childless couple; when Ursula (born in 1896!) died first, Sir John lived alone at his Blockley family property in the Cotswolds near Oxford. Fortunately younger economists on the Oxford scene helped him travel to conferences in Italy and elsewhere.

To the end Sir John Hicks was as he had been throughout his life: a loner scholar, for whom the sun rose in the morning when first he opened his eyes. His works constitute his immortality.

### REFERENCES

Bliss, Christopher, 1987. "Hicks, John, R." in J. Eatwell, M. Milgate and P. Newman, eds., *The New Palgrave A Dictionary of Economics*, Vol. 2, London. Macmillan.
Hicks, John, R., 1932, 1963. *The Theory of Wages*. London. Macmillan.
Hicks, John, R. 1937. *La Théorie Mathématique de la valeur end régime de libre concurrence.*. Trans. G. Lutfalla. Paris: Hermann.
Hicks, John, R. 1939, 1946. *Value and Capital*. Oxford: Clarendon Press.
Keynes, John Maynard. 1936. *The General Theory of Employment, Interest and Money*. London. Macmillan.

---

[1]Wanting to square the books before it was too late, John Hicks in private at Saltzesbaden expressed worry that he had been remiss in properly citing my works parallel to his. Long earlier I had made the optimal adjustment to his manner of composition and I could see no point in worrying a doughty warrior at that stage of life. Therefore I assured him that always I had learned much from him (a literal truth); and that indeed I had early known the brief 1937 French version of his developed 1939 classic. Reassured, he confided: "Now that I am old and working alone, getting the big books off the library shelf is quite a chore and that inhibits my bibliographical accuracy". When I told Bob Solow this story I added: "Those books were always heavy on Sir John's shelves".

# CHAPTER - 2

# JOHN AND URSULA HICKS – A PERSONAL RECOLLECTION

*Colin Simkin*

## ABSTRACT

In this article I describe an association with John Hicks and his wife Ursula that began during the Second World War and lasted until his death in 1989. I first wrote expressing a wish to do post-graduate work under him, and he encouraged me to come to Oxford for that purpose after the war. In 1947 I joined him at Nuffield College, before it had its own permanent buildings and when there was an exciting atmosphere of academic pioneering. My two years there resulted in a friendship which gave me introductions to British and foreign economists, and warm hospitality at Porch House, their Cotswold home. They also resulted in D Phil and the publication of a book based on my thesis. After my return to Auckland I kept in touch by correspondence and by two visits to England in 1958 and 1966–67, and arranged academic hospitality for them at Sydney during their visit to Australia in 1976. When I retired in 1980, I paid further visits to England, during which I received more hospitality at Porch House. In all these ways I came to form a long and rewarding friendhsip with John and Ursula, from whom I received much kindness, intellectual benefit and professional help. I was, of course, only one of many who could express deep indebtedness to these two remarkable people, but my account may convey something of what they meant to those fortunate enough to know them well.

## 1. INTRODUCTION

I have had the good fortune to know two men of something like genius, both of whom became life-long friends and from whom I received much personal kindness as well intellectual benefit. And I cannot think of them apart from their two exceptional and friendly wives.

The first was Karl Popper whom I met in 1939 when I went to Canterbury University College where he was the senior lecturer in philosophy, and gave him some help in writing the great *Open Society and its Enemies*, and also *The Poverty of Historicism*, both written with secretarial and other help from his devoted wife Hennie. But I got much more from him than I could give; insight into scientific method, probability theory and mathematics in its application to economics. I recall particularly his elucidation for me of R.G.D. Allen's mathematical half of the *Reconsideration of the Theory of Value* which was written in collaboration with J.R. Hicks in 1934,[1] and his encouragement to persevere with the study of *Value and Capital* which Hicks published in 1939. This germinal work, together with Jan Tinbergen's *Statistical Testing of Business Cycles* (1938) gave me new insights into economics and its possibilities, reinforced by reading current volumes of *Econometrica*,[2] again aided by Karl. In them I found John's important article, *Mr Keynes and the Classics*, and also his useful survey of monopoly theory. I had not then read his first book, a neo-classical one, *The Theory of Wages*, although I had learnt something of its ideas from studying R.G.D. Allen's *Mathematical Analysis for Economists*.

I was not able to proceed far in such directions because I entered the Royal New Zealand Air Force in 1942 and had a tour in the Pacific Islands (as a meteorologist). But when it became clear that Nazi Germany and Imperial Japan could be defeated, I decided to try building a bridge to my future by writing to John Hicks, then Professor of Economics at Manchester. I sent him two articles, which I had published, in *The Economic Record* on budgetary reform, drawing a good deal on Swedish theory and practice of counter-cycle budgeting. It turned out that Ursula Hicks, who had a strong interest in public finance, had helped Erik Lindahl prepare the English edition of his *Studies in the Theory of Money and Capital* (1939) when he came to the LSE to arrange for this[3]. She and John, moreover, collaborated during the war years in work on local authority rating and other aspects of public finance.[4] My joint articles were thus well received and John encouraged me to plan coming to Manchester to do a PhD under his supervision.

---

[1] I also read *Theorie Mathematique de la Valeur* (1937) in which John set out his basic analysis of value theory, before *Value and Capital* appeared.

[2] I could read most of it then.

[3] John also gained from Lindahl's visit by becoming aware of Swedish ideas on economic dynamics and temporary equilibria, ideas which were used in *Value and Capital*.

[4] In 1948 John published a small book on *The Problem of Budgetary Reform*, and had asked my opinion on some of its content.

Later he wrote to say that he was leaving Manchester to take up an official fellowship at the new undeveloped Nuffield College in Oxford, and suggested that I should plan to come there for my postgraduate study.

But the War ended in 1945, Karl left to take up a readership in Logic and Scientific Method at the London School of Economics and I, quite unexpectedly, was appointed to the vacant chair of economics at Auckland University College. I wrote to John explaining this appointment and saying that nevertheless I hoped to join him before long for postgraduate work. He answered expressing doubts about that, and I had them, too. Then came two unexpected strokes of luck. The Rockerfeller Foundation offered me a generous fellowship for two years of overseas study, and the council of the College approved my taking leave (on half pay) for this purpose. I wrote to John with this news and also enclosing an article which I had written, *Notes on the Theory of Discriminating Monopoly*. This was published before the end of 1947 in *The Review of Economic Studies*, of which Ursula was an editor. Greatly elated I set out for Oxford and arrived there in January 1947.

My wife and I were soon invited by John to a lunch at what was then Halifax House with Ursula and Herbert Frankel, a South African who held the chair of economic development and whom John had known during the year he served as a temporary replacement lecturer at the University of Johannesburg. It was a very pleasant personal introduction to the Hicks, both friendly and Ursula warm where John was shy or reserved, and good to meet Herbert, a fellow 'colonial' and an able economist. They were very encouraging and John soon arranged that I should become a research fellow of Nuffield (unpaid), that he should be my supervisor for a thesis on what I took to be business cycles in New Zealand, introduced me to the excellent facilities of Rhodes House and got me a room in the Institute of Statistics where I benefited from contact with Patrick Moran and David Champernowne. I attended his weekly seminar for Nuffield students and heard interesting exchange between him and a visiting Paul Samuelson on the valuation of the social income; and Ian Little, then a research student, astounded us with a brilliant paper on revealed preference. I also attended the lectures John was giving in 1948 on Keynesian theory – lectures which became the basis of *A Contribution to the Theory of the Trade Cycle* which he published in 1950. All this was inspiring, although I was somewhat less impressed by his style of lecturing than by his superb writing. Much, too, was gained from the Friday dinners for fellows of the College,[5] an able lot presided over genially by Henry Clay. The conversation was good and there were often interesting guests, including on one occasion Lord Nuffield, then the only founder of an Oxford College who could dine with its fellows. Unlike the distinguished ecclesiastics and nobles who had much earlier founded the other colleges, Nuffield was the son of a farm labourer who began his career with a bicycle shop in Oxford, going from that to become the leading British manufacturer of automobiles. The college which he had endowed in 1938, on the urging of Alexander Lindsay, was also distinctive in being an institution for research and post-graduate work in the social sciences, and in being bisexual although, when I was there, the students were all men many of whom, like me, had done war service.[6]

Ursula was also teaching and supervising postgraduate students in the field of public finance, and taking a particular interest in African or Asian students, one of whom was Gamini Corea who later became governor of Sri Lanka's central bank. During term she and John lived in a Nuffield flat but at other times in Porch House at the Cotswold village of Blockley. This house had belonged to John's uncle who left it to John's sister, from whom Ursula bought it. A fairly large historic building, once a country residence of the bishops of Gloucester, it had been divided into two sections the larger of which was occupied by a distinguished woman who had retired from the Civil Service and the smaller one used by Hicks. There they spent weekends and vacations with their constant companion Sammy, a very appealing cat. John's secretary, young Pat Rathbone, also lived in Blockley with her father and his wealthy second wife. Porch house had a large garden which gave scope for Ursula's considerable interest in things botanical. Painting, especially interesting scenery, was another of her hobbies, They seemed very happy, content with each other[7], revelling in their professional lives,

---

[5]These were held in an old vicarage in Woodstock Road; it also provided the fellows' common room. The College's buildings were still being planned. Classes and administration were conducted in an old house plus army huts in Banbury Road, and fellows, including the Warden, were housed in flats of converted Victorian houses. There were, of course, disadvantages in these interim arrangements but they also were associated with a fresh spirit of academic pioneering.

[6]he senior fellow of the College, however, was Margery Perham, a colonial historian.

[7]I recall once hastily entering a carriage on the train from Paddington to Oxford and found myself sitting, by accident, next to John and Ursula. They told me, happily but

which often extended beyond their much loved Oxford, and enjoying their spells in the lovely Cotswolds. We Nuffield students, as one of us put it, appreciated Ursula's warm heart and John's remarkable brain.[8]

My wife and I were glad to be invited to Porch House for a day trip twice and to make friends with Sammy. So, when the Hicks were to spend a month of the summer vacation in the United States,[9] we were offered the use of their part of Porch House so that we could care for Sammy. It was a wonderful experience. The weather was exceptionally good, the Cotswolds were largely empty of tourists and motor cars and so little commercialised. We had good times exploring charming villages on our bikes – when I was not working on my thesis. Then in September, John generously arranged for me to go instead of him to an international conference of economists held in Genoa, where we were lavishly entertained by its communist mayor. I was visited at my hotel by a local professor who, having seen from the conference programme that I came from Oxford, wanted to know whether John was doing more work to develop general equilibrium theory. He explained that he and other Italian economists were very interested in this theory and admired *Value and Capital*, but had been cut off by the war from access to English or American journals.

In March we set out for Scandinavia, supplied by introductions from John to his friends Erik Lindahl in Uppsala and Carl Iverson in Copenhagen, both of whom treated us well. Next month the foundation stone for Nuffield College's building was laid with great ceremony, involving a Chancellor's procession and a lunch at Christ Church for university officials, fellows of the College and their wives, and many academics from other universities. There were, of course, speeches which referred to the contribution Nuffield College could make to the social sciences and to the University. Lord Nuffield made a rather different speech, in which he said that he had always found the entrance to Oxford from the railway station unimpressive and that the College, when built, would improve things in that respect.

---

rather shyly, that the day was their wedding anniversary and they had had a celebratory dinner in a favoured London restaurant

[8]A possible exception was Ian Little who, after having had John as his supervisor, had differences with him and transfered to supervision by Phillip Andrews.

[9]On his visit John saw old friends such as Schumpeter and Viner, and met their younger colleagues, Samuelson, Arrow, Friedman and Patinkin all of whom were influenced by *Value and Capital* in working on neo-classical synthesising.

In August John and Ursula went on another overseas trip and we were again in Porch House for a month of glorious weather. Sammy welcomed us by jumping from an open skylight into the bathroom. We were back again at Porch House in December. By then, I had passed my examination for a D Phil,[10] had a modified version of the thesis accepted for publication by the Clarendon Press, booked our return passages to Auckland, and had a farewell party given for us by the Nuffield fellows, at which I become the first to sign the Nuffield Register.

Our weekend visit to Porch House was also a farewell by the Hicks, who had succeeded in getting possession of the whole of it. We helped them move furniture and books from the smaller to the larger part of the house. The other guest there was Sandy Henderson and the three of us had to join a search led by a concerned Ursula to find Sammy before returning with them to Oxford by car.[11] On the 16th we had to go by train to Southampton to embark, and were farewelled at this station by both the Hicks and the Poppers. John and Ursula were themselves about to set off from England for Nigeria to advise about its new constitution, especially about the financial aspects.

In these two years I thus had the good fortune to be helped by a man who was still taking a leading role in shaping what Maurice Peston has called 'the golden days of economic theory' – days when economics was exciting, promising to offer much and not yet so entangled with mathematics or ideology as to limit its appeal or intelligibility. John Hicks and Paul Samuelson between them were largely founding what came to be called neo-classical economics, although John's interests were much wider, embracing history, European literature and music. In many respects, he was a splendid example of plain living and high thinking, combined with a tolerant and democratic humanitarianism that extended to all countries, developed or underdeveloped economically.

After our return to Auckland we corresponded with the Hicks and sent the fruit cakes which they valued, under the tight rationing that still held in Britain, to provide refreshment for the younger Oxford economists who attended John's regular seminar on economic theory. (It was started

---

[10] Ian Little and I were the only Nuffield students of our year to complete this qualification. Most of the rest had been absorbed into one or other of the many prevailing opportunities for employment as academics or as recruits to government and the new international agencies.

[11] It was driven by Ursula; John did not drive.

because of his concern that some youngish people had been appointed to tutor in the colleges before they were fully equipped in economics.) But before long rationing ceased. In 1952, John was appointed to the Drummond Chair of Political Economy which went with a fellowship of All Souls College, a connection which he greatly valued. He had to resign from Nuffield as an Official Fellow with teaching duties, but retained his close connection with it by becoming one of its Faculty Fellows. During the 1950s and 1960s the British Empire was breaking up and some of the newly independent countries called on British economists for advice. John and Ursula thus received and accepted invitations, after Nigeria, from the West Indies, India and Ceylon, as Sri Lanka was still called. In many cases they were welcomed there by former students. He was also able to develop valued contacts with Italian economists some of whom, too, were former students. (He had gained a reading knowledge of Italian at his school, Clifton, and had used it to study Pareto, his inspiration for the theory of value, and to read Dante and other Italian authors.[12])

I did not see John again until he came to New York in April 1958 when I was there for a short time during tenure of a Carnigie Travelling Fellowship. He kindly invited my wife and me to a dinner he was giving for a few American friends, among them Ragnar Nurske who had me to lunch at Columbia a few days later. After leaving the States I spent a few months in Stockholm and the Hague before coming to Oxford to complete my sabbatical leave. There I rented Francis Seton's flat, which was below that occupied by Ursula and John. We thus saw them fairly often.[13] I had dinner with John at All Souls, and we had another few days at Blockley where they had us witness their wills. Shortly after our return to Auckland, I learnt that John had recommended me for a chair at Southampton and went there for an unsuccessful interview. After it I came to Blockley for a few days where I was helped to lick my wounds.

---

[12] I was told that when he was ill in hospital in the mid 1960s, and could not read, he passed the time by trying to recall passages from Dante's Divine Comedy. Another poet who greatly attracted him was Yeats. A copy of whose Tower he gave us after enthusiastically pointing out subtle Classical allusions in it. This reminds me that Ursula once told me of John's way of passing time on long journeys when he had run out of reading matter; he would recreate a proof of some mathematical theorem or attempt solving some mathematical puzzle.

[13] Both were taking an active interest in developing Nuffield's gardens.

Then in 1966–67 I had a Commonwealth Visiting Professorship at the new University of Essex where I had an interesting time. In my Masters' course on economic dynamics I made considerable use of *Capital and Growth*, which John had published in 1965, the year in which he also retired from his chair, and was glad to see how well the better students took to this book. I left Essex at the start of the summer vacation of 1967 and came to Oxford, where Nuffield provided me with academic hospitality, including a room, and the Hicks gave us the use of their new flat near the Observatory in Woodstock Road as they were spending their vacation in Blockley and again going overseas. But before they did we were their guests at the Oxford Encaenia, involving presentation of honorary degrees in the Sheldonian Theatre, lunch in the Codrington Library and a garden party. During my period in Essex I had written *The Traditional Trade of Asia* and John was helpful in arranging for it to be published by the Oxford University Press in London.

Back in Auckland I found conditions for my Department were worsening so much that I decided to apply for a vacant chair at Sydney University, and was strongly supported by both John and Karl (among others). My application was successful but before I could go to Sydney my wife died of a sudden heart attack. Ursula and John wrote me sympathetic letters about that. In 1972 I married again, this time to a Yorkshire lady living in Sydney, the same year that John received his Nobel prize. I went with her on sabbatical leave in 1974, spending short periods in Hull and Manchester as a visiting professor and spending my last months in Oxford. There, of course, we saw the Hicks, visited Blockley and, at their request moved into Porch House for a few weeks while they were away – but this time there was no Sammy or replacement for him.

Two years later the Hicks came to the Australian National University at Canberra, where Ursula had been asked to contribute to a study on federal financial systems. On the way they stopped at Singapore to have hospitality from Lim Chong Yah, Head of the Department of Economics and Statistics at the National University there, who had also gained a D Phil under John's supervision. While they were there Ursula had the misfortune to fall and break her hip, which meant hospitalisation. Before that happened Ursula had indulged her passion for botany by visiting the public gardens. The accident prevented further visits so that John used his camera to take her shots of the parts of the gardens she had wanted to see again. I had a letter from him telling me this, that he and Ursula would be arriving in Sydney on their way to Canberra, and asking me to ensure that she got a wheel chair at Sydney's airport before going on a connecting flight to Canberra. I did so and greeted them when they arrived. When I asked Ursula if she would like a coffee I received an answer that what she needed was not coffee but a stiff whisky – it was promptly provided and drunk before they set off for Canberra.

While they were there, I had John invited to Sydney to deliver the Mills memorial lecture, and he gave us *Must Stimulating Demand Stimulate Inflation?*[14] He also gave a talk which was eagerly attended by economists from all three metropolitan universities. After Ursula had completed her work in Canberra, I arranged that they should have academic hospitality in Sydney where John was also consulted by the Reserve Bank. We gave them also private hospitality and Ursula, struck by the fine view from our apartment, got out her sketch book to make drawings from which she later did a painting and gave it to us. During that visit they suggested that, on my retirement, we should come to live in the reconditioned smaller part of their Porch House under a life tenancy for Anna, a generous offer which we could not accept.

I retired from the University of Sydney in May, 1980, and immediately set out on a tour which brought us in July to England, where we stayed for some months during which we had another stay at Porch House. On my return I was asked by UNESCAP to go to Bangkok to work on an energy project, and then to do the annual economic survey of Asia for 1982. While I was completing it I had a letter from John, who was again in Singapore with Lim Chong Yah. He suggested that I break my return journey to Sydney by spending a few days in Singapore with him and Ursula. I did that and was invited to dinner with them at Lim's house, a very pleasant occasion. Not long after I reached Sydney a letter came from Lim saying that, on John's recommendation, I was offered a visiting professorship at the National University forthwith. I was glad to accept, and had a rewarding fourteen months with good colleagues and good advanced students.

In 1984 we were once more in Britain, and had another stay with the Hicks at Porch House, where we witnessed their signatures to new wills.[15] Back in Sydney I had a letter from John saying that Ursula was

---

[14]This appears in Volume Two of his Collected Essays, *Money, Interest and Wages.*

[15]They were presumably connected with Ursula's election to a fellowship of the new Linacre College, to which Porch House went after John's life tenancy expired.

so ill as to be confined to bed, that he was looking after her with some difficulty because Porch House was not suited for nursing the sick. I was saddened next year to hear that she had died. In 1986 we returned to England and spent a week at a hotel in Chipping Camden from which we visited John, now living alone in Porch House. He spoke appreciatively of visits from his Oxford successor and also of a visit to Taipei organised by the Academia Sinica who had sent one of their men to escort him from England. While there he gave two important lectures which the Academia had printed in January 1986. One was *Towards a more General Theory* and the other *Managing Without Money*. He was also completing his last book, *A Market Theory of Money* (published in 1989),[16] helped by useful advice from Tom Wilson, an old colleague who had written the *Times* obituary for Ursula. He had difficulty walking but seemed to be well enough otherwise.

My last contacts with John were in 1988. We had again come to England and spent a few days in July at a hotel below Porch House and were invited to see him there. He was pleased about going soon to Italy for a gathering of leading economists from a number of countries to discuss the impact that *Value and Capital* had had upon economic thought. We took him to lunch the next day. Before leaving England in October I rang John. He had enjoyed the conference, but seemed rather depressed about his health. Within six months he was dead, and I had lost a valued friend who had done much to shape my thinking and my career. But, of course, I am only one of many who could say this the same about this gifted and kindly man.

---

[16]Although John was dismissive of monetarism, this book was well reviewed by David Laidler, a strong monetarist whom John described to me as 'very clever'; in telling of a symposium in which both had participated at the Bank of England.

# CHAPTER -3

# HICKS, A WORLD ECONOMIST

## *O.F. Hamouda*

### ABSTRACT

In this chapter, Hicks's work is examined in the light of his striking qualities: his powerful theoretical mind, his practical awareness, and his sense of the historical time dependence of intellectual contributions. Hicks's theoretical sweep is discussed via four areas: the theory of value and price determination; price and quantity determination; the complications related to fixed capital; and the definition of money and the dichotomy between the real and money sector. The issue here is not Hicks's success in resolving dilemas, but rather his constant, constructive approach which they highlight. Hicks's concern with practical issues in applied economics (labour, unemployment, inflation, trade, balance of payments and international finance, and development) is then discussed. To illustrate, through examples, how Hicks consistantly handled the intricate issue of policy intervention with delicacy. Lastly, it is observed that while theory or practical application might appear to have been Hicks's intermittant dominant concern, something more sophisticatedly measured is reflected in any pauses. Hicks's renown sequential (re-)treatment of ideas was a reflection of another of his essential qualities: his sense of the historical time dependence of both theoretical and practical contributions. He was able both to put each into time perspective and to address thereby all unresolved issues again and again.

## 1. INTRODUCTION

Hicks is one of the immortal economists who now belong to the history of thought. Like Adam Smith, before him, Hicks owes most of his economic contributions to his astute sense of observation of the world around him and to his deep and wide knowledge of the works of his predecessors and contemporaries. It was his early work, both on micro and macro-economics which earned him the Nobel Prize. In micro-economic theory, his contributions to general equilibrium, the theory of value, and welfare economics, in macro-economic theory, his work on the IS-LM and money shaped the foundations of ensuing standard text-book economics. It is these contributions which made him an economist's economist, appreciated by the world economics community.

Having had a very good education with a strong interest in British and world history, having been tempted in his twenties by and experienced journalism for a very short period, and having travelled extensively around the world for most of his life, Hicks, over the years developed, however, a universal, humanistic vision and attitude which were not always shared by his contemporaries (most of whom were more focused on the technicalities of economics). Four qualities combined made Hicks a truly outstanding economist. a) He had a powerful theoretical mind.b) He had a tremendous awareness of the practical economic problems of the world in which he lived. c) He was terribly conscious of the time-dependence of ideas, in terms of their reception and in terms of the importance of history, in the moment when new ideas are set out and in the placing of those ideas in their historical context. d) He was conscious that the fate of an idea, once in the public domain, is out of the hands of the author, such that it goes forth with a life of its own.

To place Hicks and his achievements in the development of the economic ideas, it is perhaps worthwhile to restrict the present chapter to providing an account of the general aspects of Hicks's work and to leave its details to be discussed by other contributors (Also, for a more elaborate assessment of Hicks' work, see Hamouda 1996). Hicks's three intellectual qualities (a powerful theoretical mind, an awareness of practical concerns, and a strong sense of the historical time dependence of both theoretical and practical contributions) always played an important part in his analytical preoccupation and were evident in virtually all his works. Hicks was, as a good Ricardian, able to build simple, elegant models from which he and his readers could infer a rich sense of the direction of economic forces. As he matured, Hicks further became, like Marshall, so aware of the human dimension that amidst the mechanical aspects of economics, his theories touched many aspects of the human being – specifically, time and the state of the evolution of the economy, at whatever stage – and he contemplated policies which might be derived from them. The perspective taken in this chapter is thus that

Hicks was a theoretical, applied and historically conscious economist of the world.

## 1. THEORETICAL MIND

The generation of Hicks, which includes Samuelson and Kaldor, to name a few, constituted a generation of its own, and each member will undoubtedly in retrospect be considered a classic economist in his own right. To gain appreciation of each one's contribution is, however, a different exercise than that presented to historians of thought by earlier generations of economists. Hicks's giant predecessors, Smith, Ricardo, Mill, Wicksell, and Marshall, for example, had each written a treatise on economic principles, in which the attempt was to discuss and analyse every aspect of economics. Their principle books, for each author, his magnum opus, went through numerous revised-editions and reprints with redefining changes here and there. The generation of Hicks and others, which followed, touched just as many theoretical aspects of economic foundations – in fact, these economists investigated each topic in more technical depth than had their predecessors – but their ideas were more spread out, to be found in many, many journal articles, books, and lectures, spanning a lifetime. To evaluate the overall contribution to economics of Hicks and Hicks's generation, one has, therefore, to search for and relate together the bits and pieces throughout all their writings, (which for some means those stemming from five or more decades of an active career), to reconstitute, as it were, their respective treatises of their *Principles*.

To take the case of Hicks, in particular, he wrote on both micro- and macro- issues as applicable, whether in statics or dynamics, whether in the context of labour-, good-, capital- or money markets, whether in the treatment of welfare and compensation principles, whether in a state of competition, asymmetrical or symmetrical information, or risk, whether they be consumer surplus, substitution of factors of production, or elasticity of expectations, whether they be growth, business cycle, inflation, trade, or (un)employment. Further, Hicks did not consider the assertions about whatever topic he studied at any one point definitive and left himself a margin for improvement or reconsideration. This careful attitude allowed him to make bridges between various parts of his theory or between his earlier and later works. For the reader, Hicks's work as whole is, therefore, a type of puzzle for which the pieces must be collected through time to grasp his attempts to satisfy himself with respect to the above numerous topics. For example, many, especially in America, received his *Theory of Wages* (1932) with excitement, yet to Hicks's mind it remained an unsatisfactory work for a long time. His *Value and Capital* (1939) is considered by most economic theorists to be a jewel; also, however, in Hicks' opinion, it had weaknesses which bothered him for a long time.

Reasons for Hicks's unhappiness with his treatment of a topic in any one text can be found here and there, as can his ways of addressing it. Hicks's rehabilitation of Walras' general equilibrium and his invention of devices, such as the elasticity of expectation and the IS-LM, which bear his name, will be lasting major technical contributions to economics, for which he deserves to have received many Nobel Prizes. Underlying his ingenious way of developing prototype model and clever techniques, however, Hicks had a much more ambitious goal. His energy was mostly consumed in attempting to resolve the major fundamental theoretical problems which preoccupied the discipline of economics and which had led to controversies since Adam Smith.

The most difficult theoretical issues for Hicks which persist well up to today were four: a) the theory of value and price determination, b) price and quantity determination, c) the complications related to fixed capital, and d) the definition of money and the dichotomy between the real and money sector. How did Hicks do with respect to each issue? Hicks, very early, knew that these four themes represented the heart of the theoretical foundation of the economics of a free market. He was well aware of the past and current controversies surrounding each one. He expressed uneasiness with the success of his early contributions derived from his sense that a technical and temporary solution to these difficult issues was not good enough. This also explains why he came back to hammer at the same issue and to face his own unanswered questions again and again.

With regard to the theory of value and price determination, since Jevons had declared that value and prices are the same (which was not the position of many who struggled greatly to explain the distinction between the two), the marginalist school had adopted prices as an expression of marginal utilities (and marginal productivity). In his *Theory of Wages* Hicks explicitly expressed his satisfaction with the usefulness of the marginal theory. He also applied it again a couple of years later to his banking theory in his "Simplifying the Theory of Money" (1935). By resuscitating Walras' general equilibrium Hicks fell happily within the sphere of marginal theory. Furthermore, with regard to the theory of equilibrium, by slowly weeding out the economic foundation of Marshall's indeterminateness and by hedging in favour of Edgeworth's determinism, which culminated in his *Value and Capital* (1939), the synthetic pinnacle of marginalism, Hicks led the way to the post-war development of rigorous microeconomics.

Aside from his having left out of his theory of value the role of the government, risk and uncertainty factors, and non-competitive aspects, Hicks's own growing unhappiness with *Value and Capital* (1939) stemmed from the realisation that his general equilibrium theory i) was unable to deal with simultaneous price and quantity determination, ii) did not handle properly the concept of fixed capital, and iii) was unable to integrate money. These are the three difficult and controversial issues which, especially the last two, continued to frustrate economic theorists and have led to endless debates yet to be resolved. Hicks would tirelessly spend his entire life attempting to resolve them. From about the mid-nineteen-fifties and thereafter he tried to build a single theory that could accommodate both the fix-price and the flex-price theories. Even, however, in Hicks's most elaborate theoretical construct, *Capital and Time* (1973), the dichotomy between the two remained, despite his determined efforts to integrate them.

Hicks wrote three entire books on capital, *Value and Capital* (1939), *Capital and Growth* (1965) and *Capital and Time* (1973), not to mention his numerous articles dedicated to dealing with both circulating and fixed capital. He was aware of the tremendous difficulty that fixed capital poses. In the end, even in his most sophisticated approach, *Capital and Time*, the dichotomy between fixed capital and circulating capital remains. Hicks found, in fact, an ingenuous way of making fixed capital disappear entirely from his theory, to avoid the Wicksellian problem of technical reversal. Indeed he believed that his Austrian simple model of traverse (two sectors, two periods) was immune to the re-switching problem, all the while not daring to venture into more sophisticated cases. Hicks avoided entirely dealing explicitly with the problem of fixed capital.

Hicks was extremely aware of the importance and the role of money both at the micro level in value determination and at the macro level in the establishing of the general price. Nonetheless he developed his theory of money in parallel with his real sector theory. Even in his last book *A Market Theory of Money* (1989) where he attempted to integrate both the monetary sector and the real sector, however, the dichotomy remained.

The point here is not to evaluate Hicks's success, or otherwise, in resolving the greatest issues of economics, but rather to highlight both his constant constructive way of bringing the theoretical issues of the discipline to the fore and of putting them in perspective, and his way of reminding economists that the difficult task of facing unresolved issues remains. Even if he did not supply all the solutions, he laid the ground for further research and provided a reminder of just how difficult the tasks facing economists really are.

A direct implication of the extreme difficulty of theoretical issues which carries over for all economists into the instances of attempts to come up with practical suggestions for change is the problem of trying to link theoretical causal relations to practical issues. In an economic theory one can posit the necessary causal relations to come up with a proto-type model which can explain specific phenomena. In a theoretical construct it might be easy to come up with a set of policy conclusions, however, as Hicks was aware, dynamics and the working of a real economy are far more complex in cause and effect relations than models can encompass. Thus for Hicks, any of his simple prototype theories would have to be interpreted with great caution for policy applications.

## 2. PRACTICAL ECONOMIC ISSUES

Hicks was concerned with every practical economic issue that might imply macroeconomic policy, whether in the form of rules of regulation or de-regulation, or in terms of fiscal and monetary prescriptions. His attitude, however, was not always clear, and sometimes it was subtle to the point of almost being non-committal. Consider, for example, this passage:

> I ... try to construct a theoretical framework which may help us in our thinking about the condition of the world at the present time. ... Keynes did in fact give us another model even more exactly parallel to the kind of thing I want to attempt in this paper – the theory of a war economy which he used as a foundation for his "How to pay for the War". I cannot indeed hope in this paper to get as far as Keynes could be relied upon to do; I shall try to diagnose, but I shall not venture far into the field of prescription. Perhaps I shall tempt you to do some prescribing on the basis of my diagnoses; or perhaps the diagnoses themselves will give you enough to discuss. (Hicks, 1959, p. 3)

The issue of intervention for Hicks was very intricate. On the one hand, economic activity is a human institution in which in all situations there is undoubtedly some unfairness and reaping of advantage by a few, which calls for something to be done to prevent abuse. But how can this be done? The first regulator which comes to mind to intervene to rectify the imperfections, would perhaps be a government. To Hicks's mind, however, since government itself is a human institution, why should one trust it over any other group of people? Hicks believed that, whenever possible, the setting for economic activity should be one in which a large number is involved and no monopolies are allowed in any form, because to a great extent, competition itself provides checks and balances on abusive behaviour. Since this is, however, not always possible, some form of regulation may have to be introduced.

Examples could be found in Hicks's treatment of virtually every area of applied economics. Here, however, discussion of five examples will serve to illustrate his policy approach. The first example concerns his attitude toward unions and monopolies in the labour market. While visiting South Africa in the late twenties during his early years as an interim teacher, Hicks was preparing his *Theory of Wages* (1932). He saw first-hand how the labour movement was not interested in defending the welfare of the working class as a whole, or of all the poor. It was only concerned with the interests of the white workers, leaving all black workers unprotected, subjected to exploitation and victimised by sustained apartheid. This experience gave his thinking clear direction, as to how the free market and competition would have, at the expense of the "sheltered" workers' wages, provided greater wage equalisation. This observation of the world led Hicks to formulate the *Theory of Wages* (1932) in the way he did, relying nonetheless more on unconstrained, (harmonious) forces than on superimposed (arbitrating) policies to resolve conflict. He did, however, provide some discussion on conciliation and arbitration in industrial disputes and also on wage regulation at the firm level.

The discussion of wage labour in the *Theory of Wages* (1932) was only one aspect which had practical ramifications; another theoretical area, which provides another example of a potential for policies, now from a purely macroeconomic perspective, is that of employment and unemployment. His interest in employment and unemployment stemmed from, on the one hand, his discussions of Keynes and Keynesian economics, which began with his publication of "Mr. Keynes's Theory of Employment" (1936), and on the other, wide-spread contemporary application of Keynesian policies. Hicks did not ignore the existence of unemployment, but initially made a (non-Keynesian) distinction between temporary unemployment and normal unemployment: he saw the former as the result of economic downturns, part of the expected business cycle, and the latter as due to the fact that the individual's potential to provide adequate work as an employee is lacking, due to insufficient training, ability or due to disability. By virtue of these very definitions, Hicks could assume full employment (or a state in which rectification of unemployment is unnecessary) in his models, taking temporary (cyclical) unemployment to improve rapidly with changes in the competitive environment and normal unemployment having only a social, not an economic solution.

Nonetheless Hicks was drawn to address directly the root of cyclical unemployment, as noted, the periodic downturn of one or more sectors of the economy. In an ideally flexible world, Hicks's theoretical remedy was for market forces to jump-start production again, but, he recognised, in a world of economic imperfections, including monopolies, trade unions, etc., some practical form of government controls and incentives would likely have to be introduced. However absent any concrete policy suggestions of his own for stimulating production, Hicks maintained that no policy, whether its goal was to increase production efficiency with existing sources of primary products or to develop new sources of raw materials supply, should be implemented at the expense of inflation or a national economy's balance of payments (Hicks, 1977, pp. 104-7). For Hicks, a country's policy decisions to rectify internal economic problems, such as unemployment, could easily spill over into jeopardising its domestic and its international economic strength, should the connection between labour-market remedies, for example, and other components of a national economy not be fully considered. Inflation was, however, for Hicks so directly related to unemployment that contemplation of a remedy for one had to take the other into account. An inflationary impact would, for example, according to Hicks, result from any government policy aimed directly towards rectifying cyclical unemployment by enlisting spending or taxation measures. Hicks was, however, loathe to see tolerating sustained unemployment as an acceptable practical approach to the threat of inflation and so chose to tackle inflation in its own right, another example of Hicks's applied economics.

Hicks' analysis of the causes of inflation in the latter half of the twentieth century reflected a) his assertion that inflation was not "a monetary matter" and b) his conception that a causal chain of effects linked rising money wages, or falling real wages, back to rising prices, or the rising "money values" of things, back to decreasing production levels, or a weakening of the economy. Since Hicks felt that "what is bad about inflation is principally not its effects", he turned both theoretically and practically to address first its root cause. It was the familiar "weakening of the economy which is the cause of the evil. If that is cured, inflation, with only a little help from monetary policy, will cure itself". (Hicks, 1989, p. 135) In his discussion of inflation Hicks did entertain tax's transfers to entrepreneurs as a production-stimulating policy treatment, but to "cure" only extreme production weakness, as in a post-war circumstance (Hicks, 1982, p. 152). A more accessible level of the economy for policy measures to combat inflation was, for Hicks, the consumer level:

> The only anti-inflationary measures which are available, under the Labour Standard, ... are price control and, if necessary, rationing; it is one of the costs of the Labour Standard that these measures require to be introduced in order to deal with slighter and more temporary falls in real wages than would previously have required such drastic treatment. Further, though this is the only way out, it is difficult to make it wholly effective; if it is not wholly effective, it brings other troubles with it. (Hicks, 1952, p. 95)

Hicks acknowledged that wage controls had been tried in some circumstances, but viewed them himself as a very last resort (Hicks, 1974 and 1975).

Hicks wrote a lot on trade and balance of payments, and other international questions, but it is the specific issue of the European Monetary Union and its related issues of a European currency and a central bank which best illustrate his practical involvement, from a distance, in an active, financial, topical debate. As in virtually all of his analyses of critical theoretical circumstances, Hicks derived the scope of his discussion from the real-world situation. In this case, "Should Britain enter or not enter, or partly enter, the European Monetary System (EMS)?" (Hicks, 1989, p. 121) Hicks's response was non-political, to say the least. His conviction in the possibility of a non-interventionist solution to the as-then undecided role of Britain in the existence of the ECU, and more importantly in the role of the pound sterling, which for most of the nineteenth century, before the US Dollar Standard, had been the currency of "a sort of central bank for the whole world economy" (Hicks, 1986, p. 21), derived from his extrapolation from historical record. For the last two hundred years, currency leadership had not been "acquired by a decision of the 'central' government, or of its banking system". It had come "from decisions by others, who choose to make the currency of that country their chief "international"" (Hicks, 1989, p. 130) or through market forces, "without any treaty having been needed to establish it" (1989, p. 127). So the question for Hicks was really whether circumstances had changed so significantly as to require now umbrella policy measures on a currency standard, to which he, briefly, answered "no". Even in the current case of adoption of the ECU and decision on a possible locus for its central bank, it was not up to any governmental agency, whether national or international to orchestrate the changes (Hagemann & Hamouda, 1991). At the very most such an institution might give its acknowledging rubber stamp to such decisions which would already have been taken by the amorphous, unrestricted financial-trade-consumer collective.

The last example of Hicks's practical approach to economics is to be found in perhaps the most obvious area: development economics. Hicks, especially due to his first-hand observations during travel to parts of the developing world, observed that certain socio-economic conditions needed remedy. The three he noted most troubling were poverty, malnutrition and rapidly increasing population. Granting that poverty and malnutrition, both potentially life-threatening to the current generation, require the most immediate remedies, Hicks gave the widest range of possible interventionary measures to circumstances of increasing population. All of the applications Hicks was to propose, even if directed first and foremost to the economic dangers of over-population, would, however, in time have a positive impact on reducing the threat of poverty and especially malnutrition. The immediate sector they were designed to influence was that of agriculture, or food production.

Hicks advocated the fostering of expansion first and foremost in the quantity of agricultural production and secondly in product diversification generally. While some development economists might advocate methods of intervention designed to effect directly changes in population reproduction rates, Hicks saw his task as "a matter of finding places for the rising generation that is already there", through "horizontal expansion" non-uniformly across a country's economy (Hicks, 1959, p. 197). In the exemplary case of Ceylon, Hicks advocated at least seven distinct policy measures for enhancing agricultural production:

> What Ceylonese agriculture seems to require is **better organisation, better methods of production,** not a lot of capital investment. Improvement on these lines involves **a good agricultural advisory service,** and (no doubt) **some credit facilities;** it probably involves **some rationalisation of holdings;** and it no doubt requires **a system of incentives,** which will *impel* cultivators to a **utilisation of the facilities offered.** (bold emphasis added; Hicks 1959, p. 202)

By his system of agricultural incentives Hicks meant a reward subsidy concentrated at the high margin of production, financed by a universal land tax on "normal" output.

To enhance product diversification generally, Hicks first considered, in the case of Ceylon again, the situation of existing products in the overall economy. He did not advocate policies fostering products which were already or would prove to be, through lack of local primary resources, dependent upon outside or imported materials. Nonetheless he did envisage instances in which new industries should be supported through infant industry protection (in the form of the public supplying of energy resources, export taxes, budgetary assistance for employment costs, and no fixed demands for increases on return). More surprisingly, perhaps, Hicks did not object to the establishment of public enterprises for some products, to give time to the private sector to develop. A public corporation must, he wrote, however, be "manned by persons of authority who are independent of government and who yet possess an unimpeachable public reputation, so that they can command, on their own reputations, the full confidence of the public" (Hicks, 1959, p. 208).

The above few examples of Hicks' approach to policy recommendation show his open-mindedness. Whenever the socioeconomic processes are at work in a well-established institutional, legal, and technological setting whose forces of interest are counter-balanced, in many instances, he felt, solutions to practical economic problems could be found with some guidance and very little intervention. This translated, thus, for Hicks, into a more distanced role for the policymaker. When, however, a portion of a country's population is in significant need and the mechanisms for counter-balancing interest are not adequate, then Hicks could be quite forceful in his interventionist policy recommendations.

### 3. THEORY AND POLICY IN TIME

Of Hicks' two intellectual qualities, his powerful theoretical mind and his awareness of practical concerns, one might appear that at any one point in his life to have been the more dominant. For example, from the end of the nineteen-twenties until the early – fifties, theoretical issues unquestionably preoccupied him most. Hicks spent his travel time mostly in Europe and America, associating with others with whom he could have theoretical discussions. Practical issues began, however, to surface strongly in his writing with his exposure, through wider travel, to the geographic context of ideas. The resounding impact of his early trip to South Africa in the nineteen-thirties and his involvement in his wife Ursula's absorption with national accounting during the war and fiscal development thereafter in the fifties became evident in his work. John and Ursula Hicks co-authored numerous articles over a series of trips to the developing countries and her studies of their financial policies, and he began reflecting practical fiscal concerns in his own writings. Hicks's receipt of many honorary degrees during the nineteen-sixties and onward, each tied to an invitation to lecture to a wider audience, might explain in part his pondering yet other aspects of economics, methodology and philosophy. As a more mature traveller and lecturer, he seems no longer to have contemplated economics only in terms of pure theory, but in a much broader, even historical sense.

Clearly, however, there is something more sophisticated and measured being reflected than a simple predominance of theory over practice or practice over theory at various points in Hicks's intellectual life. He was an extremely eclectic theoretician who would pick up an issue to work it through as best he could at one point in time, only to pick it up later, in the same state he had left it decades earlier, either to change it or to drop it again. He was a sophisticated thinker in the sense that he could let whole parts of his intellectual person a exist without working on them. He was measured in the sense that he had multiple theoretical interests and looked at their many aspects at many different periods throughout in his entire life. Hicks also, however, had many different approaches to the many different aspects, such that, as the examples above were intended to illustrate, he might pursue first a very theoretical approach, then a relatively pragmatic one, for almost all of them. In the latter part of his life, he would push the connections between theory and practice even farther to explore through an examination of economic methodology and philosophy the root of the fundamental difficulties in economic theory and the sources of the necessary ambiguity in deriving policy applications from theory.

Sequential treatment and re-treatment of ideas was a reflection of yet another essential quality of Hicks: his strong sense of the historical time dependence of both theoretical and practical contributions. The origin of this awareness may have been his slow, self-conscious awakening to the early conviction he had manifested in the *Theory of Wages* (1932), that any theory could be generalised and applied anywhere in the world at any time. Theory as specific to its time and place made apparent to him through critiques of his theories, through travel, and through his exclusion from direct participation in wartime planning. In retrospect, it struck him that the disastrous reception of his first book (at Oxbridge) was due to poor timing – although he would say that its place was well defined. As Hicks grew older, he increasingly saw problems and their solutions as time and locale specific.

What he probably ought to have concluded instead was that he and his works marched perforce to tunes of different drummers. He might have emphasized the conviction of which he was very conscious: that the fate of an idea, once in the public domain, is out of the hands of the author. It goes forth with a life of its own and its fate is very much the product of the time and place of its reception. Nonetheless what Hicks wrote was mistaken, by him even, for himself, for it ensued so completely from his collecting experience and reflection and his extensive mulling over of both of them. Although he was not a visionary, or at least he did not let himself be cast in that role, he certainly acknowledged the importance of the issues of the day, and his characteristic was to observe the current state of the issues, whether theoretical or practical, in the conviction that one cannot anticipate answers before collecting information and knowledge. Should, however, as much effort now be turned to understanding the whole corpus of Hicks's work as has been dedicated by economists to his earlier technical works, slowly the realisation of how rich and profound the full legacies of both Hicks and his works really are will come to light.

## REFERENCES

Baumol, W.J., 1972. "J.R. Hicks' contribution to economics", *Swedish Journal of Economics*, 74: 503–27.

Hagemann, H. and Hamouda, O.F., 1991. "Hicks on the European Monetary System", *Kyklos*, vol. 44, fasc. 3: 411–23.

Hamouda, O.F., 1993. *John R. Hicks. The Economist's Economist* Oxford/Cambridge, MA: Blackwell Publishers.

Hicks, J.R., 1932. *The Theory of Wages* London: Macmillan.

Hicks, J.R., 1935. "A suggestion for simplifying the Theory of Money", *Economica* February: 1–19; rpt. 1967. *Critical Essays in Monetary Theory* Oxford: Clarendon Press,
pp. 61–82; rpt. 1982. *Money, Interest and Wages. Collected Essays on Economic Theory*, vol. II Oxford: Basil Blackwell, pp. 46–63; rpt in Helm, 1984. *The Economics of John Hicks* Oxford: Basil Blackwell, pp. 168–85.

Hicks, J.R., 1936. "Mr Keynes's Theory of Employment", Economic Journal June, 238–53; rpt. 1982. *Money, Interest and Wages. Collected Essays on Economic Theory*, vol. II Oxford: Basil Blackwell, pp. 84–99.

Hicks, J.R., 1939. *Value and Capital* Oxford: Clarendon Press.

Hicks, J.R., 1959. *Essays in World Economics* Oxford: Clarendon Press.

Hicks, J.R., 1965. *Capital and Growth* Oxford: Clarendon Press

Hicks, J.R., 1973. "The mainspring of economic growth", *Swedish Journal of Economics*
December: 336–48; rpt. 1977 *Economic Perspectives. Further Essays on Money and Growth* Oxford: Clarendon Press.

Hicks, J.R., 1973. *Capital and Time*. A Neo-Austrian Theory Oxford: Clarendon Press.

Hicks, J.R., 1974. *The Crisis in Keynesian Economics* Oxford: Basil Blackwell.

Hicks, J.R., 1975. "The permissive economy" in "Crisis '75 ..." *Institute of Economic Affairs*, Occasional Papers, 43.

Hicks, J.R., 1977. *Economic Perspectives: Further Essays on Money and Growth* Oxford: Clarendon Press.

Hicks, J.R., 1982. *Money, Interest and Wages. Collected Essays on Economic Theory*, vol. II Oxford: Basil Blackwell.

Hicks, J.R., 1989. *A Market Theory of Money* Oxford: Clarendon Press.

# CHAPTER - 4

# "MR. KEYNES" AND HICKS'S VALUE AND CAPITAL

## Michio Morishima

### ABSTRACT

After pointing out that Hicks' theory of the firm is not adequate as the base from which investment functions of firms are to be generated, it is further pointed out that his ideas of IS and ML curves are inconsistent with his general equilibrium approach in *Value and Capital*. In the present paper it is also shown that the theory of the firm which I have proposed in an earlier book of mine is able to derive both the demand and supply functions of money and securities and the physical investment function. It is important to have one entire theory that can explain financial and physical aspects of investment behavior of entrepreneurs simultaneously.

## 1. INTRODUCTION

1. As soon as Keynes's *General Theory of Employment, Interest and Money* was published in 1936, Hicks wrote "Mr. Keynes and the Classics: A Suggested Interpretation", *Econometrica* 1937 [1]. Obviously, he was then writing *Value and Capital* [2]. In fact, we find a passage in its introduction: "Mr. Keynes's [book] appeared at a time when my own work was well under way, but was still incomplete in several respects. Since we are concerned with similar fields, it was inevitable that I should be influenced by Mr. Keynes' work to a very great extent. The latter half on this book would have been very different if I had not had the *General Theory* at my disposal when writing. The final chapters of Part IV, in particular, are very Keynesian./When I began to work on Capital, I had the hope that I should produce an entirely new Dynamic

Theory – the theory that many writers had demanded, but which none, at that time, had produced. These hopes have been dashed, for Mr. Keynes has got in first. Yet I still think it worth while to produce my own analysis, even if it looks pedestrian beside his. A more pedestrian approach has the advantage of being more systematic; further, I think I have cleared up several important things he left not very clear".[1]

But Hicks's approach is very different from Keynes' because it is based on the general equilibrium analysis in terms of demand for and supply of commodities and their prices, whilst Keynes' on the income approach in terms of output, input, consumption, and investment. To put these two in the same framework, Hicks assumes that outputs are sold out as soon as they are produced, and inputs are bought from other firms when they are used. These assumptions are usually made in the static analysis, but do not generally hold true in dynamics, as they are valid in the stationary state only. An excess of supply over output, as well as input over demand creates a decrease in the stock of relevant commodities. Hicks' theory of the firm does not pay any attention upon stocks, so that investment is absent in his dynamic analysis of production in [2].

Consequently we have to say his interpretation of Keynes in [1] does not follow from his main work [2]. In order to achieve his aim of deriving Keynes from [2], his theory of the firm must be expanded so as to include not only input and output, but also demand and supply as well as stocks. Regardless of these basic differences, Hicks characterizes the final chapters of [2] as "very Keynesian". It is true that they may be called Keynesian, but it must be noticed that his results have been derived in a more or less intuitive way but do not follow from a rigorous analysis of his own model. Unless we make some serious amendments, the general equilibrium theory of his type is unable to serve as a foundation of Keynesian economics.

2. As said above, Hicks' theory of the firm is based on two assumptions: (I) For any product the equation, output = supply, holds, and (II) for any factors of production, demand = input holds. In fact, following the sentence that a firm "will reduce its cash balance by any acquisition it makes of factors of production, increase it by any sales of products"[2] Hicks transforms the equation whichO. Lange refers to as Walras' Law:[3]

---

[1][2], p. 4.
[2][2], p. 156.
[3]See [4].

Acquisition of cash by trading = Value of sales of products

– Value of demand for factors – Interest on debts (1)

– Value of securities issued (or sold) – Dividends

into:[4]

Acquisition of cash by trading = Value of output – Value of input

– Interest on debts + Value of securities issued (or sold) (2)

– Dividends.

On the other hand, we have for any private individual

Acquisition of cash by trading = Receipts (3)
(including interest on securities owned) – Expenditure

– Value of securities acquired,

We then find, in view of (2) and (3), that one of the four equilibrium conditions,

Expenditure by private persons = Value of net output of commodities, (4)

Receipts by private persons = Value of input of the primary

factors of production + Interest on debts + Dividends, (5)

Value of securities bought = Value of securities issued or sold, (6)

Total acquisition of cash by trading = 0, (7)

follows from the rest. They determine prices, wage rates and the rate of interest.

The assumption (I) and (II) are crucially important in obtaining Hicks' equilibrium conditions (4)–(7). Otherwise, the supply of products and the demand for factors of production remain unexplained; Hicks' theory of the firm in terms of inputs and outputs cannot determine them.

3. There are, however, the following obvious relationships between output and its supply and also between input and its demand:

the value of output of product $i$ – the value of its supply = $G_i - G_i'$

---

[4] [2], p. 156 and p. 158.

the value of demand for factor $j$ – (the value of its input + the maintenance and improvement costs of the stock of $j$) = $G_j - G_j'$

respectively, where $G_i$ is the actual value of product i the firms have at the end of period and $G_i'$ the value of i the firm have at the beginning of the period; $G_j$ and $G_j'$ are similarly defined for factor $j$.

Adding up above equations for all products and for all nonprimary factors of production (i.e. capital goods), we write; $G' = \Sigma G_i + \Sigma G_j$ and $G' = \Sigma G_i' + \Sigma G_j'$ Following Keynes we denote the total supply of the products by A, the total demand for capital goods, i.e. the total demand for capital goods that entrepreneurs purchase from other entrepreneurs by $A_1$, and the total sum on maintenance and improvement of capital goods B. We then obtain[5]

the total value of output – the total value of input

$$= A - A_1 + [G - (G' - B)].$$

Obviously the part in the square brackets stands for the increment in the value of the entrepreneurs capital goods beyond the net value they inherited from the previous period, it therefore represents investment $I$. The lefthand side of the same equation is nothing else than the total value of net outputs, $Y$. If $A - A_1$ equals the amount which individuals want to buy, i.e. $C$, as it should be in the state of equilibrium, then the above equation is reduced to

$$Y = C + I,$$

that is the aggregate market equilibrium condition for the whole economy. This corresponds to equation (4) under Hicks' assumptions (I) and (II). Our notation above enables us to put (4) in the expression, $C = Y$, which implies $I = O$. Thus we find that (I) and (II) are the assumptions which are inadequate for discussing Keynes' *General Theory*. Hence we must say that Hicks' *Value and Capital* is not adequate for providing a microfoundation for Keynesian economics, or we cannot say that his "Mr. Keynes and the Classics" is a simplified version of his major book.

4. This has been pointed out in my *Dogakuteki Keizai Riron* (1950), which at last appeared in English in 1996 with the title of *Dynamic*

---

[5] [3], p. 66.

*Economic Theory.*[6] It explicitly distinguishes between output, supply, and the stock of product, and similarly between input, demand and the stock of factor (or capital good). Throughout the following we neglect the maintenance and improvement costs for the simplicity sake.

Let us now use the notation in these two books instead of Keynes' one above. Let $x''_{it}$ be the stock of commodity $i$ at the end of period $t$. The stock at the end of period $t$ equals the initial stock of period $t$, $x''_{it-1}$ *plus* the increment during the period, which is, if $i$ is a product, the output of $i$ *minus* its supply during the period and if $i$ is a factor of production, the amount of the factor that the firm purchases (i.e. the demand for $i$) *minus* the input (the amount consumed for production) during the period. Hence, for product $i$

$$x''_{it} = x''_{it-1} + \text{output of } i \ (x'_{ti}) - \text{supply of } i \ (y_{it}) \tag{8}$$

and for factor $i$

$$x''_{it} = x''_{it-1} + \text{demand for } i \ (x_{it}) - \text{input of i } (y'_{it}) \tag{9}$$

Hence the equation, $x''_{it} = x''_{it-1}$, is obtained for product $i$ at t if and only (I) holds and for factor i if and only if (II) holds. We thus see that the two assumptions due to Hicks rules out investment.

Hicks had no theory of supply and demand of the firm. The supply of each product and the demand for each factor of production are equal to the corresponding output and input which are determined such that the discounted value of the stream of surpluses (= the discounted value of outputs minus the discounted value of inputs) takes on a maximum value. Then from (I) and (II) it follows the stock of commodity at the end of each period $x''_{it}$, equal to its initial stock $x''_{it-1}$, so they are all equal to the stock at the beginning of period 0, $x''_{it-1}$.

How should the theory of production be formulated, once (I) and (II) have to be given up?[7] This is the most basic point of the microeconomic foundation to the Keynesian economics. To do so, I consider, in my two books above, an entrepreneur whose production plan extends from period 0 to period $T$. We assume that he knows his subjective probability that when he is provided with a stream of money ($x_{00}, x_{01}, ..., x_{0T}$), securities ($x_{10}, ..., x_{1T}$) and stocks of commodities ($x''_{20}, x''_{30}, ..., x''_{nT}$), the adaptability of his business in the future will be at least as high as a

---

[6][5], pp. 21-3 and [6l, pp. 14-5.
[7][5], pp. 23-7 and [6l, pp. 15-7.

34

given degree $\xi$. Let it be $Q(\xi)$, which depends on interest rates, $r_t$, and prices $(p_{2t}, \ldots p_{nt})$, $t = 0, 1, \ldots, T$. We then write $Q(\xi) = Q(X, \xi)$, which is a probability distribution function, where

$$X = (x_{00}, \ldots, x_{0T}, x_{10}, \ldots, x_{1T}, x''_{20}, \ldots, x''_{nT}, p_{20} \ldots, p_{nT}, r_0, \ldots, r_T). \quad (10)$$

To each distribution $Q(X, \xi)$ we attach a positive number $\phi$; as we explain later the functional $\phi(Q(X, \xi))$ describes the entrepreneur's liquidity preference.

Next we define his net revenue (or dividends) in period 0 as:

Dividends $(R_0)$ = the value of supply of products – the value of demand

for factors of production – the value of new securities bought + the value of old securities sold + interest from old securities

– acquisition of cash of the firm.

This follows from (1) and may be put in symbols in the form:

$$R_0 = \Sigma p_{i0} \, y_{i0} - \Sigma p_{i0} x_{i0} - (x_{00} - x_{0-1}) - x_{10} + x_{1-1} + r_{-1} x_{1-1},$$

where the first summation $\Sigma$ applies to products only, while the second one to the factors of production only. In the economy of short period lending that we assume, old securities $x_{1-1}$ are sold and the new securities are bought by $x_{10}$. Where the firm has old securities, it receives interest on them, while where it has issued them as is assumed in equation (1), interest on debts must of course be deducted. Dividends in the future periods are defined in a similar way. We assume that the entrepreneur maximizes the discount value of the stream of dividends. We may then note that Hicks' discounted value of the stream of surpluses is nothing to play in the scheme of decision making of the entrepreneur, in the general case of (I) and (II) being ruled out.

We now formulate the theory of the firm as the problem of maximizing $\Sigma \beta_t R_t$, with the discount factor $\beta_t$ defined below, subject to (8) and (9), and

$$\phi(Q(X, \xi)) \geq \gamma, \quad (11)$$

where $\phi$ is set such that $\phi(Q(X_0, \xi)) >, = , < \phi(Q(X_1, \xi))$ according as the entrepreneur judges the distribution $Q(X_0, \xi)$ to be more, equally, or less preferable to the distribution $Q(X_1, \xi)$ from the viewpoint of liquidity. The constraint (11) implies that the entrepreneur chooses a production plan whose index of liquidity preference is at least as high as $\gamma$, a given number. In addition, we have an implicit production function of the Hicksian form:

$$f(x_0, x_1, ..., x_T; y'_0, ..., y'_T) = 0, \tag{12}$$

where $x'_t$ the output vector of period $t$ and $y'_t$ the input vector. Solving the conditions for optimum, we obtain the equilibrium values of supply and demand, and stocks of commodities, as well as those of output and input. Because there are no constraints that should equate supply to output, and demand to input, the stocks of commodities may change from period to period. Obviously, the increment (or decrement) of the stocks which gives investment (disinvestment) does not necessarily vanish.

A microeconomic foundation of Keynes' economics which contains investment as a crucial variable can be obtained on the basis of such a microeconomic theory which includes investments on commodities as variables to be determined. In this theory the adaptability or liquidity preference function $\phi(Q(X, \xi))$, plays an essential role, so that we may refer to the investment theory of this sort as a liquidity preference theory of investment. At first sight it looks different from Keynes' production theory of investment saying that it is made as long as it yields net product more than the interest rate.

5. In this section I am concerned with restating the liquidity preference theory of investment in terms of Keynes' production theory of investment, i.e. the theory of marginal efficiency of capital. For this purpose I begin with a state of the firm's plan being settled at an optimum point discussed in section 4. Let us now suppose that the input of capital good k in period 0 by one unit and the output of good j in period 1 by $\alpha$ units, all other inputs and outputs in every period $t$, $t = 0, ..., T$, being kept constant. The demands for and supplies of all goods, securities and money in every period do not change. Obviously, then these imply, in view of (9), that the stock of capital good k increases in period 0 by one unit and this increase is kept until the end of period $T$, and, in view of (8), that the stock of good $j$ diminishes by $\alpha$ units throughout periods 1, ..., $T$. The productivity $\alpha$ is decided such that the liquidity of the firm is kept unchanged at the wanted level of $\gamma$.

Thus we have seen that the marginal increase in input $y'_{k0}$ for production of output $x'_{j1}$ implies substitution between $x''_{k0}, x''_{k1}, ..., x''_{kT}$ and

$x''_{j0}$, $x''_{j2}$, ..., $x''_{jT}$. There must be a certain relationship between the marginal rate of substitution between $x''_{kt}$ ($t = 0, 1, ..., T$) and $x''_{jt}$ ($t = 1, ..., T$) and that between $y'_{ko}$ and $x'_{jl}$. This is seen in the following way. At the point of equilibrium we have the marginal conditions:

$$\lambda\phi_{it} = \beta_2 p_{it} - \beta_{it+1} p_{it+1}, t = 0, ..., T-1, \tag{13}$$

$$\lambda\phi_{iT} = \beta_{T+l} p_{iT},$$

for all $i = 1, ..., n$, where $\lambda$ is the Lagrangean multiplier of the maximization problem being applied to the constraint (11), $\phi_{it}$ the partial derivative of $\phi$ with respect to $x''_{it}$, and $\beta_t$ the discounting factor,

$$\beta_t = \frac{1}{(1+r_0)(1+r_1)...(1+r_{t-1})}$$

with $r_t$ being the rate of interest in period $t$. Note, however, $\beta_o = 1$. Where one unit of the stock of commodity $k$ is increased in each period $t$ from $t = 0$ to $T$, $\phi$ increases by the amount

$$\phi_{k0} + \phi_{kl} + ... + \phi_{kT} = p_{k0}/\lambda \text{ because } \beta_o = 1. \tag{14}$$

Also from the fact that $x''_{jt}$ diminishes by i units in each period $t$, $t = 1, ..., T$, we see that $\phi$ decreases by the amount

$$[\phi_{j1} + \phi_{j2} + ... + \phi_{jT}]\alpha = \alpha\beta_1 p_{j1}/\lambda. \tag{15}$$

In order for $\phi$ to remain unchanged, we have from (14) and (15)

$$[\phi_{k0} + ... + \phi_{kT}] + [\phi_{j1} + ... \phi_{jT}]\alpha = 0$$

Therefore,

$$\alpha = -p_{k0}/\beta_1 p_{j1}. \tag{16}$$

On the other hand, (9) states that one unit increase in $x''_{k0}$ is made by one unit decrease in input $y'_{k0}$, so that $dy'_{k0} = -1$, and (8) implies that $\alpha$ units decrease in $x''_{j1}$ creates $\alpha$ units decrease in output $j$ in period 1, i.e. $dx'_{j1} = \alpha$. As we have equilibrium conditions,

$$\mu f_{k0} = -\beta_0 p_{k0} \text{ and } \mu f_{j1} = \beta_1 p_{j1}, \tag{17}$$

where $\mu$ is the Lagrangean multiplier applied to the implicit production function (12), and $f_{k0}$ and $f_{j1}$ are partial derivatives of f with respect to $y'_{k0}$ and $x'_{jl}$, respectively, we have in view of (16)

$$f_{k0} \, dy'_{k0} + f_{j1} \, dx'_{j1} = 0. \tag{18}$$

That is to say, $dy'_{k0} = -1$ and $dx'_{j1} = \alpha$ are technically feasible[8].

We now define the ratio of the marginal decrement of the net output to the marginal decrement of the value of input as:

$$\rho = \frac{p_{j1}dx'_{j1} - p_{k0}dy'_{k0}}{p_{k0}dy'_{k0}} \tag{19}$$

Taking (17) and (18) into account, (19) can be put in the form $(1/\beta_1) - 1$ which equals $r_0$ in view of the definition of $\beta_1$. Thus $\rho = r_0$.

This result obtained for $dx''_{k0} < 0$ follows in the case of $dx''_{k0} > 0$ too. In this case, though we have $dy'_{k0} > 0$ and $dx'_{j1} > 0$, we still have $\rho = r_0$.

We may call $\rho$ the marginal efficiency of input $y'_{k0}$. It is decided so as to be equal to $r_0$. Note that in this argument the demand for $k$, $x_{k0}$, is kept constant, so that (9) implies a relationship between investment and input such that

$$d(x''_{k0} - x''_{k-1}) = -dy'_{k0}$$

This completes the proof of Keynes' proposition that the level of investment is decided so as to establish an equality between the marginal efficiency of capital[9] and the rate of interest. In other words, the liquidity theory of the firm's production plan over time and the theory of marginal efficiency of capital are equivalent in the sense that the equilibrium conditions of the former implies the condition of the latter.

6. We have seen so far that it is impossible to derive IS and ML curves from the original system of Hicks' *Value and Capital*, because investment is absent there by virtue of the assumptions, supply = output concerning products and demand = input concerning factors. In this section we derive the curves from the corrected version of the system that has been discussed in the previous sections. For simplicity, we classify commodities, other than money and securities, into four groups: (1) consumption goods, (2) capital goods, (3) capital services, and (4) primary factors of production. Let $\delta_i$ be the rate of depreciation of a capital good i when it is used normally for production. Then the use of $1/\delta_i$ units of capital good $i$ means a loss of unit of it completely. Input of capital good i for producing other commodities is measured in terms of the loss of the capital good calculated in this way. Also assumed below

---

[8][3], p. 137.
[9] [2], p. 276.

are the prices belonging to each group always changing proportionately, so that commodities in the same group are treated as if they are components of a single commodity (according to Hicks' theory of group of commodities).

We write the prices of the commodity groups (1) and (2) as $p_1$ and $p_2$. $O_1$ and $S_1$ for group 1 denote the output and supply in period 0. $\overline{X}_1$ and $X_1$ are stocks at the initial and terminal points of time of period 0. For the sake of simplicity, throughout the following discussion we omit the subscripts signifying the period 0.

Then we have

$$X_1 = \overline{X}_2 + O_1 - S_1, \tag{8'}$$

Similarly for the producers of commodities of group (2)

$$X_2 = \overline{X}_2 + O_2 - S_2 \tag{8''}$$

and for the users of the same commodities

$$X_2' = \overline{X}_2' + D_2 - Q_2,$$

where $X_2'$ and $X_2$ are the users' stocks of commodities at the initial and terminal points of time of period 0, and $Q_2$ the input of the same commodities. We then have the value of net output, $Y$:

$$Y = p_1 O_1 + p_2 (O_2 - Q_2) = p_1 S_1 + p_2 (S_2 - D_2)$$
$$+ p_1 (X_1 - \overline{X}_1) + p_2(X_2 + X'_2 - \overline{X}_2 - \overline{X}_2') \tag{20}$$

Because we have the market equilibrium conditions

$$S_1 = D_1, S_2 = D_2, \tag{21}$$

where $D_1$ is the demand for consumption oods by individuals, so that $p_1 D_1 = C$, the above equation is reduced to:

$$Y = C + I, \tag{22}$$

where $I$ is investment: $I = p_1(X_1\ X_1) + p_2 (X_2 + X'_2 - X_2 - X_2')$. In addition to (21) we have the equilibrium conditions for primary factors of production, money and securities. Thus we have five conditions altogether, one of which follows from the rest because the Walras law holds. The remaining four determine $p_1$, $p_2$, $w$, $r$. We then write:

$$Y = Y(p_1, p_2, w, r), I = I(p_1, p_2, w, r) \tag{23}$$

As for consumption $C$, we assume that it depends on the national income earned $Z$ as well as $p_1, p_2, w, r$, given as:

$$Z = p_1 O_1 + p_2 (O_2 - Q_2) + w(N^S - N^D),$$

where $N^S$ and $N^D$ stand for the supply of and the demand for primary factors of production. Obviously, $wN^S$ is the current income the suppliers of the primary factors expect and the sum of the remaining terms on the righthand side of the above equation gives the current income of the enterprises the entrepreneurs expect. $Z$ is referred to as the expected income earned, and we may write

$$Z = Z(p_1, p_2, w, r) \tag{24}$$

It is equal to the national income produced in the state of equilibrium of factor markets,

$$N^S - N^D \tag{25}$$

so that

$$Z = Y. \tag{26}$$

From the first expression of (23) together with (24) we have the inverse relationships:

$$p_1 = p_1 (Y, Z, w, r), p_2 = p_2 (Y, Z, w, r) \tag{27}$$

Because $p_1 S_1 = p_1 D_1 \ C(p_1, p_2, w, r)$, $S_2 = D_2$, (26) and (27), we may write (20) in the form:

$$Y = C(Y, w, r) + I(Y, w, r), \tag{28}$$

and similarly the equilibrium condition for money, $M = D_0 (p_1, p_2, w, r)$, is put in the form:

$$M = L(Y, w, r). \tag{29}$$

Clearly, the last two equations are Keynes' macroeconomic equilibrium conditions. To eliminate the wage rate from them, he was concerned, as is well known, with two cases. Where $w$ is fixed at a certain conventional level, say $\overline{w}$, the labour market is cleared by adjusting the actual amount of employment $N$; the difference between quantity offered voluntarily at $w$, max $N^S(w)$, and the labour actually employed $N = N^D$ gives the involuntary unemployment, while the difference between the existing amount of labour $N$ and the maximum amount offered voluntarily gives the voluntary unemployment.

Where $w$ is flexible, Keynes measures $Y$ in terms of wage unit, i.e., $Yw = Y/w$, and assumes $C$, $I$, $L$ being proportional to w: we thus have

$$C_w = C_w (Y_w, r), \quad I_w = I_w (Y_w, r), \quad L_w = L_w (Y_w, r)$$

where $C_w$, $I_w$, and $L_w$ are given in terms of wage unit, $C_w = C/w$, etc. In this case, as is well known,

$$Y_w = C_w(Y_w, r) + I_w (Y_w, r), \tag{30}$$

$$M_w = L_w (Y_w, r). \tag{31}$$

We have thus converted the revised Hicksian type equilibrium conditions in terms of prices into those of the Keynesian type in terms of income, from which we may derive IS and ML curves. This shows the equivalence of the two systems under some added assumptions.

7. Let us now concentrate our attention upon the situation where the wage rate is fixed at W and the demand for and the supply of the primary factors of production are equated by adjusting the involuntary unemployment. Then $N^s - N^D$ vanishes from the equation of the Walras law. We get

$$Y = C(Y, r) + I(Y, r) + L(Y, r) - M - E_1 \tag{32}$$

where $E_1$ represents the excess supply of securities. The functions $C$, $I$ and $L$ do not explicitly contain $w$ as an argument because it is fixed at $w$. Or alternatively, (32) may be written:

$$p_1 [O_1(p_1, p_2, r) - C(p_1, p_2, r)]$$
$$+ p_2 [O_2(p_1, p_2, r) - Q_2 (p_1, p_2, r) - p_1/p_2 (X_1(p_1, p_2, r) - \overline{X}_1) \tag{32'}$$
$$- X_2 (p_1 p_2, r) + X'_2 (p_1, p_2, r) - \overline{X}_2 - \overline{X}'_2)]$$
$$+ [M - L(p_1, p_2, r)]] + E_1 = 0$$

where the parts within the first, second and third pairs of square brackets represent excess supply of consumption goods, capital goods and money, respectively. We notice a parallelism between the income analysis and the price analysis as they satisfy (32) and (32') respectively. In the former we may eliminate $E_1 = 0$ wherever the two equilibrium conditions (28) and (29) holds. The working of this system may be examined in terms of the IS curve and the ML curve derived from (28) and (29) respectively.

In the latter analysis, however, we have three markets of consumption goods, capital goods and money and eliminate the market of securities. The analysis is three dimensional in this case, but may be simplified into a two dimensional one by assuming proportional change between $p_1$ and $p_2$. In the last three chapters of *Value and Capital*, Hicks took this two dimensional approach, although in his own case the part standing for investment,

$$p_1 (X_1 (p_1, p_2, r) - \overline{X}_1) + p_2 (X_2 (p_1, p_2, r) + X'_2 (p_1, p_2, r) - \overline{X}_2 - \overline{X'_2})$$

should disappear, because of the fatally damaging assumptions, supply = output for products and demand = input for factors that Hicks made. We now observe that the equivalence between IS–ML analysis and the Hicksian general equilibrium price analysis is established whenever we get rid of the assumptions and construct the theory of the firm in a proper way, though we have to simplify the latter analysis by making the assumption of proportionality of prices of commodities.

8. Assuming as if he himself constructed a general equilibrium model which is saved from the damaging effects of the assumptions mentioned above, Hicks has dealt, in Chapter XXII on the temporary equilibrium of the whole system, with an examination of effects of investment. He makes an assumption of proportional change of prices of all commodities and aggregates markets of all consumption and capital goods into one which he calls the market of "commodities". He translates the laws obtained from a model of three goods into "terms of the triad Commodities, Securities, and Money", among which the market of Securities is eliminated by virtue of the Walras law. This system has two variables, one being the price of Commodities and the other the rate of interest.

Then Hicks writes: "Let us say that there is an increase in the demand for some particular commodity; expectations are inelastic, so that the increase in demand must be understood to be temporary, and all consequential changes in prices must be understood to be temporary too. The increase in demand will then be met, so far as is possible, by drawing on stocks or accelerating production." However, no drawing on stock is possible in his own original model that assumes all stocks remaining constant through time.

In the same way, the following sentences of Hicks, which are not intelligible within his own model, do perfectly fit the revised model. "If the increased 'investment' is financed by borrowing, the net change is an increased demand for commodities in terms of securities; this will raise the price level of commodities, and raise the rate of interest."[10] It is obviously true that Hicks' own model, though it is appropriate for dealing with stationary states of no investment, is useless in examining the process of capital accumulation. This is also true for his discussion on the trade cycle. The final two chapters of [2] dealing with capital accumulation and trade cycle should not be regarded as logically rigorous derivation from his own model, but as a description written intuitively on the basis of his economic common sense. They are mostly correct and consistent, because they fit the revised model presented above. Finally, it must be said that although the liquidity preference theory is usually regarded as a theory of choice concerning money and securities, stocks of commodities also have to be included in the list of items of choice. Otherwise the stocks of commodities to be held at the end of the present period 0 will be zero for products as well as for factors of production; so no sensible investment function will be obtained.

## REFERENCES

[1] Hicks, J. R., "Mr. Keynes and the Classics: A Suggested Interpretation," *Econometrica*, Vol. 5, No. 2, 1937, pp. 147–59.
[2] ditto, *Value and Capital*, Oxford University Press, 1939.
[3] Keynes, J. M., *The General Theory of Employment, Interest and Money*, Macmillan, 1936.
[4] Lange, O., "Say's Law: A Restatement and Criticism," *Studies in Mathematical Economics and Econometrics*, ed. by O. Lange et al., Univesity of Chicago Press, 1942.
[5] Morishima, M. *Dogakuteki Keizai Riron*, Kobundo, 1950.
[6] ditto, *Dynamic Economic Theory*, Cambridge University Press, 1996.

---

[10] [2], p. 277.

# CHAPTER - 5

# HICKS ON CAPITAL

## Syed Ahmad

### ABSTRACT

'Capital' was a major theme of many of Hicks's work, and the main purpose of
the present paper is to consider briefly how he treated this theme in his various
works. In modern times, capital has been looked at in at least three different
ways: (i) exactly like any other factor, (ii) as a produced means of production
and (iii) as representing the role of time in the production process, and Hicks
contributed to theories in all these frameworks. In the latter two, he also dealt
with the question of reswitching and capital reversal, which, however, he believed not a likely phenomenon. In his later work, he also got interested in 'historical' time in contrast to 'analytical' time, a distinction which as is well-
known, has particular significance for the theory of capital.

## 1. HICKS AND CAPITAL THEORY

Among Hicks' six major teatises in economic theory, all except the *Revision of Demand Theory* [1956] deal directly with capital and its ramifications; three of these include 'capital' in their titles. Thus it is not
surprising that capital also appears to be the subject of his most abiding
interest; his earliest major work, *Theory of Wages* [1932], and his last,
*Capital and Time* [1973],[1] both have capital as a major theme and this
interest continues in his later work.

In the recent literature on the subject, capital has been treated (i)
exactly like any other factor – simply as factor $x$; (ii) as a produced
means of production; and (iii) as representing the role of "time"[2] in the

---

[1]Not treating his *A Market Theory of Money* (1989) as one of his major treatise.

[2]Hicks, in later years, became keenly interested in the distinction between an event
taking place "in time" and "out of time" [e.g. 1976]. Here the discussion is not of
production 'in time'. We briefly return to this at the end of the paper.

production process. For purposes of association, rather than as a complete description, we may relate (i) to J.B. Clark and Wicksteed, (ii) to Marx and Sraffa and (iii) to the Austrians. Hicks comes close to making these associations in one of his later papers [1973A] but the parallel is not exact.[3]

It is somewhat intriguing, although given the length of the period over which, and the variety of context in which, Hicks has made his contribution, not surprising, that he has used each of these concepts of capital on one occasion or another. In describing such uses in the following paragraphs, I shall, for the sake of clarity perhaps draw sharper distinctions than Hicks intended.

The concept of capital he first used, in his *Theory of Wages*, was the Clarkian one[4] – the one still used in standard textbooks and for that matter in the new classical and endogenous growth literature. It is through this view of capital that he defined his famous "elasticity of substitution" – which still remains attached exclusively to his name in spite of his generous attempt [1970A] to share credit with Joan Robinson [1933]. "Substitution" is the central theme of this approach, and requires that an increase in wage rate cause a substitution of capital for labour. This was immediately attacked by Shove [1933] in his review of the *Theory of Wages*, from both the Marx-Sraffan and Austrian points of view. He wrote

"If capital means concrete capital goods, these are themselves the product of labour, so that, it would seem, the rise in wages must cause a proportionate rise in their cost of production and consequently (if there is no change in the rate of interest) in the annual charge in employing them. Similarly, if "capital" be identified with "waiting", the rise in wages causes a proportionate rise in the amount of waiting involved in the creation and use of a given instrument...".

Shove's was one of the most fruitful comments on the subject. This criticism forms the basis of the powerful "simple" and "general" non-substitution theorems published decades after this contribution.[5] Hicks's

---

[3]Hicks' distinction between the "fundists" and the "realists" [1973] is somewhat related, but not the same. The distinctions in the text relate mainly to the process of production, the distinction here is best seen as the producers view of "capital" whether he sees it in value or physical terms.

[4]Hicks himself feels [1963] that it was an awkward amalgam of the Clarkian and Austrian concepts, but in my view the Clarkian characteristic dominates.

[5]Samuelson [1949, 1966], Sraffa [1960], Mirlees [1969].

own reaction [1963] was perhaps an unparalleled example of integrity and magnanimity in the history of our subject. In spite of the book having become the standard reference, and almost an instant classic, he refused Macmillan's request to reprint it for the next thirty years! And when he did allow it to be reprinted in 1963, he included Shove's critical review as an appendix, strongly recommending it to the reader![6]

Hicks own use of capital as a produced means of production, the second concept in our classification, first appears in a rather pale form, in his *Contribution to the Theory of Trade Cycle* [1950]. Most of the argument of the book is couched in terms of a one-commodity economy, and hence the question of relative price never becomes significant. Therefore the complications which arise when commodities are produced by commodities do not appear. Hicks, however, uses a more developed form of this concept in his *Capital and Growth* [1965]. Here the produced means of production is different from the final good; to emphasise this difference, he calls them simply "machine" and "consumption good" respectively. Issues relating to both quantities and prices are discussed, and the questions of reswitching and capital reversal (more of which is in the following section) are raised, but, understandbly, the role of time in the production process is ignored. It is this omission which is attacked in Kennedy's powerful criticism in his contribution to a book written in Hicks' honour [1969]. Hicks' response [1970, 1973, 1977] was characteristically graceful. He accepted the validity of the criticism. but expressed dissatisfaction with Kennedy's solution and proceeded to provide his own, in an entire treatise in fact, *Capital and Time* [1973]!

This brings us to the third, the Austrian concept of capital. In *Capital and Time*, Hicks returns to his old interest in the Austrian approach, which, as he tells us [1984], dates back to a period even prior to the publication of his *Theory of Wages*, although, it is in his *Value and Capital* [1939] that he explicitly discusses this for the first time. Even then his interest in the Austrian concept predates his interest in and use of the Marx-Sraffa concept by at least a decade.

---

[6]See Hicks [1963], in which he attributes his reluctance to the reprinting of the book to other causes as well, including the Keynesian influence. See also his more recent attempt to explain his approach in *The Theory of Wages*, in a non-equilibrium context.

The main original contribution of *Value and Capital* is contained in the later parts of the book, where it deals with "dynamics"; the earlier parts are essentially only a systemization of Hicks' own earlier writings. Since "dynamics", as defined in *Value and Capital* is the analysis of situations in which "every quantity must be dated", it is not surprising that the Austrian concept of capital finds a congenial context. He not only uses this concept but goes on to redefine Böhm-Bawerk's period of production, as the elasticity of capital value with respect to the discount rate, $1/(1 + r)$. Although, his assessment of the Austrian approach in *Value and Capital* is negative, it is not a dismissive negative, but an appreciative one. In *Capital and Time*, and in the Menger volume [1973A], both published almost thirty five years later, and also in *Economic Perspective* [1977], he returns to the Austrian concept in a positive spirit.

One of the main critics of Hicks' use of the Austrian concept of and approach to capital in his *Capital and Time* is Burmeister [1974]. His main contention is that by not using the von Neumann approach [1932] which simultaneously incorporates produced means of production and time in the production process, and using instead the Austrian approach which incorporates only the latter,[7] Hicks is needlessly restricting his analysis to a less general case. Hicks' reply [1977] to this criticism is clear and definite. He says that although von Neumann approach to capital can take account of both aspects of capital, it can do so only for the steady state; outside this state it can take account of neither. Hicks' preference for the Austrian concept and approach, in spite of its apparent shorcoming, is based on his belief that it can be used in non-steady state situations as well, in particular, in what he calls the "traverse", the situations between the steady states.[8] Since an actual economy is never in the steady state, Hicks claims that from the point of view of application Austrian approach is superior to von-Neumann's. He could also

---

[7]That the Austrian approach does not take account of produced means of production needs clarification. All this means is that the produced means of production does not enter the analysis as such, and not that it does not exist in the system, since it is impossible for labour, which perishes at the moment of its creation, to coexist if performed at different points of time, unless it is incorporated into some produced means of production.

[8]In *Capital and Time* he discusses "traverse" as situations between two steady states, but later in [1977], he suggests that no reference to steady state is necessary for the argument.

claim that from the theoretical point of view also his case is not less general than von Neumann's since Hick's approach applies to situations to which the other does not.

## 2. HICKS AND RESWITCHING

It would have been surprising, considering the time he was writing his last major work, if capital reversal and its special case (Garegnani, 1970) reswitching, did not come up for discussion and indeed they did.

Hicks' contribution to the reswitching debate ranges from the discussion of the nomenclature and the shape of the tools of analysis to the reasons for and the significance of the phenomenon.

As is well-known, the usual tools of analysis of the reswitching phenomenon are wage-interest $(w - r)$ curves and wage-interest frontiers. Samuelson, who first named them [1962] called them "factor-price" curves and frontier. The argument used against these designations has been that the interest rate is not the price of a "factor", and the critics [e.g. Garegnani, 1970] changed the designation to wage-profit curves and frontiers. Hicks criticises [1973] both designations because of their unwarranted association with the distribution of income, which can at best be their secondary characteristic; he regards their relation to the efficiency of production as more basic and calls them respectively "efficiency curve" and "efficiency frontier". This is similar to, but not the same as, the criticism of defining the elasticity of substitution with reference to the relative income share of the inputs, rather than defining it strictly in terms of the productive characteristics of the inputs, such as their marginal product etc. However, Hicks' attempt at this disassociation with distributional concepts turns out to be only partially successful, since in his discussion also the distributional terms appear.

It may be noted that reswitching may occur because of the production process employing produced means of production, or requiring multiplicity of periods. Since Hicks employs both these concepts of capital, he discusses the shape of the efficiency curves in both these cases. In his *Capital and Growth* he deals with the former. In that case, the efficiency curves are usually "curves", but they can also be straight lines. In *Capital and Time*, he deals with the latter, and shows that now it cannot be a straight line (p. 40), since it cannot touch the wage axis, although at some point it touches the interest axis.

His more important contribution, of course, lies in his attempt to find the economic reasons for the reswitching phenomenon, and also to assess its importance and significance.

In trying to sort out the reasons for the reswitching phenomenon he attacks the issue from two related, but different directions, so to say. One is somewhat traditional, the other not so traditional. The attempt from the traditional direction is to relate it to the question of "complementarity". The implication is that just as in other areas of economics, complementarity spoils some of the simple results of economic theory, such as the simple negative relation between the price and quantity demanded, it does something similar in the context of the switching of techniques, by spoiling the simple relationship between the rate of interest and "capital intensity". He does not provide a full-blown argument on this issue, but usually only hints at it, particularly in the footnotes of *Capital and Time*. Perhaps this hint led attempts by others to provide formal proofs that complementary is a necessary condition for reswitching (or capital reversal), for example by Hatta (1976), (1988), but more recently shown by Steedman (1990) to be less general than Hatta had claimed.

The attack from a less conventional direction is Hicks' use of a special time structure of inputs and outputs, from which he concludes that reswitching cannot be a likely, or at least not a frequent, phenomenon. "That could happen; but it looks like being on the edge of the things that could happen" (1973, p. 44).

The special time structure he uses for this demonstration is what he calls the *Simple Profile*, with infinite horizons.

| Weeks | 0 to $m - 1$ | $m$ to $\infty$ |
|---|---|---|
| Inputs | $a_c$ | $a_u$ |
| Outputs | 0 | 1 |

In this framework there is a "construction period" of $m$ weeks (weeks 0 to $m - 1$) in which $a_c$ input per week is used, but there is no output. Then comes the "utilization period" in which $a_u$ input is used every week to produce 1 unit of output till the end of time. One technique differs from another only with respect to $a_c$, $a_u$, or $m$. By defining $m_1 = 1$ for one of the techniques, technique 1, he obtains from the manipulations of the efficiency curves derived from techniques 1 and 2, the relationship

$$a_{c2}[(1 + r)^{m2} - 1] = a_{u1} - a_{u2} + a_{c1}r$$

HICKS ON CAPITAL

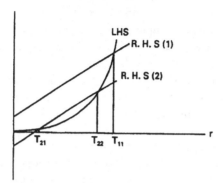

**Figure 1.**

He then plots the two sides of this equation against $r$ by assuming, without loss of generality, that $m_1 = 1$, and $m_2 > 1$, and then discusses two alternative situations with the help of the figure above. This gives the curve representing L.H.S. its origin at zero and its slope and curvature as drawn in the diagram.

The two alternative situations discussed are when the R.H.S. has a positive or a negative intercept, which depends, as we can see from the above equation, on whether $a_{u1} - a_{u2} < 0$. Reswitching may occur only in the latter case, as illustrated in the diagram. This implies that in the above profile reswitching can occur only if the operating cost is higher for a technique (technique 2 in this case) which also has larger gestation period ($m_2 > m_1 = 1$) but inspite of this, the technique is more profitable than the other. Hicks considers this unlikely, since this would require that the "double disadvantage" noted above is more than compensated by $a_{c2}$ being sufficiently lower than $a_{c1}$. From this he reaches the conclusion quoted above.

Hicks' attempt to give economic interpretation to what is usually presented as a bland mathematical characteristic is commendable, but his conclusion that this is an unlikely phenomenon is based on his speculation on a special case of the profile of his choice. There are simply innumerable cases which are not covered by Hicks' example, but in which reswitching can take place. (Ahmad, 1991).

Although Hicks considers reswitching a phenomenon not often likely to occur, he believes that "...its importance is not on its own account; it is for the much more substantial issue that lies behind it". [1973, p. 44]

The "substantial issue" is the possibility of finding any *one* index of capital intensity. Going back to his example he says that if $m_1 = m_2$, no reswitching can occur; techniques can be ordered in a manner such that one of them is unambiguously more efficient at higher rates of interest than the other, a higher ratio of $a_c/a_u$ represents higher capital intensity, etc. No such simple indices are available once additional features, such as difference in $m$, the length of the construction period, are added.

Hicks does not explicitly consider but implies by the above, is something which has been ignored by most other writers: the insufficiency of the ordering itself for the purposes for which the concept of capital is used. Let us say that we could find the necessary and sufficient conditions for such ordering, then could we go about using capital in our production functions, once these conditions were fulfilled? The answer has to be in the negative. For using "capital" in the production function, we need the *cardinal* and not the ordinal measure of the variables we use as input in the system – recall that even when utility is "measured" ordinally, the inputs that produce that utility still need cardinal measurement. Hence, not only reswitching is not necessary but only sufficient for capital reversal (Garegnani, 1970), capital reversal itself is not necessary, but only sufficient for the unsuitability of capital to be treated as an input in the production function.

### 4. LOOKING BACK AND AHEAD

This rather brief and sketchy review of Hicks' work on capital theory confirms the earlier stated view in Hicks' passionate desire to seek "the truth". In this search he moves from one concept of capital to another, and yet to another, and back. What he has already written never comes in the way of what he wants to write; if it contradicts his earlier writing, so be it. He simply acknowledges this and moves on. His attitude to economics has, by and large, been constructive; he has tried to forge tools which could be used for application - he wrote as early as 1939 that "... the place of economic theory is to be the servant of applied economics". However, he never hesitated in attacking a popular concept or tool of application, even if, or particularly if, he was himself its author – once he found it fundamentally flawed. One of such concepts, closely related to capital theory, is that of time as used in traditional economics. Although his awareness of an analysis being 'in time' or 'out of time' dates back to very early period, he had, in later years become increasingly concerned with the fact that most economic analysis, including some of his own widely acclaimed contributions are not 'in time', even when they do incorporate 'time' in the analysis in the traditional way. However, characteristically, he did not stop after criticising the traditional approach, but proceeded to deal with the issue in a constructive way [1976]. No doubt he had a long way to go, and he would have been the first to admit it, but this never deterred him from starting on his new journeys of discovery.

### REFERENCES

Ahmad, S. (1991) *Capital in Economic Theory*. Aldershot, Edward Elgar.

Burmeister, E. (1974) "Synthesising the Neo-Austrian and Alternative Approaches to Capital Theory" A Survey, *Journal of Economic Literature*.

Garegnani, (1970) "Heterogenous Capital, The Production Function, and the Theory of Distribution", *Review of Economic Studies*.

Hatta, T. (1976) "The Paradoxes in Capital Theory and Complementarity of Inputs" *Review of Economic Studies*.

Hatta, T. (1988) 'Capital Perversity' in J. Eatwell, M. Milgate and P. Newman (eds.) *The New Palgrave*, London, Macmillan.

Hicks, J.R. (1932) *Theory of Wages*, Macmillan.

Hicks, J.R. (1939) *Value and Capital*, Oxford.

Hicks, J.R. (1950) *A Contribution to the Theory of the Trade Cycle*, Oxford.

Hicks, J.R. (1956) *A Revision of Demand Theory*, Oxford.

Hicks, J.R. (1963) *Theory of Wages*, Second Edition, Macmillan.

Hicks, J.R. (1965) *Capital and Growth*, Oxford.

Hicks, J.R. (1970) "A Neo-Austrian Growth Theory" *The Economic Journal*.

Hicks, J.R. (1970A) "Elasticity of Substitution Again: Substitutes and Complements", *Oxford Economic Papers*.

Hicks, J.R. (1973) *Capital and Time: A Neo-Austrian Approach*, Oxford.

Hicks, J.R. (1973A) "The Austrian Theory of Capital and its Rebirth in Modern Economics" in *Carl Menger and the Austrian School of Economics*, Eds. J.R. Hicks and W. Weber, Oxford.

Hicks, J.R. (1976) "Time in Economics" in *Evolution, Welfare and Time in Economics*, Festschrift in honour of Nicholas Georgescu-Roegen, Ed. Tang. Reprinted in Hicks (1984).

Hicks, J.R. (1977) *Economic Perspectives*, Oxford.

Hicks, J.R. (1979) "Formation of an Economist" *Banca Nazionale del Lavoro Quarterly Review*, Reprinted in Hicks [1984].

Hicks, J.R. (1984) *Economics of John Hicks*, Ed. Helm, D.

Hicks, J.R. (1989) *A Market Theory of Money*, New York, Clarendon Press.

Kennedy, C. (1969) "Time, Interest and the Production Function" *Value, Capital and Growth: Essays in Honour of Sir John Hicks*, Ed. Wolfe, J.N.

Lutz, F. (1951) *Theory of the Investment of the Firm*, Princeton.

52

Mirlees, J.A. (1969) "The Dynamic Non-Substitution Theorem" *Review of Economic Studies*.

Robinson, J. (1933) *Economics of Imperfect Competition*, Macmillan.

Samuelson, P. (1951) "Abstract of a Theorem Concerning Substitutability in Open Leontief Models" *Activity Analysis of Production and Allocation*, Ed. Koopmans, T., Wiley.

Samuelson, P. (1961), "A New Theorem on Non-Substitution" *Money, Growth and Methodology*, published in honour of Johan Akerman, Lund.

Samuelson, P. (1962), "Parable and Realism in Capital Theory: The Surrogate Production Function" *Review of Economic Studies*.

Shove, (1933) Review: (Hicks Theory of Wages) *Economic Journal*.

Sraffa, P. (1960) *"Production of Commodities by Commodities, A Prelude to a Critique of Economic Theory"* Cambridge.

Steedman, I. (1990) 'Perversity without Complementarity' *Review of Political Economy*, 2, 138–48.

von Neumann, J. (1932, 1939, 1945–46) "A Model of General Equilibrium" *Review of Economic Studies* (1945–46).

# CHAPTER - 6

# HICKS AND ECONOMIC THEORY

## *Frank Hahn*

### ABSTRACT

In this issue devoted to Hicks his main works are considered, that is to say 'Value and Capital' and his books on growth. His considerable originality and contribution are noted, but also his occasional lack of technical expertise and his very English reluctance to read other people's work. It is argued that while his work was clearly in the Neo-classical tradition he was, it is argued, especially in his later years, uncomfortable in it. One of his great achievements was to propose a framework for dynamic analysis (based on a simple periodisation, "the week"): His work here was very influential. He returned to it in his later work on growth where he studied "the traverse" from one growth path to another. (But the complexity of this task was really to high for crisp results). This paper also re-evaluates the famous "Mr. Keynes and the Classics" which has lately been much derided. It is argued however that with the exception of his Trade Cycle book, Hicks never published anything which did not carry the marks of distinction. The "Revision of Demand Theory" and "A Suggestion for Simplifying the Theory of Money" are instances offered in evidence.

Most people, when asked, would class Hicks as a neoclassical economist. After all, Value and Capital rivalled Samuelson's *Foundations of Economic Analysis* as a neo-classical bible. What are the essential ingredients of this approach? Certainly rational self-interest of agents is one. The interaction of agents in markets is another, the outcome of which is captured by market equilibrium. Hicks and Samuelson were both faithful to Marshall in distinguishing short, medium and long period equilibrium. And yet, in spite of all these familiar features, Hicks cannot be regarded as a neo-classical economist in the contemporary American way. This will be my first topic for discussion.

I shall then speculate on the extent to which Hicks lacked modern technical equipment and how that lack may have affected his economic "Weltunschauung". Since I regard the latter as preferable to that of his more technically gifted successors, it will be found that this will not be the occasion of pejorative comparison.

I shall conclude with some critical remarks. These will be provoked by what, for a better term, I call "Oxford hubris".

# I

The first three chapters of Value and Capital were regarded by young theorists in Britain during the war, as setting a standard of excellence which Marshall and indeed most of Hicks' predecessors could not attain. Instead of a boy picking blackberries under diminishing marginal utility of berries we were given an account free from imponderables and, as we thought, operational. Hicks taught us that there was no need to measure utility for a positive theory of choice. (Later Samuelson maintained that we did not need utility at all but only consistency in choices.) All this was like a blast of fresh air, but had we been less provincial and read Italian we could have experienced its salutary effects earlier. Of course this exercise in Occam's razor was only a beginning. Income and substitution effects followed, as did compensating and equivalent variations, and it was crowned by the Slutsky equation. Later the whole was rather beautifully reworked and added to, in Hicks' Revision of Demand Theory. What we now had were theorems deducible from simple axioms.

This fruit of non-obvious implications from simple postulates was not always appreciated. For instance, Joan Robinson believed that the theory said no more than that an agent will choose what he prefers and preferences, being changeable, this was not much of a prediction. But it must be clear that the empirical content of the theory is a certain minimal stability of preferences. That is the hypothesis of importance, and it allows us to deduce the "fundamental law of demand" as well as quite unobvious implications like the symmetry of the substitution term. This still leaves the question of the most convenient way of thinking of preferences so as to endow them with as much stability as possible.

There are two questions here not much discussed by Hicks although there can be no doubt that he was aware of them. One of these concerns the "domain" of preferences. If it always commodities then inevitably the domain will keep changing with the discovery of new goods. Moreover the consumption of some goods is bound to affect preferences, e.g. consumption of education or of classical music. Some thought readily convinces one that one cannot expect stable preferences over commodities. But one could instead think of preferences over characteristics of goods: taste, appearance, smell, etc., characteristics embodied in different proportions in different goods. While that will not get one out of all difficulties it will go some way. But except for Lancaster [1966] and Gorman [1963] it has been rarely pursued although it is, for instance, clearly important for the construction of cost of living indices. (Fisher and Shell, [1972]).

Much of this will be familiar. But there is a connection to Welfare Economics of these problems which, perhaps, has been less frequently discussed. We owe the insight to Samuelson, Hicks, Kaldor and Scitovsky, that one cannot in general pass from agents' budget data to judging their welfare. To do so we would need the axiom of revealed preference to hold for aggregate data. Scitovsky for instance found it easy to produce paradoxical welfare judgements when that was not the case. There was much debate and Hicks wrote a fine summing up. [1975]. But it was left to Hildenbrand [1994], Grandmont [1992] and to some extent to Arrow-Hahn [1971] to show what properties of wealth and preference distribution led to the desired result. In other words, global results require some global information. Just as Arrow's celebrated theorem led to a search for special cases, (i.e. those which did not obey Arrow's restrictions), but were nonetheless interesting and allowed welfare ranking, so the "New Welfare Economics" of the immediate postwar years has drawn in its horns (although this may not be universally agreed).

But all of this, while no doubt important, was really secondary to Hicks' initial aim. That was to build an equilibrium theory from "the bottom up". That is, firmly founded in the theory of rational choice and market interactions of rational agents. Something rather surprising happened. Hicks fully understood the importance of future consequences of present action and that their evaluation was uncertain. He invented various tools, e.g. the elasticity of expectations, to deal with that, but of course could only reach classificatory conclusions of the kind "if the elasticity of expectations is less than one then..." In a famous passage he said that imperfect competition had to be ignored not because it was unimportant but because neither he nor anyone else knew how to deal with it on an economy-wide basis. He refused to use tatonnement dynamics and so produced somewhat peculiar ideas like "perfect stability". But compare him with his successors in Chicago or indeed in most graduate schools. Where these believe not only in the beneficence of the market system (for all I knew they are right), they also firmly hold that they understand what is required for strong advice or opinions. For that I can see no warrant but, what is more to the point here, neither could Hicks.

I believe that this characterisation of Hicks is of some interest. He was in the first place an English economist to whom the system building of continentals (e.g. Walras) and later Americans, was not serious. Champernowne, another economist in this mould, used to refer to almost all mathematical economic exercises as "toys". Hicks did not go as far as that and, indeed, was fascinated by technical analysis. But I warrant that when advising government, or suggesting remedies, he used it extremely roughly. That is an English characteristic: one is more averse to appearing pretentious than being wrong. Compare French and British philosophy to see something similar at work. In any case the idea of, for instance, an economy with "rational expectations" from now to the end of time would not have recommended itself to Hicks as a basis for actual economies as opposed to "Gedanken experiments".

I shall soon be arguing that Hicks paid a price for all of this, although I for one think that he was right to do so. One Mas-Colell is a great benefit, two or three produce the possibility of interaction, but dozens and dozens lead to a decisive change in subject matter. The same goes for one Lucas: let there be a relentless following of a textbook track. It will surely have some benefits. But when a school develops then there is time to call a halt.

It was Milton Friedman's "as if" theory which with rare exceptions has never recommended itself to Europeans. To do so we would need the precision of particle physics. So Hicks was never, as far as I know, tempted to write that the British economy behaved "as if" governed by a Ramsey maximiser. While he was reworking the Keynesian heritage to the end he neither abandoned nor, in the final analysis, endorsed it. His manner of proceeding was too literary and broad to allow this. On the other hand on the way he delivered various illuminations: for instance in his analysis of the precautionary motive.

This, at a somewhat late stage, brings us to "Mr. Keynes and the Classics". That it was one of the most influential papers ever written in economics is widely agreed. But it now has many many enemies. Most of these do not realise that the diagram is a cross-section of a very much larger one in which there are magnitudes of various dates and types. This makes it less suitable for our simple exercises, but it does not make it wrong. One can easily use it to discuss money neutrality etc. In fact there is a paper by Geanakoplos and Polemarchakis [1986] which does just that. It remains true, that for its date the Hicks paper deserves to be regarded as outstanding.

At the time "Mr. Keynes and the Classics" greatly enhanced Hicks' standing in the profession. But of course it could not survive the rather more complete analysis which included above all a well articulated financial sector and a theory of prices. There were also difficulties in distinguishing "stocks" and "flows" and much else besides. What is therefore striking is that, as Solow noted, [1984], as a first approach to a study of a policy change, it remained serviceable. But not adequate. However a not dissimilar short-cut - the real Phillips curve - is still widely accepted in spite of its repeated (empirical) failure. Moreover, it was also based on rather ad hoc theorising: mistakes made by workers and employers in the short run. This may have been a real psychological insight, although in the nature of the case it would be hard to establish. I conclude that macro-economists use whatever short cuts they can get away with, and that Hicks was in no way special here. He took prices as relatively constant in the short run and certainly a short run possibility of non-clearing labour markets. In retrospect this does not mean a set of very extravagant assumptions.

## II

Hicks' work covered a very wide range and whatever he touched he improved. But it was inevitable as the subject changed as dramatically in its method of analysis that Hicks' work would appear a little out of date not in content but in method. He had mathematical gifts but in many areas not enough mathematics. I rather suspect that he would have liked to have had more but never stood ready to sacrifice his latest economic pursuit to learn more.

A good example is his essay on the turnpike which he called a "mare's nest". He early on discovered that convergent efficient production could not be translated into convergent prices without some special attention to the nature of duality. But he got it wrong and concluded that the turnpike was a mare's nest. He was plainly interested in, even fascinated by, a technical problem, but could not reach the right conclusion. Very similar remarks apply to his work on separable intertemporal utility which he needed for some of his work on growth. Here he was saved from a number of errors by Professor Gorman, although he did not acknowledge his debt. Perhaps out of pride.

The obvious question is: does any of this matter? Except from the bad book on the Business Cycle, almost everything he wrote, whether sometimes technically flawed or not, was important and productive. From "Simplifying the Theory of Money" to a Theory of Economic History, to his reconsideration of Keynes, he made important contributions and provided new insights. It is, for instance, notable that in his Theory of Wages [1963] he suggested a bargaining theory with many points of similarity to the well known Rubinstein construction. He would not have been capable of providing a proof a la Rubinstein nor would he have been able to make the connection with Nash, but he nonetheless seems to have seen his way to the essentials.

Above all, Hicks had a vision in which the "atomic" theory of agents' decisions was reasonably well integrated in that of the economy as a whole. The Mathematical Appendix to Value and Capital showed this first attempt and the analysis of the "Traverse" in later growth work got quite close to his aim. But of course this is a difficult undertaking which, if at all feasible, has very recently been made so by the advent of the computer. But it should be emphasised that Hicks always understood that, for instance, macro and micro economics were not two different subjects. In macro-economics he was of course influenced greatly by Keynes. But he was never a "straightforward simple Keynesian", as must be obvious from his writings. His attempt at a formal "fix price" analysis was influential but not in the end as successful as it might have been. He traced the economy from "week" to "week" where the latter was a period of time over which prices were not altered. But the history of the past weeks helped to determine the price set at the beginning of the present one. This was a true dynamic set up but fiendishly hard to study under any generality. Hicks did not provide the generality but concentrated on expectations (single-valued).

I have no doubt that Hicks was on the right track with this dynamic set-up (think of menu cost), but I believe that the whole enterprise requires much more technical expertise than Hicks (or almost any one man) has and, of course, a lot of fairly new economic analysis. For instance, "herd" behaviour as well as "conventional" behaviour needs to be formulated and put into the story. The latter of course also needs to be supplemented by an investment story and account of technological innovation. It may well be that economic analysis of this complexity is impossible and that Hicks was right to stick to "British commonsense" with a little extra!

### III

There is no doubt that Hicks thought well of himself as do most successful people. There is nothing wrong with that. But it has a price which is, on the one hand what the Swedes saw as "excessive striving for originality" in British economists and a disregard of the work of others, whether predecessors or successors.

That Hicks read a rather limited subset of the economic literature which was relevant to what he was doing, is quite clear. Certainly it meant that he "rediscovered" results. But it also led him to write in a tone of voice which was not always felicitous, and indeed could lead to ridicule. This occurred in his well-known introduction to his Trade-Cycle book where he told us "that he could have kicked himself" for not seeing a point which had been clear to Harrod, thereby of course implying that he could well have seen it himself.

On the other hand this style of his kept Hicks free - almost alone amongst recent economists - to write in the "grand" manner. I do not only mean that he touched on "grand" issues but that there was a seriousness of purpose which was discernible in almost everything he wrote. For he did not only take himself seriously, he took the subject seriously, and never gave up hope of constructing something which would outlast other efforts. Yet he was sound on economics as a "science" - it was at best a pseudo-science and destined to remain so. The reason was, I believe, old-fashioned - economic states can never be shown to repeat themselves sufficiently clearly for valid empirical generalisations. Of course this is not something to which econometricians (or for that matter Chicago economists) can readily agree. I do not know the answer but having imbibed the local culture I rather believe that Hicks was right on this.

## CONCLUSION

I hope the reader will not conclude from my critical remarks that Hicks was other than admired by me. He had a profound effect on my own development and there are many parts of his oeuvre which will surely last. But I was not writing hagiography and felt that this was the occasion on which long-held views could be expressed.

### REFERENCES

Arrow, K.J. and Hahn, F: (1971) General Competitive Analysis, San Francisco: Holden-Day

Fisher, F. M. and Shell, K. (1972): The Economic Theory of Price Indices, Academic Press, New York and London.

Geanakoplos, J. and Polemarchakis, H. (1986): "Existence, Regularity and Constrained Sub-optimality of Competitive Allocations when Markets are Incomplete" in Heller, Starr, Starrett (eds.), Essays in Honour of Kenneth Arrow, Vol.3, Cambridge

Gorman, W. M. (1963): "The Structure of Utility Functions", Review of Economic Studies No. 104, xxxv(4), pp. 367-390 Grandmont, J-M. (1992): "Transformations of the Commodity Space, Behavioral Heterogeneity and the Aggregation Problem", Journal of Economic Theory.

Hicks, J. R. (1975): "The Scope and Status of Welfare Economics", oxford Economic Papers, 27.

Hicks, J. R. (1963): The Theory of Wages, 2nd edition, Macmillan, London.

Hildenbrand, W. (1994): Market Demand: Theory and Empirical Evidence, Princeton University Press.

Lancaster, K. (1966): "A New Approach to Consumer Theory", Journal of Political Economy, 74, 132-157.

Solow, R. M. (1984): "Mr. Hicks and the Classics", Oxford Economic Papers, New Series, Vol. 36, Nov 1984 Supplement, pp. 13-25, reprinted in D. Collard, D. Helm, M. Scott and A. Sen (eds.), Economic Theory and Hicksian Themes, Oxford University Press, 1984.

CHAPER - 7

# MONETARY CAUSES OF THE BUSINESS CYCLES AND TECHNOLOGICAL CHANGE: HICKS VS. HAYEK

*Harald Hagemann*

### ABSTRACT

The economics of Keynes and Hayek were a lifelong challenge for Hicks in developing his own theory. Whereas the first is well known to a wider public, and can be expressed in four letters, IS-LM, Hayek's influence on Hicks is of a more critical nature and still only known to a small group of academic economists. Hicks always had been sceptical about Hayek's claim that the economy would be in equilibrium if there were no monetary disturbances. Although he took over from Hayek the idea that the impact of an impulse on the real structure of production is most important, it is very clear for Hicks that, unlike in Hayek, the divergence from a steady-state path and the dynamic adjustment process are not caused by monetary but by real factors like technological change. Hicks's position has much in common with Adolph Lowe whose contributions to business-cycle theory in the 1920s were the major challenge for Hayek. Finally it is shown that despite the fact that Wicksell's analysis of the cumulative process provided an important building block of Hayek's business-cycle theory, Wicksell essentially held a real view of the cycle, a view which was shared by Hicks. This is a fundamental disagreement with Hayek for whom monetary disorders were of first and not of secondary importance.

## 1. INTRODUCTION

The economics of Keynes and Hayek were a lifelong challenge for Hicks in developing his own theory. Whereas the first is well known to a

This Chapter is based on the Paper presented at the *Journées d'Étude "Hicks"*, sorbonne, Paris, October 23–25, 1997 and at the second Annual Conference of the *European Society for the History of Economic thought* Bologna, February 27–March 1. 1998.

wider public, and can be expressed in four letters, IS-LM,[1] Hayek's influence on Hicks is of a more critical nature and still only known to a small group of academic economists. After Hicks's dramatic *Hayek Story* (1967), which caused Hayek (1969) to write his late "elucidations" of the Ricardo effect which had come to occupy a central place in the theory of industrial fluctuations when emphasis shifted from money and interest to capital and profit (see Hayek, 1939: 3 ff.), it has become commonplace to state that Hayek's business-cycle theory largely failed to gain general acceptance because of the quick success of Keynes' *General Theory* after 1936. Apart from the inconsistencies in Hayek's combination of Cantillon and Ricardo effects (see Hagemann and Trautwein, 1998), that, 'what Hayek was saying appeared to have little relevance' compared 'to the opportunities that had been opened up by the *General Theory*' (Hicks, 1967: 205). As Hayek had next to nothing to say about the later stages of the cumulative process of deflation and the lower turning point of the cycle, his theory seemed utterly out of step with the reality of the Great Depression.

Hicks always had been sceptical about Hayek's claim that the economy would be in equilibrium if there were no monetary disturbances. This is already manifest in his early essay on equilibrium and the trade cycle which essentially is the result of Hicks's grappling with Hayek's *Prices and Production* and Hayek's 1928 concept of intertemporal equilibrium. Here we find Hicks arguing against Hayek's statement 'that a change in the effective volume of monetary circulation is to be regarded as an independent cause of disequilibrium. I cannot accept this in its literal sense, though I am prepared to agree that in a world of imperfect foresight monetary changes are very likely to lead to acute disequilibrium' (Hicks, 1982 [1933]: 32). Hicks realized that to analyze money one must consider uncertainty and expectations. He had a long struggle to present an inherently dynamic version of the economy in which agents' present decisions represent attempts to cope with an uncertain future in view of monetary and real constraints imposed upon them by past actions. But although Hicks made important contributions to monetary theory over a period of almost six decades,[2] he did not become too tired

---

[1]For greater details see Hamouda (1993, chpt. 8).

[2]This dates from his 1935 'Suggestion for Simplifying the Theory of Money', a landmark in the evolution of the theory of liquidity preference with which Hicks became a very influential monetary economist, via his 1967 *Critical Essays in Monetary Theory* to his last book *A Market Theory of Money* (1989).

to emphasize 'the *real* (non-monetary) character of the cyclical process' (Hicks, 1950: 136). Indeed it had been one of the main objectives of his *Contribution to the Theory of the Trade Cycle* 'to show that the main features of the cycle can be adequately explained in real terms' (ibid).

## 2. FROM HAYEK'S LSE SEMINAR IN THE EARLY 1930S TO THE NEO-AUSTRIAN THEORY IN CAPITAL AND TIME

It was one of Hayek's major contributions to have shown the importance of the temporal structure of production processes for cyclical fluctuations. Hicks repeatedly pointed out how much he had been influenced by Hayek in whose seminar at the London School of Economics he participated between 1931 and 1935. In particular Hayek had introduced him to the work of Wicksell, who had linked Böhm-Bawerk with Walras, and had made Hicks think of the productive process as a process in time. However, there is a remarkable difference. For Hayek cyclical adjustment problems arise because of monetary factors, like changes in savings behaviour and in particular credit expansion which distorts the system of relative prices. Hicks, on the other hand, always had been sceptical about Hayek's claim that the economy would be in equilibrium if there were no monetary disturbances. Although he took over from Hayek the idea that the impact of an impulse on the real structure of production is most important, it is very clear for Hicks that, unlike in Hayek, the divergence from a steady-state path and the dynamic adjustment process are not caused by monetary but by real factors like technological change.

> Where ... I do not go along with him [Hayek] is in the view that the disturbances in question have a monetary origin. He had not emancipated himself from the delusion ... that with money removed 'in a state of barter' everything would somehow fit. One of my objects in writing this book has been to kill that delusion. It could only arise because the theory of the barter economy had been insufficiently worked out. There has been no money in my model; yet it had plenty of adjustment difficulties. It is not true that by getting rid of money, one is automatically in 'equilibrium' – whether that equilibrium is conceived of as a stationary state (Wicksell), a perfect foresight economy (Hayek) or any kind of steady state. Monetary disorders may indeed be superimposed upon other disorders; but the other disorders are more fundamental.

(Hicks 1973: 133–4)

Thus it becomes clear that Hicks's neo-Austrian model is designed as a barter-type economy in which money is at best the medium of exchange. It therefore cannot be granted 'that some anti-Say's law prevails, as in Keynes's *General Theory* model' (Morishima, 1989: 185). Since Hicks's own neo-Austrian theory has nothing to say about the problems of a monetary economy, it cannot take account of Keynesian unemployment but it can allow for the employment consequences of a physical restructuring of capital due to increased mechanization, i.e. technological unemployment. Hence Hicks's finding that the introduction of improved machinery may lead to a temporary contraction in output, and in employment, in the early phase of the traverse does not, in itself, contradict Say's law of markets. It is manifest that this type of 'neo-Austrian' theory is as much inspired by Ricardo as by Böhm-Bawerk and Hayek, a fact openly admitted by Hicks (1985: 156): 'So where we have come to on this Austrian route, is close to Ricardo ... to his latest insights, which he did not live to follow up. The Austrian method is indeed a Classical method'.

By the late 1960s Hicks had clearly become fascinated by the *Ricardo machinery effect*, i.e. the employment consequences of the introduction of a different, more 'mechanized' method of production. Hicks came to the defence of what he regarded as the central message of Ricardo's analysis of the machinery question: there are important cases in which the introduction of a new type of machinery might reduce both real output and employment in the short run, the harmful effect might persist for quite a time, but the increased investment caused by higher profits due to the increased efficiency of a new production process should eventually lead to a path of output and employment which is above that one which could have been achieved with the old production process.[3]

Hicks has not been the last of many great economists who have been attracted by Ricardo's chapter on machinery. In his *Path of Economic Growth*, Lowe (1976) characteristically starts his investigation of the macroeconomic consequences of technological change and of the necessary conditions for bringing an economy back to an equilibrium growth path from Ricardo's analysis of the machinery problem. Recently Samuelson (1988, 1989) has set out to vindicate Ricardo's propositions that machinery can hurt wages and reduce output and employment.

---

[3]For a detailed analysis of Hicks's discussion of the employment consequences of the introduction of new machinery see Hagemann (1994b).

Samuelson's exposition contains numerical examples that lead to a new long-run equilibrium position with unemployed labour, i.e. to *permanent* technological unemployment. In Ricardo's numerical example, the economy takes off from a stationary state equilibrium and the evolution of the gross and net produce is calculated for three successive periods, depicting the effects of the construction and utilization of machinery on aggregate output (Ricardo, 1951: 388–90). There is, however, no indication that the economy will arrive at another uniquely determined equilibrium, i.e. the subsequent development of profits, investment, output and employment is largely left in the dark. For that reason Ricardo's example can be regarded as an 'early and rude type of traverse analysis' (see Kurz, 1984) which contains a capital shortage theory of *temporary* technological unemployment. According to Ricardo's view capital accumulation and output expansion will in the long run act as a compensating factor to the initial displacement effect of machinery. This has been fully grasped by Hicks who in the late 1960s set out to accomplish Ricardo's traverse analysis.

The employment consequences of technological change had been in the centre of the life-long research interest of Adolph Lowe whose writings on business cycle theory, particularly on the methodological requirements a theory of the business cycle has to fulfill, were the major challenge for the young Hayek.[4]

### 3. THE PROBLEM OF THE BUSINESS CYCLE: METHODOLOGICAL REFLECTIONS

In his 1926 article 'How is business cycle theory possible at all?' Lowe (1997) emphasized not only the relevance of the departmental scheme to the analysis of the business cycle but also that the concept of equilibrium that has been central in all systems of economics since the Physiocrats is logically bound up with a closed interdependent, and therefore a static, system. Lowe's critical analysis of the existing literature on business cycle theories led him to the following conclusion:

> The business cycle problem is no reproach *for*, but a reproach *against* a static system, because in it it is an *antinomic* problem. It is solvable only in a system in which the polarity of upswing and crisis arises analytically from the conditions of the system just as the undisturbed adjustment derives from the condi-

---

[4]The following two sections are based on Hagemann (1994a).

tions of the static system. Those who wish to solve the business cycle problem must sacrifice the static system. Those who adhere to the static system must abandon the business cycle problem. J. B. Say, who consciously took this step, came with regard to reality in the logical neighbourhood of Palmström, who deduces with razor-like sharpness, '*dass nicht sein kann, was nicht sein darf'*. (Lowe, 1997: 267)

Lowe stated the problem clearly: if economic theory is satisfactorily to explain the business cycle, it cannot do so simply by outlining the consequences of a disturbing factor exogenously imposed upon an otherwise static economy. Rather, it must seek for some causal factor endogenous to the system itself which can distort the rigid interrelations implied in the system of static equilibrium.

How did Hayek react to Lowe's claim for a fundamental revision of the methodological foundations of business cycle theory? First, there are important elements common to both Hayek's and Lowe's positions. Hayek (1933: 28) explicitly agreed with Lowe's view on the relation between *empirical* observation and *theoretical* explanation:

Our insight into the *theoretical* interconnections of economic cycles and into the structural laws of circulation has not been enriched at all by all these phase descriptions and calculations of correlations. ... Now it would of course mean to misunderstand the logical relationship between theory and empirical research to expect an immediate furtherance of the *theoretical* system from an increase in *empirical* insight (Lowe, 1997: 246).

Furthermore, Hayek accepted Lowe's seminal argument that all existing theories of the business cycle suffer from the fundamental weakness that they rely on *exogenous* shocks or disturbances and adjustments to such shocks in an equilibrium framework. Such a procedure could hardly result in a satisfactory theory to explain economic fluctuations which occur in a somewhat regular fashion. The logic of equilibrium theory

properly followed through, can do no more than demonstrate that such disturbances of equilibrium can come only from outside i.e. that they represent a change in the economic data and that the economic system always reacts to such changes by its well-known methods of adaptation, i.e. by the formation of a new equilibrium (Hayek, 1933: 42–3).

Trade cycle theory, like any other economic theory, must fulfil two criteria of correctness to avoid the pitfalls of creating cyclical fluctuations via the introduction of exogenous shocks into an otherwise static system.

Firstly, it must be deduced with unexceptionable logic from the fundamental notions of the theoretical system; and secondly, it must explain by a purely deductive method those phenomena with all their peculiarities which we observe in the actual cycles. Such a theory could only be 'false' either through an inadequacy in its logic or because the phenomena which it explains do not correspond with the observed facts (Hayek, 1933: 32-3).

Hayek explicitly points to the parallels of his argument with the views expressed by Lowe (1928). Most important, however, is his making common cause with Lowe in identifying the incorporation of cyclical phenomena into equilibrium theory as the crucial problem of business cycle theory and in the demand for an endogenous factor causing the cycle.

Nevertheless, the two authors differ fundamentally in the conclusions drawn from their methodological reflections. This holds in particular for the role of the concept of equilibrium. While Lowe claims that the traditional concept of a static equilibrium has to be replaced by a new concept of a dynamic system in which the polarity of upswing and crisis takes the same position as the equilibrium in a static system (see, e.g., Lowe, 1926: 267–8), Hayek adheres to the concept of equilibrium as an indispensable tool for economic theory in general and the understanding of intertemporal price relationships in particular. To start from the assumption of equilibrium therefore is essential for Hayek's explanation of cyclical fluctuations. *Prices and Production is* characterized by Hayek's 'conviction that if we want to explain economic phenomena at all, we have no means available but to build on the foundations given by the concept of a tendency towards an equilibrium' (Hayek, 1935: 34). For the analysis of dynamic questions it is essential to incorporate the element of time into the notion of equilibrium and to take into consideration differences in the prices of the same goods at different points in time.

Hayek's adherence to the concept of equilibrium in his business cycle analysis has theoretical as well as empirical reasons. While he regards the free market economy as inherently stable so that all movements can essentially be regarded as equilibrating adjustment processes, Lowe is convinced of disorderly tendencies in uncontrolled industrial markets in which profit maximization has lost its classical determinacy. Hence his later plea for interventionism in order to combine political and economic freedom with the goal of collective rationality (see Lowe, 1965).

Hayek's business cycle theory rests on the idea that prices determine the direction of production. The function of prices as an intertemporal co-ordination mechanism is to give entrepreneurs the required information for their investment and allocation decisions. If in an equilibrium framework supply and demand are equilibrated via the price mechanism, how is it possible that cyclical fluctuations are a regular phenomenon, since no change *within* the system can give rise to it?

> The obvious, and the only possible way out of this dilemma, is to explain the difference between the course of events described by static theory ... and the actual course of events, by the fact that, with the introduction of money ..., a new determining cause is introduced. Money being a commodity which, unlike all others, is incapable of finally satisfying demand, its introduction does away with the rigid interdependence and self-sufficiency of the 'closed' system of equilibrium, and makes possible movements which would be excluded from the latter. Here we have a starting point which fulfils the essential conditions for any satisfactory theory of the Trade Cycle. (Hayek, 1933: 44–5)

### 4. IDENTIFYING THE ENDOGENOUS FACTOR: MONEY AND CREDIT VERSUS TECHNOLOGICAL CHANGE

It was Löwe's closest collaborator, Fritz Burchardt, who in his outstanding 1928 paper on the history of monetary trade cycle theory, which even his main opponent Hayek (1929a: 57) praised as 'very valuable in its historical part', showed how structural changes in economic history alter the character of theory. During the nineteenth century crisis theory evolved into trade cycle theory. Credit expansion and interest-rate movements became more important as symptoms of the cycle. Recognizing monetary influences in particular manifesting themselves through changes in the price level, Burchardt concluded that monetary factors alone cannot explain cyclical phenomena. In his view non-monetary factors have to play an important role. This holds especially for technical progress which is recognised as the central determinant of the cycle. With reference to Wicksell's influential theory, for example, Burchardt emphasized that, although changes in the market rate of interest are important for movements of the price level, the real impulse for the disturbance of equilibrium of an economy is given by technical progress which leads to an increase of the natural rate (see Burchardt, 1928: 119).

Hayek, on the other hand, pointed out that any theory of business cycles must take the influences arising from money (and credit) as its starting point. A theory of the monetary economy therefore could explain processes like cyclical fluctuations characterized by disproportionate developments that are unthinkable in the equilibrium system of a barter economy. The starting-point for the explanation of crises has to be a change in the money supply automatically occurring in the normal course of events, and not evoked by any forcible interventions (see Hayek, 1928b: 285–6).

Hayek not only regarded his trade cycle theory most decisively as a monetary one but also emphasized that a theory of cyclical fluctuations other than a monetary one is hardly conceivable. Accordingly, he saw the main division in trade cycle theory to be that between monetary and non-monetary theories. However, in a new footnote to the English translation of *Geldtheorie und Konjunkturtheorie,* Hayek made an important qualification:

> Since the publication of the German edition of the book, I have become less convinced that the difference between monetary and non-monetary explanations is *the most important* point of disagreement between the various Trade Cycle theories. On the one hand, it seems to me that within the monetary group of explanations the difference between those theorists who regard the superficial phenomena of changes in the value of money as decisive factors in determining cyclical fluctuations, and those who lay emphasis on the real changes in the structure of production brought about by monetary causes, is much greater than the difference between the latter group and such so-called non-monetary theorists as Prof. Spiethoff and Prof. Cassel. On the other hand, it seems to me that the difference between these explanations, which seek the cause of the crisis in the scarcity of capital, and the so-called 'underconsumption' theories. is theoretically as well as practically of much more far-reaching importance than the difference between monetary and non-monetary theories. (Hayek. 1933: 41)

This change of emphasis is not surprising since Hayek from the beginning stressed two arguments:

1. His trade cycle theory essentially is a monetary one. But while *monetary* factors *cause* the cycle, *real* phenomena *constitute* it. Although cyclical fluctuations caused by monetary factors, in particular credit expansion, are unavoidable in modern industrial economies, it is the impact on the real structure of production which is most important.

2. Monetary theory has by no means accomplished its task when it has explained the absolute level of prices. Thus he argued against sim-

plified quantity theories which focus exclusively on the relationship between the quantity of money and the general level of prices. The classical dichotomy has to be seen as a cardinal error of economic theory. A far more important task of monetary theory is to explain changes in the structure of relative prices caused by monetary 'injections' and the consequential disproportionalities in the structure of production which arise because the price system communicates false information about consumer preferences and resource availabilities. Misallocation of resources due to credit expansion may even occur despite price level stability, i.e. constant prices cannot automatically be regarded as a sign of monetary stability, as Hayek (1925) has pointed out with reference to US monetary policy during the prosperous 1920s.

These arguments also form the basis for Hayek's reaction against the criticism which has been raised by Burchardt and Lowe against monetary theories of the trade cycle. On the one hand, Hayek explicitly agrees to several points of criticism. In particular he views Lowe's most important argument against contemporary monetary theories of the cycle as

unquestionably valid, even with reference to the theory as it has been developed earlier by his admired tutor Mises. The argument concerns the *exogenous* character of the theory as it comes in by taking arbitrary interferences on the part of the banks as the starting point. Hayek thus dedicates the whole Chapter IV of *Monetary Theory and the Trade Cycle to* the issue raised by Lowe and to show that he neither has to rely on arbitrary interferences on the part of the banks nor on the general tendency of central banks to depress the money rate of interest below the natural rate but that the fundamental cause of cyclical fluctuations is of an *endogenous* nature.

> The situation in which the money rate of interest is below the natural rate need not by any means originate in a *deliberate lowering* of the rate of interest by the banks. The same effect can be obviously produced by an improvement in the expectations of profit or by a diminution in the rate of saving which may drive the 'natural rate' (at which the demand for and the supply of savings are equal) above is previous level; while the banks refrain from raising their rate of interest to a proportionate extent but continue to lend at the previous rate, and thus enable a greater demand for loans to be satisfied than would be possible by the exclusive use of the available supply of savings. The decisive significance of the case quoted is not in my view due to the fact that it is probably the commonest in practice, but to the fact that it *must inevitably recur* under the existing credit organisation'. (Hayek 1933: 147–8)

The most important reason for an improvement in the expectations of profit which leads to an increase of the natural rate is the occurrence of technical progress, an argument which exactly had been made before by Wicksell and was repeated by Burchardt. However, when Hayek maintains that a discrepancy between the natural and the money rate of interest does not presuppose any deliberate action by the monetary authorities, and that technical progress may cause an increase in the natural rate which is not matched by an immediate adjustment of the money rate, the important question then is whether this discrepancy, and hence money and credit, is or is not *essential* for the emergence of cyclical fluctuations. Lowe would argue that it is not, i.e. that, although the fluctuations may be intensified if excessive credit is given to innovators, the latter would also occur in the absence of additional credit money. Hayek, on the other hand, insists that a satisfactory model of business cycles must be a monetary one. Whereas he recognizes the importance of non-monetary factors, such as technical progress, as a propagation mechanism for cyclical fluctuations, he nevertheless views monetary factors as the ultimate cause.

We can identify here Hayek's most innovative achievement. While Wicksell in his cumulative process analysis concentrated on changes in the purchasing power of money and never developed his monetary theory into a business cycle theory, Hayek accomplished precisely that task. He combined Wicksell's analysis of the cumulative process with the classical concept of forced saving to produce a monetary theory of cyclical fluctuations (especially in the production of capital goods) in which the expansion of bank credit leads to disturbances in the system of relative prices and distortions in the time structure of production via discrepancies between the natural (equilibrium) rate and the market rate of interest.

The main point of criticism levelled by Hayek against Burchardt and Lowe is that they follow Wicksell supposing

> that only general price changes can be recognized as monetary effects. But general price changes arc no essential factor of a monetary theory of the Trade Cycle; *they are not only unessential, but they would be completely irrelevant if only they were completely 'general' – that is, if they affected all prices at the same time and in the same proportion.* (Hayek 1933: 123, original italics)

With regard to the role of technical progress we find a significant change in Hayek's writings over time. In *Monetary Theory and the*

*Trade Cycle*, Hayek supported Wicksell's argument that monetary expansion is frequently induced by changes in the 'capital rate', i.e. from improvements in profit expectations. Hayek (1933: 191–2) mentioned technical progress as a major factor behind such changes. Thus he recognized the importance of technical progress as part of the impulses and implicitly also of the propagation mechanism for cyclical fluctuations. In later writings he payed little attention, if any, to technical progress. Apparently he did not want to modify his insistence on the inevitability of crisis and the return to the original equilibrium position. However, reducing the Ricardo effect to a choice-of-technique problem required a switch in the assumptions about the cause of monetary expansion, from technological change to an autonomous lowering of interest rates (see Hagemann and Trautwein, 1998).

In contrast to economists like Hayek who regarded the cycle as caused by monetary factors, Lowe emphasized the role of *technical progress*. Indeed, technical progress was seen by him as the central determinant of both the cycle and the long-run growth trend, i.e. he denied the possibility of separating these two aspects from each other. The research programme of the Kiel school consisted in the attempt to develop a theory of accumulation, technical progress and structural change. Against the background of the microelectronics revolution it turns out that the programme as well as the methods used are pronouncedly up-to-date in many respects. The main research interest of the group was on the construction of a theoretical model of cyclical growth with the basic working hypothesis that a satisfactory explanation of industrial fluctuations must fit into the general framework of an economic theory of the circular flow as it was developed by Quesnay and Marx. The first step consisted in the construction of a model that incorporated both the physical and the value dimensions and that could be made amenable to dynamic transformation. For Lowe and the other members of the Kiel school the physical and technical aspects represent a fundamental determinant of an economic system, especially as important constraints on structural change and behaviour during transition processes. This structural dimension could only be neglected if the production factors were perfectly flexible, mobile and adaptable in the face of change. In order to develop a frame of reference for a sectoral study of economic growth the attention of the Kiel group was directed back to classical analysis, since neither the Lausanne nor the Cambridge school, with their emphasis on price variables and the far-reaching exclusion of the physiotechnical structures, offered a fruitful starting-point. Lowe's attempt to develop a theory of accumulation, technical progress and structural change culminated more than 40 years later in *The Path of Economic Growth* (1976). It shows Lowe as the second pioneer, after John Hicks, in the field of traverse analysis, i.e. in studying the conditions that have to be fulfilled in order to bring the economy back to an equilibrium growth path after a change in one of the determinants of growth, such as the supply of labour or technical progress.

## 5. CONCLUSIONS

By the late 1960s, when Hicks came to the defence of the Ricardo machinery effect he based his traverse analysis on a *neo-Austrian* representation of production structures in which time as the essence of capital enters production in a twofold way: as the duration of the process by which labour inputs are converted into consumption goods, and in the sense of intertemporal joint production of final output at different dates, a sequence generated by the fixed capital goods. Capital is thus an expression of sequential production. By dealing explicitly with fixed capital goods, Hicks' theory differs from that of Böhm-Bawerk and the Hayek of *Prices and Production*, who confined their models to working capital and, therefore, could only work with production processes of the flow input – *point* output type. Since Hicks regarded capital goods to be the source of a whole stream of final consumption goods at different dates, i.e. he considered productive processes to be of the *flow* output type, he explicitly abandoned typically Austrian concepts such as Böhm-Bawerk's construction of the average period of production or the notion of the degree of roundaboutness. Thus Hicks saw the decisive advantage of his neo-Austrian approach over that of the 'old' Austrians in the incorporation of fixed capital, the lack of which had been the Achilles' heel of the Austrian model, first pointed out by Burchardt (1931/32).

Hayek responded to Burchardt's critique by conceding that the stages model or vertical approach, which he had used in *Prices and Production* "gives the impression of a simple linearity of the dependency of the various stages of production which does not apply in a world where durable goods are the most important form of capital" (1939: 21–2). However, in his business cycle theory he stuck to the Austrian model and thus continued to neglect circular flows.

The analysis of the impact of process innovations on industrial structures is the strength of the horizontal or sectoral model whereas it has some difficulties in coping adequately with product innovations and in defining the time profile of the interindustry adjustments in the system. Hicks saw the decisive advantage of the Austrian method in its ability to cope with the important fact that process innovations nearly always involve the introduction of *new* capital goods which cannot *a priori* be physically specified. It is exactly this argument which had caused Hicks to move away from the horizontal model of *Capital and Growth* (1965) to the vertical model of *Capital and Time* (1973), since in process innovations

> the only relation that can be established [between the capital goods that are required in the one technique and those that are required in the other]runs in terms of costs, and of capacity to produce final output; and this is precisely what is preserved in an Austrian theory (Hicks 1977: 193).

Thus Hicks, the life-long critic and modifier of Hayek's original construction in business-cycle theory, returned not only to Austrian capital theory. He also reappraised the message of Ricardo's machinery chapter in a passage that seems to reproduce the broad message of the Ricardo effect in Hayek's business-cycle theory:

> To industrialize, without the savings to support your industrialization, is to ask for trouble. That is a principle which practical economists have learned from experience. It deserves a place, a regular place, in academic economics also (Hicks 1973: 99).

But there is one decisive point which Hicks had in common with Wicksell whose ideas provided the starting point for Austrian trade cycle theory as it was developed by Mises and Hayek. Hicks always treated the cycle as fundamentally a real phenomenon reflecting technological change and the fluctuations in investment that accompanied them. Monetary disorders may be superimposed upon the real disorders but they are only of secondary importance. Wicksell also essentially held a real theory of the business cycle.[5] Wicksell's business-cycle analysis remained a fragment. Nevertheless his two articles 'The Enigma of Business Cycles' (1953) and 'A New Crisis Theory' (1998), both written in 1907 and influenced by the writings of Tugan-Baranowsky and Spiethoff make clear the importance he attributed to the cycle phe-

---

[5]See, for example, Boianovsky (1995) and Leijonhufvud (1997).

nomenon as well as the identification of the unsteady stream of innovations as the 'deepest' cause of fluctuations. With regard to the central role of technical progress Wicksell is "far closer to the Marx-Schumpeter tradition in cycle theory than to any monetary tradition" (Laidler 1991: 145). This marks a decisive difference to Hayek for whom the cycle essentially is caused by monetary factors although real phenomena constitute it. Wicksell emphasizes technology shocks and perceives in real factors which lead to a change in the natural rate of interest the essential reason for business cycles. Nevertheless he does not suit for being identified as a forerunner of modern equilibrium business cycle theories since he is not only miles away from making the market-clearing hypothesis as a methodological principle but also accentuates intertemporal coordination problems as the essence of his economic thinking. Hicks, who in his late writings an monetary theory[6] came very close to a neo-Wicksellian approach, shared with Wicksell also the view that the business cycle is basically a real phenomenon. This is a fundamental disagreement with Hayek for whom monetary disorders were of first and not of secondary importance.

## REFERENCES

Boianovsky, M. (1995). Wicksell's business cycle, *The European Journal of the History of Economic Thought* 2: 375-411.

Burchardt, F.A. (1928), Entwicklungsgeschichte der monetären Konjunkturtheorie. *Weltwirtschaftliches Archiv* 28: 78-143.

Burchardt, F.A. (1931-2). Die Schemata des stationären Kreislaufs bei Böhm-Bawerk und Marx. *Weltwirtschaftliches Archiv* 34: 525-64; 35: 116-76.

Colonna, M. (1990). Hayek on Money and Equilibrium. *Contributions to Political Economy* 9:43-68.

Colonna, M. and Hagemann H. (eds)(1994). *Money and Business Cycles. The Economics of F.A. Hayek*, Vol.I, Aldershot: Edward Elgar.

Cottrell, A. (1994). Hayek's Early Cycle Theory Re-Examined. *Cambridge Journal of Economics* 18: 197-212.

Hagemann, H. (1994a), Hayek and the Kiel School: Some Reflections on the German Debate on Business Cycles in the Late 1920s and Early 1930s. In Colonna and Hagemann (1994: 101-21).

Hagemann, H. (1994b), Employment and Machinery. In H. Hagemann, O.F. Hamouda (eds.), *The Legacy of Hicks*, London: Routledge, 200-224.

---

[6]See, for example, Hicks last book *A Market Theory of Money* (1989).

76

Hagemann, H. and Trautwein, H.-M. (1998), Cantillon and Ricardo Effects – Hayek's Contributions to Business Cycle Theory. *European Journal of the History of Economic Thought* 5, 292–316..

Hamouda, O.F. (1993), *John R. Hicks. The Economist's Economist*, Oxford: Basil Blackwell.

Hayek, F.A. (1925), The Monetary Policy of the United States after the Recovery from the 1920 Crisis, in F.A. von Hayek (1984), 5–32.

Hayek, F.A. (1984 [1928a]). Intertemporal Price Equilibrium and Movements in the Value of Money. In R. McCloughry (ed.), *Money, Capital and Fluctuations. Early Essays of F.A. Hayek*, London: Routledge. 71–117.

Hayek, F.A. (1928b), Einige Bemerkungen über das Verhältnis der Geldtheorie zur Konjunkturtheorie, in K. Diehl (ed.), *Beiträge zur Wirtschaftstheorie. Zweiter Teil: Konjunkturforschung und Konjunkturtheorie*, Schriften des Vereins für Sozialpolitik, 173/II, Munich and Leipzig: Duncker & Humblot.

Hayek, F.A. (1933 [1929]). *Monetary Theory and the Trade Cycle*, New York: Kelley (Reprint, 1966).

Hayek, F.A. (1935). *Prices and Production* (2nd ed.). New York: Kelley (Reprint, 1967).

Hayek, F.A. (1939). *Profits, Interest and Investment and Other Essays on the Theory of Industrial Fluctuations*. London: Routledge.

Hayek, F.A. (1942). The Ricardo Effect. *Economica* 9: 127–52.

Hayek, F.A. (1969). Three Elucidations of the Ricardo Effect. *Journal of Political Economy* 77: 274–85.

Hicks, J. (1982a [1933]). Equilibrium and the Cycle. In *Money, Interest and Wages. Collected Essays on Economic Theory*. Vol. II, Oxford: Clarendon Press. 28–41.

Hicks, J. (1935), A Suggestion for Simplifying the Theory of Money. *Economica* 2: 1–19.

Hicks, J. (1950), *A Contribution to the Theory of the Trade Cycle*, Oxford: Clarendon Press.

Hicks, J. (1965), *Capital and Growth*, Oxford: Clarendon Press.

Hicks, J. (1967). The Hayek Story. In *Critical Essays in Monetary Theory*, Oxford: Clarendon Press. 203–15.

Hicks, J. (1973). *Capital and Time. A Neo-Austrian Theory*, Oxford: Clarendon Press.

Hicks, J. (1977). *Economic Perspectives. Further Essays on Money and Growth*, Oxford: Clarendon Press.

Hicks, J. (1985). *Methods of Dynamic Economics*, Oxford: Clarendon Press.

Hicks, J. (1989). *A Market Theory of Money*, Oxford: Clarendon Press.

Kurz, H.D. (1984). Ricardo and Lowe on machinery, *Eastern Economic Journal* 10: 211–29.

Laidler, D. (1991). *The Golden Age of the Quantity Theory*, London: Philip Allan.

Laidler, D. (1994). Hayek on Neutral Money and the Cycle. In Colonna and Hagemann (1994: 3–26).

Leijonhufvud, A. (1997). The Wicksellian Heritage, *Economic Notes* 26: 1–10.

Löwe, A. (1997) [1926]. 'How is Business-Cycle Theory Possible at all?' *Structural Change and Economic Dynamics* 8: 245–270.

Lowe, A. (1928). Über den Einfluß monetärer Faktoren auf den Konjunkturzyklus, in K. Diehl (ed.), *Beiträge zur Wirtschaftstheorie. Zweiter Teil: Konjunkturforschung und Konjunkturtheorie*, Schriften des Vereins für Sozialpolitik, 173/II, Munich and Leipzig: Duncker & Humblot.

Lowe, A. (1965). *On Economic Knowledge. Toward a Science of Political Economics.* New York: Harper & Row.

Lowe, A. (1976). *The Path of Economic Growth,* Cambridge: University Press.

Morishima, M. (1989). *Ricardo's Economics. A General Equilibrium Theory of Distribution and Growth,* Cambridge: Cambridge University Press.

Neisser, H. (1990) [1932]. The Wage Rate and Employment in Market Equilibrium. *Structural Change and Economic Dynamics* 1: 141–163.

Neisser, H. (1934). Monetary Expansion and the Structure of Production. *Social Research* 1: 434–457.

Ricardo, D. (1951 [1821]). *Principles of Political Economy, and Taxation* (3rd ed.), ed. by P. Sraffa, *Works and Correspondence of David Ricardo,* Vol.I, Cambridge: University Press.

Samuelson, P.A. (1988). Mathematical vindication of Ricardo on machinery. *Journal of Political Economy* 96: 274–82.

Samuelson, P.A. (1989). Ricardo was right! *Scandinavian Journal of Economics,* 91: 47–62.

Trautwein, H.-M. (1996). Money, Equilibrium and the Cycle: Hayek's Wicksellian Dichotomy. *History of Political Economy* 28: 27–55.

Wicksell, K. (1953) [1907a], The Enigma of Business Cycles, *International Economic Papers,* 3: 58–74.

Wicksell, K. (1998) [1907b], Eine neue Krisentheorie, in: E. Streissler (ed.), *Studien zur Entstehung der ökonomischen Theorie. Vol. 18,* Berlin: Duncker & Humblot.

Wicksell, K. (1934 [1913]), *Lectures on Political Economy,* Vol.I. London: Routledge.

# CHAPTER - 8

# CAPITAL AND GROWTH: ITS RELEVANCE AS A CRITIQUE OF NEO-CLASSICAL AND CLASSICAL ECONOMIC THEORIES

## Joseph Halevi

### ABSTRACT

This paper argues that Hicks' *Capital and Growth*, and its rewritten version Methods of Dynamic Economics, constitute a critique of both Neo-classical and Classical economics.The critique of the Neo-classical side is explicit: it appears in the series of explanations concerning the necessity to abandon the Temporary Equilibrium method of *Value and Capital*. Furthermore, the way in which Hicks argues against the assumption of a given aggregate saving ratio takes him straight into the Kaldor-Pasinetti Cambridge Equation. Having jettisoned both the Temporary Equilibrium and the Harrod type Fixprice methods, Hicks ends up with Sraffa type prices of production. By inserting those prices into the saving equation he obtains a model where any change in the natural growth rate implies a change in the distribution of income à la Kaldor with the underlying prices being determined à la Sraffa.

Up to this point the analysis runs in terms of comparing alternative equilibrium positions. Nothing has been said about how the system can get into equilibrium. The paper shows that Hicks' Traverse represents the analytical framework dealing with this specific Robinsonian preoccupation. The outcome of Hicks analysis is particularly inimical to the Neo-classical idea of convergence, yet it provides also all the elements for a critique of Classical economics. The essence of the Classical view on the basis of which a change in the wage rate implies an inverse change in the profit and growth rates, is criticised by using Hicks' own Traverse model. The difference vis à vis Hicks' lies in that it is assumed that investment is exogenously determined à la Kaldor and that the techniques of production are uniform across the two sectors. In this way we obtain a Kaldorian-Classical model where Kaldorian adjustment is not possible. It is then argued that Kaldor's theory of distribution is so rooted in Classical economics that the refutation of the Kaldorian adjustment process is an indirect refutation of the Classical mechanism. In this context, the structural Traverse is used to show that Classical adjustments are derailed by the emergence of the problem of effective demand.

## I. INTRODUCTION

In 1975 Geoff Harcourt organised a symposium on the old and the new political economy which appeared in the *Economic Record*, the journal of the Australian Economic Society (Harcourt, 1975). The participants were Maurice Dobb, Frank Hahn, John Hicks. The contribution of Hicks was most interesting. The author of *Value and Capital* argued that there were by now two Hickses to speak of: the J.R. Hicks of *Value and Capital*, and John Hicks of *A Theory of Economic History* (1969, 1975).

Just the same, a substantial change in Hicks' own outlook on the foundations of economics is found already in *Capital and Growth* (1965) which culminates in the chapter on the two sector disequilibrium Traverse. This was to be followed by a reappraisal of the neo-Austrian theory of production undertaken in *Capital and Time* (1973). The themes developed in *Capital and Growth* continued however to provide the foundations for Hicks' new approach to the issues of growth and equilibrium. Indeed in his last book on dynamic processes - titled *Methods of Dynamic Economics* (1985) - thirteen out of the fourteen chapters of the book are a revised version of chapters already included in *Capital and Growth*. The neo-Austrian Traverse appears in the last chapter in the guise of a concluding essay. Furthermore, in the paper, read by Casarosa, sent to the 'Sraffa Conference' held in Florence in the same year, Hicks argued that there was a basic similarity between his approach and Sraffa's, only that he started where Sraffa had ended (Hicks, 1990). The similarity can be evinced from chapter 12 of *Capital and Growth* where a Sraffa type price system is set up in order to build a growth model containing Kaldorian features.

It may be useful, at this preliminary stage, to remind the reader that Hicks' 1965 disequilibrium Traverse is nothing but the quantity dual of the reswitching case developed by Pasinetti (1966) and Garegnani (1970) in the context of capital theory. Just as in Marginalist theory the adjustment to full static equilibrium requires an inverse monotonic relation between capital per head and the rate of interest (profit), in Solow-Swan-Phelps models convergence to a growth equilibrium depends upon an inverse relation between capital per head and the growth rate. Hicks - using a two-sector model - then showed that such a convergence will not as a rule occur. The assumed inverse relation turned out to depend on a unique type of technological configuration requiring that the consumption goods sector be more capital intensive than the capital goods one. To be fair to the economic literature of the time, it was not Hicks who discovered this possibility. The non-convergence case emerged already in the two sector Neo-classical growth models developed by Shinkai, Inada and Uzawa in the 1960-62 period, as well as in a little valued paper by Ronald Findlay (1963) which addressed Joan Robinson's theory of capital accumulation[1].

Yet the attention paid to the stability properties of the models led to ignoring the significance of the non-convergence case[2]. It is in this context that Hicks' growth theoretic contribution acquires both a methodological and an epistemological significance. As will be argued in the second and third sections of this paper, the intellectual project of *Capital and Growth* up to chapter 16 dealing with the Traverse, combines a critical rethinking of the method of *Value and Capital* with a dialogue with the theoretical evolution taking place in Cambridge. In so doing Hicks integrated Sraffa's approach to prices of production with the Kaldor-Pasinetti theory of growth and distribution. The adoption of the Cambridge theory of distribution and of Sraffa's prices represented only a stepping stone to build a model of structural disequilibrium. In this case imbalances cannot be corrected just by resorting to either a flexible distribution of income - à la Kaldor - or to flexible production coefficients - à la Solow.

---

[1] Findlay proved that full employment (state of bliss) in Joan Robinson's theory of accumulation could be attained only upon satisfaction of the capital intensity condition (Robinson, 1956; Findlay, 1963).

[2] The MIT produced what they thought would become the dominant graduate textbook on macrodynamics. It was written by Duncan Foley and Miguel Sidrauski (1971). In many respects it is still the best book on neoclassical growth. It is entirely based on a two sector model of the Inada-Uzawa type and right from the start the capital intensity condition is presented as the necessary requirement for the validity of the whole story told in the book. Overall, this means that capital per head will move inversely to changes in the steady state growth rate. The short lived nature of that book was not due to the impact of the capital controversies - which in the United States was minimal but to the rise of Lucas' economics.

Structural disequilibrium is nothing but the first Hicksian Traverse dealing with the relations between productive sectors. In this paper I will try to show that the methodology of the structural Traverse can be developed in order to criticise also the Classical-Marxian process of accumulation. Interestingly enough, Keynes' concept of effective demand comes out not only unscathed but indeed strengthened. Thus, section four will sketch out the simple disequilibrium Traverse while section five will introduce the effective demand conditions. Finally section six deals with the implications concerning Classical-Marxian economics.

## II. THE EXIT FROM TEMPORARY EQUILIBRIUM

For the distinguished Oxonian economist Temporary Equilibrium constitutes the appropriate framework for the study of a flex-price system. In this case the problem of stock equilibrium would not arise nor, unlike the Intertemporal Equilibrium case, decisions would have to be taken once and for all for the entire life span of economic agents (Pasinetti, 1977). *The Value and Capital* model is exclusively concerned with perfect competition in which markets clear but no uniform rates of return are required. Hence its temporaryness relative to the Walras-Wicksell view of long run equilibrium characterised by the tendency towards a uniform rate of return. To use a term coined by Pierangelo Garegnani, Hicks' method of Temporary Equilibrium brought about a 'change in the notion of equilibrium' by delinking it from the requirement of a uniform rate of return (Garegnani, 1976).

In terms of analytical connections, the dialogue with the theoretical evolution taking place in Cambridge represented the most significant factor contributing to Hicks'departure from the method of *Value and Capital*. Two sets of observations can be marshalled in support of the above view.

The first concerns the absence of any influence stemming from the results obtained within the framework of Arrow-Debreu theory. In developing his own critical reflections on the limitations of the Temporary Equilibrium method Hicks made no reference to the problems which were found to beset the Intertemporal Equilibrium approach, such as existence, stability and uniqueness. In my opinion this is due to the fact that the Hicksian 1939 *Value and Capital* method is conceptually more flexible than the Intertemporal Equilibrium one. It does not require that decisions be made once and for all, it is not particularly damaged by the whole discussion concerning the issue of large and regular economies, typical of the existence and stability problems engulfing the Arrow-Debreu system. This last aspect is due to Hicks' clear view about the methodological role played by the notion of perfect competition for whom 'a universal adoption of the assumption of monopoly must have very destructive consequences for economic theory' (Hicks, 1939, p. 83).

The second set of observations concerns the construction of the model presented in chapter 12 of the 1965 book where Sraffa prices and the Cambridge equation form the core of the Hicksian growth model. But this will be discussed in the subsequent section. Before we do that it is necessary to show how Temporary Equilibrium was abandoned by its founder.

In both *Capital and Growth and Methods of Dynamic Economics* Hicks wrote :

> The fundamental weakness of the Temporary Equilibrium method is the assumption which it is obliged to make, that the market is in equilibrium - actual demand equals desired demand, actual supply equals desired supply - even in the very short period, which is what its single period must be taken to be. This assumption comes down from Marshall, but even in a very competitive economy, such a short-run equilibration is hard to swallow; in relation to modern manufacturing industry, it is very hard to swallow indeed. It was inevitable that the time should come when it had to be dropped (1965, p. 76; 1985, p. 81).

The proposed new method is called *Fixprice* because prices are not determined by the equilibrium between supply and demand relations. It does not mean that prices will not vary, Hicks lists specifically the cost of production as a factor generating such a change. It simply means that prices do not move in the manner postulated by Mariginalist theory. What is required from prices is that they cover costs and, if competition prevails, that the rate of profit be the same across industries. In relation to the foregoing discussion it is worth observing that the *Fixprice* method does not lead to a Temporary Equilibrium of the kind developed by Clower, which is Walrasian all but in name, but to a Sraffa type system. As we shall see shortly, it is by merging Sraffa's prices of production with the Kaldor-Pasinetti Cambridge equation, that Hicks obtains his own particular growth model.

# III SRAFFA PRICES AND THE CAMBRIDGE EQUATION IN *CAPITAL AND GROWTH*

The adoption of the *Fixprice* method has led Hicks onto the path of dynamic macroeconomic analysis. As long as we have unused capacity and unemployment, prices can be kept fixed and changes will occur via the standard procedures related to the stock adjustment principle, provided certain difficulties are taken into account (Hicks, 1965 chapters 8 to 11). In Harrodian dynamics, by contrast, the fixprice system can work as long as the warranted rate does not hit the ceiling of the natural growth rate. Alternatively fixprices rule in growth equilibrium, but if the latter undergoes a change the relative price structure must also change unless techniques are uniform across sectors. Thus Harrodian equilibrium constitutes also the limit to which the *Fixprice* method can be stretched.

Yet, to discuss changes in the equilibrium growth it is necessary first to set out the price and quantity relations. Having rejected the supply and demand approach to prices of the Temporary Equilibrium method, and having imposed only the condition that they cover costs, the price equations are identical to those of Sraffa. The only differences consist in that the uniform rate of profit is calculated without any depreciation and the model is reduced to a Marxian-Robinsonian two sector framework.[3] The quantity system is written in terms of the standard linear two sector model. Yet, here I prefer to think in terms of the Fel'dman-Mahalanobis version of the model where $\lambda$ defines the ratio of capital stock installed in the capital goods sector over the total stock. When $\lambda$ is multiplied by the output-capital coefficient $\lambda$ of the capital goods sector, the growth rate G of total capital is determined:

$$G = \alpha\lambda \tag{1}$$

Now, if the conditions for equilibrium undergo a change, such as an increase in population growth, then a necessary but non sufficient requirement is that $\lambda$ should be increased as well[4]. The absolute level of total employment is not only determined by the higher value of $\lambda$ but also by the employment capacity of each machine according to the sector where it is installed. A structural equation linking the equilibrium growth of capital to full employment must therefore be satisfied.

---

[3]All this happens in chapter 12 of Capital and Growth - not included in the 1985 book - well before the discussion of the Traverse which takes place in chapter 16.

[4]The sufficient conditions are examined in the chapter on the Traverse.

Consider the case in which the growth rate $\alpha\lambda_0$ was in equilibrium for some time when a new growth rate of labour came into being at time $t_1$ at the rate $g^* > \alpha\lambda_0$. Given the labour-machine ratios in each sector, say '$m$' for the tractors operating in the capital goods sector and '$n$' for those operating in the corn sector, the equilibrium structural equation is;[5]

$$g^* = [(1+(\alpha\lambda_0)(h\lambda_1+n) - (h\lambda_0+n)]/(h\lambda_0+n) \quad h = m - n) \tag{2}$$

The value of '$h$' may be positive, negative or zero, each value having specific implications which will be dealt with subsequently. If the value of $h = 0$, the model displays uniform techniques of production. With $h = 0$, equation (2) admits a solution only when $\alpha\lambda = g^*$. Economically this is very interesting and will be used to build a Hicksian Traverse of a Keynesian - but un-Kaldorian - nature.

The real unknown in (2) is $\lambda_1$ and we do not know yet if it exists or whether it yields a stable solution. This is a matter of the Traverse and the Fel'dman-Mahalanobis formulation brings it out more sharply than Hicks' own construction. For the time being it suffices to assume that $\lambda_1$ exists, with $h \neq 0$. The new equilibrium growth rate of capital will then be

$G^* = g^* = \alpha\lambda_1$, where $\lambda_1 > \lambda_0$. The identification of the appropriate level and composition of the capital stock required for the new growth equilibrium can be derived therefore entirely from the technical side of the system.

To each variation in $\lambda$ there may or may not correspond a variation in the saving ratio and in the rate of profit. This is precisely the point where the Cambridge equation enters into the model of *Capital and Growth*. More specifically, in Hicks the Cambridge equation emerges from the junction of the Sraffa price system with the quantity system.

In *Capital and Growth* the chapters separating chapter 7, where the Fixprice system is presented, from chapter 12, where the quantities and price relations are outlined, deal with Keynesian and Harrodian dynamics. Thus

---

[5]Equation (2) is derived in the following manner. Assume full employment and full capacity to prevail at period t0, then the stock of capital in the same period will generate a level of employment equal to :
$L_0 = K_0[(m-n)\lambda_0 + n]$, where $(m-n) = h$.
For full employment to be maintained in the subsequent period t1, it is necessary that:
$L_1 = K_1(h\lambda_1 + n)$. We also know that $L_1 = L_0(1+g^*)$ and that $K_1 = (1 + \alpha\lambda_0)K_0$. Since we know the expression for $L_0$ we can solve for $g^*$ and obtain equation (2).

in those chapters the saving ratio is taken as given. In chapter 12 a model is set up in order to examine changes in the equilibrium growth rate. This involves studying the behaviour of the saving ratio and the rate of profit relative to variations in growth conditions. The saving equation is given as follows.

Let '$p$' and '$q$' be the price of the capital and consumption goods respectively, while $M$ is the output of capital goods and $C$ that of consumption goods. $Y$ is total money income. If we start from a give propensity to save '$s$' and set the standard equality between saving and investment, we have:

$$Y = pM+qC \tag{3}$$

$$s(pM+qC) = pM = S = I \tag{4}$$

$$(p/q)(M/C) = s/(1-s) \tag{5}$$

The above equations are self-explanatory.

The ratio $M/C$ contains the growth rate of the system allowed by the initial value of $\lambda$. If K is the total stock of capital and $\lambda$ and $\lambda$ are the output-capital coefficients in the capital and consumption goods sector, in terms of the Fel'dman-Mahalanobis formulation we obtain:

$$M = \alpha\lambda K = \Delta K \tag{6}$$

$$C = \beta(1 - \lambda)K \tag{6a}$$

$$(M/C) = \alpha\lambda/\beta(1-\lambda) \tag{7}$$

We already know that $\alpha\lambda$ is the growth rate of the capital stock, thus without any loss of information we can set:

$$[\alpha\lambda/\beta(1-\lambda)] = \sigma \tag{8}$$

Similarly the ratio s/(1-s) may be written as:

$$[s/(1-s)] = \varphi \tag{9}$$

Lastly, the ratio between the price of the consumption good and the price of the capital good is defined as :

$$(q/p) = x \tag{10}$$

Substituting equations (8), (9), (10) into equation (5), and solving for $\sigma$ we obtain the link between the growth rate and the saving ratio:

$$\sigma = x\varphi \tag{11}$$

The value of x is nothing but the relative price ratio, which in Hicks corresponds to a Sraffa system[6]. It is the presence of the rate of profit in the price equations which enables Hicks to establish a link between the growth rate, the saving ratio and the distribution of income. In so doing Hicks merged Sraffa's approach with the macroeconomic theory of distribution of Kaldor and Pasinetti. In fact, from footnote 6 we have the expression for x which when substituted into equation (11) yields:

$$\sigma = \varphi[(rz+d)/b] \tag{12}$$

According to equation (12) a constant saving ratio, i.e. a given $\varphi$, is compatible with an increase in the growth rate, i.e. with a rise in $\sigma$, whenever '$z$' is positive or negative. If the value of '$z$' is zero any change in $\sigma$ would have to be accompanied by a parallel change in $\varphi$. The value of '$z$' is the determinant, with an inverted sign, of the matrix of the Sraffa-Hicks price equations. It therefore bears a strict relation to the value of '$h$' in equation (2). When '$z$' is positive, negative or zero, so is '$h$'[7]. Clearly with $z = 0$, an increase in the rate of growth can be met only by a rise in $\varphi$. With $z \neq 0$ and $\varphi$ given, as in Solow's model, changes in the growth rate involve changes in the rate of profit '$r$'. We should expect the rate of profit on capital to increase with the rate of growth, otherwise why should firms invest at all? With a Solow type saving function, this is possible if $z > 0$; that is: $m > n$. Such a condition is consistent with a well behaved production function when applied to a linear two sector model (Spaventa, 1970).

The factor that brings Hicks to jettison the assumption of a given saving ratio and opt for the Cambridge equation is what, from the stand point of Neo-classical capital theory, amounts to the well known case of

---

[6] Hicks used a Sraffian model where: $p = par+wb$, $q = pcr+wd$.. Where a and c are the coefficients of machines necessary to produce one unit of machines and one unit of consumption goods; r and w are the profit and wage rates, while b and d are the labour inputs needed to produce one unit of the respective goods. Solving for $q/p$ we get: $x = (rz+d)/b$, where $z = (cb-ad)$, which is nothing but the determinant (with an inverted sign) of the coefficients matrix forming the equations for $q$ and $p$.

[7] Since: $h = m-n$, where '$m$' is the $L_m/K_m$ (employment to capital ratio)ratio in the machine sector and '$n$' is the the $L_n/K_n$ ratio in the consumption goods sector, whenever '$z$' is positive, negative or zero, $m>n$ and $h>0$, m<n and $h<0$, $m=n$ and $h=0$. This is because from the equation for '$z$' given in footnote 6, $(b/a)=(L_m/K_m)$ and $(d/c)=(L_n/K_n)$.

reswitching of techniques. In Hicks' two sector model this happens when $z < 0$ which means that $m<n$. Under these circumstances, the sign of the derivative $d\sigma/dr$ is negative, implying that, with a given saving ratio, the rate of profit must fall when the growth rate rises. The result whereby the highest growth rate requires the lowest rate of profit, instead of being viewed as perverse, is used by Hicks to move towards the Cambridge equation. He writes:

> I think that several things have gone wrong (....). The simplest thing which has gone wrong is that we have carried the assumption of saving proportional to total income, over from the Harrod-type theory (where it belongs) to the present theory, where it is much less at home. As soon as we make the distinction between factor shares (as in the Harrod-type theory we did not have to do), the question must arise: will not the saving-income proportion be affected by income distribution? (Hicks, 1965, p. 145).

The suggested way out is 'to introduce a direct effect of income distribution on saving' (pp. 145-6). The assumption of all savings being out of profits, although judged extreme, 'is a very convenient assumption which simplifies things considerably, so that - purely in order exhibit the properties of the model - it is one that I shall largely use' (p. 146). The model is then reduced to two basic equations.

The first equation is the Sraffian wage rate-rate of profit equation (called by Hicks the wage equation) stating that the two distributive variables are inversely related:

$$w = (1-ar)/(rz+d) \tag{13}$$

The second is the Cambridge equation, which Hicks calls the saving equation:

$$G = s_r r \quad \text{Where } s_r \text{ is the saving ratio out of profit.} \tag{14}$$

It follows that :

> If the real wage (w) is given, the rate of profit is determined from the wage equation, and the rate of growth is then determined from the saving equation. The higher the real wage, the lower the rate of profit, and the lower (therefore) the rate of growth. If it is the rate of growth that is given, the same two equations work the other way round. The rate of profit (which is consistent with this rate of growth) is then determined by the saving equation, and the rate of real wage from the wage equation. The lower the rate of growth, the lower the rate of profit, and the higher the real wage. This is all that there is to be said (1965, pp. 146-7).

However once we know what should happen in order to be in the new equilibrium position, we know nothing about whether or not we can attain it. From this perspective issues of choice of techniques become secondary because, as Hicks noted in a fully Robinsonian flavour:

> in the real world changes in technology are incessant; there is no time for an economy to get into equilibrium (if it was able to do so) with respect to January's technology, before that of February is upon it. It follows that at any actual moment, the existing capital cannot be that which is appropriate to the existing technology; it inevitably reflects past technology; to existing technology it is more or less inappropriate (Hicks, 1965, pp 183-4)[8].

## IV THE TRAVERSE

Any change in the equilibrium growth rate, i.e. in the Harrodian natural rate, requires an adjustment determined by the Cambridge equation independently from how and by what means it is achieved. The Traverse chapter deals precisely with the issue of how to get into the new equilibrium.

From Harrodian theory and the *Fixprice* method we know that an economy in long-run equilibrium can adjust to a change in its growth rate only if the average saving ratio varies via changes in the distribution of income. Yet the adjustment requirements are not to be confused with the process of getting into the new position:

> let us suppose that the Harrod difficulty has been got over: that a suitable change in the propensity to save, for whatever reason has occurred - will that be the end of the trouble? (Hicks, 1965, p. 185; 1985, p. 131).

It is well known that Hicks' answer is in the negative. It is based on the same analytical elements which brought him to discard the flexibility of prices as a means to attain a new equilibrium growth rate with a given saving ratio. It may be recalled that the compelling reason why a given saving ratio would not do when the long run equilibrium growth rate changes, lies in the technological structure of the economy inherent in equation (11):

$$\sigma = x\varphi$$

---

[8] This passage has been omitted in the 1985 book.

The relative price ratio 'x' contains the technological structure of the system - 'z' - as well as the rate of profit. A negative 'z, i.e. a negative 'h', would generate absurd results if the saving ratio remains unchanged. By the same token, a negative 'h' would be incompatible with stable full employment. To see this let us reproduce equation (2):

$$g^* = [(1 + \alpha\lambda_0)(h\lambda_1 + n) - (h\lambda_0 + n)]/(h\lambda_0 + n \quad h = (m - n)$$

If we assume, with Hicks, that the composition of the stock of capital is at full employment equilibrium at time $t_0$, the growth of the stock of equipment from $t_0$ to t1 will be $\alpha\lambda_0$. It may also be assumed that the growth of the labour force moves away from equilibrium and, between the two periods, grows at a rate

$$g^* > \alpha\lambda_0$$

In this context, a solution for $\lambda_1$ consistent with raising the growth rate of capital to $g^*$ is possible only with a positive 'h'. In other words, if we want the new proportion of the stock of capital allocated to the capital goods sector to emerge as a solution consistent with the new equilibrium growth, the capital goods sector must be less mechanised than the consumption good sector. Hence if we keep the Kaldorian hypothesis of $G = s_r r$, the adjustment to $g^*$, while requiring a change in the distribution of income à la Kaldor, still needs the technological condition that 'h' be positive. This condition - being a special case - is rejected by Hicks who concludes that 'the chief lesson that we learn from these exercises is that smooth adjustment may not be possible'(1965, p.195; 1985, p. 137).

For each configuration of 'z' ('h'), the prices ruling during the Traverse are always the right ones. They are prices of production determined by Sraffa type equations. Yet they are not equilibrium prices, or, more specifically, the lack of smooth adjustment is not caused by the absence of price flexibility (Bhaduri, 1975; Halevi, 1992). The strict analogy between the quantity and the price Traverse is a very important aspect of Hicks' contribution since it shows that prices cannot give much guidance about production decisions in a macrosectoral framework.

## V FROM THE TRAVERSE TO EFFECTIVE DEMAND CONDITIONS

Hicks' results have been obtained by finding the value of $\lambda$ as the solution to the problem of how to distribute the stock of capital between the two sectors. This procedure is legitimate if we want to endogenously determine the adjustment path to the new equilibrium growth rate.

However, Hicks' procedure completely by-passes the question of effective demand. Take the case in which the technological configuration leads to a state of disequilibrium. The level of effective demand never comes into the picture. Produced capital goods are allocated in such a way as to grope towards an equilibrium solution which, unfortunately, will turn out to be unstable.

It is preferable, therefore, to follow Kaldor more closely and set the full employment level of investment. exogenously. Obviously, in this case the shape of the technology would no longer be the main factor determining whether or not structural disequilibrium will emerge. The main threat to stability would come, instead, from unemployment due to a lack of effective demand.

Assume that at time $t_l$ the new long run growth rate of the labour force is $g^* > G$, where $G$ is the equilibrium growth rate ruling until $t_0$. At time $t_0$ the stock of capital was in equilibrium and full employment prevailed. Depending on the value of '$h$', for $h \neq 0$, any change in the composition of the stock of capital at $t_0$ would have led to structural unemployment, due either to too many machines relative to the available number of workers, or to too many workers relative to the number of machines. Consider now the case in which at time $t_l$ the transfer of the stock of capital to the capital goods sector is implemented by exogenous decisions, so that the value of $\lambda_1$ generates the full employment growth rate $g^*$. Yet, at the dawn of $t_l$ the stock of capital would have grown, in relation to $t_0$, by $\alpha\lambda_0 < g^*$. With $h = 0$, $\lambda_1$ would absorb an amount of labour exactly equal to the old growth rate. With $h < 0$, the intake of labour would be even less because the transfer to the capital goods sector implies a smaller crew per each unit of capital good installed there. Unemployment U would then be:

$$U = [(1+g^*)(h\lambda_0+n)-(1+\alpha\lambda_0)(h\lambda_1+n)]K_0$$

where: $h \leq 0$, and : $\lambda_1 > \lambda_0$ 

(15)

The unemployment rate u is thus:

$$u = [1-(1+\alpha\lambda_0)(h\lambda_1+n)/(1+g^*)(h\lambda_0+n)]$$

(16)

This rate of unemployment cannot be absorbed unless $\lambda$ is raised temporarily above the equilibrium level $\lambda_1$. However a value of $\lambda$ greater than that required by the new equilibrium rate involves a higher growth rate of capital which will have to be lowered at a later stage. In a structural context with limited shiftability of capital, the reduction of the growth rate of capital cannot be obtained without the formation of unwanted unused capacity. At any rate with $\lambda$ raised to the level of $\lambda_1$, the economy will start absorbing labour at the rate equal to full employment growth only from time $t_2$ onward. Indeed the stock of capital - being set at its fully adjusted composition at time $t_1$ - will have, by time $t_2$ - expanded exactly at the equilibrium rate $g^*$.

Barring the case of raising $\lambda$ temporarily above the equilibrium value $\lambda_1$, the backlog of unemployment will stay for ever. Yet its proportion over the total labour force will decrease with time as the numerator of equation (16) remains unaltered, while the denominator gets larger and larger. Just the same, the progressive dwindling of the rate of unemployment can take place only if capacity remains normally utilised. In other words, raising $\lambda$ to the level of $\lambda_1$ is a necessary but not sufficient condition for equilibrium growth to occur after $t_2$. The additional requirement is that at $\lambda_1$ both sectors keep operating at the normal capacity utilisation rate. In this context, it is the consumption goods sector to face a threat to its normal rate of capacity utilisation. If the unemployment rate ruling in the initial period of adjustment is such as to induce a fall in money wages, uncompensated by a fall in prices, then real consumption demand will decline engendering a reduction in the level of employment in the consumption goods sector. Unemployment will thus rise further with additional negative results for the state of consumption demand. At this point, it is likely that firms operating in the consumption goods sector will start revising their investment plans downward, thereby causing unused capacity to emerge also in the capital goods sector.

As a consequence the economy will find itself mired in Keynesian unemployment being, therefore, unable to get into the new equilibrium rate of growth. It must be pointed out that no over-accumulation of capital has occurred here since the value of $\lambda$ was raised to the equilibrium level of $\lambda_1$ from the outset. The thrust towards disequilibrium comes entirely from the effective demand side, i.e. from the negative impact of unemployment on the level of money wages. Disequilibrium is due to the system's structural inability to absorb immediately into production the additional amount of labour stemming from the higher growth rate. Yet, the derailment of the economy from its long run growth rate is determined by the events happening within the short period. Under these new circumstances prices, which at the beginning were assumed to be of a Sraffian nature, have become Kaleckian prices in every respect. In fact, if consumption goods prices were to be perfectly flexible in relation to variations in money wages, employment in the consumption goods sector would remain unchanged. Hence, structural unemployment will not be reabsorbed. By contrast, if prices do not change in the light of a fall in money wages, the appearance Keynesian unemployment would be due to the rise in the mark up. Both cases are purely Kaleckian. Price flexibility does not eliminate unemployment, it simply prevents further rises in its level.

From a strictly analytical perspective, full employment can be positively ensured as of time $t_l$ whenever the economy is conceived in terms of only one commodity. In such a system any amount of consumption goods can be made into capital goods. It follows that if at $t_l$ the number of corn made machines does not suffice to employ all the available population of working age, a part of the corn allocated for consumption can be switched to operate as 'corn machinery'. As long as the wage rate does not fall below subsistence, any amount of corn can be transformed into capital goods. This means that the share of corn functioning as investment can be reduced at a later stage just by raising the wage rate. In a one commodity world the adjustment to a higher or a lower growth rate can be attained without any danger of encountering the problem of effective demand.

It is indeed a pity that Hicks did not analyse this aspect of the Traverse because it would have, on one hand, strengthened his scepticism towards equilibrium adjustments, while tempering, on the other, his hostility towards the 'fanfare of the Keynesian orchestra' (1985, p.131).

## VI CONCLUSION: A CRITIQUE OF CLASSICAL ECONOMICS

The application of the Traverse method to the one commodity case shows that the problem of effective demand cannot be taken into account by the theoretical framework of Classicala and Marxian economics. In Classical theory growth and accumulation are guided by parsimony. The impossibility to introduce the level of effective demand into the Classical system was indeed seen very clearly by Hicks in the early stages of *Capital*

and *Growth* and of *Methods of Dynamic Economics*, in the chapter devoted
to Adam Smith and David Ricardo:

> There is no problem, in the Original Model, about the transmission of saving
> into investment, for in that model there is no money. Indeed there is hardly
> any exchange. One would be quite entitled to think of landowners (or
> capitalists) into whose possessions the harvest comes just piling it up in their
> store-houses; then doling it out to those whom they employ, productively or
> unproductively. If they are paid in money, then spend the money on their
> 'corn' consumption, the money just comes back where it was without making
> any difference (Hicks, 1985, pp. 34-5).

In relation to the Original Model, the method of the Traverse shows
that Classical accumulation, whether analysed in terms of prices of
production or labour values, is not compatible with Keynesian principles
and breaks down as soon as heterogeneity is introduced into it. The
formation of the money capitalist, as Marx pointed out in the third *volume
of Capital*, is strictly connected to the emergence of separate sectors of
production and, in particular, to the separation of the capital goods from
the consumption goods sectors. But this very factor requires a different
theory of output and of dynamic processes from the Classical one where
a higher rate of profit (a lower real wage rate) unambiguously entails a higher
growth rate.

To clinch the theoretical incompatibility between Classical dynamics
and the structural dynamics of a Hicksian type, let us transform the case
in which $\lambda$ is exogenously raised to $\lambda_1$ into a numerical example. Assume
that at t0 the stock of capital is made of 100 undepreciating machines, of
which 10 are in the capital goods sector and 90 in the consumption goods
sector. The coefficient $\lambda$ is thus 0.1. Each of the 10 machines produces one
machine. Hence by the end of t0 the growth rate of capital will be 10%.
Assume also that each machine, irrespectively of the sector where it is
installed, employs one worker. Total employment is therefore 100 and, for
balanced growth to be maintained, the labour force should grow by 10%.
Within each period the equilibrium effective demand for consumption goods
is ensured by the following Robinson-Harcourt equation (Harcourt, 1963):

$$w(N_i + N_c) = q*C \qquad (17)$$

Where $q*$ is the price of consumption goods which is no longer derived
from a Sraffian procedure; w is the money wage rate, and $N_i$ and $N_c$ are

the number of workers in the capital and in the consumption goods sectors respectively. On the basis of the assumptions made hitherto and substituting equation (6.a) into equation (17), we obtain:

$$wK = q*\beta(1-\lambda)K = q* C \tag{18}$$

The real wage rate (w/q*) becomes:

$$(w/q*) = \beta(1-\lambda) \tag{19}$$

Thus if (19) is allowed to operate freely, there will never be an effective demand problem in the consumption goods sector.

At this point, if the growth rate of the labour force has turned out to be greater than that of the stock of machines, unemployment will emerge even if investment is raised to the equilibrium level. Assume that by the end of $t_0$ the growth rate of labour is - say - 12%. It follows that with the new equilibrium growth set at 0.12, it is necessary that at the beginning of period $t_1$ $\lambda$ be raised to 0.12. Assume it is; with $\alpha$ equal to unity the ensuing growth rate will be equal to 12%. But the new equilibrium growth rate will materialise only at the end of period $t_1$ and its persistence will be rather uncertain. The Kaldorian decision to increase the rate of investment to the full employment level at the beginning of $t_1$ only increases the proportion of the workforce employed in the capital goods sector, but it does not create additional employment at the outset. In our example, at the beginning of $t_1$ there are 110 employable workers ($n = 1$ and $K = 110$) while the labour force is 112 units. By raising $\lambda$ to 0.12, we increase the number of workers in the capital goods sector to 13.2 out of a total of 110. Two workers have no other option but to remain unemployed.

Dynamic adjustment would involve more trouble under conditions of greater uncertainty. Indeed, if during period $t_1$ the unemployed workers start affecting negatively the real wage rate, thereby altering the equilibrium relation (19), the consumption goods sector will be piling up unwanted inventories, while the capital goods sector keeps working at full capacity. Thus by the end of $t_1$ the firms operating in the consumption goods sector will have to find a way of getting rid of the unwanted inventories and of how to use the machines which produced them. A straightforward adjustment procedure would be to reduce the demand for new machines by an amount equivalent to that which produced the undesired level of inventories. In Keynesian terms, this is equivalent to a decrease in real investment demand. Unused capacity will appear also in the capital goods sector which - at time $t_2$ - will lay off a proportional number of workers. The ensuing decline in consumption demand will trigger a further round in the negative multiplier. The economy will be, by now, well and truly out of equilibrium growth.

The above case of the Traverse shows that the Kaldorian adjustment mechanism does not eliminate the problem of effective demand even if investment is initially raised to the full employment level of output. The source of the disequilibrium is structural and its evolution is of a Keynesian type. By contrast if output were homogeneous with capital, the adjustment to full employment would not involve any difficulty[9].

The criticism of the Kaldorian process brings into sharp relief the shortcomings of the Classical, especially Marxian, view of accumulation. From an analytical perspective Kaldor's mechanism of income distribution is completely Classical only that it is tied to the hypothesis that investment is set at the level of full employment. Just the same, like the Classics and Marx, whenever the distribution of income shifts towards profits, the rate of growth should rise as long as unemployed labour is available. When the warranted rate hits the ceiling of the natural rate, the distribution of income should shift to wages, thereby enabling the system to stay, roughly, on a full employment path. Within the limits determined by the natural rate, the dynamic process is exactly as in Marx : share of profit up, rate of profit and rate of growth up!

In this context Kaldor thought that an economy with too little capital to employ the whole of the workforce would be characterised by Marxian

---

[9]Consider a one good model of the following kind:

(i)    $\alpha K_0 = Y_1$ and, because K is homogeneous with Y, we have:

(ii)    $K_0 + Y_1 = X$. Furthermore: (iii) $Y_1 = (1+g)Y_0$. Where g is the growth rate of output from period $t_0$ to $t_1$. Now, if the growth rate of the labour force is $\gamma > g$, and n is the labour to capital coefficient, we have to find the proportion $\varepsilon$ of $X$ which is to become capital in order to employ the whole of the labour force at $t_1$. Hence :

(iv)    $\varepsilon n X = L1$    We know also that: (v) $L_1 = (1+\gamma)L_0$; and that (vi) $L_0 = nK_0$, and, from (i) and (iii):

(vii)    $K_0 = [(1+g)/\alpha]Y_0$ Substituting and solving for $\varepsilon$ in equation (iv), we obtain:

(viii)    $\varepsilon = (1+\gamma)/(1+\alpha)$. The coefficient $\varepsilon$ is nothing but the accumulation ratio calculated over X which includes K. As long as $\gamma < \alpha$, a meaningful solution for $\varepsilon$ exists without any effective demand problem. Full employment is ensured. The Classics by treating capital as fully circulating worked, in fact, on the basis of equation (ii).

unemployment; whereas an economy with too much capital would be affected by Keynesian unemployment. This definition, because of its simplicity, is very appealing indeed. Yet, it fails to capture the difference between the economics of effective demand (Kalecki and Keynes) and the economics of cyclical growth (Marx and Goodwin). The modified Hicksian Traverse presented above brings that difference to the surface in an equally simple way. At the beginning of period $t_i$ there are more workers than the number employable by the existing stock of capital, although investment has been fixed at a level allowing for an equilibrium expansion of the stock of capital. The mere existence of unemployed workers suffices to push the system out of its equilibrium path. The shift is due entirely to the negative impact on the level of effective demand of a decline in real wages. In other words, even when the level of investment is secured by anchoring it to the full employment level, there is no guarantee that it will stay there. The decline in real wages, while bringing about a notional increase in the rate of profit, actually causes a rise in unused capacity in the consumption goods sector with negative consequences for the demand of capital goods.

It is not difficult to see that the criticism which, on a Hicksian basis, can be levelled against Kaldor's adjustment mechanism can be more forcefully directed against the Classical approach to income distribution and growth. In the Marx-Goodwin growth model effective demand plays no role at all. If we were to outline the Marx-Goodwin path in a two sector framework, we should be arguing as follows.

Whenever the Reserve Army of Labour brings down the real wage rate, the rise in unused capacity in the consumption goods sector should be interpreted by capitalists as a signal that notional profitability is rising. With perfect information and perfectly rational expectations in the dynamic properties of the Marx-Goodwin growth cycle, capitalists ought to shift investment towards the capital goods sector, giving rise to a new upward cycle. By contrast, it is far more likely that in the face of a fall in consumption demand, investment and accumulation will suffer as well. In a single good model the Classical story is not only credible but actually very powerful. It provides a firm belief in a set of objective laws sustaining the whole dynamic process over-time.

Keynes and Hicks, the latter perhaps unwittingly as far as Marxian growth is concerned, contributed - in different but not incompatible ways

- to the demolition of the belief that economic systems are propelled by immanent and objectively identifiable forces.

## REFERENCES

Bhaduri, Amit (1975), 'On the Analogy Between the Quantity and the Price Traverse', *Oxford Economic Papers*, 27(3): 455-61.

Findlay, Ronald (1963), 'The Robinsonian Model of Accumulation', *Economica*, 30(117): 1-12.

Foley, Duncan.and Sidrauski, Miguel (1971), *Monetary and Fiscal Policy in a Growing Economy* (New York: Macmillan).

Garegnani, Pierangelo (1970), 'Heterogeneous Capital, the Production Function and the Theory of Distribution', *Review-of-Economic-Studies*; 37(3): 407-36.

Garegnani, Pierangelo (1976), 'On a Change in the Notion of Equilibrium in Recent Work on Value and Distribution', in Brown, Murray; Sato, Kazuo; Zarembka, Paul (eds.), *Essays in Modern Capital Theory* (Amsterdam and New York: North Holland).

Halevi, Joseph (1992), 'Accumulation and Structural Disequilibrium', in Halevi, Joseph., Laibman, David., Nell, Edward. (eds.), *Beyond the Steady State* (London: Macmillan).

Harcourt, Geoffrey C. (1963), 'A Critique of Mr. Kaldor's Model of Income Distribution and Growth', *Australian Economic Papers*, 1(1): 20-6.

Harcourt, Geoffrey C. (1975), 'Decline and Rise: The Revival of (Classical) Political Economy', *Economic-Record*, 51(135): 339-56.

Hicks, John R. (1939), *Value and Capital* (Oxford: Oxford University Press).

Hicks, John R. (1965), *Capital and Growth* (Oxford: Clarendon Press).

Hicks, John (1969), *A Theory of Economic History* (Oxford: Clarendon Press).

Hicks, John R. (1973), *Capital and Time* (Oxford: Clarendon Press).

Hicks, John R. (1975), 'Revival of Political Economy: The Old and the New', *Economic-Record*, 51(135): 365-67.

Hicks, John (1985), Methods of Dynamic Economics (Oxford: Clarendon Press).

Hicks, John R. (1990), 'Ricardo and Sraffa', in Bharadwaj Krishna and Schefold Bertram (eds.), *Essays On Piero Sraffa. Critical Perspectives on the Revival of Classical Theory* (London, Boston, Sydney, Wellington: Unwyn Hyman)

Pasinetti, Luigi L. (1966), 'Changes in the Rate of Profit and Switches of Techniques', *Quarterly Journal of Economics*, 80: 554-65.

Pasinetti, Luigi L. (1977), *Lectures in the Theory of Production* (New York: Columbia University Press).

Robinson, Joan (1956), *The Accumulation of Capital* (London: Macmillan).

Spaventa,-Luigi. (1970), 'Rate of Profit, Rate of Growth, and Capital Intensity in a Simple Production Model', *Oxford-Economic-Papers*; 22(2): 129-47.

# CHAPTER - 9

# EQUILIBRIUM, EXPECTATIONS AND ISLM

*J.W. Nevile*

## ABSTRACT

The ISLM model that Hicks produced to "elucidate the relation between Mr Keynes and the 'classics'" became one of the most widely used models in economics in the second half of the 20th century. However, it came to be supported much less wholeheartedly by its creator than by the majority of the economics profession, who use it for many purposes including deriving the aggregate demand curve in aggregate demand and aggregate supply analysis. Hicks' reservations relate to the equilibrium nature of the analysis and especially to the implications of this for expectations. This article contrasts the way equilibrium and expectations are handled in ISLM and the *General Theory* and discusses issues arising from that contrast. The conclusion is reached that ISLM may be of some help to economic historians interpreting the state of an economy in the past, but is unsuitable for the analysis of policy changes or forecasting more generally.

## INTRODUCTION

Perhaps the most influential article that Hicks ever published was written early in his career. The ISLM model, that he produced to "elucidate the relation between Mr Keynes and the classics", became one of the most widely used models in economics in the second half of the 20th century. For many generations of students it was as close as they ever got to the ideas of the *General Theory*. For a generation of professional economists it became the basis of their thinking about macroeconomic events. Following Tobin, Solow described ISLM as the trained intuition of many of us (1984, p. 16). ISLM neglects the supply side. Yet when the profession changed to aggregate demand and supply models as the usual way of teaching, and thinking about, macroeconomics, ISLM was

[98]

widely used to derive the aggregate demand curve in these models. Thus, it still occupies an important place in macroeconomics.

However ISLM came to be supported much less wholeheartedly by its creator than by the majority of the economics profession. In what he called his post-Keynesian, or neo-Wicksellian phase (1982, p. xii) Hicks became increasingly dissatisfied with ISLM. In "IS-LM – An Explanation" (1980–1) he spelt out the reasons for this dissatisfaction. They arose from the way time is treated in the model and in particular how this is reflected in the concepts of equilibrium and expectations in ISLM.

Hicks denotes a substantial proportion of "IS-LM – An Explanation" to describing how his original 1937 article "Mr Keynes and the 'Classics': A Suggested Interpretation" cast Keynes' analysis into a Walrasian general equilibrium framework. He points out that the model is one which describes the equilibrium position of an economy in a particular period, with a past, that has determined the capital stock and various other variables, and a future about which expectations are exogenous and fixed throughout the period. The period had to be quite long since in Keynes analysis "quite a lot of things had to happen" (1980–1, p. 141) for equilibrium to occur. It also had to be not too long since Keynes assumed a constant stock of capital. "We shall not go far wrong", Hicks says, "if we think of it [the period] as a year" (ibid.). Hicks points out that in his model the economy had to be treated as if it were in equilibrium over the whole period, the whole of this "year", and that this is true both for the IS relationship and the LM relationship (1980–1, p. 151). Since ISLM is a Walrasian general equilibrium model this is surely correct. Equally surely, as Hicks points out, this causes problems.

At first sight, the most serious of these is that the requirement of full equilibrium over the whole period appears to cause insuperable problems with respect to the LM curve. To quote Hicks:

"there is no sense in liquidity unless expectations are uncertain. But how is an uncertain expectation to be realized? When the moment arrives to which the expectation refers, what replaces it is fact, fact which is not uncertain" (1980–1, p. 152)

Hicks does suggest a way of overcoming this problem, though he remarks that "I do not have much faith in it" (ibid.). His solution treats expectations, not as single-valued expectations but expectations that variables will fall in a particular range. As long as the observed variables do fall within this range throughout the period equilibrium is possible.

However, a second problem about expectations in ISLM is more important. Treating expectations as exogenous variables restricts the use of ISLM to explaining what has already happened. It cannot be used to analyse policy change since the assumption of exogenous expectations implies that everything is to go on as expected. It may be hoped that at some point in the future after a policy change, the economy will settle at a new equilibrium with a new set of (exogenous) expectations, but this cannot happen immediately. In the period following the policy change many things may happen which may change the new equilibrium position or even prevent any equilibrium position being reached. In Hicks' terminology, "there must always be a problem of traverse" (1980–1, p. 153). Of course ISLM has been very largely used to analyse policy changes, and this, together with complete disregard of the problem of traverse may have heightened Hicks' doubts about the model.

This paper accepts these doubts that Hicks expressed about ISLM. It argues that the problems are created or heightened by the attempt to cast Keynes' analysis in a Walrasian general equilibrium framework. The paper should not be interpreted as a criticism of ISLM as being an incorrect or inadequate representation of what Keynes was saying. It treats ISLM as a model in its own right, which it has proved to be over the last 60 years. However, it argues that the weaknesses Hicks identified in it occurred because it was written in his "Walrasian" phase not his "post-Keynesian" phase.

### MARSHALLIAN VERSUS WALRASIAN EQUILIBRIUM

Walrasian general equilibrium analysis provides information about the conditions that must be fulfilled if equilibrium is to exist: the necessary and sufficient conditions for equilibrium. If all these conditions are fulfilled, if an economy is in equilibrium, well and good: it will stay in equilibrium until some shock to one or another variable moves it out of equilibrium. However, strictly speaking general equilibrium analysis cannot provide any information about what will happen when an economy is not in equilibrium. If shocks are small and random, departures from equilibrium may be trivial and not cumulative[1] so that it is appropriate to ignore then and assume that the economy remains in equilibrium. In this case descriptions of the characteristics and consequences of equilibrium are useful. But this is the limit of general equilibrium analysis. It cannot be used when analysing the effects of a policy change designed to move an economy from an existing equilibrium position to another one.

More generally, equilibrium analysis cannot be used to predict what will happen when an economy is in a position of structural disequilibrium, because of a policy change or for any other reason. All it can do is set out the conditions that are consistent with equilibrium. This statement about equilibrium analysis applies to some extent to Marshallian analysis, but it is particularly clear cut in the case of Walrasian general equilibrium. There are no causal relationships in Walrasian general equilibrium. Everything is determined simultaneously.[2] One should not say that a change in "a" causes a change in "b". All that the theory states is that if an economy is thrown out of equilibrium by a change in an exogenous variable 'a', then 'b' will have to change by a specified amount if the economy is again to be in equilibrium (assuming that the values of other exogenous variables do not change).[3]

Hicks was already steeped in Walrasian analysis when he wrote "Mr Keynes and the Classics". It is not surprising that he recast the core of Keynes' theory into a Walrasian equilibrium framework. However, Keynes' purpose in writing the *General Theory* was not just to increase understanding of the economy and what has happened in the past, but to lay the basis for policies to remove substantial involuntary unemployment, policies to shift an economy from point A with unemployment to point B with much less. Walrasian equilibrium theory is not suitable for this purpose, which may be why Hicks became increasing sceptical of

---

[1]This is more likely if the equilibrium is stable. However, static analysis cannot provide a definitive answer about stability.

[2]This gives rise to the problem of "false trading" or trading early in the period before the equilibrium prices have become established. If "false trading" occurs the final equilibrium values will be changed. Thus general equilibrium theory has to use artificial devices like the Walrasian auctioneer or Edgeworth's recontracting to ensure that the economy is in equilibrium throughout the period.

[3]This assumes that the equilibrium position is not path determined.

the value of ISLM.[4] There is always the "problem of traverse", to which Hicks devoted a great deal of attention in his later life.

Quite a different concept of equilibrium underlies Keynes' thinking. As in much else, Keynes training as a pupil of Marshall was important here. Keynes thought of equilibrium in terms of Marshall's particular equilibrium models.

Clearly macroeconomic analysis cannot use Marshallian particular equilibrium models unchanged. A macro model cannot be for a particular industry. It can be for a particular country, as opposed to the whole world, but that is not the point. The distinction to be made is not between the coverage of the models, but the methods of analysis. On the one hand general equilibrium analysis treats all variables not determined by the model as exogenous. They are either policy determined variables (Tinbergen's instruments) or variables assumed to have constant values irrespective of what happens to the instruments or the variables determined by the model (Tinbergen's data). On the other hand Marshallian particular analysis proceeds on the basis that the values of a number of variables can be assumed to be constant, or approximately constant, for the purpose in hand.

The distinction is much more than the contrast between the exact assumptions of general equilibrium theory and Marshall's somewhat fuzzy concept of approximately constant for the time being. Calling variables exogenous leads to a different mode of thought than that encouraged by the assumption that for the purpose in hand the variables are at least approximately constant. Exogenous variables can be changed at will and an examination made of the effects of a change of a single exogenous variable on the conditions for equilibrium. It is far less easy to vary at will the values of variables that are assumed to remain approximately constant, locked "for the time in a pound called *ceteris paribus*" as Marshall put it (1920, p. 366). The assumption that a number of variables remain approximately constant does not imply that one variable can change significantly while all the others remain the same. When discussing the demand for an individual commodity, say soap, microeconomic textbooks commonly assume that money income and the prices of all other commodities are held constant. They certainly do not imply that it is useful to consider the effects of a large increase in money

---

[4]Certainly Hicks (1980–1, p. 153) explicitly warns against using ISLM to analyse the effects of policy changes.

income on the demand for soap, while keeping the assumption that the prices of all other commodities remain the same. One must take into account the effects of changes in the prices of other commodities. Similarly, at the macro level if policy changes one variable in the *ceteris paribus* pound, one has to consider if this will change the values of any of the other variables in that pound. The problem of traverse must be faced.

Keynes was, of course, well aware of this as can be neatly illustrated by comparing his discussion of the effects of an increase in the money supply with that of textbooks which adopt the Walrasian ISLM approach. The textbook analysis is well known. With a larger money supply, the rate of interest is lower and hence, the textbooks say, output and employment are higher. The textbooks imply, when they do not say it outright, that there is a causal chain running from a larger money supply to a lower rate of interest to an increase in output and employment. Most textbooks show no discomfort in adopting this approach, though some of the better ones have in the past. For example, after tracing through the effects of a structural change using the ISLM framework, Ackley comments:

"we tread perilously close to misleading statements in the foregoing, as well as being forced to bring dynamic considerations into what is supposed to be static analysis" (1961, p. 372).

In contrast to the textbook ISLM approach, Keynes was cautious about the claim that an increase in the money supply can increase employment significantly:

"A moderate increase in the quantity of money may exert an inadequate influence over the long-term rate of interest, whilst an immoderate increase may offset its other advantages by its disturbing effect on confidence" (1936, pp. 26-7).

It is not only textbooks that use the ISLM model to analyse policy changes. When Solow called it the trained intuition of many of his generation of economists, it was intuition in relation to policy changes that he had in mind. To quote him again:

"If I pick up the morning paper and read that the US Congress may soon pass a package of tax and expenditure measures intended to reduce the Federal deficit by $180 billion over the next three years, I know that my mind naturally draws IS and LM curves and shifts them" (1984, p. 14).

While it is clear that to use a Walrasian general equilibrium model to analyse a change in a policy variable is formally incorrect does it help intuition towards the correct answer or is it often misleading? It is most likely to be misleading if changing one exogenous variable causes a change in another exogenous variable. If Keynes' statement about the effects of increasing the volume of money is translated into ISLM terms, he is arguing that a large increase in the volume of money will certainly shift the LM curve to the right, which, if nothing else changed, could be expected to lower the rate of interest and increase investment, but that, through its effects on expectations, it may also shift the IS curve to the left. Hence, even intuitively, it is not clear whether investment, output and employment will increase, decrease or stay the same.

Expectations are the variables ISLM treats as exogenous which are most likely to change when there is a policy change. The reason Hicks gave why ISLM could not be used to analyse policy change was its assumption of exogenous constant expectations (1980–81, p. 153). The quotation from Keynes about the effects of an increase in the money supply shows that he was sensitive to policy changes affecting long run expectations.[5] In the 1950s and 1960s, when ISLM reigned supreme, most western economies were almost always close to full employment and long term expectations were probably fairly stable. Now all that has changed. Expectations are again unstable and hence important. Placing them in Marshall's *ceteris paribus* pound is far less likely to lead to error than calling them exogenous.

### THE ROLE OF EQUILIBRIUM IN KEYNES' ANALYSIS

Not only does the Marshallian framework of the *General Theory* make less likely the neglect of possible changes in other exogenous variables following a policy change, but also the role of equilibrium in that book overcomes to some extent the criticism that the analysis can say nothing about an economy which is not in equilibrium. Unlike ISLM the *General Theory* does not consist solely, or even mainly of equilibrium analysis. Keynes is not primarily concerned with the values of variables that hold in equilibrium. That may have been his starting point, but as he

---

[5]In his formal short period analysis Keynes put long period expectations in the *ceteris paribus* pound. However, a large part of the discussion in the *General Theory* emphasises the instability of long period expectations.

said himself, the *General Theory* "evolved into what is primarily a study of the forces which determine changes in the scale of output and employment as a whole" (1936, p. vii). Moreover, towards the end of the *General Theory*, Keynes claimed "to have shown in the preceding chapters what determines the volume of employment at any time" (1936, p. 313).

This is not to say that Keynes did not use equilibrium analysis. He did, and one of his concerns was to prove that a stable equilibrium position with substantial unemployment was possible. However, he did not see equilibrium analysis as solving a set of simultaneous equations to find the values of the endogenous variables which satisfy the conditions for equilibrium. If equilibrium was attained it was the result of a causal process.

Keynes' theorising highlights the fact that production takes place over time and that fixed investment and production decisions made at the beginning of the period cannot be changed until the beginning of the next period. There can be unintended inventory investment and disinvestment, but as far as the short period is concerned (fixed) investment is predetermined and is not affected by what happens during the period. This is probably because in Keynes' mind not only was the marginal efficiency of capital constant in the short run but also finance was arranged, through borrowing, at the beginning of each period at the rate of interest prevailing at that time (i.e. the rate determined by conditions in the previous period and ruling at the end of that period).

The process by which equilibrium is determined is as follows (1936, pp. 248–9). Start with a given marginal efficiency of capital schedule and a predetermined rate of interest. These determine investment and, given investment, consumption is also determined, through the multiplier, determining aggregate demand. This, in conjunction with aggregate supply, determines employment, output, price and income for the period. If there is unintended inventory investment this leads to downward revision of expectations and a lower income in the next period (and vice versa for unintended inventory disinvestment). However, Keynes usually thought of the period as long enough for desired investment, and consumption, to be equal to actual investment and consumption. Once income is determined, given the stock of money and the liquidity preference function this will determine the rate of interest. If this is the same as the rate of interest at the end of the previous period the economy is in equilibrium. If the rate of interest is higher than this, in the next period investment and income will be lower leading to a fall in the interest rate'and vice versa when the rate of interest is lower at the end of the period than at the beginning. There could be oscillations, but the system quickly converges to the equilibrium position in which the rate of interest, investment and income are constant from one period to the next.[6]

Keynes did not argue that the volume of employment was necessarily stable. On the contrary he stressed the volatility of the long period variables that he had assumed constant in the short period, commenting that "there is not one ... which is not liable to change without much warning, and sometimes substantially" (1936, p. 249). But equally an equilibrium with substantial involuntary unemployment could persist for a long time, for a large number of short periods. This would be the case if in a depression net investment was a negligible positive or negative amount each period, so that the capital stock remained approximately constant and if the economy received no shocks from policy changes or other variables assumed to be constant.

One could be tempted by the above description of Keynes' model to think that he had a fully dynamic model. In one sense this is true, he had a model which shows how the economy moves towards equilibrium and reaches it in a succession of short periods. Keynes' short period was shorter than the "year" Hicks mentioned as the length of the period in ISLM analysis. Keynes defined the short period as "the shortest interval after which the firm is free to revise its decision as to how much employment to offer" (1936, p. 47n).[7] It is appropriate to think of "Hicks' year" as the sum of the number of Keynes' short periods that is required to reach equilibrium. Within this horizon the analysis is fully dynamic. Given today's capital stock, and today's long-term expectations the short period model will trace out the path towards the equilibrium position and do this as long as the capital stock and long-term

---

[6]Particularly since Keynes thought that the rate of interest at the end of a period was unlikely to be so different from that holding at the beginning that a large change in investment occurred in the following period (1936, p. 250).

[7]Keynes also often considered the short period long enough for there to be no unintended investment (or disinvestment) in inventories. He believed that such unintended investment was a very temporary phenomena (1936, pp. 124–5). There is an interesting parallel between Marshall's view that "false trading" could be neglected and Keynes' treatment of unintended inventory investment as unimportant.

expectations remain approximately constant. In this sense it does deal with the "problem of traverse" if only in a limited way. It can deal with relatively small policy changes, but as Keynes implies in Chapter 5 of the *General Theory*, the adjustment following a large policy change will take long enough that it is unlikely that all the variables in the *ceteris paribus* pound will remain even approximately constant.

Keynes' theory is not fully dynamic. While it is dynamic within a period that can be called a "Hicks' year" i.e. the succession of Keynes' short periods in which equilibrium is established, there is no way to link one "Hicks' year" with the next. Once short period equilibrium is reached that is the end of the story until one of the variables assumed to be constant changes for reasons outside the scope of the model. There is no theory linking any changes in long period expectations about interest rates or the marginal efficiency of capital with what happens in one or more short periods. The most obvious lack of any relationship between the short and long period variables concerns the capital stock. If net fixed investment is significantly different from zero it will change the capital stock in the long period and hence the marginal efficiency of capital. Some of the variables assumed to be constant in the short run analysis may vary systematically in the longer run. There is no formal analysis of this either. There is a lot of discussion in the *General Theory* about the instability of long period expectations and the constant need to be alert for changes in them. There is even a chapter headed "Notes on the Trade Cycle", but it is just that: notes not a formal analysis. The *General Theory* only solves the "problem of traverse" for relatively small traverses, and for traverses in which there is no relationship between current events in succeeding short periods and long period variables, especially long period expectations.[8] Nevertheless, Keynes' analysis can legitimately go further in analysing policy change than can ISLM. It also provides a better basis for recursive or historical models which can integrate short period and long period dynamic analysis.

## EXPECTATIONS AND THE LM CURVE

As was noted in the introduction, in later life Hicks found the Walrasian requirement of equilibrium throughout the period in conflict with the

---

[8]There is in passing (on pp. 48–49) a sketch of what may happen in a traverse which takes longer than a "Hicks' year" to complete.

rational of the LM curve. While there are often difficulties in combining flows and stocks in one model, Hicks seems unduly hard on ISLM in this case. A study of the way the analysis in the *General Theory* side-steps the problem suggests a way out. Keynes' basic method is to ana-lyse the movement towards and attainment of equilibrium in a small number of very short periods while assuming that long period variables remain constant. While the interest rate will change in each of these very short periods until equilibrium is reached, the long period expectations about monetary conditions which form the basis of the speculative mo-tives for holding money remain unchanged. For example, there may be a general belief that interest rates will rise substantially in the future but not necessarily in the current short period and such an expectation could remain unchanged over a succession of very short periods in which there were only minor fluctuations in interest rates. A similar type of argu-ment can be used to legitimize the liquidity preference underpinning the LM curve in ISLM.

In any case the whole problem has become much less important with the deregulation of financial markets. In countries where there are deregulated financial markets, not only is the money supply endogenous but changes in it have little correspondence with changes in interest rates, at least during and for some time after the process of deregulation. Substantial rises in interest rates may be accompanied by a large rise in the money supply. For example, it is generally agreed that the prolonged recession in Australia in the early 1990s was precipitated and made more severe by very tight monetary policy. Annual reports of the Re-serve Bank of Australia described monetary policy as tight from the June quarter of 1988 to the June quarter of 1990, and interest rates rose from June 1988 to December 1989 and then remained constant for the first few months of 1990. Yet over the year to December 1989 M3 in-creased by 22 per cent and broad money by 14 per cent. Nominal GDP increased by 9 per cent over the same period. Expectations and liquidity preference still affect the demand for money but the central banks' in-strument is now the interest rate and the volume of money is endoge-nous. For the majority of OECD countries, with deregulated financial markets, the LM curve is horizontal at the current rate of interest.[9]

---

[9]The assumption of exogenous interest rates is less true for long term interest rates than for short term rates, but can be used as a reasonable approximation in a model with the purposes of ISLM.

## CONCLUDING REMARKS

Hicks (1980–1, p. 153), warned against using ISLM to analyse policy changes. Nevertheless this has been, and remains the major use of the ISLM model. This paper also has suggested that ISLM is not suitable as the basis for thinking about macroeconomic policy even just in the role of trained intuition. The major reasons why this is the case stem from the Walrasian general equilibrium nature of ISLM. The analysis of macroeconomic policy involves changing the value of a variable taken as given in the model used, and tracing through the results of the economy. Calling such variables exogenous gives the impression not only that they can be changed at will, at least in principle, but also that the changes will have no effect on other exogenous variables. This is precisely the way ISLM has been used. If a Marshallian model is used, policy instruments are not exogenous but only variables that, among others, are assumed to be more or less constant for the time being. Changing one of these variables may cause changes in others of them as well as in the variables endogenous to the model. Once one breaks the *ceteris paribus* assumption, the natural first step is to see what is an appropriate new set of values for the variables to which *ceteris paribus* applies, not to assume that one can be changed at will without affecting the others.

It is unlikely that a Walrasian model will be able adequately to analyse policy change because it is a profoundly static model in which everything is determined simultaneously. All it can do is give the conditions for equilibrium. It can say nothing about how an economy moves from one equilibrium situation to another. Marshall's particular equilibrium approach is also a static equilibrium method, but as Hicks remarked it is "a last stage in the evolution of static method, it gets very near to dynamics. It is the beginning of a transition to dynamics" (1985, p. 51). Marshall's pupil, Keynes, continued this transition. While not fully dynamic the method used in the *General Theory* is partly dynamic and better suited to help economists think about macroeconomic policy changes.

Does this mean that ISLM is of no value at all? Hicks (1980–1, p. 149) suggests that it is useful when one is concerned solely in understanding the past. Looking back we know that in any given year it is unlikely that an economy is in equilibrium, but in many years no great problems flow from the assumption that departures from equilibrium within the year are random, and can be neglected. In such years ISLM can give a useful understanding of the economic situation. However, this is not true of all years. As Hicks himself pointed out (1980–1, p. 150), turning points are years when this assumption is dangerous. Even when confined to looking at the past the use of ISLM is limited.

## REFERENCES

Ackley, G. (1961). *Macroeconomic Theory*, New York, Macmillan.

Hicks, J.R. (1937). "Mr Keynes and the 'Classics': A Suggested Interpretation", *Econometrica*, Vol.5, No.2, pp. 146–59.

Hicks, J.R. (1980–1). "IS-LM an explanation", *Journal of Post Keynesian Economics*, Vol.3, No.2, pp. 139–154.

Hicks, J.R. (1982). *Money, Interest and Wages, Collected Essays on Economic Theory*, Oxford, Basil Blackwell.

Hicks, J.R. (1985). *Methods of Dynamic Economics*, Oxford University Press.

Keynes, J.M. (1936). *The General Theory of Employment, Interest and Money*, London, Macmillan.

Solow, R.M. (1984). "Mr Hicks and the Classics" in D.A. Collard, D.R. Helm, M.FG. Scott and A.K. Sen. (eds), *Economic Theory and Hicksian Themes*, Oxford University Press.

# CHAPTER - 10

# THE FUNCTION OF THE HICKSIAN ECONOMIC INSTITUTION

## B.B. Price

### ABSTRACT

Some analysts of Sir John Hicks write of an evolution in his thought, but his ideas on the economic institution demonstrate a constancy in his conviction that it can serve three significant functions: to allow for economic activity, to facilitate both individual and collective economic activity, and to exercise checks and balances on economic activity. Seemingly Hicks asked how societies could create the most effective economic institutions to carry the burden of allowing market forces to work best, while at the same time providing checks and balances to these same market forces.

The focus of this study is the role of the Hicksian insitution, considered either as economic (a producer or conveyor of goods and/or services), or at least in its economic context, a complex milieu where social interdependences are organized by custom and/or authority. To help understand the importance Hicks placed on economic institutions in their capacity to serve the three significant functions, a second section addresses what he perceived to be the sources of instability in economic activity. Specific institutions – non-merchants, competition, cooperation /coordination, regulation(political and legal), resources, merchants, and price – are then examined to see whether they might be likely candidates for assuming part of the Hicksian functions. The result is a survey of some ideas on the role of institutions in the fostering, facilitating and regulating of Hicks' vision of economic activity at its most efficient, productive best.

Some analysts of the work of Sir John Hicks write of an evolution in his thought. On the subject of institutions, however, it would appear that over the course of his long career Hicks mainly elaborated his ideas on institutions rather than changed them in any dramatic way. He sustained his perspectives, for example, on markets as institutions from his reflections in *Value and Capital* (1939), and on the role of the financial

[111]

centre among financial institutions from their expression in letters to Patinkin in the 1950s to their echo in his last work, *A Market Theory of Money* (1989). This does not reduce the importance of his ideas. Quite to the contrary, they seem to stand as affirmed and reaffirmed throughout his writing and to demonstrate the constancy of Hicks' conviction in his ideas that economic institutions serve three significant functions:[1]

(1)  to allow for economic activity (at least 'market exchange')
(2)  to facilitate both individual economic activity (measured in profit), and collective economic activity (measured in GNP or standard currency)
    a)  to exercise checks and balances on some economic activity
    b)  to allow for economic activity and/or
    c)  to facilitate economic activity.

Hicks' main concern in contemplating the role of economic institutions seems to have been to answer the question, 'How do societies create the most effective economic institutions to carry the burden of allowing market forces to work best, while at the same time providing checks and balances to these same market forces?'[2] It is a tall order, but one for which Hicks found answers largely in his analysis of the steady historical and contemporaneous changes, both conscious and unconscious, in the context in which economic activity occurs.

## I

The focus of this study is thus the role of the institution, considered either as economic or at least in its economic context. To define the Hicksian institution, the entity of interest to the economist, is not a totally simple task. To give examples is far more easily done: the family,

---

[1] This conviction on the part of Hicks is simply asserted, although one could refer to the following works for respective corroboration: (1) *A Theory of Economic History* (1969); (2) *Value and Capital* (1939), *A Revision of Demand Theory* (1956), and *Capital and Time* (1973); and (3) specific essays in *Economic Perspectives* (1977) and *A Market Theory of Money* (1989).

[2] In one of his works devoted to the analysis of economic institutions, Douglass North sets up a slightly more restricted but methodologically analogous type of investigation, inquiring as to "what combination of institutions permits capturing the gains from trade inherent in the standard neoclassical (zero transaction cost) model at any moment of time?" (North 1990, pp. 118,11-16.)

the school, the firm, business or enterprise (e.g. manufacturers, stock-option companies, trading companies), the market, political collectives (e.g., State), the contract, money, credit, etc. Institutions for Hicks are more than "the rules of the game in a society" or "the humanly devised constraints" of Douglass C. North.[3] Hicks' institution, however, is the *human organization* which functions according to rules or constraints, as Hicks states it, "an organization, now revealed as a structure of rules and understandings" (Hicks 1969, p. 11).

For Hicks, the institution is revealed as the structure of an internalized combination of the two root sources of social rules, or understandings": custom and authority. Customary rules derive from tradition. They seem to spring from generally accepted practices which, while they prescribe "individual function" or "allotted task", have been being followed collectively, even without being recognized as the organization's rules or constraints as such (Hicks 1969, pp. 13, 14). Authoritative rules, on the other hand, derive from organizing decisions made at a specific time and place by one person or a subgroup of persons concerned. Hicks refers generically to the source of these rules variously as the social "centre" or its "top" (Hicks 1969, pp. 12, 13).

The Hicksian economic institution epitomizes the combination of what defines virtually any institution. It is most commonly one in which certain rules delimit the domain in which each individual can take decisions in order to reach the specific objectives, commonly fixed by the authority (Hicks 1973, p. 20; see also 1939, p. 111). It is important to note that Hicks entered into the much debated issue, launched in the thirties, of the relationship between economic institutions and the market.[4] From his ideas, it can be asserted, for purposes of this discussion, that he did not define economic institutions as such by virtue

---

[3]North 1990, p. 3. The discussions in the definitions of North and Hicks are quite significant, especially as North tackled some of the same concerns which Hicks addressed in the context of analyzing institutions, how to improve the "performance characteristics of economies" (North 1990, p. 69). Both are persuaded that institutions "are the underlying determinant of the long-run performance of economies" (North 1990, p. 107).

[4]Hicks does not seem to have been working in an intellectual void at either of his 1939 or 1973 foray into the issue of economic institutions: of Coase's reflections in 1937 on firms and markets as different organizations while performing some of the same economic functions, and Arrow's 1964 published comments, deriving from his presidential address to the Institute of Management Sciences in 1963, on firms and markets as distinct institutions for the organization of economic activity.

of their connection to a market. The firm or enterprise, Hicks' quintessential economic institution, was, for example, specifically an "economy without a market". The question thus presents itself as to what an economic institution, distinct from any other social institution, was for Hicks.

Institutions are economic institutions by virtue of the fact that they produce or convey goods and/or services. Each alone is a combination of non-human and human resources. Although Hicks is not explicit about this point, it is perhaps his recognition of the importance of the non-human resources in the activities of economic institutions which caused him to incorporate more than the notion of human constructs (i.e., rules or constraints) into the definition or configuration of economic institutions.[5] It is, however, not explicit in Hicks; perhaps even, by the 1980s as financial institutions were coming recognizably close to creating a pure credit economy, he might have felt an insistence on material resources dated his ideas and restricted the desired universality of his institutional analysis. Nonetheless, Hicks' interest in the non-material aspects of the economic activities of production and distribution are trademarks of many of his contributions to economics: the traverse equilibrium model, primary vs secondary goods markets analysis, production functions, key elements of capital theory, and even his early liquidity analysis and the multiplier effect. Of course, for Hicks, as for virtually all economic theorists who are not materialistic determinists, human beings are the ultimate determinants of economic institutions, if only because they are the cause of an organization's being 'born'.

The human element of the economic institution is especially important. Non-human resources do not exist as economic products (or components of services) unless intentionally procured to that end, either by purchase or local production. Further, rarely can they be conveyed 'as is' as 'product'.[6] Only when used in combination with labour (the basic human economic resource), can they be produced into the goods or services capable of being sold (see Hicks 1956, p. 90). Thus in most economic institutions human beings are critical in the valuation, production, and conveyance of all non-human resources, underlining the

---

[5]See above North's definition of institution and note 2.

[6]One is led to think here of the proverbial fruit falling, edible, from the tree straight into the mouth.

importance of both human and non-human elements in economic institutions.

Either due to the process of creating or to the result of having created goods and services, economic institutions need connections between each other, frequently by establishing the intermediary of the market. Hicks identified market types according to the parties for whom the market served as the intermediary: "(1) dealings between merchants, (2) dealings between merchants and non-merchants, (3) direct dealings between non-merchants" (Hicks 1976, p. 148).[7] While the issue was for him in part who the parties meeting at the market were, Hicks emphasized a further distinction, between "organized" and "unorganized" markets.[8] Harking back to his definition of institution as "an organization, now revealed as a structure of rules and understandings" (Hicks 1969, p. 11), it is clear for him that 'organized' markets are institutions, while 'unorganized' ones are not. Organized markets work under the rules, "of a club", as it were, beyond those of raw supply and demand, and restrict access only "to those who promise to keep the rules" (Hicks 1977, p. x).[9]

Hicks pushed his reflections on markets toward all the elements of their organization or institution. The rise of the market is the starting point for his studying the parties to exchange (reflected in the definitions above),.the rules made for internal market organization, and the 'logic of the system of private enterprise'. Although specialization and division of labour presented themselves before there was "any market (or any dependence upon a market)", Hicks saw in 'specialization', among other things, the key to shifts in the character of market parties (Hicks 1969, p. 22). Initially, however, even without

---

[7]Hicks' examples of each market type offer further identification of the parties: (1) as traders, or at least "parties to an agreement [who] are doing the same kind of business" and by definition in frequent contact with the market (Hicks 1969, p. 35; see also Hicks 1976, p. 148), or as "professionals" in the case of the credit market", (2) as independent shopkeepers [merchants] and producers/wholesalers [non-merchants] (Hicks 1976, p. 148) or as merchants and consumers, of which the non-merchant party may or may not come frequently to the market, and (3) as parties to "the market in private dwelling-house", who are infrequently in market relationship with one another (Hicks 1976, p. 148).

[8]This distinction is couched within one connected to the history of economic ideas, namely the identification of "unorganized markets" as Marshallian, and the "organized", as Walrasian. For further discussion of this link, see Hamouda, 1993, pp. 68–70.

[9]"and who are willing to pay the costs of administering them" (Hicks 1977, p. x).

116

"deliberate and creative specialization", early traders gave organizing structure to their market, through rules, for verifying property rights and for policing their contracts (Hicks 1969, p. 36). In these very earliest historical beginnings of economic 'clubs', no enterprise, however specialized by default, provided, as Hicks sees it, organizational subterfuge[10] to pure trade competition based on available supply and focused demand.[11]

Hicks' references to the interventions of the State open toward an understanding of the context of economic institutions generally and of the market in particular. Hicks firmly asserted it "advisable to see some actions of the State as non-economic",[12] especially in the examination of economic institutions "conducted with the aid of different methods, analogous to those of the specialist in economic history" (Hicks 1956, p. 6). It was Hicks' sense that economic history "sticks to economic activity and does not imply that economic motives underlie apparently non-economic behaviour", including that of political entities. As Hicks observed, the first "government intervention on the market" was in the form of insisting that markets be held "under some sort of licence", since "[A]ny government . . . must set its face against brawling and rioting (or what counts as brawling and rioting by its standards); for they present an obvious danger *that is purely political*" (emphasis added; Hicks 1969, p. 33). He felt strongly that the political, supervisory role must exist for the State, if an economy is to have "the power of growth, of spreading itself continually into new fields and new applications" (Hicks 1969, p. 38).[13]

The multiplicity of markets, fostered historically by State support, drew Hicks to analyse the institution of the firm or enterprise. In economies of greater and greater entreprenerial specialisation, he wrote, "What we have need of most of all is a technique permitting the study of the connections between markets". (Hicks 1956, p. 2). At their nexus

---

[10]Hicksian innovation implies the installation of competition among politico-economic groups.

[11]Issues of price determination still arose. These will be addressed below.

[12]This citation stems from the chapter devoted to Hicks and history in Hamouda 1993, p. 281, and derives from his expression of it in Hicks 1977, p. 125. It is asserted that the date of publication of the these ideas is not the earliest date of Hicks' affirmation of them.

[13]"What is also necessary is that they [the rulers], together with their judges and administrators, should have a 'feel' for trade, so that they can give the kind of help, or rather recognition , that it needs." (Hicks 1969, p. 38)

he saw the firm, representative both of pure 'unproductive' traders non-hierarchically horizontally organized and of the productive organization vertically integrated top to bottom. A truly representative firm is, of course, a fiction, but one could be posited which might carry out either or both production and marketing functions. Over the course of his writing, Hicks analyses the phenomenon of multiple markets and, especially in *Theory of Economic History* (1969), the long history of market activity, and the enterprise and its entrepreneur at its intersections.

Just as the enterprise is a representative, fiction, so is the enterpreneur. Some one or group of persons is, however, in the case of each production or service organization principally responsible for organizing its production/service and exchange. For Hicks, within the dimensions of the firm, the portions devoted to production and marketing are determined by its choice of specialization. Hicks identifies the growing difficulty in directing an enterprise once its scale of activity develops (1956, p. 73). On the marketing side too challenges present themselves, for aside from the problems simply of organization, entrepreneurial decisions depend on expected profits for a certain duration of the institution's processes (Hicks 1956, p. 69). The 'entrepreneur' and his institution must thus collect and synthesize crucial decision-guiding information arriving simultaneously from the pertinently related different (and possibly large number of) sourcing, purchasing, and competing markets.

The model for leadership decision-making Hicks designed initially was that of a Walrasian temporary equilibrium.[14] Although this model did not allow for decisions to be implemented within its defined period of the 'week', it did take into consideration the existence of more than one period for entrepreneurs and thus of their need to plan both for and beyond one 'week'. Its entrepreneurs thus consider "those actions devoted to the present ends and those actions which are directed to the future" (Hicks 1939, pp. 123–4). On 'Monday' and only on 'Monday' when the "market" opens can desired actions be put into effect, and as Hicks notes, all "proceeds quickly and smoothly to a position of temporary equilbrium" (Hicks 1939, p. 123). By keeping everything except deliberations constant and all changes in the economy confined to "Monday", this model de-emphasized, if not ignored, any push for

---

[14]See Hicks' discussion of it in Hicks 1934.

change during the period stemming from on-going deterioration of capital equipments, imperfect contemporaneous knowledge, a need for price-re-determination, or exhaustion of supply or excess of demand.

As his adoption and modification of the model reflect, Hicks saw institutions as not predisposed to change, but rather to a working stasis or equilibrium. He did, however, not want to foster any misconceptions: "our method seems to imply that we conceive of the economic system as being always in equilibrium" (emphasis added; Hicks 1939, p. 131). While organizations, not in situations of change or not aware of surrounding change, do not indeed change, modifications seemed nonetheless to him almost inevitable in the case of most institutions. As stated by Douglass North, "[I]ncremental change comes from the perceptions of the entrepreneurs in political and economic organizations that they could do better by altering the existing institutional framework at some margin" (North 1990, p. 8). Hicks further emphasized the human component of change: "The immediate cause of an economic effect is, nearly always, a decision by someone; or it may be the combination of decisions that were made by different people" (Hicks 1979, p. 88). This discussion might probe further whether change is solely attributable to 'perceptions' or rational expectations, or vis-versa, but the point here is that individuals in economic leadership or authoritative positions do react, whether to stasis or to change, in such a way as to cause changes. Whether institutional economic change is endogenously self-induced or exogenously suggested, institutions alter themselves, however voluntarily, in a responsive way. In such situations, each institution attempts to control the situation to its own benefit (i.e., survival), by introducing presumed beneficial modifications. Hicks identified nonetheless certain characteristics common to all economic changes. As noted above, their cause is predominantly human. Their effects are chronologically irreversible.

## II

To help understand the importance Hicks placed on economic institutions and their capacity to serve the three significant functions of allowing for economic activity, facilitating it and exercising on it, when and where needed, some checks and balances, one might examine what he perceived to be the sources of instability, or disequilibrium, in economic activity. Once he had identified some of its causes, Hicks could turn to his main purpose in examining the role of economic institutions, to answer the question, 'How do societies create the most effective economic institutions to carry the burden of allowing market forces to work best while at the same time providing checks and balances to these same forces?'

In the environment of the free market, the context predominantly assumed by Hicks, falling profits or decreasing returns is perhaps the greatest source of instability to an economic institution. Institutions face both internal and external conflicts, but Hicks sees problems of internal organisation as being most responsible for pulling enterprises into the zone of decreasing returns.[15] If, for example, the institution lacks a strong hierarchical structure or respect for its leadership, according to Hicks,

> it will unable to respond to new emergencies, emergencies that differ in some essential respect from those that have been previously experienced. It is hardly possible for an organization to respond to a new emergency without some central decision, and a central decision that can be made effective . . .

> Hicks 1969, p. 12

External stimuli are, however, the far more abundant sources of an organization's instability. In an active economy, the risk of disequilibrium is not negligible. For example, new producers can enter the market and incite competition over product and price. Demand fluctuations can cause excessive excitement over a product or undue pessimism over expenditures. Collective illiquidity may constrain economic activity.

The keys to the moderation of these and the many other modern economic instabilities are multiple and different, dependant upon three conditions: their source, their context and the indeterminacy of economic causality. The potential 'resolution' of economic instability differs depending on whether its source is internal or external. Otherwise stated, each economy is the combination of the integration (or interdependence) of the elements most critical to the 'internal' face of the individual organization and the differentiation of the elements most acute for the 'external' face of the whole economy. Although coordination of all economic actions happens, consciously or unconsciously, it may not always lead to stability. The variety of an

---

[15]Most explicitly perhaps in *Value and Capital* (1939).

economy's elements, the complexity of the context of economic activity, and the potentially wide-ranging impact of economic actions are all possible reasons.

If the source of an institution's economic instability is internal, the problems causing the instability ought to find resolution, according to Hicks, in 'altruism'. Following Hicks' notion that internal instability derives from too little cohesion to a central determinant (or determiner) of purpose and plan, 'altruism' as its key to a solution might best be understood to mean the collective or wide-spread individual imposition of an increased number of internal constraints affecting choice. The instincts of participants within the organization must be 'domesticated' to allow it to function well. This would refer most directly to behavioural restrictions of the customary type, for in a purely customary system, individuals adhere to routines founded on a culture which generates some constraints for each one. It might also entail, however, the collective adoption of additional 'legal' prescriptions. Appreciation of the impact of individual action on the viability of the institution at large, another understanding of 'altruism' perhaps, would guide the formulation of the new restrictions toward those which would foster the institution's ability to sustain sufficient return by means of bargaining strength, and production and marketing efficiency.

Consideration of the broader economic context in which instability is present may also hold the key to its reduction,[16] for if the source of an institution's economic instability is external, the problems causing the instability ought to find resolution, according to Hicks, in relative increases in efficiency and profit, among producers, traders and/or financial interests. Hicks does not seem specifically to have envisaged stability to derive necessarily from the elimination of specific organizations within the economy as a whole. As a first step, producers, better informed of the existence and plans of their competitors, can try to foresee their impact on their own pricing sequence over the course of

---

[16]Hicks' hypotheses regarding access to other external economies facilitating the survival of an specific firm, or set of merchants, i.e., freedom from the classic problem of decreasing return, reflect such an awareness for the case of internal instability:

This, I think, is one of the main reasons why the city-state form of organization is so important. It is particularly favourable to the growth of a diversified trade; so it provides a way round the first form of the 'diminishing returns' obstacle to trade expansion.

Hicks 1969, p 16.

a projected future and try thereby to increase their profit margin. Obviously competition itself can eliminate institutional inefficiency within a group of institutions, but here the aim is to consider the possibility of all to prosper within the collective – a Pareto optimality of sorts. Although the fact remains that small firms manage to coexist with big firms, it seems nonetheless possible to infer from Hicks' emphasis on efficiency that for him stability in a free market can be maintained in the environment of efficiency afforded by the presence of even a small number of competitors in most areas of production rather than necessarily derived from the welfare benefit to consumers of a 'competitive' choice between many firms, small and large.

Merchants or traders epitomize recognition of the broadest context of economic activity; not only are they the key traditional link between producers and consumers within one economy, the economy of which they are a part is most often "dependent upon trade with peoples outside it", effected by them (Hicks 1969, p. 49). Faced with the inefficiency and risk of stock fluctuations (and their accompanying explosive differentiations in price) they often seek to guide producers, discouraging the too optimistic expectations which might put an unsatisfiable demand on supply or stimulating demand to meet supply in cases of unjustified pessisimsm. Hicks perceived an increasing eliding of the parties of merchant and producer, the result of the instability in stocks and pricing which the distinction permitted. In his analysis of the institutional shift from Marshallian to Walrasian markets, Hicks identified the role of the merchant as having been "transferred" to producers who to a large extent have thereby become more important in dictating market terms" (Hamouda 1993, p. 69). Although he emphasized the new price-setting role of producers in this transformation, Hicks also presumably considered their approach to stock production (and reduction) to have become more efficient, if only due to the elimination of an intermediary information relay, or 'listening point', to use the terminology of A Market Theory of Money (1989).

Another contextual condition which could lead to excessively strong institutional disequilibrium is the risk of illiquidity. The intervention of merchants can avoid what in their absence only the producers, conditioned to be without access to credit, could endure and can help them sustain efficiency and profit, if not increase both.

> To the merchant, in any age, financial dealings are a natural extension of trade dealings; he finds himself passing, almost imperceptibly, from one to the other. Even before the invention of money, goods that were owned by one person must often have been entrusted to another, for him to trade with them on behalf of the owner . . . After the invention of money, it will often be more convenient to replace such physical entrustings by a money loan.

Hicks 1969, p. 73

Prices are presumed to be abnormally high or low, without the demand by traders wishing to sell them. Merchants' anticipation of future sales in the market tends, even during periods of illiquidity, to retain an end-price at a level acceptable to most producers, save those who would be constrained by having to seek usurious loans. Merchants providing the key to the resolution of producers' illiquidity would seem to be an excellent instance of what Pavel Pelikan (1987) might describe as the application of adaptive efficiency within the broader economic context in which instability is present: except for the resorting to usury, perhaps for ideological reasons, an example of individuals' option for preferences for solutions which are not adaptively efficient, merchants' sustaining demand is an example of institutions exhibiting willingness to assume risk in order to resolve at a particular point in time an economic problem or logjam.

Understanding the keys to the moderation of economic instabilities is also dependent upon an appreciation of the indeterminacy of economic causality. For Hicks, both the dual sources of instability, the internal and the external, and the broad context of economic activity preclude a deterministic approach to analysizing, let alone resolving, institutional instability. Any process, whether equilibrating or disequilibrating, cannot be considered to be one 'which, once begun, must necessarily complete itself; it can be interrupted by external causes, or it can run into internal difficulties which it has no means of escaping" (Hicks 1973, p. 15). This conviction derives both from his theoretical look at economic history and his examination of economic causality.

> We can continue the [historical] sequence (. . .) right up to the rise of Industialism, and to the reaction against the market which has followed (or appears to have followed) upon it. But we shall not be able (as a deterministic theorist might think he was able) to extrapolate into the future; all we shall be able to do all the economist is ever able to do, is to speculate about things which, more or less probably, may happen.

Hicks 1969, p. 8

Particularly since "all economic data are dated", they "can never do more than establish a relation which appears to hold within the period to which the data refer ... we cannot even reasonably guess that it will continue to hold for the next fifty years" (Hicks 1979, p. 38).

## III

Thus, Hicks appears to have asked, who or what is or could be responsible for an economy's able, if not equilibrated, functioning? Who or what is or could be most capable of reducing instability and raising efficiency and profit?

Given is the environment in which Hicks' institutions exist – a complex milieu where the interdependences among the agents is organized by custom and/or authority. There exists thus within the mileu certain deliberately constructed collective rationalities, and perhaps even one 'umbrella' economic one. The particular group of institutions, structured currently to assure coordination among contemporary economic agents is for Hicks the undoubted product of a chronological change he has traced more than once. If realization of an absolutist economic optimisation is not his purposeful goal, in question is at least whether the existing elements of the economic whole or the 'superstructure' itself do not require modification (1) to allow for economic activity, (2) to facilitate both individual and collective economic activity, and (3) to exercise checks and balances on some economic activity both to allow for economic activity and to facilitate economic activity.

For the balance of this article, specific institutions will be examined to see to what extent they might to Hicks' mind be likely candidates for assuming part of the outlined undertaking: those of non-merchants, competition cooperation/coordination, regulation, resources, merchants, and price.

### The institution(s) of non-merchants, i.e. firm and entrepreneurs/producers

Equilibrium models were principally developed by Hicks from the point of view of the entrepreneurs, as was seen above in the case of the temporary equilibrium model based on Walras. Their more or less static environment permits the institution of the firm or enterprise some assurance of a certain permanence in the rules of conduct which provide for its organization. Enterprises do not just spring up, and the enterpreneur/producer who develops an enterprise does so only if he is capable of tapping within the system the principles of coordination among potential individuals for his own institution and among those needed outside it. Much has been written about the qualities of the representative 'good' entrepreneur. For Hicks' having an aptitude to foresee the effects of substitution among resources,[17] to offer a recognized specialization to those desirious to entering into contracts, to retain a necessary capital liquidity for expenditures and loans, to establish long-range plans which incorporate merchandizing are all valuable qualities.

'Equilibrium' in the preoccupations of firms seems to spell the search for the satisfactory size for utmost efficiency and attention to innovation as the means of forestalling diminishing return. The enterpreneur can thus play a significant role, especially with regard to (1) allowing for economic activity of production and (2) facilitating the individual economic activity of the merchant and the collective economic activity of the producing institution. His biggest challenge is in short to manage the complexity the enterprise presents. Since, according to Hicks, increased confidence is tightly linked to the possibilities to reduce risk, the more confidence the enterpreneur instills in his organization and merchants, the more effectively he sustains a stable economic environment. Nonetheless as Knight soberly reminded his readers on a similar topic, there are limits to how much confidence even the most ideal of entrepreneurs can create:

> the question of diminishing returns from entrepreneurship is really a matter of the amount of uncertainty present. To imagine that a man could adequately manage a business enterprise of indefinite size[18] and complexity is to imagine a situation in which effective uncertainty is entirely absent.
>
> Knight 1965, pp. 286–87

## The institution of competition

---

[17]A particular firm's organisation might render a great number of efficient possible combinations of factors of production for its given scale of production.

[18]Smallness of size might, however, indicate, according to Hicks, not a great degree of uncertainty, but simply lack of capital (see Hicks 1969, p. 118).

Hicks identified the institutions of relatively perfect competition and imperfect competition. A more perfectly competitive environment preferred a free market, i.e., one of open entry and free pricing, i.e. supply – demand determined without collusion. Hicks represented imperfect competition in a time-sequence of three periods: a period of construction (before production), a 'closed' period of production (during which would-be competitors have not had the time to catch up and compete), and an 'open' period of production (during which competitors have had the time to adapt and engage in competition). For Hicks both perfect and imperfect competition, despite their different rules, create an institutionalized environment in which returns are growing collectively. Nonetheless, since Hicks does not translate into economic instability the casualty, noted earlier, which competition can bring to specific firms or individuals, by the same token, mere existence of the institution of, while it might be seen to help (1) allow for economic activity generally, competition does not per se in Hicksian economics provide the key to economic stabilization or improvement.

*The institutions of economic cooperation/coordination*

The obvious alternative to institutionalized competition would appear to be organized cooperation or coordination of economic activity external to the single institution. Its desirability seems to turn on the problem of access to information about the future possibilities of markets, given that producers do not know or know poorly the plans of their competitors. A 'connection between producers', particularly if perceived as a 'connection between markets', especially in a fundamentally competitive environment, is something which has to be established by a deliberate act of entrepreneurs. Such coordinating networks can effect a sort of entering selectivity or filtering (perhaps in the guise of 'quality control' or industrial standards'), which is undoubtedly a form of check on economic activity. This effect of enterpreneurial aggregation is offset, Hicks would seem to advance, by the microeconomic tendencies by which consumers exercise the control over firms. A combination thus of cooperation on the supply side and individual consumer preference on the demand side, although not strictly speaking, one institution nor even the interface of two institutions, might be recognizable as a symbiosis of check and balance. In terms of facilitating or fostering economic activity, however, the interrelationship seems of relatively little consequence to Hicks.

Hicks developed instead the narrower contextual perspective that potential gains for all could be realized in a climate favourable to 'supply' institutions, particularly if the authority of the firm and the customs of the market support each other cooperatively and if both 'commerce' and 'industry' are allowed to exercise their "real tendences to increasing returns" (Hicks 1973, p. 56). More specifically, however, Hicks, as will be seen below, placed greater hope in market coordination than in production collaboration to increase, facilitate and enhance economic activity. Presumably, as identified in the discussion of competition and alluded to just above, even institutionalized cooperation between producers need not, for Hicks, be designed specifically to allow for more entrants into the production sector nor to facilitate the activity of its struggling members. Further, the concluding observation above that no alliance of producers could be Hicks' mind mitigate fluctuations due to the vagaries of 'taste' virtually eliminates the role of producers' cooperatives in potentially moderating, even to their own advantage, supply abherations or radical price shifts. Cooperation or collaboration, at least among the production institutions, although it might lead to some risk and hostility reduction, was thus not Hicks' answer to greater economic stability and strength.

*The institutions of organizational regulation*

The regulation of economic organizations can take many forms. Among those discussed most by Hicks were State interventions and legal codes.

For Hicks the role of the State seemed strong at the 'start' of economic history. He depicts its forms chronologically:

- a particular feudal entrepreneur, such as a Pharaoh, King or Emperor,[19] in competition with the other entrepreneurs for its share

---

[19]The economy of a neolithic or early medieval village, as well as tribal communities which have survived until lately in many parts of the world, was not organized by its Ruler (if such existed); it was based on a corpus of tradition. . . . It is important to emphasize that the 'head' of the organization (King or Chief or High Priest or Council of Elders) would himself be part of the traditional structure.

of the agricultural surplus to support himself and is 'civil service' bureaucracy (Hicks 1969, pp. 15–24);

- the city-state, in which trade is the economic base and "the rulers themselves are merchants or are deeply involved in trade themselves" (Hicks 1969, p. 38);

- the Mercantile Monarchy, in which the market owes its consolidation to the possibility of an agreement settling on the sharing of the surplus between the State with its predatory tendencies and the community of merchants (Hicks 1969, pp. 60–72); and

- the administrative nation-state, in which "the State has taken the place of the landlord . . . reserving for itself no more than the minimum duties of a Protector", for which "it must exact a payment for its services" (Hicks 1969, p. 115), in which it serves "as partner, or provider of capital" (Hicks 1969, p. 120), and in which "the most thoroughgoing [device] of all is the bringing of those who make the decisions about trade and investment under the direct control of government" (Hicks 1969, p. 163).[20]

The form of State intervention in economic activity is different accordingly as the type of State effecting it is different. Thus in the case of the feudal entrepreneur, the first interventionary role his 'government' of civil servants assumes is the collection of revenue in the form of agricultural surplus (Hicks 1969, p. 19). Further to meet his needs for other than food and to exploit more than agricultural production, ancient and medieval monarchs sponsored sites for market exchanges, by expending resources to establish market places or even whole cities (Hicks 1969, p. 32). Thus, what Hicks called "the first reason for government intervention", the potential political danger of economic gatherings, presented itself, as did the government interventionary response, the issuing of market licences (Hicks 1969, p. 33).

Only slightly later, government sponsorship[21] was also critical in the role of money within an economy. The State came in to provide the

---

[20]See Hamouda 1993, pp. 270–71 for the distillate of Hicks' own classifications of chronological changes into three different possible states of society and four phases of economic change. Extraction of his chronology of State development seems to cut across these two classifications.

[21]Military protection was occasionally another form government sponsorship took.

'public service' of minting coinage according to standard quality and weight. Hicks notes that "it may indeed have been the merchants [of the city-state] who, in the first instance insisted upon some guarantee", seeking, as it were, support for acceptance of a stamped money (Hicks 1969, pp. 66–7). By the time of the Mercantile Monarchy, however, "it was so clearly an advantage to him [the king] that it should be used that he would not abandon it" (Hicks 1969, p. 68). Initially the monarch appreciated his ability to procure the direct profits of seignieurage from minting, but his own coinage also afford him greater flexibility in what he could ultimitely acquire than had previous taxation payments in goods.[22] Next came State intervention in the value of the currency. To meet their neediness, kings manipulated the money supply, through currency inflations, "by debasement or otherwise", reissuing the coinage with more alloy added [Hicks 1969, pp. 88–9). Hicks concludes his chronology of State intervention in economic currency and financial institutions noting that in our era "the control of the State over the [national] money supply . . . has become complete" (Hicks 1969, p. 96).

Another mode of State intervention is taxation. In the Mercantile Monarchy, the State exercised its predatory tendancies on the community of merchants by intervening where possible to levy duties on external trade into their ports or across their borders.[23] The administrative nation-state, however, no longer pursues taxation in such a piecemeal fashion:

> the taxing power of the State, which for long ages was so rudimentary, has in these last few centuries been immensely fortified. The income taxes, the profits taxes, the sales taxes, even the capital taxes such as death duties ... In all of these ways the taxing power of the State has been fortified

Hicks 1969, p. 98

---

[22]He had a direct profit from minting (a profit which became more considerable whenever token coinage was acceptable); but the indirect advantage that accrued was surely more important. If he could get his revenue in the form of money (and he would soon be seeking to do that, so far as he could), he would be able to spend it, through channels of trade, so as to get a flow of real goods, that had greater variety, and therefore greater 'utility', than he could get directly from taxation paid in kind (Hicks 1969, p. 68)

[23]Some such regulation of trade through tariffs was clearly for national political purposes. Hicks generalizes from this instance to all such economic interventions which serve "as a means to national objectives of all sorts, including the pursuit of influence over other nations, of prestige and of power" (Hicks 1969, pp. 161–2).

According to Hicks, the State's increased power of tax intervention is due both to mercantile development as well as to the fact that the great wealth which the wealthiest citizens possess is now within the government's technological reach

Of course, the noted examples of expropriation of a territory's or a people's resources, whether directly in kind or through taxes, is an economic interventionary strategy, but hardly regulatory. Over time, state intervention has, however, increasingly been implemented to exercise political control over the economy, its leaders and its institutions. Hicks offers this summary to his historical chapter on the finances of the sovereign:

> The Mercantile Economy, in its First Phase, was an escape from political authority – except in so far as it made its own political authority. Then in the Middle Phase, when it became formally back under the traditional political authority, that authority was not strong enough to control it. It might destroy, but it could not control. In the Modern Phase, into which we have now passed, that is changed. Largely because of the internal evolution of the Mercantile Economy, control over it has become immensely easier. This is so, whatever is the political structure, and whatever are the ends of the controllers. Their powers will serve them alike for War or Peace, for the solving of social problems or for smothering them.

> Hicks 1969, p. 100

Expropriation, mainly in the form of taxation, has thus transformed itself, in principle, from an economic method used by the State to sustain its leaders and their administration, to a political tool used to regulate the economic aspects of the political entity of the State. It is important to remember that since Hicks' position was that economic strength did not derive inherently from any particular political system, the State's relation to economic activity can only be seen as primarily self-serving. From the economist's perspective, thus State interventions and assumptions of control are presumed to be more to foster its own political ends than the ends of its jurisdiction's economic activity, notwithstanding that at least in recent decades enlightened leaders see the unavoidable necessity of promoting both together. In this very journal issue Hamouda treats in a less specifically historically based discussion Hicks' rationale for government intervention, arriving at a similar, if not sceptical, at least cautious, conclusion that for Hicks only analysis of the specific conditions in a particular economy and their time and place allows determination of the appropriateness of State intervention to permit economic activity, to facilitate both individual and collective economic activity, and even to exercise checks and balances on some economic activity.

The other form of organizational regulation to absorb some of Hicks' thinking was legal codification of economic behaviour. Just as custom lies at the root of all economic organization, it is to be found in legal codes which apply to economic activity. The first legal codification of economic activity seems to have stemmed from two needs: protection of properly and protection of contract (Hicks 1969, p. 33). The 'customs' of the merchant, (1) to "have properly in the things in which he trades" and identifiable right to that property, and (2) to have "a general understanding of what is to happen if there prove to be obstacles to the performance" of an exchange, became integrated thus into the Roman world of law (pertaining to economics) (Hicks 1969, p. 34). The role of the legal encoding of customary rights and understandings did more, however, than preserve the customs and give legal recourse to disputes which arose from them. Legal codification served also to foster the predominantly authoritarian system of some early economic institutions, since, however permeated with dictates, in law-bound institutions an individual does not have 'to expect to receive just any order' and authoritarianism can be less arbitrary.

Although Hicks concluded, as noted above, that the political tail does not way the economic dog, he was less sanguine about the effect of legislative and juridic declarations. In relatively short order, the legal regulation of economic institutions made some old doctrines give way to new formulations and economic practices, either by way of consequential adherence to the new code or as a side effect of a rigidified position. Money and the law became more than superficially linked as money became the means of valuating and compensating the guilty deed. By extension perhaps, merchants' capital losses, by reason of non-repayment of loans by a monarch, became the price to pay by the community of merchants for legal recognition of their customary privileges. Further, both the condemnation of loans with interest and the acceptance of just loans with interest seem to have resulted from the instantiation of merchants' customs in law.

The economic system with a monarchical centre became, in addition to merchant law, another source of law. To reinforce the centre, new rules in the form of laws were imposed on vassals of the sovereign and were generated and proclamed by a new intellectual elite created through a costly bureaucracy. The development of property titles and contracts had the repercussion nonetheless of leading the State and feudal lords, as well as the Church, to limit their own previously customary rights of, for example, 'le droit de seigneur' or involuntary tithing.

Although, as Hicks recognized (1973, p. 149), both legally bound elements and elements without legal binds can and do coexist within many economic institutions, as, for example, protected labour and work without statutory protection, he felt that certain legal codes could play a stabilizing role. For example, laws 'defining' some term contracts commit its parties to long-term lending/borrowing at a non-negotiable fixed rate. Effective application of the law to economic activity presupposes the State's having assumed the functions of Justice (law enforcement) and Defence and the existence of specialized intermediaries. Hicks reminds his readers that

> the appearance of a government that is strong enough to perform them [Justice and Defence] adequately is not a thing which happens automatically. To look for the adequate performance of these functions from the governments . . . , weak both financially and administratively, would usually have been impossible.
>
> Hicks 1969, p. 104[24]

For Hicks the institution of the law guiding economic activity is an extremely relevant one. The most important key to its efficacy, from the perspective of 'the smooth working of the economy', is "that even on the more difficult matters clear decisions should be given". There will undoubtedly be casualties, but "though one contract may be invalidated, further contracts will not be invalidated; those who enter into contracts will be able to know what can be enforced and what can not" (Hicks 1969, p. 36).

*Resource institutions*

Economic resource institutions, whether offering goods, or labour or financial capital, afford opportunity. It takes the continuous flow of factors and intermediary products, which constitutes the Pigouian 'lake',

---

[24]Hicks went on to attribute partly the longevity of and wide-spread resorting to the lord-and-peasant system to its ability to provide a form of justice and defence.

to feed a continual flow toward finished products. Firms which have recourse to a network of sourcing merchants can reduce the risk attached to their business. When a firm's expenses and receipts do not coincide, financial resourcing institutions may provide the rescue. Continuity of financial infusions may be the sustaining resources until a firm's receipts appear, delays being possibly as long as several Hicksian 'weeks' of continuing expenses. In the end, of course, when capital equipment costs, the inevitably principal drain on expenses, are ammortized, despite the constant costs of production resources, the running net revenue might be positive and the major outlay would then be for basic goods resources. The result of further economic calculation would determine if and how soon the installation of new equipment was foreseen, and what is often seen conventionally as an investment cycle would continue.

As Hicks grew older, issues surrounding financial capital recources drew his attention more than the sourcing of all other production needs. He saw suppliers of financial capital as creating virtually a new age of essential intermediaries. Already, in 1957, however, in a letter to Patinkin focused primarily on a discussion of the Quantity Theory of Money,[25] Hicks had outlined his perspective on the relationship between the Monetary Authority, a central source of financial resources, and the end users of the money, on the matter of interest setting. Explaining his own diagramatic depiction of a concentric circular relationship, he wrote "that the Monetary Authority fixes its own 'inner' rate of interest, and that this is transmitted through the rest of the financial system into an 'outer' rate, which is the rate which effectively acts as investment" (Hicks to Patinkin, Dec. 31, 1957, p. 4). By *A Market Theory of Money* (1989) in which the diagram resurfaced, Hicks' Monetary Authority had become explicitly at the central bank.

Hicks saw the key to both the viability and stability of the highly developed economic system to lie in the various responsibilities of a properly organized financial resource sector. First of all, his model had to have layers, his concentric circles; otherwise, "[T]he distinction between the inner and the outer rate [of interest] will have disappeared"

---

[25]Cited here is the letter of 1957 (made newly available on the internet http://scriptorium.lib.duke.edu/economists/patinkin/1957-12-31-p4-72.jpeg), rather than equally concise passages of *A Market Theory of Money* (1989) to emphasize the longevity of Hicks convictions, as well his sources of inspiration: Keynes and Wicksell.

(Hicks to Patinkin, Dec. 31, 1957, p. 4). Admitting that "[T]here will only be a full control of the outer rate if the Monetary Authority lent an industry directly, . . . as industry required at the rate of fixed [interest]",[26] he, like Keynes, opted for "imperfect control", a sort of feedback relationship between the Monetary Authority, as ultimate lender, determining the Quantity of Money, and the borrowers, with their Liquidity Preference ultimately determining the interest rate. As Hicks described his own model in 1957, it is "drawn up under the assumption that the rate of interest (the outer rate) is an independent variable: thus . . . it must be supposed that the Monetary Authority is able to make each particular rate of interest effective" (Hicks to Patinkin, Dec. 31, 1957, p. 4).

Hicks presented the credit market generally as a 'market of professionals' which avoids turbulences. By virtue of its structure, however, he also recognized its inherent necessity to cope with the potentially destabilizing waves of unbrided competition at the intermediary level. In *A Market Theory of Money* (1989) he explicitly introduces a central bank as a means of overcoming the tension between the tendency toward competition "with knives drawn" between the financial intermediaries, primarily the banks, and the tendency toward cooperation. One finds in numerous places in Hicks the idea that specialized agents play an important role in the realization of an equilibrium, and for him agents providing financial resources were no exception. He believed that the group of financial intermediaries, allbeit in a position of competition, has an strong interest in realizing equilbria and that as a group the financiers can form 'plans' for a future which, while conceived undoubtedly not as stationary, can nonetheless allow for explicit coordination among them. Professional capitalists can thus operate in a system of coherent interest rates (Hicks 1956, p. 157), the central monetary authority and the financial intermediaries permitting avoidance of discrepancies' becoming to excessive.

This exercise of financial power was, however, for Hicks, a concomittant element of a truly stable economy or at least an economic situation perceived as stable. Since "the level of the interest rate measures in fact the intensity of the risk factor, the variations in interest which are compatible with calm maintenance of organized markets are of weak amplitude" (Hicks 1956, pp. 244–45). An interest rate created

---

[26]"but, then, of course, we are back at what I called above the Wicksellian model" (Letter, Hicks to Patinkin, Dec. 31, 1957, p. 4)

through intermediaries would be "too weak to be able to exercise a real influence on the situation in the near future" and the risk factor projected by borrowers would be "too important for interest to be able to exercise a real influence on the far future", and the risk factor projected by borrowers would be "too important for interest to be able exercise a real influence on the far future" (Hicks 1956, p. 210).[27] The end result then of a concentric system of institutions of financial capital resources was for Hicks a very fostering and stabilizing one. The intermediairies made the resources available; the regulation of them by the authority and the competition and cooperation among them made the rates of interest neither extreme in absolute terms nor in terms of discrepancies, the dual division of sourcing funds made for the economic efficacy of each interest rate; etc.

## The institution of the merchants

For product markets, the intervention of merchants as intermediary agents was until relatively recently the rule, and in the case of specialized products, still is. As a result of the part they play as conveyors, merchants guide the formation of prices, reducing transaction costs in the face of consumers of changing tastes. In Hicks the merchants likely to have the most stabilizing role are the traders who play a 'regulating' role. In diffusing information on workable prices, they can reduce the reliance on anticipated pricing of producers. They can, for example, buffer producers' limiting their supply to avoid the strong consumer reactions to take advantage of producers' reactions to the anticipations of other producers' limiting upward wholesale price adjustments . . .

Given that they do not know or know poorly the plans of their competitors, all producers suffer to some degree from the problem of access to information about the future possibilities of markets. Merchants are, however, in a position to be able to learn about and to synthesize the tendencacies. Due to the fact that they are in competition among themselves and also because it is not to their longer range advantage either to reduce or to stimulate demand in an exhaggerated way, whatever the propensity of the merchants to speculation, they have

---

[27]For example, a drop in interest rates (present or anticipated) would have to be very large in order to compensate for the anticipations of a drop in price.

to conserve a reasonable attitude. For the combination of these reasons, they can therefore fill the function of smoothing anticipated price fluctuations. This makes of the institution of merchants and their markets a very positive (1) fostering, (2) facilitating, and (3) regulating economic force.

## The institution of price

Issues of pricing tie into virtually every institution thus far discussed, and their connection to the functioning of a stable, productive, and efficient economy is not hard to see. In the context of a discussion of the effects of the institution of the price, two observations seem particularly important. First, competition has a stabilizing effect on price formation, since the purest rules of the marketplace most significantly effect the formation process. As has already been seen, the market is an institution which frames the actors and their rules of actions and in so doing functions to facilitate the most efficient exchange. It is also thereby able to facilitate the equilibrium-price formation, either through a process of mutual discovery by all parties concerned through bargaining or by further delimiting the range of 'workable' prices already adopted by merchants coming to market.

Hicks had much to say about price formation, price determination, the factors of price, etc., Among its aspects which economists have contemplated for centuries is the issue of non supply-demand based pricing. This usually translates into price regulation, and since it was not mentioned above in the context of regulatory institutions, it would seem appropriate to do so here. The medieval approach to price formation was juridic along the Roman model. The just price was legally determined and enfor- ced with the requisite moral formulation of prohibitions. The State's role in price determination has been less moralistic and far more inter- ventionary, however, dependent upon legislative formulation. Briefly, and as the second important point here, Hicks seems to have felt in general that there may well be a place for the regulatory role of the State in periods of price aberrations. In 1938, he constated, not for the first nor last time, for example, that "[E]xistence of a type of rigid pricing has stabilising effects in periods of deflation" (Hicks 1938, p. 247).

## CONCLUSION

A discussion on economic institutions might address its focus either to an institutional 'superstructure' or to the individual institutions which comprise the system as a whole. Since, however, it would seem that such issues as modifications of law, as, for example, in the case of the institutionalization of merchant contracts, have been considered transformations of the 'superstructure', the distinction between a wholistic and an elemental approach may not be that enlightening. Here, the aim has been to see to what extent specifically economic institutions, such as the market, the firm, price, competition, etc., can and do work effectively in a wholistic system which includes as well the regulatory institutions of the State and the legal code. The evaluative standards proposed, (1) to allow for economic activity, (2) to facilitate both individual and collective economic activity, and (3) to exercise checks and balances on economic activity as necessary, require both the 'individual' actors (merchants, producers, consumers, etc.) and the whole contextual system inside which to function. To isolate one from the other and both from such 'outsiders' as the State and the Law, would have little meaning or purpose. Indeed perhaps categorical rigour has suffered here slightly, but it is suggested that the trade-off might be a better understanding of Hicks' own approach to institutions within and without the large arena of economic activity.

One might note as well in closing that the areas of economic thinking devoted to the contemplation of economic institutions and even economic thought devoted to institutions are riddled with the usual partisan position and the devisiveness which ensues. Hicks, on the other hand, seemed to have ridden above this incidious problem. In *A Theory of Economic History* (1969), for example, he does not disguise his sympathies with Marx; Keynesian ideas, just as those noted in this article, are a frequent refrain. Hicks was, however, also clearly intrigued, if not inspired, by his contemporary Hayek; many of Friedman's ideas on the free market and the value of competition were far from offensive to him. It is this profoundly independent ecclecticism of Hicks' ideas which makes him such an interesting thinker for study. A examination of Hicks on economic institutions provides a particularly rich and stimulating array of examples of the conventional 'right' and 'left' conjoined. Here they have not been identified as such, nor has the analysis been intended to speak to a synthesis. The result is instead simply a survey of some ideas on the role of institutions in the fostering, the facilitating and the regulating of Hicks' vision of economic activity at its most efficient, productive best.

## REFERENCES

Arrow, Kenneth, 1964. "Control in large organizations", *Management Science* 10 (April): 397–408.

Coase, Ronald, 1937. "The nature of the firm", *Economica N.S.*, 4: 386–405; (rpt 1952) in G.J. Stigler and K.E. Boulding, eds, *Readings in Price Theory* Homewood, illinois: Richard D. Irwin, pp. 332–47.

Eggertsson, Thráinn, 1990. *Economic behaviour and institutions* Cambridge Surveys of Economic Literature Series Cambridge: Cambridge University Press.

Hamouda, O.F. 1993, *John R. Hicks; The Economist's Economist* Oxford: Basil Blackwell.

Hamouda, O.F. and Price, B.B., 1991. *Verification in Economics and History* London: Routledge.

Hicks, John R., 1934. "Leon Walras", *Econometrica* 2, October: 338–48; rpt. 1983, in *Classics and Moderns, Collected Essays on Economic Theory* Vol. III Oxford: Basil Blackwell.

Hicks, John R., 1939. *Value and Capital* Oxford: Clarendon Press.

Hicks, John R., 1956. *A Revision of Demand Theory* Oxford: Clarendon Press.

Hicks, John R., 1969. *A Theory of Economic History* Oxford: Oxford University Press.

Hicks, John R., 1973. *Capital and Time: A Neo-Austrian Theory* Oxford: Clarendon Press.

Hicks, John R., 1976. "Some questions of time in economics", in A.M. Tang, F.M. Westfield and J.S. Worley (eds), *Evolution, Welfare and Time in Economics: Essays in Honour of Nicholas Georgescu-Roegen* Lexington, MA: Heath, Lexington Books, pp. 135–51; rpt. 1982 in *Money, Interest and Wages. Collected Essays on Economic Theory* Vol II Oxford: Basil Blackwell, pp. 282–300; rpt. 1984 in D.R. Helm, *The Economics of John Hicks* Oxford: Basil Blackwell, pp. 263–80.

Hicks, John R., 1977. *Economic Perspectives; Further Essays on Money and Growth* Oxford: Clarendon Press.

Hicks, John R., 1979. *Causality in Economics* Oxford: Basil Blackwell

Hicks, John R., 1989. *A Market Theory of Money*

Knight, Frank H., 1965. *Risk, Uncertainty and Profit* New York: Harper & Row.

North, Douglass C, 1990. *Institutions, Institutional Change and Economic Performance* Cambridge: Cambridge University Press.

Pelikan, Pavel, 1987. "The Formation of Incentive Mechanisms in Different Economic Systems", in Stefan Hedlund (ed.). *Incentives and Economic Systems* New York: New York University Press.

Williamson, Oliver E., 1985. *The Economic Institutions of Capitalism; Firms, Markets, Relational Contracting* New York: The Free Press/London: Collier Macmillan Publishers.

# CHAPTER - 11

# HICKS AND THE CRISIS IN KEYNESIAN ECONOMICS

*John Lodewijks*

### ABSTRACT

In 1973 Hicks attempted to revise and update the Keynesian system. His reformulation was in the spirit of Keynes and not a reversion to pre-Keynesian thinking. This paper examines three recent texts (Mankiw, Parkin and Taylor) for their correspondence with Keynesian ideas.

Twenty-five years ago, Sir John Hicks gave the Yrjo Jahnsson Lectures in Helsinki. The revised version of these lectures was later published as The Crisis in *Keynesian Economics*. Hicks, in these lectures, was responding to the widespread questioning of the intellectual basis of Keynesian economics and attempted to provide a more satisfactory revised version of Keynes's views. His "reformulated Keynes is much more like Keynes than it is like the cruder forms of 'neo-classical' doctrine" (Hicks 1974:84).

In this paper we look at the current state of thinking about the intellectual basis of Keynesian economics. However, we proceed not by examining the scholarly journal literature but instead focus on three recent principles texts. Textbooks introduce students to macroeconomic enquiry and their influence on the profession cannot be underestimated (Kuhn 1970:136-143).

### MANKIW, PRINCIPLES OF MACROECONOMICS

Mankiw's text which has just been published will not be popular among those who identify themselves as Keynesian. There are seven chapters on "the real economy in the long run" followed by only three chapters on short-run fluctuations. This is an extraordinary change of emphasis. Most Keynesian macro texts might spend a chapter on long run growth and the vast bulk of material is on developing analytical models to explain short-run cyclical instability.

Chapter 13 is on financial markets, saving and investment. It is unusual to start here as most texts would start with the income-expenditure model and only later introduce monetary detail. Readers will be amused to see the Pre-Keynesian loanable funds model. This is just the classical theory they have taught generations of students to disregard. The underlying theme that the long run is a classical world will not be accepted easily. Nor the proposition that all a budget deficit achieves is higher interest rates, crowding out and lower national saving. Most economists do not accept this view, contrary to the author's assertion. What Mankiw is presenting is the "Treasury View" that Keynes so devastatingly attacked (Hicks 1974:20).

Chapter 14 on Unemployment will be equally savaged. There is no mention of aggregate demand. The only causes of unemployment are minimum wage laws, unions, efficiency wages and job search. In this chapter we just deal with the natural rate, that is, structural and frictional unemployment. Cyclical unemployment is relegated to the last few chapters.

Chapter 15 and 16 are on money and prices in the long run and they provide a monetarist approach to inflation. Most macroeconomists might be comfortable with a long run monetarist explanation (or in the case of hyperinflations). But to only look at inflation from a long period perspective is questionable at best.

Finally with chapter 19 we treat short run fluctuations and AS-AD (there is no income-expenditure model or IS-LM in the text). The focus is now on short run deviations from the long run equilibrium - expressing it this way seems to belittle its significance. Chapter 20 is the first mention of macro policies (particularly fiscal policy) and their impact on aggregate demand. This topic consumes a large number of chapters in conventional Keynesian texts. The problem many instructors will have is reconciling a loanable funds story for interest rates in the long run and a liquidity preference story for interest rates in the short run. The authors explanation of this inconsistency is unconvincing.

This text concentrates on the classical principles of macroeconomics and is a savage departure from the fundamental principles of Keynesian thought.

## PARKIN, ECONOMICS

Parkin's text is well-known and widely adopted in many countries, however, it provides us with a number of methodological concerns. As is well known, there are certain conceptual difficulties with using AS/AD analysis. As a result, in most texts their derivation is handled quite cautiously, with great circumspection. Most texts are careful to point out that while they may look like the micro supply and demand, they are quite different animals.

Not so with this text. This treatment has no regrets. It goes further in equating AS/AD with the micro supply and demand than perhaps any other text, note especially the stress on price changes as the adjustment mechanism instead of the traditional Keynesian quantity adjustments and the focus on output as price determined instead of price determining. Students will like this; they will think its just the same as in micro, and have no difficulties with accepting it. But as scholars we need to make them aware that all is not what it seems, and there are grave conceptual difficulties with these constructs.

The section on inflation in chapter 24 implies that we are all monetarists now. Parkin's use of "cause" in this context is philosophically unsound (Hicks' book on *Causality in Economics* clearly brings this out). Note that in his scholarly work, even Friedman never uses the word cause - he is too methodologically sophisticated to fall into that old trap. With respect to the material on money demand, Keynesians would stress far more the role of expectations and uncertainty and the instability in money demand function.

On unemployment, Keynesians take Keynes' position that even if wages were flexible you might still get involuntary unemployment through deficient aggregate demand. In Parkin it is just a matter of insufficient wage flexibility, ignoring the variety of Keynesian explanations for persistent unemployment. Parkin's text always seems to have unemployment at the natural rate with deviations rare and transitory. Only a small minority of the profession would take this seriously.

The traditional neo-classical Labour demand treatment in this text seems to run counter to abundant empirical observations. Let me list a few:

1.  Why does North American data show a positive relationship between output and labour productivity (contrary to the text story on declining marginal product of labour)?

2.  Why have non-union employers with no explicit contractual obligations granted general wage increases when they had abundant applicants, no vacancies, and negligible quit rates?

3.  Why is there on the job underemployment, during declines in economic activity (contrary to text that assumes workers will always be retrenched)?

4.  Why in situations of excess demand do many firms increase unfilled orders rather than raise prices to exploit tight market conditions?

The sticky wage models in the Keynesian literature are far more richer than the ones presented in this text (an *explicit* contracts story). These richer accounts include efficiency wages, insider-outsider models, *implicit* contracts and Akerlof-Yellen social norms. For a simple treatment of these see chapter 2 "Persistent Unemployment" of Robert Solow, *The Labour Market as a Social Institution*, Blackwell Oxford 1990. Solow clearly and simply explains the various sticky wage approaches and why the flexible wage story is found wanting.

## JOHN B. TAYLOR, ECONOMICS

Taylor's text is only a few years old yet is quite controversial from a Keynesian (or Hicksian) perspective. There is a very simplistic cycle theory in the second half of chapter 12 and far richer accounts can be found in Haberler's *Prosperity and Depression* or Hicks's *Contribution to the Theory of the Trade Cycle*. Taylor fails to recognize that both governments and the private sector can instigate economic instability. He also places far too much weight on "the" interest rate in the story he tells. Monetary disturbances can cause instability but so can many other factors. The author seems to exclude from consideration the volatility of the exogenous components of aggregate demand, while supply factors only get less than a page from the author. Many readers might argue that it is the exogenous components of aggregate demand that cause the major fluctuations, not the endogenous ones influenced by interest rate changes

Chapter 20 sets forth a very ambitious task, namely a complete theory of growth and fluctuations. The author fails to note that his "theory" is just one of a number of possible explanations for growth and instability. His account contains a simplistic "crowding-out" story, with no mention of a possible crowding-in with the complementarity between private and public investment. Again what seems fragile is the excessive weight placed on the interest rate in influencing the components of expenditure. Other variables clearly affect Investment (profits, expectations), Consumption (income) and net exports (imports are a function of income). The treatment of consumption is very classical and the author fails to note that while Consumption is a function of income and interest rates, it is the former that predominates. Similarly, the treatment of crowding-out seems to assume perpetual full employment (again a classical presumption).

Taylor's text, like Mankiw, is modern, but it is also idiosyncratic. It is precisely the classical principles that dominate these texts that dismay those economists that still call themselves Keynesian.

## CONCLUSION

I have selected three leading texts and examined their main departures from Keynesian thinking. I have not tried to provide an overall evaluation and it should be stated that there are many valuable sections in all the books. My focus has been a narrow one of investigating the areas where these texts depart from standard Keynesian approaches. The departures are significant and alarming to those not of a classical persuasion. The "Treasury View", quantity theory of money and Say's Law are all found in modern guise. Long term growth issues are increasingly central and cyclical instability is relegated to a minor role and automatically equated with inappropriate government policies and excessive wage demands. I am not sure at all that this is what Hicks would have intended when he set out to revise the intellectual basis of Keynesian economics twenty five years ago.

# REFERENCES

Hicks, J. 1974. The Crisis in Keynesian Economics. Oxford: Basil Blackwell

Kuhn, T.S. 1970. The Structure of Scientific Revolutions. Chicago: University of Chicago

Mankiw, N.G. 1998. Principles of Macroeconomics. Sydney: Dryden

Parkin, M. 1996. Economics. Sydney: Addison-Wesley

Taylor, J.B. 1995. Economics. Sydney: Houghton Mifflin

# A NOTE ON DON PATINKIN'S MISSPECIFICATION OF KEYNES' CONSUMPTION FUNCTION AND MISINTERPRETATION OF KEYNES' ELASTICITY ANALYSIS IN CHAPTER 10 OF THE GENERAL THEORY

*Michael Emmett Brady*

## ABSTRACT

This note examines the claim of Don Patinkin that he had found a mathematical error in Keynes' elasticity analysis contained in a footnote on page 126 of Chapter 10 of The General Theory. A re-examination of the footnote demonstrates that no error is present with respect to the model of the consumption function specified by Keynes in the General Theory. Don Patinkin failed to consider that the linear model used to demonstrate Keynes' multiplier result was distinct from the complete Theory of the consumption function, which included the probability of a non-linear relationship.

## 1. THE CONSUMPTION FUNCTION

J.M. Keynes, in the General Theory (GT), consistently used elasticity analysis in Chapter 10, 20-21 to analyze and illustrate his theories of Employment and Effective Demand. Thus, Keynes's use of elasticity analysis in Chapter 10, 20, and 21 is crucial to any evaluation of the GT. It will restrict the analysis to Chapter 10 of the GT, where Keynes applies elasticity analysis to his aggregate demand function.

Keynes made four assumptions about his consumption function. First, he assumed that actual aggregate consumption expenditure was a stable function of aggregate (disposable) income. Second, he assumed that the marginal propensity to consume (MPC) was positive and less than one, i.e., $0 <$ MPC $<$ I. Third, he assumed that as income increases the average propensity to consume (APC) declines so that APC $>$ MPC, where APC = C/Y and O $<$ APC $<$ I Keynes' final assumption was that as income increases, the MPC declines. However, this fourth assumption was viewed by Keynes as *not* being on aas solid a foundation of "the detailed facts of experience" as were the first three assumptions. Thus,

"The marginal propensity to consume is not constant for all levels of employment, and it is probable that there will be, as a rule, a tendency for it to diminish as employment (income) increases:

......(Keynes, 1964, p.120:author's underscore).

Thus, when it came to develop his consumption function *mathematically*, Keynes chose a *linear* version, not a non-linear version. Keynes' first three assumptions can be correctly modeled using a linear consumption-income model. The fourth assumption would require a non-linear version.

Keynes specifies his linear consumption function on pages 114-117 of the GT, with additional results appearing as footnotes on pages 116 and 126. First, Keynes defines actual, realized current income *(Y)* to equal actual current consumption $C$ plus new actual current investment (I). Thus, Y = $C + I$. Note also that by definition $Y = C + I = C + S$. Therefore, $I = S$, so actual current investment always equals actual current savings. Of course, $I = S$, so actual current investment always equals actual current savings. Of course, $I = S$ could occur at an optimum, where $I = S = D_2$ at $e_0 = e_0 = 0$, or $I = S$ could occur at I = S $< D_2$, a nonoptimal state.

Let us now differentiate Y. We obtain $dY = dC + dI$ or $I = (dC/dY) + (dI/dY)$, which can be written as $I - (dC/dY) = dI/dY$. Now let "$dY = kdI$". Then $(1/k) = dI/dY$, so that $I - (dC/dY) = dI/dY = I - (dC/dY) = 1/k$. Thus, $I - (1/k) = dC/dY = MPC$. Let us denote the $MPC = b$. Then $I - (1/k) = b$, given that $k = dY/dI$.

Now consider the usual linear textbook derivation, where $Y = C + I$ and $C = a + bY$, where a, autonomous consumption, is $>0$. After substituting $C$ into $Y = C + I$ and solving for $Y$ one obtains $Y = (a + I) I(1 - b)$. Thus, $dY/dI = 1/(1 - b)$. For Keynes, however, $dY/dI = k$. Thus k must equal $1/(1-b)$, where $b = 1 - (1/k)$. If Keynes' model and the textbook version are consistent, then after substituting $b = 1 - (1/k)$ into $k = 1/(1 - b)$ we should obtain $k=k$. Now $k=1/(1-[1-(1/k)])=1/[1-1+(1/k)]=1/(1/k)=k$. Thus, Keynes' model from Chapter 10 of the GT is consistent with the usual textbook result. Thus, for Keynes, $Y=[1/(1-b)]I$ so that $dY=[1/(1-b)]dI$ and $1-b=dI/dY$ or $1-dC/dY)=dI/dY$. The reader should note that Keynes' actual expenditure function is $C=bY$, not $C=a+bY$.

However, Patinkin (1979, p. 176, 1982, p. 151) has insisted that Keynes' exposition of his model in Chapter 10 was non-linear, i.e., $d_2C/dY_2<o$. He specifically makes this point with respect to Keynes' footnote 2 on page 126, concerning Keynes' verbal discussion of his elasticity result $[1-(C/Y)]/[1-(dC/dY)]$. The reader should note that an elasticity is always defined as the ratio of a marginal function to an average function. For linear functions, the second derivative will always be zero. Following Patinkin, let $Q=[1-(C/Y)]/[1-(dC/dY)]$. Now Keynes verbally states the $dQ/dY$ is positive where the sign

$$dQ/dY=sign \ [([1-(dC/dY)([C/Y^2][1-n_{cy}])+([1-(C/Y)][d^2C/dY^2])].$$

(1)

The term $n_{cy}$ is the actual income elasticity of consumption. Patinkin states that Keynes assumed $d^2C/dY^2<0$. Now clearly this is exactly what Keynes states verbally in his assumption 4. However, because Keynes had clearly specified a linear model to work with, in order to simplify the mathematical analysis, $dC/dY=b$ and $dC^2/dY^2=0$. Given Keynes' reservations about the soundness of his fourth assumption, it made sense to use a linear model where the second derivative would be zero.

Thus, Keynes' verbal statement that $n_{cy}<1$ does imply that the sign of $dQ/dY>0$, because the signs of $[1-(dC/dY)]$, $[C/Y^2]$, and $[1-ncy]$ are all positive. The second term in (1) will equal zero, given that $d^2C/dY^2=0$. Keynes' intuitive, mathematical "good sense", led him to choose a linear consumption function to work with instead of a non-linear one 1,2. It would not make sense for Keynes to complicate his analysis by using a non-linear function, given his belief that "it is probable" that there is only a "tendency" for $dC/dY$ to diminish. Given that the mathematical model used to derive $Q$ in the GT is identical to the model of pages 114-117, Keynes' verbal description is correct as stated.

What caused Patinkin to believe that Keynes' consumption function specification was

$$C=a+bY+b_1Y^2$$

*or*

$$C=bY+b_1Y^2,$$

instead of Keynes' own clearly defined specification

$$C=bY \ ?$$

Again, Patinkin had been lead to believe through personal correspondence with Richard Kahn that Keynes was deficient in his knowledge of applied mathematical economics and microeconomic theory. Patinkin then proceeded to ignore the mathematical specification of the model provided by Keynes on pages 114-117 of the General Theory and used Keynes' verbal statement in the text to override the fact that $C=bY$. In other words, Patinkin was looking to find an error that wasn't there. He, therefore, created an error that did not exist! However, in the back of Patinkin's mind was Kahn's claim that Keynes had been a poor mathematician since 1927 (Skidelsky, 1992, p 288). Patinkin, in his own mind, was only confirming what Kahn had already said.

(1)     Note that this is different from Keynes' expectations elasticity analysis in Chapters 20 and 21 of the *GT*. *dQ/dY* would be equal to the ratio *(1-D/D)?(1-dD/dD)*, where $D=D_1+D_2$ states that expected income equals expected consumption expenditure plus expected investment expenditure. Only if the actual, current elasticity, $e_e$, on page 116, ft. 1 equals the expected elasticity, $e_e$, on page 283, is the realized, current result equal to the expected result. For an economy wide optimum, this result would also require $e_e=e_o=$zero.

(2)     Following Patinkin, let

$$Q=[1-(C/Y)]/[1-(dC/dY)]$$

then $dQ/dY=[1-(dC/dY)].[1-(C/Y)]dY-$
$$[1-(dC/dY)]dY/[1-(dC/dY)]^2$$
$d[1-(C/Y)]/dY=d([Y-C]/Y)/dY$
$$=Y[1-(dC/dY)] - [Y \cdot C]1/Y^2$$

$$=Y\text{-}Y(dC/dY)\text{-}Y+C/Y^2$$
$$=C\text{-}Y(dC/dY)/Y^2$$
$$=C/Y^2[1\text{-}[(Y/C)(dC/dY)]]$$
$$=[C/Y^2][1\text{-}n_{cy}]\quad\text{where}\quad n_{cy}=(Y/C)(dC/dY).$$
$$[1\text{-}(dC/dY)]dY=d[1\text{-}(dC/dY)]dY=0\text{-}(d^2C/dY^2).$$

Combining terms, we obtain $dQ/dY=$
$$[[1\text{-}(dC/dY)](C/Y^2)(1\text{-}n_{cy})+[1\text{-}(C/Y)](d^2C/dY^2)/[1\text{-}(dC/dY)]^2.$$

Keynes specifies $C = bY$, so $dC/dY = b = $ mpc, $0< b< 1$. Given that $dC/dY> 0$ and $C/Y = $ APC$<1$, then the following signs apply: $\{1\text{-}(dC/dY)] > 0$, $C/Y^2 > 9$, $1 - n_{cy}>0$, $[1 - (C/Y)] > 0$. But, since $dC/dY=b$, then $d^2C/dY^2=0$. Patinkin claims $d^2C/dY^2<0$. The sign of Q is thus

$$[(+)(+)(+)+(+)(0)]/(+)$$

or

$$[(+)+(0)]/(+)$$

or

$$[(+)]/(+)=+$$

Keynes' conclusion is correct for a linear consumption function. What about Patinkin's claim for a non-linear consumption function? Instead of a (0) in the second term in the numerator, we would get a (-). Patinkin would be correct, since the sign of $Q$ would be indeterminate. However, nowhere in the *GT* is a non-linear consumption model specified. Unfortunately, Patinkin never considers the case of a linear consumption function at all! Instead, he simply ignores all of the analysis Keyness presented on pages 114-117 of the GT and creates his own specification based on Keyne's heavily qualified verbal comments. Thus, while Keynes' theory allows for the probable existence of a non-linear relationship between consumption and disposable income, Keynes' *model* specification is *linear*. Patinkin appears not to have understood the difference.

### REFERENCES

Keynes', J.M. (1964). The General Theory of Employment, Interest and Money. Harcourt, Brace and World, New York.

Patinkin, D. (1979). "A Study of Keynes' Theory of Effective Demand". Economic Inquiry, 17, 155-76.

Patinkin, D. (1982). "A critique of Keynes' Theory of Effective Demand". In Patinkin Don. Anticipations of the General Theory? Oxford: Basil Blackwell.

# CHAPTER - 13

# MONEY, INDIVIDUAL CHOICE AND FRICTIONS

## Carlo Benetti

### ABSTRACT

The aim of this paper is to evaluate the effect of Hicks's 1935 "simplification" on the contemporary analysis of the integration of money into the value theory. Hicks's methodological suggestion is based on two central concepts: individual choice and frictions. Since 1935 the development of the monetary theory has been characterized by the search of relevant frictions so that individuals choose money at equilibrium. We show that, while these concepts are well adopted to analyse money as a store of value it is not possible, on this basis, to obtain (construct) a model where the theories of money and prices are successfully integrated. After a critical examination of the main results of the recent monetary theory, we sketch an alternative solution based on a scheme of price formation where money, as a medium of exchange, is a condition of the price system. In this framework money can be integrated into the price theory without making use of the Hicksian concepts of individual choice and frictions.

## 1. INTRODUCTION

This paper is not a study of Hicks's monetary theory. In a more limited way, its aim is to evaluate the effect of Hicks's famous 1935 "simplification" on the subsequent analysis of the integration of money into the value theory.

Hicks poses the monetary problem at its deepest level, that is at the junction with the theory of value. Starting from the microeconomic theory of individual choice, and introducing the concept of frictions, he establishes the logical relation between the neoclassical price theory and the monetary theory. This result is all the more remarkable as it was found about 20 years before the clarification of the general equilibrium price theory (to which Hicks contributed). Our criticism does not imply any negative judgment on Hicks's contributions to the monetary theory. His position changed. But no one of his subsequent contributions has been as influential as his 1935 article.

Hicks's methodological suggestion is quite well adapted to analyze money as a store of value. We will show that, on this basis, it is not possible to integrate money into the price theory. To do this, money must be conceived as a medium of exchange. Recently, this function has been modelled by using Hicks's method, but so far the results seem doubtfull. Such disappointing conclusions justify the necessity to look for some sort of solution which is different to what Hicks suggested. The one we propose rests on the idea that the integration of money into the value theory is not mainly a problem concerning the monetary theory, but it has to do, first of all, with the theory of value.

The first three sections contain an outline of Hicks's simplification, its relation to the position of the most relevant authors who preceded him, its influence on the subsequent monetary theory. In section 4 we discuss the concept of friction. The criticism of the equilibrium with a zero-price for money (section 5) is used in the 6th section where we will show the limitations of the application of Hicks's method to the problem of integrating money into the theory of value. In section 7 we sketch what we consider an alternative solution: money as a condition of prices, independently of any reference to frictions and individual choice.

## 1. HICKS'S "SIMPLIFICATION"

As usual in the field of the monetary theory, the starting point is the complaint on the underdevelopment of the theory of money with respect to the general economic theory, in fact the theory of value.[1] Fisher's equation is at the core of the monetary theory at that time. Hicks observes that value theoreticians know it very well since this equation was as important for them as for money theoreticians when they speak about value as "a ratio between demand and supply". But this was "in the mid-

---

[1] In the same sense, see Hayek 1931, chap. 1 and, 40 years later, Hahn 1969, 195: "Economic theory still lacks a 'monetary Debreu'". A (implicit) criticism of this idea will be found in section 7.

dle of the last century". Since then, another equation has been discovered, "which states that the relative value of two commodities depends upon their relative marginal utility". Since "it was marginal utility that really made sense of the theory of value; and to come to a branch of economics which does without marginal utility altogether! No wonder there are such difficulties and such differences! What is wanted is a 'marginal revolution'! That is my suggestion" (Hicks 1935, 62).

In order to fill the gap between the monetary and value theories, Hicks proposes a methodology in which two concepts are central, individual choice and frictions.

Concerning the first one: "the marginal utility analysis is nothing else than a general theory of choice, which is applicable whenever the choice is between alternatives that are capable of quantitative expression. Now money is obviously capable of quantitative expression" (ibid. 63). The method consists in considering "the position of an individual at a particular point of time and enquire what determines the precise quantity of money which he will desire to hold" (ibid. 64). For the main part, the monetary theory is a theory of demand of money.

This leads to what Hicks considers as the "critical question", that is: "what has to be explained is the decision to hold assets in the form of barren money, rather than of interest – or profit – yielding securities [...] This, as I see, is really the central issue in the pure theory of money. Either we have to give an explanation of the fact that people do hold money when rates of interest are positive, or we have to evade the difficulty somehow" (ibid. 66).

It is here that frictions come into the picture: "Of course the great evaders would not have denied that there must be some explanation of the fact. But they would have put it down to 'frictions' and since there was no adequate place for frictions in the rest of their economic theory, a theory of money based on frictions did not seem to them a promising field for economic analysis. This is where I disagree. I think we have to look frictions in the face, and see if they are really so refractory after all" (ibid. 67). Hicks stresses two types of frictions: transaction costs, that is "the cost of transferring assets from a form to another" (ibid.), and the uncertainty about the expected period of the investment and its expected product.

This method is then "simply an extension of the ordinary method of value theory". In the theory of money as well as in the theory of value, the individual is supposed to reach his optimal position. The difference is that in the second case it is a matter of an "income account" whereas in the first one it is a matter of a "capital account, a balance sheet" (ibid. 74).

In his writings, Hicks comments his preceding works, often criticizing them. It is interesting to note that he maintains a most positive opinion on his 1935 essay. For instance, in 1982, he writes: "I would still stand by what I said in it, so far as it goes. It is no more than a statement of what might now be called the 'micro-foundations' of monetary theory; but these are stated very clearly and I believe correctly. By themselves, they are no more than a beginning; but to begin with them is the right way to begin". This positive judgment goes far beyond the purely analytical aspects. Hicks states that the 1935 simplification has played an important part in building his scientific personality, in particular in his intellectual independence from different doctrinal movements. This article shows that the mere use of money makes the market system unstable. Thus, monetary institutions are explained as a remedy (necessarily imperfect) to this instability. On the other hand, the Keynesian theory has evolved towards "something more mechanical than [Keynes] probably intended". The conclusion is: "So in the end I had to go back to 'Simplifying', and to insist that its message was a Declaration of Independence, not only from the 'free market' school from which I was expressly liberating myself, but also from what came to pass as Keynesian economics" (Hicks 1982, 9–10).

## 2. PIGOU, HAYEK AND KEYNES

The idea that the integration of money into the theory of value must rest on individual choice is not Hicks's discovery. It is a part of the Cambridge tradition as it is shown, for instance, by the explanation Pigou gives of the superiority of the Cambridge equation over Fisher's equation. The principle of decreasing marginal utility is easily admitted, and "an exactly analogous proposition holds good of the satisfaction yielded by successive units of resources held in the form of titles to legal tender". This is expressed by the $k$ variable of the Cambridge equation. It follows that although this equation is not "truer" than Fisher's equation, it has "a real advantage, because it brings us at once into relation with volition – an ultimate cause of demand – instead of with something what seems at first sight accidental and arbitrary" (Pigou, 1917–18, 47 and 53).

In the same spirit, in his 1931 lectures at the London School od Economics, Hayek goes much farther when he proposes a radical criticism of Fisher's equation. As Hicks will do some years later, Hayek explains the underdevelopment of the monetary theory by the domination of this equation: "What I complain of is not only that this theory in its various forms has unduly usurped the central place in monetary theory, but that the point of view from which its springs is a positive hindrance to further progress. Not the least harmful effect of this particular theory is the present isolation of the theory of money from the main body of general economic theory". The reason is the same as the one Hicks will give later: "For so long as we use different methods for the explanation of values as they are supposed to exist irrespective of any influence of money, and for the explanation of that influence of money on prices, it can never be otherwise" (Hayek, 1931, 4).

But the closest filiation, actually the only one Hicks admits explicitely, is with Keynes.[2] In the *Treatise on Money* Hicks discovers the dependence of the price level on the "relative preference of the investor – to hold bank-deposit or to hold securities". His theory is related to Keynes's intuition. From this point of view he will be "more Keynesian than Keynes" (Hicks 1935, 64). Frequently, Hicks will come back on the relation between his simplification and Keynes's theory. In particular, he mentions a letter of December 24th, 1934 which Keynes sent him after reading the proofs of his paper: "I agree with you that what I now call Liquidity Preference is the essential concept of Monetary Theory" (Hicks 1982, note 12). Let us remember that in 1937 Keynes posed the problem in the same terms as Hicks: besides being a unit of account and a medium of exchange, money "is a store of value. So, we are told, without a smile on the face. But in the world of classical economy, what an insane use to which to put it! For it is a recognized characteristic of money as a store of wealth that it is barren; whereas practically every other form of storing wealth yields some interest or profit. Why should

---

[2]However, let us note that, according to Hicks, the direct origin of the "simplification" is a previous work with R. Allen on demand: "it was obvious ... that there were a parallel; the same technique that we had been using in demand theory could be used in this other context", the theory of money. The difference is that the first is concerned by a "flow problem", whereas the second raises "a stock problem; the role of uncertainty here was far more important than it was there". see Hicks 1982, 8–9.

154

anyone outside a lunatic asylum wish to use money as a store of wealth?" (Keynes 1937, 115–116).

### 3. HICKS'S SIMPLIFICATION AND THE MONETARY THEORY

Since 1935 the development of this theory is characterized by the search of relevant frictions so that individuals choose money at equilibrium.

The conception of money as a store of value chosen by individuals is largely dominant. On this common basis, the monetary theories differ from one another according to the choice of frictions (in particular the Hicksian frictions such as temporary equilibrium, transaction costs and uncertainty, or frictions expressed by the overlapping generation models).[3]

We can distinguish two logical consecutive steps. The first (the demonstration of the existence of an equilibrium) is central in the neoclassical approach and secondary in the Keynesian one. The second one, which is common to both keynesians and neoclassicals, consists in the explanation of Hicks's "paradox" (and Keynes's, see the last section): "the main challenge facing monetary theory is to face up to the frictions that lead people to hold low-yielding money, monetary-like assets" (Wallace, 1988, 25).

Beyond this direct influence, Hicks's method has been extended to model money as a medium of exchange: the individual is no more conceived as a bank making a portfolio choice, but an agent making trades. This recent approach is derived from Hicks's simplification in the sense that it rests on the two central concepts of his method, individual choice and frictions (see sections 4 and 6).

### 4. THE CONCEPT OF FRICTION

The clarification of the general equilibrium theory (the "Arrow-Debreu model") leads to extend the role of frictions beyond to what Hicks said. This concept is used not only to explain the coexistence, at the monetary equilibrium, of assets whose rate of return is different. It has become necessary in order to justify the existence of money itself.

---

[3]"...what sort of frictions? On that there is not agreement, which is to say there is no widely accepted theory of fiat money", Wallace 1980, 50.

The two central hypotheses of the Arrow-Debreu model which are related to the monetary question, are:

(i)   The existence of a complete set of markets.
(ii)  The existence of a centralized system allowing for the execution of transactions without cost and money.

Hypothesis (i) leaves out money as a store of value, more generally all kind of assets by means of which the intertemporal allocation of resources can be made. This is guaranteed by the future markets. Hypothesis (ii) excludes money as a medium of exchange. The centralized "accounting system" or the central "clearing house" is the name given to the device allowing the economy to work without a medium of exchange.[4]

In this model money does not exist and cannot be introduced. Every positive quantity of money has a zero equilibrium price (see section 5). In order to pose the monetary problem, these hypotheses must be eliminated. Strangely enough this is identified with the introduction of frictions in a perfect market system: "In order to get a theory of money, one must generalize the Walrasian model by including in it some sort of frictions, something that will inhibit the operation of markets. On that there is agreement" (Wallace, 1980, 50). And: "In a Walrasian model, at least, money cannot facilitate exchange: the non-monetary competitive equilibria are Pareto optimal. ... Thus, to get money into a model something must inhibit the operation of markets" (Townsend 1980, 265). The ambiguity of this widespread position is remarkable. If, in this model, money does not facilitate exchange, this is not because the equilibrium is an optimum, but because the exchange itself (spot and future) is absent and replaced by a centralized organization of transactions. As a consequence (decentralized) markets are non-existent and we do not see what it means to inhibit their working.

Anyway, the concept of friction has a very different meaning if we consider the first or the second hypothesis. We will show that this concept is justified only in the first case.

Since the problem is to allocate resources over time, hypothesis (i) allows individuals to make, at the present date, all decisions concerning their trades of present and future goods. When this hypothesis is

---

[4]"No theory of money is offered here, and it is assumed that the economy works without the help of a good serving as medium of exchange". (Debreu 1959, 28).

suppressed, these decisions are made in a different context. Individuals need at least one commodity in order to transmit value to the future periods and a budget constraint for each period replaces the unique budget constraint. This is a necessary condition for a positive demand of money as a store of value. However, the friction consisting in eliminating hypothesis (i) is not sufficient to explain the coexistence, at the monetary equilibrium, of different assets having different rates of return. We must introduce here what is to be considered as a second friction, that is an "imperfection" such that individuals choose to keep a part of their wealth in the form of an asset (money) whose rate of return is inferior to the rate of return of other existing assets. This is admitted. The only difference concerns the kind of imperfection which is chosen: uncertainty and transaction costs (Hicks), legal restrictions which prevent assets like the Treasury bills to circulate as money (Wallace, 1983), or frictions used in the search theory (Kiyotaki and Wright 1989, 951, see also section 6).

A very different situation is created by the elimination of hypothesis (ii). Now the problem concerns trades (at general equilibrium prices). The consequence of this hypothesis is not to make them possible in ideal conditions, but to suppress them. In this model, trades are not included in the set of individual activities. The agent is a consumer and a producer. He is never a trader. What is called the perfect trade system is, actually, the perfect absence of trade.

Obviously, it is not impossible to imagine property transfers by means of some centralized accounting system. But, contrary to the production and consumption plans established under hypothesis (i), these trades are outside the theory and, in this sense, they are non-existent. We know only one non-monetary transaction system where trades are an individual activity and leading to the equilibrium allocation: Ostroy and Starr's chains of trades which have nothing to do with a perfect market (see Ostroy and Starr, 1972).

N. Kiyotaki and R. Wright consider that: "The use of monetary exchange helps to overcome the difficulty associated with pure barter trade in economies where trade is not centralized through some perfect and frictionless market" (1993, 63). If centralization is understood properly, once more the "perfect and frictionless market" is nothing but the complete absence of market. If centralization is understood as the Walrasian organization of markets, frictions are superfluous since the difficulties of the barter trades through such a "perfect and frictionless market" are already there.

The elimination of hypothesis (ii) does not mean the modification of the conditions of the individual economic activity. It leads to the formation of this activity. The perfect market without money does not exist. Consequently, the Hicksian concept of friction is not relevant for money as a medium of exchange.

### 5. THE PROBLEM OF THE EXISTENCE OF AN EQUILIBRIUM WITH A ZERO-PRICE FOR MONEY

The discussion of the approach of money in terms of individual choice which we propose in the following section is based on the negative answer to this question. We give here a justification.[5]

"We therefore reach the rather displeasing conclusion that the Patinkin model always contains a 'non-monetary' solution" (Hahn 1965, 150). This conclusion has been widely accepted.[6]

Let us consider an exchange economy. The general equilibrium is a non-negative price vector and a consumption allocation such as it maximizes the utility function of every agent under his budget constraint. Let us distinguish 4 kinds of economies:

(i) Economy (W) which is composed of commodities, agents and a centralized accounting system or a central clearing house allowing for the realization of transactions without cost. Arrow and Debreu demonstrated the existence (under some conditions) of a price vector $p \geq 0$ for which there does not exist any positive excess demand. In the W-type economy this result is sufficient to get the equilibrium allocation.

(ii) Economy (M) where the centralized accounting system is suppressed and replaced by one medium of exchange. In this economy the equilibrium exists: first the vector price $p$ is determined and then the monetary trades at these prices lead to the equilibrium allocation.[7]

(iii) Economy (T) which is obtained by suppressing the medium of exchange of the previous ecoonmy. Trades at prices $p$ do not lead, in

---

[5]The argument used here is developed in Benetti 1996.

[6]See also Starr : "A model of fiat money may be expected ... to include an equilibrium where price of money is nil" (1989, 293).

[7]A demonstration of this proposition as well as of (iii) and (iv), is found in Ostroy and Starr 1972.

general, to the equilibrium allocation. In this economy the equilibrium does not exist.

(iv) Economy (C) which is obtained by adding to the previous economy a chain system of bilateral trades, where the place of each agent is assigned in a centralized way according to his excess demand vector. In this economy the equilibrium exists.

Let us consider a M-type economy where the equilibrium exists and let us examine the consequences of the zero-price for money. The demand for money is nil, so that the excess demand of money is negative. The zero-price of money is then an equilibrium price. Economy (M) transforms itself into a T-type economy where, in general, the equilibrium does not exist.[8] The equilibrium with a zero-price for money exists only if: (i) either we reutilize the centralized accounting system (or the central clearing house) of the economy (W) which was suppressed in order to introduce money, but this is incoherent; (ii) or we add the trade chain system of the C-type economy, but in this case Hahn's proposition is incorrect.[9]

### 6. HICKS'S "SIMPLIFICATION" AND THE INTEGRATION OF MONEY INTO THE PRICE THEORY

1. The dominant approach according to which money is conceived as a store of value is directly derived from Hicks's method.

The origin of this idea is Keynes. An important aspect of his monetary conception is the opposition he makes between the "real-exchange economy", where money is nothing but a medium of exchange which is "neutral in its effect", and the "monetary economy" (Keynes, 1933). According to Keynes, the orthodox theory is not adapted to study the second and limits itself to the first, precisely the one in which money is insignificant: "By acting as a money of account it facilitates exchanges without its being necessary that it should ever itself come into the picture as a substantive object. In

---

[8] It exists only in particular cases such as the overlapping generation model with only one good and identical agents whose difference is only the date of birth, or if the condition on the double coincidence of wants is verified.

[9] The most delicate point is to see what Hahn's demonstration demonstrates. We showed that the result he obtains is not the existence of a non-monetary equilibrium in the economy (M), but the impossibility of a monetary equilibrium in the economy (W). This is not surprising in an economy which is refractary to the introduction of money. See Benetti 1996.

this respect it is a convenience which is devoid of significance or real influence" (Keynes, 1937, 115).

The same position is found in the contemporary orthodox theory: "In general equilibrium theory money has one function. It is a store of value" (Gale 1982, 290–291). Consequently, the monetary theory coincides with the theory of the demand of money. The only differences are the analyses of such a demand.

When money is considered as a store of value it can be studied by means of the Hicksian concepts of individual choice and frictions. The integration of money into the price theory consists in demonstrating the existence of a monetary equilibrium (with a positive price for money). Knowing that a zero-price for money is an equilibrium price, the problem is to look for the conditions at which the price of money does not fall to zero (at a sufficiently low price of money, the excess demand for money is always positive).

2. In the temporary equilibrium model (Grandmont 1974), the equilibrium with a positive price for money depends on particular and unexplained expectation functions. This condition is not sufficient. We must add another one, namely that there should not exist any asset having a higher rate of return than money.

In the transaction costs theory (Hahn, 1971) the monetary equilibrium exists only if the structure of the transaction costs is such that the spot trade is preferred to the future trade and if the positive rate of interest on assets is more than compensated by costs on asset transactions.

In both cases, the existence of a monetary equilibrium depends on unexplained parameters. Besides, in these finite horizon models, individual choice leads necessarily to a zero demand for money at the final period and, by recurrence, in all periods. Such a difficullty can only be eliminated by means of *ad hoc* hypotheses, for instance agents are constrained to hold the same stock of money at the terminal and the initial periods, or to pay at the final period a monetary tax properly calculated, or to bequeath money to the following generation. The **artifice** is obvious: the existence of money depends on a constraint and not on a choice.

3. Infinite horizon models must then be used (even if it makes it more difficult to prove the existence of equilibrium). The most remarkable
result has been provided by the overlapping generation models where the existence of an equilibrium with a positive price for money has

been proved. This explains why it is considered that "the friction in Samuelson's 1958 consumption loan model overlapping generations, gives rise to the best available model of fiat money" (Wallace, 1980, 50).

The result which is obtained is of the same kind as that of the previous models. According to the initial parameters (in this case, endowments, technique and utility functions) the stationary equilibrium can be monetary or non-monetary (where the value of money at each period is nil). This is explained by the fact that by comparing, in terms of efficiency or welfare, two kinds of equilibria (with or without money as a store of value) the agents choose the best asset they can attain in order to make the intertemporal trade.

It is certainly interesting to explore the conditions at which money is the preferred store of value. The difficulty arises when this kind of model is used in order to solve the completely different problem of integrating money into the price theory. In this case, the equilibrium with or without money as a store of value means the equilibrium with money or without any money at all.

Now, as we have seen, the so-called non-monetary equilibrium does not exist, in general, or it only exists if a centralizaed transaction system is introduced. Consequently, the integration of money into the price theory which is made by using Hicks's method implies meaningless comparisons between either equilibrium and the absence of equilibrium, or between market economy and non-market economy. It is clear that individuals choose between transfering or not transfering their purchasing power over time by means of money. At the stationary equilibrium the price of money as a store of value can therefore be positive or nil. It depends on the specification of the initial parameters. But it does not mean that, acting in this way, individuals choose between a decentralized and a centralized organization of trades and that the latter is always preferred in economies defined by adequate initial data.

The only way to avoid this strange conclusion is not to identify money with its function as a store of value, and thus to admit that, by making a zero demand for money as a store of value, individuals do not eliminate money. In other terms, money must have another function than that of store of value, which subsists even when the latter desappears. Obviously, this function is the medium of exchange.

Thus, the choice of the best way of transfering the purchasing power over time does not imply any comparison between a monetary equilibrium and a so-called non-monetary equilibrium. The comparison individuals make is between two equilibria, both with a medium of exchange, where the purchasing power is transferred by means of money in one case and by means of another asset in the other.

Starting from the idea that: "money cannot act as a medium of exchange if it does not also act as a store of value" (Hahn, 1971, 101) the dominant research program conceives the integration of money into the price theory as a search for an equilibrium with a positive price for money. We can conclude that this program has failed. It is not right to state that the overlapping generation models "do successfully integrate value and monetary theory" (Wallace, 1980, 77). Under well-identified conditions, the Arrow-Debreu model always has a solution. This is not the case of models with money as a store of value. Thus, the problem is not that in these models equilibria are "tenuous" as stated by Wallace (ibid. p. 50). This would be correct only if these models always had a solution, monetary or non-monetary. But since, in general, the latter does not exist, the monetary theory elaborated in this way is "vacuous".[10]

4. Until recently, it was commonly admitted that the monetary theory developed on the basis of Hicks's methodological suggestion failed to study money as a medium of exchange. This is the meaning of Clower's criticism to Patinkin. This originates the "cash in advance" models where the medium of exchange is introduced by means of an *ad hoc* constraint, such that goods only can trade with money.

This state of things has been radically changed by the use of the search theory in order to model the medium of exchange.[11] In this respect, Wright's models are exemplary, since they give a central role to the Hicksian concepts of individual choice and frictions (transaction costs which are minimized by the monetary trade, or uncertainty derived by the occurrence of bilateral meetings and the double coincidence of

---

[10]In the sense of Debreu's statement: "Walras and his successors were aware that his theory would be vacuous in the absence of an argument supporting the existence of its central concept" (1987, 131.

[11]See however the explicit reference to Hicks's "simplification" in Starr 1972, 143.

wants). In short, they propose a solution of the monetary problem as formulated by Menger, by using Hicks's methodology.[12]

Since they are built on the basis of Hicks's simplification, it is not suprising that we find the traditional results concerning the store of value, this time applied to the medium of exchange. According to individual choice, the equilibrium can be monetary or non-monetary (the former, when it exists, being superior to the second). All depends on exogeneous data: the parameters of the productive sector, the intertemporal utility functions, the expectation of the value of money or the subjective probability of its acceptation by other agents, the structure of trades defined by randomly bilateral meetings.

In the model with endogenous prices (Trejos and Wright, 1995) there always exists an equilibrium with a zero-price for money, whatever the hypothesis concerning the existence or the exclusion of direct barter trades. In this latter case, we obtain a state of the economy without prices, production and trades. Since, by hypothesis, nobody can produce services for his own consumption, the latter is also nil. It seems to us that such a state of autarky has nothing to do with an equilibrium. In fact, it represents a non-viable economy (the non-existence of an economic solution). Moreover, when the equilibrium price of money is positive, the rates of exchange are endogeneously determined by bilateral trades. They do not verify the condition of the unique price for each good (see the following section).

The interpretation of such ambiguous results is not easy. Let us only note that in Wright's models the market institution is absent. When they occur, trades are made by means of bilateral meetings and not, as in the general equilibrium theory, on organized markets where at the same time all sellers and all buyers of the same commodity participate, and where the price is unique, known and accepted by all traders.[13] Wright is

---

[12]Let us recall Menger's problem: "What is the nature of those little disks or ducuments, which in themselves seem to serve no useful purpose, and which nevertheless, in contradiction with to the rest of experience, pass from one hand to another in exchange for the most useful commodities...?" (Menger 1892, 69)

[13]In the search model proposed by Iwai (1988), the trades are made on the organized markets à la Walras, where the equilibrium prices are determined before trades. When it exists, equilibrium is locally stable, so that a strong perturbation is necessary in order to obtain the monetary equilibrium. Contrary to Trejos and Wright's model, the "non-monetary equilibrium" does not exist in an economy where the direct barter is excluded. In this situation, "some individuals may have no choice but to suffer the misery of autarky with the utility level of $-\infty$", (p. 40).

right in stating that the general equilibrium model does not explain how the equilibrium allocation is obtained and that his model proposes an explanation. But it is not clear why the second fills a gap of the first.

5. Let us conclude. Hicks's method is certainly adapted to deal with the problem of money as a store of value, that is the coexistence at the equilibrium of assets having different rates of return. But Hicks suggests that his method applies also to the distinct problem of integrating money into the value theory. This program of research, dominant since more than half a century, leads to a dead end[14]. Let us note that an additional ambiguity rose, due to the fact that those who studied the first problem stated that this is the central monetary question, and discarded the other functions of money, in particular the medium of exchange.

The above analysis suggests that the origin of such disappointing results cannot be ascribed to some difficulties peculiar to the theory of money, or to a (unexplained) weakness of the monetary analysis (this is confirmed by the quality and quantity of monetary works). This justifies a reexamination of the basis of this analysis, that is the general equilibrium price theory, in particular two of its central features: the determination of prices independently of (and previously to) trades and the realization of these latter at the equilibrium prices.

### 7. MONEY AND PRICES: A SKETCH OF A NON-HICKSIAN APPROACH

In a private property economy, individual decisions are decentralizaed in the sense that individuals act without knowing the general state of the economy which results from their actions. Consequently, it can be different from what individuals expected. Besides, all price theories admit that, in a competitive economy, individual decisions concern quantities only. Prices are determined on anonymous markets.

In these conditions, the first task of the price theory is to determine the social evaluation (the exchange values) of private activities. What are the market prices (at which trades are made) corresponding to a set of private actions decided at given parametric prices (expected by indi-

---

[14]It would be interesting to examine if this conclusion is modified by the recent contribution to Walras's monetary theory proposed by Rebeyrol. In the temporary equilibrium framework, money is conceived as a medium of exchange, whose demand is calculated at the begining of the period. If this solution of the monetary equilibrium problem is accepted, the difficulty is shifted from money to the price theory (see section 7).

viduals or communicated to them by an auctioneer)? The general equilibrium theory does not provide any answer to this question. The best formulated version of the search theory answers by eliminating markets.

Let us call "market mechanism" the algorithm allowing to calculate the market prices and the allocations resulting from a given set of individual decisions. A simple principle is provided by Cantillon (and used also by Smith): "Prices are fixed on the markets by the proportion of commodities brought to market and money which is supplied in order to buy them".[15]

Let us introduce it in the general equilibrium model and sketch a non-Hicksian approach of the relation between money and prices in the easiest case of an exchange economy.[16] In an economy with $n$ commodities, there exists $n(n-1)/2$ trading posts. In the $(i,j)$ trading post, agents have a supply for $i$ (resp. $j$) and a demand for $j$ (resp. $i$). If $s^h_{ij}$ is the quantity of $i$ used by the agent $h$ in order to buy $j$, the exchange rate $v_{ij}$ (the price of $i$ in terms of $j$) is equal to $(\sum_h s^h_{ji})/(\sum_h s^h_{ij})$. Whatever the way in which supplies and demands are calculated, in this generalized barter system trades generate prices which are incoherent in the sense that, in general, condition $v_{ik} v_{kj} v_{ji} = 1$ is not verified. Each commodity has a different evaluation depending on the trade post where it is traded.

In order to suppress this incoherence a unique medium of exchange (and unit of account) must be introduced. Let us start from a (parametric) price vector $\mathbf{p}$ communicated by an auctioneer. We can use the microeconomic theory of consumer behaviour to calculate individual supplies and demands. As in the general equilibrium theory, trades are made in organized markets: all buyers and all sellers of a specified commodity participate in trades on the corresponding trading post. Obviously, we eliminate the condition of exogeneous market prices which actually are nothing but the parametric prices used by the agents in their optimization calculus. It follows that the agents act in the ignorance of the outcomes of their actions.

Let $s_{hi}(\mathbf{p})$ and $d_{hi}(\mathbf{p})$ be agent's $h$ supply and demand at prices $\mathbf{p}$. Here we must introduce a monetary system such that agents can obtain the money they need to finance their demand. The quantity of money agents get by selling their commodities is returned to the monetary sys-

---

[15]Cantillon, 1755, 7. This rule has been adopted in the strategic market games models (see Shubik, 1990)

[16]For more details, see Benetti and Cartelier, 1994.

tem. This kind of money is then a pure medium of exchange. For agent $h$, we have $m_h = \Sigma_i p_i d_{hi}(\mathbf{p})$. Since $m_{hi}(\mathbf{p}) = p_i d_{hi}(\mathbf{p})$ is the quantity of money spent by agent $h$ on market $i$, the market price $v_i$ is determined by the ratio: $\Sigma_h m_{hi}(\mathbf{p})/\Sigma_h s_{hi}(\mathbf{p})$. On different markets are formed monetary prices from which relative prices are derived.

If parametric prices do not coincide with market prices, the budget constraint which is verified to calculate supplies and demand at prices $\mathbf{p}$, is violated in trades at prices $\mathbf{v}$. The disequilibrium is defined by both individual positive or negative monetary balances (whose algebraic sum is zero), and individual real disequilibrium wich is measured by the difference between $m_{hi}$ and $m_{hi}$ $(p_i/v_i)$.

The adjustment process is both a monetary and a real one. It depends, on the one hand, on the reaction of the monetary authority to the individual balances and on the other hand, on the interpretation individuals make of the gap between parametric and market prices. Such an interpretation determines market prices expectations. These expected prices (which can be different for each agent) are the new parameters used to calculate individual supplies and demands. Monetary trades in the trade posts generate a new (unique) vector of market prices.

While synthetic, this presentation of the scheme of price formation is sufficient. Let us come back to the relation between prices and money and make 5 points.

1. Because of the absence of a market mechanism, in the general equilibrium theory only parametric prices exist. Consequently, on the one hand, this theory determines the market outcome only for particular vectors of parametric prices, at which there does not exist any positive excess demand. In this case, by definition, parametric and market prices are identical. (But the theory cannot explain how such a situation is obtained). On the other hand, as we saw, the process of changing prices takes place in the absence of any kind of auctioneer. It is the absence of a market mechanism and not the perfect competition hypothesis that explains why the general equilibrium theory needs the auctioneer to modify the prices. As it is commonly admitted, this is one of the weaknesses of the theory.[17]

2. Since the equilibrium is the stationary point of a real and monetary process, it is not surprising that we have not significant results yet. We

---

[17]For more details, see Benetti, 1995.

limit ourselves to a comparison between equilibrium concepts, which is enlightening for the monetary question. In the above scheme, the equilibrium is defined by the equality between market and parametric prices. When this condition is verified, individuals obtain their desired allocation. In the general equilibrium theory, once the existence of a price vector such that there does not exist any positive excess demand is demonstrated, it remains to explain how, at these prices, individuals obtain their equilibrium allocations (to which the criterion of Pareto-optimality is applied). There are only two possibilities: (i) as in the basic general equilibrium model, this question is evaded by means of *ad hoc* hypotheses (see section 4), (ii) The problem is posed and we face the difficulties of integrating money which was put aside in order to build the price theory.

By eliminating the traditional dichotomy between prices (determined as a solution of a system of simultaneous equations) and trades, which is common to all value theories (labour theory of value, prices of production, general equilibrium theory) the introduction of a market mechanism eliminates at the same time the separation between the problem of money and that of prices.

3. We saw that, in a moneyless economy, prices are incoherent. A comparison with Walras's theory is instructive. Let us consider a given set of incoherent prices, known by all agents. Trade decisions at these prices are such that, on each market, if supply (resp. demand) is positive, demand (resp. supply) is nil. In Walras's theory where trades are made at exogeneous prices, the excess demands can be defined, allowing to elaborate a price adjustment process which (if it is stable) leads to coherent prices. This is the well-known Walrasian arbitrage. Nothing similar can exist in the above scheme where prices are formed by trades. When prices are incoherent, on each trading post there exists only one commodity. Its price is nil and no arbitrage process can occur. Without money, not only prices are incoherent but it is not possible to obtain coherent prices by means of a non-monetary mechanism. Contrary to the Walrasian model the arbitrage is not a substitute for money. If no trade system can work without money, this is not because of the difficulties of barter trades. It is explained by the fact that money is a condition of prices.[18] In other terms, barter is not an incoherent trade system at

---

[18]This result is similar to the one which Marx obtains in his analysis of the 2nd form of value. He deduces that, since prices are not coherent, things which are traded are not commodities but only use values.

coherent prices, but a coherent trade system through which incoherent prices are formed.[19]

4. We do not study here the place and role of money in the working of market economies. Our problem is narrower: the integration of money and price theory. The above scheme provides an explanation of the existence of a commodity whose utility is dependent on its exchange value. It follows that the elementary economic world, that is the basic reference of the price theory, is necessarily composed of individuals, commodities and a monetary system.

In this framework, money is justified independently of the Hicksian concepts. Frictions are absent. The economy is a competitive one and transactions have no costs. The uncertainty on future prices only concerns the adjustment process and not the justification of the existence of money.

The individual choice does not intervene either. We do not see what the meaning of a choice between coherent and incoherent prices would be. The "choice" of money is similar to the "choice" of the division of labour. The individual is no more free to accept or to refuse money than he was when he asked himself the same question about the division of labour. Once individuals "accept" this latter, they also accept the medium of exchange, without which their acceptation of the division of labour would be meaningless. It is not reasonable to postulate the division of labour and then to ask the individual to choose between the existence or the absence of money. The microeconomic theory of individual optimization does not apply to the medium of exchange.[20]

It follows that the Hicksian concepts of individual choice and frictions are neither the necessary nor the sufficient condition of the integration of money into the price theory, as showed respectively by the scheme of price formation we sketched above and by the repeated failures of the theories which are elaborated on the basis of these concepts. However, as we have seen, they are central in dealing with the (Hicksian) problem of explaining the coexistence, at the equilibrium, of assets having differents rates of return.

---

[19]In our scheme, individuals start their trades with a quantity of money equal to the value of their demand (at parametric prices). This is Clower's condition. The difference (central in our opinion) is that it is not obtained by imposing an exogeneous constraint.

[20]Obviously, this conclusion in not acceptable by those (a majority) who identify *a priori* the theoretical explanation with the outcome of individual choice.

168

It is true that the decision of the individual concerning money depends on the evaluation of its acceptance by other agents. This can be expressed by saying that in order to be accepted in trades, money must have a positive expected price. This explains why Clower's constraint is not a solution to the monetary problem. It is supposed solved. But this feature of money does not contradict our conclusion. In the above scheme individuals act without knowing the market prices. Let us suppose that the parametric price of the existing money, as it is unanimously anticipated by the agents, is nil. There exist two possibilities: (i) a monetary change in the sense that a new money is preferred to the existing one, (ii) if no money is accepted, a deep "monetary crisis" in the sense of a desagregation of market relations (and not a non-monetary equilibrium).

In short, money poses a twofold question: it must be explained why (i) a commodity whose utility depends on its exchange value is traded; (ii) it is the commodity "a" and not "b". The individual choice concerns the second question and not the first one.[21] The individual may choose the money he is disposed to accept, but he cannot choose the kind of economy (market or non-market economy) to which he belongs.

### REFERENCES

Benetti, C. (1995). "La regla 'Cantillon-Smith' de formación de los precios y la teoría del equilibrio general", Conference *Actualidad del pensamiento clásico*, UAM, Mexico, 5–7 July, in *Análisis Económico*, vol. XIII, nº 28, 1966.

Benetti, C. (1996). "The Ambiguity of the Notion of General Equilibrium with a Zero-Price for Money", in G. Deleplace et E. Nell (eds), *Money in Motion, The Post Keynesian Circulation Approaches*, London, Macmillan.

Benetti, C. et Cartelier, J. (1994). "Money, Form and Determination of Value", Congrès *Marxian Economics: A Centenary Appraisal*. International Conference at the University of Bergamo, 15–17 december, in Riccardo Bellofiore (ed.), *Marxian Economics: A Reappraisal*, vol. 1 *Essays on Volume III of Capital, Method, Value and Money*, London, Macmillan, 1998.

Cantillon, R. (1755). *Essai sur la nature du commerce en général*, Paris, INED, 1952.

Debreu, G. (1959). *Theory of Value*, New York, John Wiley & Sons.

Debreu, G. (1987). "Existence of general equilibrium", The New Palgrave, *General Equilibrium*, London, Macmillan.

Gale, D. (1982). *Money : in Equilibrium*, Cambridge, Cambridge University Press.

---

[21]This can be expressed in Marx's terms: individual choice concerns the 4th form of value (the objectivation of the general equivalent in one particular commodity), and not the 3rd one (the existence of a general equivalent).

Grandmont, J. M. (1974). "On the Short Run Equilibrium in a Monetary Economy", in J. Drèze (ed), *Allocation under Certainty: Equilibrium and Optimality*, New York, Wiley & Sons

Hayek, F. (1931). *Prices and Production*, London, Routledge & Sons.

Hahn F. (1965). "On Some Problems of Proving the Existence of Equilibrium in a Monetary Economy", reprinted in F. Hahn, *Equilibrium and Macroeconomics*, Oxford, Basil Blackwell, 1984.

Hahn, F. (1969). "On Money and Growth", reprinted in F. Hahn, *Equilibrium and Macroeconomics*, Oxford, Basil Blackwell (1984).

Hahn, F. (1971). "Equilibrium with Transaction Costs", *Econometrica*, vol. 39, n°3.

Hicks, J. R. (1935). "A Suggestion for Simplifying the Theory of Money", reprinted in *Critical Essays on Monetary Theory*, 1967, Oxford, Clarendon Press.

Hicks, J. R. (1982). *Money, Interest and Wages*, Oxford, Basil Blackwell.

Iwai, K. (1988), "The Evolution of Money : A Search-Theoretic Foundation of Monetary Economics", University of Pennsylvania, CARESS, Working Paper n° 88-03, february.

Keynes, J. M.. (1933). "A Monetary Theory of Production", reprinted in *The Collected Writings of John Maynard Keynes*, vol. XIII, London, Macmillan, 1973.

Keynes, J. M. (1937). "The General Theory of Employment", in *The Collected Writings of John Maynard Keynes*, vol. XIV, London, Macmillan, 1973.

Kiyotaki, N. et Wright, R. (1989). "On money as a Medium of Exchange, *Journal of Political Economy*, vol. 97.

Kiyotaki, N. et Wright, R. (1993). "A Search-Theoretical Approach to Monetary Economies", *The American Economic Review*, vol. 83.

Menger, K. (1892). "On the Origin of Money", *Economic Journal*, vol. 2, reprinted in R.M. Starr (ed), *General Equilibrium Models of Monetary Economies*, Boston, Academic Press, 1989.

Ostroy, M. et Starr, R. M. (1974). "Money and the Decentralization of Exchange", *Econometrica*, vol. 42, n°6.

Pigou, A. C. (1917–18). "The Value of Money", *Quarterly Journal of Economics*, (32).

A. Rebeyrol, "The development of Walras' monetary theory", in G. Faccarello (ed), *Studies in the History of French Political Economy*, Routledge, to be published.

Shubik, M. (1990). "A Game Theoretical Approach to the Theory of Money and Financial Institutions", in *Handbook of Monetary Economies*, vol. I, chap. 5.

Starr, R. M. (1972). The Structure of Exchange in Barter and Monetary Economies", *Quarterly Journal of Economics*, vol. LXXXVI, reprinted in Starr, R.M. (ed), (1989). *General Equlibrium Models of Monetary Economies*, Boston, Academic, Press.

Starr, R. M. (ed), (1989). *General Equlibrium Models of Monetary Economies*, Boston, Academic, Press.

Townsend, R. M. (1980). "Models of Money with Spatially Separeted Agents" in *Models of Monetary Economies*, Federal Reserve Bank of Minneapolis.

Trejos A. et Wright R. (1995). "Search, Bargaining, Money and Prices", *Journal of Political Economy*, 103.

Wallace, N. (1980). "The Overlapping Generations Models of Fiat Money", in *Models of Monetary Economies*, Federal Reserve Bank of Minneapolis.

Wallace, N. (1983). "A Legal Restrictions Theory of the demand for "Money" and the Role of Monetary Policy", *Federal Reserve Bank of Minneapolis, Quarterly Review*, winter.

Wallace, N. (1988), "A Suggestion for Oversimplifyng the Theory of Money", *Economic Journal*, 98.

# PATINKIN, THE GENERAL THEORY, AND KEYNES'S AGGREGATE SUPPLY FUNCTION: A STUDY OF THE REASONS UNDERLYING PATINKIN'S MISINTERPRETATION OF THE GT

*Michael Emmett Brady*

### ABSTRACT

This paper examines the issue of how Don Patinkin, a scholar's scholar, could have gone so far astray in his periodic assessments of that part of Keynes's Theory of Effective Demand that dealt with the supply side of the economy. The six reasons that account for Patinkin's mistaken interpretation of Keynes' aggregate supply analysis are the mis-specification of the aggregate supply function, overlooking Pigou's *The Theory of Unemployment*, reliance on the unsupported claims of Richard Kahn and Joan Robinson, acceptance of Richard Kahn's claim that he developed the supply side analysis for Keynes in the General Theory, acceptance of Kahn's claim that Keynes was a poor mathematician, and acceptance of the false claims of H. Townshend.

## 1. INTRODUCTION

Consider the following gross exaggeration made by Patinkin in 1978:

"Could Patinkin, an economist who has (in Roberts' opening words) provided 'a perceptive and coherent overview of the development of Keynes's thinking on monetary problems' have been so completely incompetent as to have gotten wrong, not one or two, but every single aspect of the theory of effective demand which constitutes the basic contribution of Keynes' *General Theory*? User cost, aggregate supply, aggregate demand, equilibrium, the adjustment process, labor demand, and the price level – everything, all wrong?" (Patinkin, 1978, p. 578).

Of course, this was never the question. The question under examination in the Patinkin-Roberts exchange was whether Patinkin's interpretation of Keynes' aggregate supply function analysis in the Theory of Effective Demand was wrong. The answer to this query is yes.

The purpose of this paper is to examine how it came about that an economist of Patinkin's great intellectual caliber, training, scholarship, and erudition could have blundered so badly, over a 50 year period, in his periodic assessments of Keynes' General Theory (GT). Section 2 examines the faulty logic underlying Patinkin's misinterpretation. Section 3 derives Keynes' result by putting in the intermediate steps Keynes left out. Keynes left them out due to his belief that economists had mastered the very similar mathematical analysis contained in Part II of Pigou's 1933 *The Theory of Unemployment*. Section 4 concludes.

## 2. DON PATINKIN AND THE GENERAL THEORY – THE REASONS WHY HE WENT WRONG

There are six reasons that, taken together, account for Patinkin's failure to correctly grasp the technical, mathematical structure of the GT. The first reason was Patinkin's inability to comprehend the analysis contained in A.C. Pigou's great masterpiece, *The Theory of Unemployment*. Since Keynes chose to adapt Pigou's model and present a much improved, generalized version of it, which would incorporate price and profit expectations in the GT, Patinkin was never able to work backward, from the comparison – contrast which Keynes made between his model and Pigou's model in the Appendix to Chapter 19 of the GT, to Keynes' model.

"Having myself always had great difficulty in understanding Pigou's writings of the period, I must admit that I draw comfort from the fact that such difficulties also existed for some of Pigou's own colleagues and former students!" (Patinkin, 1976, p. 62).

Of course, Keynes eventually mastered Pigou's technique. The Appendix to Chapter 19 of the GT is the proof of that mastery. No other economist, except perhaps Seymour Harris, was able to grasp the fundamental mathematical techniques used by Pigou.

The second reason was Patinkin's misspecification of Keynes' aggregate supply function $Z$, or $Z_w$, and his conflation of the aggregate supply curve, a locus of $D = Z$ relative optimums, with $Z$, the aggregate supply function. Patinkin's misspecification followed from his failure to consider the elasticity analysis contained in Chapter 20 of the GT and his inability to follow Keynes' very clear and concise verbal specification of his D and Z functions on pages 23–25 of the GT. Keynes states:

> "The excess of the value of the resulting output over the sum of its factor cost and its user cost is the profit or...the income of the entrepreneur.... Thus, the factor cost and the entrepreneur's profit make up...the total income.... The entrepreneur's profit thus defined is...the quantity which he endeavors to maximize". (Keynes, GT, p. 23).
>
> "It is sometimes convenient...to call the aggregate income (i.e., factor cost *plus* profit)...the *proceeds* of that employment. On the other hand, the aggregate supply price of the output of a given amount of employment is the expectation of proceeds which will just make it worth the while of the entrepreneur to give that employment".[2] (Keynes, GT, p. 24).

This last sentence always gave Patinkin trouble. It is merely a verbal representation of the necessary first order condition for a profit maximum, that marginal revenue equal marginal cost. Thus,

> "The amount of employment...depends on the amount of the proceeds which the entrepreneurs expect to receive from the corresponding output[3]. For entrepreneurs will endeavor to fix the amount of employment at the level which they expectto maximize the excess of the proceeds over the factor costs". (Keynes, GT, pp. 24–25).

Again, this is a verbal way of stating that expected marginal revenue = marginal cost determines the number of workers hired.

Keynes then clearly defines his expected functions $D$ and $Z$, appending a footnote linking his discussion in Chapter 3 to his analysis in Chapter 20. Patinkin ignored this footnote.

Based on Keynes' verbal discussion above, any reasonable economist, using the following standard notation, should have been able to figure out the specification of Keynes' $D$ and $Z$ functions from Keynes' Chapter 3 discussion. Let $p$ = expected price, $O$ = output, $FC$ = factor cost, $UC$ = user cost, $P$ = expected profit, $N$ = employment, and subscript $r$ = firm or industry. Then Keynes says that the goal of the entrepreneur(s) is to

$$\text{Maximize } P_r = p_r O_r - FC_r - UC_r.$$

If we net out $UC$, set is equal to zero, or ignore it, then Keynes states that after we aggregate over all $r$ firms and industries, entrepreneurs in the aggregate

$$\text{Maximize } P = pO - FC.$$

Now "let $D$ be the proceeds which entrepreneurs expect to receive" from their sales (Keynes, GT, p. 25). $D = pO$. Then let "$Z$ be the aggregate supply price..." (Keynes, GT, p. 25). $Z = P + FC$. Define $D = f(N)$ and $Z = \emptyset(N)$. We obtain

$$D = f(N) = pO = Z = P + WN = \emptyset(N).$$

On page 41, Keynes defined factor cost to equal $E = WN$. On page 44, Keynes defines $O_r = \psi_r(N_r)$, a production function. If we aggregate over all $r$ firms and $r = 2$ industries, we obtain

$$D = f(N) = p\psi(N) = Z = P + E = \emptyset(N).$$

Patinkin never grasped the above discussion. Instead, we find the following discussion by Patinkin concerning Keynes' analysis on pages 55–56 of the GT and the second footnote on those pages. A correct analysis is contained in Section 3 of this paper.

"7. The argument of this note (which is admittedly not too clear) can be reformulated as follows. Under assumption (a) in the text here, the aggregate supply price equals total variable costs, or $Z = WN + QT$, where $Q$ and $T$ respectively represent the price and quantity of variable factors other than labor. Keynes' assumption (b) can then be expressed as $(WN + QT)/WN = k = \text{const.}$ If follows that $Z = (kW)N$, where $kW$ represents the "price" of variable-factors-of-production-in-general, whose quantity is represented by $N$. Hence $Z_w = Z/kW = \emptyset(N) = N$, so that $\emptyset'(N) = 1$.

Patinkin misspecifies $Z$ as $Z = WN + QT$. This is obviously wrong. The only variable factor in Keynes' model is the labor input $N$. On page 17 of the GT, Keynes defined that the capital stock would be held fixed in the short run. Thus $Z = WN + P$ and $Z_w = N + P_w$. Then $dZ_w/dN = 1$ or, if $Z_w = \emptyset(N) = N + P_w$, then $d\emptyset(N)/dN = \emptyset'(N) = 1$. Patinkin made the above error in six published articles in 1976, 1977, 1978, 1979, 1982, and 1989. See the references. This error is crucial because Patinkin rests his entire analytic case against Keynes' supply analysis on Keynes' supposed misidentification of the aggregate supply curve with the total variable cost curve. Of course if expected profits, $P$, or $P_w$, equal zero, then $Z = WN$ and $Z$ is equal to a linear total variable cost curve. However, Patinkin, having excluded profits from the definition of $Z$, contrary to Keynes' definition, never figured this out.

The third reason for his misinterpretation of Keynes is Patinkin's misguided reliance on the false and misleading claims made by Joan Robinson and Richard Kahn about Keynes' alleged deficiencies in mathematics and microeconomics. Patinkin incorrectly concluded that Kahn and Robinson had some special insights about the GT that they had supposedly obtained from Keynes. Nothing could be further from the truth:

> "42. See also Austin Robinson's similar testimony in Patinkin and Leith (1977, p. 79). More generally, Joan Robinson (1963, p. 79) has written: 'Keynes himself was not interested in the theory of relative prices. Gerald Shove used to say that Maynard had never spent the twenty minutes necessary to understand the theory of value'. (Gerald Shove was a colleague of Keynes' at Cambridge whose 'central interests were at that time in the rethinking of Marshallian value theory' [Austin Robinson 1977, p. 28]). In letter to me, Richard Kahn has also attributed such a remark to Shove". (Patinkin, 1982, p. 155; see also Patinkin, 1980, p. 22, and Patinkin, 1989, pp. 537–538).

There has never been a shred of evidence brought forth to support either Joan Robinson's or Richard Kahn's claim that Gerald Shove ever made such a statement. Unfortunately, the false claims of Kahn-Robinson have been severely damaging to Keynes' reputation. See, for instance, the faulty conclusions arrived at by A. Leijonhufvud, based on his assessment of this "old canard" (Leijonhufvud, 1968, pp. 32–33; 1981, pp. 342–343) as it relates to the question of Keynes' microeconomic skills. The reader should not be surprised to learn of Leijonhufvud's extensive correspondence with Joan Robinson.

The fourth reason for his misinterpretation is Patinkin's acceptance of R. Kahn's claim that he was responsible for the development of Keynes' aggregate supply function foundations in value (price) theory. (See Brady, 1994, 1995, 1996 for a refutation of this intellectual fraud.) Clearly, if Kahn's claim was true, not only is he a co-author of the GT, but he, not Keynes, should have had primary authorship:

> "In view of this absence of specific information in Kahn's book, I see no reason not to accept the evidence of his foregoing letters to me and to conclude that Kahn regarded his major contribution to the *General Theory* as being connected, not with the development of the theory of effective demand as a whole, but only with one of its components – namely, the aggregate supply function, which is the main component of the *General Theory* connected with the theory of value. This conclusion accords nicely with the fact that the properties of the supply

curve (albeit, that of a firm or industry) had been the major concern of Kahn's 1929 Fellowship Dissertation on the 'Economics of the Short Period', which was written under Keynes' supervision (1989 [1929], pp. Viii-ix). It also accords with Kahn's statement when this dissertation was published many years later (1983,p. 32; 1989, p. Xi) that 'neither he [i.e. Keynes] nor I had the slightest idea that my work on the short period was later on going to influence the development of Keynes' own thought'. (Patinkin, 1993, p. 661).

Incredibly, Patinkin just accepts Kahn's claim as true! It is obviously false. Again, the extent to which Patinkin is relying on Kahn (Robinson) as a supposed expert on the GT may possibly explain his belief that Keynes was deficient in microeconomics.

The fifth reason for his misinterpretation of Keynes was Patinkin's reliance on Kahn's false claim that "he recalled Keynes himself as being a poor mathematician by 1927" (Skidelsky, 1992, p. 288). Patinkin explicitly supported this assessment (Patinkin, 1989, pp. 537–538). This claim is also false. At this point, I must make the following conjecture. It will be established if all of the private correspondence about Keynes by R. Kahn and J. Robinson with other economists is brought out into the light of day. In their private correspondence, both Kahn and Robinson sought to disparage Keynes' reputation whenever possible, attempting to create the impression that, at least, Kahn was a co-author of the GT, just as he genuinely was the primary co-author of Robinson's 1933 book, *Imperfect Competition*. In public discourse and journal publications, Kahn would always appear to be downplaying such a belief.

The sixth and final reason is Patinkin's reliance on the error filled half-baked comments of the accountant Hugh Townshend. Townshend had mathematical training, but no training in economic theory, mathematical economics, or elasticity analysis. Townshend commits six errors. I will cover them one at a time. Townshend's first error is his claim that the "ordinary" supply curve, at the level of the firm industry, should have been written as

$$p_r = [\emptyset_r(N_r) + O_r(N_r)]/\psi_r(N_r)$$

instead of as

$$p_r = \emptyset_r(N_r)/\psi_r(N_r).$$

Contrary to Townshend, the correct way is to write

$$p_r = [\emptyset_r(N_r) + MUC_r(N_r)]/\psi_r(N_r),$$

where $MUC_r$ = expected marginal user cost and not $U_r(N_r)$ = expected user cost. Since Keynes' goal on page 44 is to discuss the aggregate supply function, and not the complications of including a marginal user cost component at the level of the firm-industry, Keynes should not have made any concession to Townshend, especially given Keynes' later discussions in Chapter 6 of the GT and its Appendix, both of which Townshend completely ignored, of precisely the question Townshend posed.

Aggregating we obtain

$$p = \emptyset(N)\!\!\not{}\psi(N),$$

where $p$ = marginal cost (Keynes, 1973, p. 236). Second, $p$ is a theoretical term which stands for the entrepreneur's expected price in the short run. In the short run, the entrepreneur aims to at least cover his factor costs or variable labor costs. User cost is not a function of labor. It is a function of the usage of the capital stock. Unfortunately, as Keynes pointed out in his footnote 1 on page 273, the intensity of capital use is not accounted for in the standard microeconomic theory of perfect or purely competitive firms. Given that Keynes, like Pigou, is holding the capital stock constant in the short run, user cost will equal a constant. The first derivative of a constant is zero. Townshend's claim that "it seems necessary to interpret all the 'prices' in the algebra of pages 283 etseq in a special sense" is incorrect, since it is clear that marginal prime cost = marginal factor cost (Keynes, 1973, pp. 240–241).

Third, Townshend's claim that "For otherwise we should not have the identity $D_{wr} = O_r p$ on which all the algebra depends" is badly flawed. While it is true that all the algebra depends on $D_{wr} = p_{wr}O_r$, and not Townshend's "$p_r O_r$", this is an equation and not an identity given Keynes' assumption of entrepreneur maximizing behavior.

The fourth error follows from errors 2 and 3. Townshend does not understand the difference in economic theory between short run variable cost and long-run fixed cost.

Townshend appears to be ignorant of the basic, theoretical approach to the short-run theory of the competitive firm, both as regards economic content and mathematical format. Townshend appears to want a *theoretical* model which will be in agreement with the *actual* long-run, real world results (see CWJMK, Vol. 29, pp. 243–245). Townshend claims that,

"...quite apart from the difficulty of supposing the book results of the complex of overlapping acts of production to be in some way analyzed into their component items, corresponding to individual output decisions, neither the factual aggregate of costs nor any of its elements, save F, appears at all, even in a derivative form, in the equations of Chapter 20 and 21. I do not think, indeed, that two of the four elements, viz the supplementary and windfall are mentioned anywhere in these chapters". (CWJMK, 1979, p. 244).

Of course, since supplementary and windfall costs are *not* functions of labor, they are, like fixed cost, treated as constants in the short-run and have derivatives of 0. They would no more "show up" in a marginal cost pricing approach than would the fixed costs. In a short-run analysis of the firm, in order to get diminishing marginal returns, the capital stock will be held fixed. The *only* variable which can change at the margin is $F$, the factor cost of the variable input, labor. Thus, this is the *only* "element" which appears in the short-run model of Chapters 20 and 21. I have demonstrated Townshend's general ignorance of basic microeconomic analysis. Since Keynes' approach to the supply side is practically the same as Pigou's and Marshall's, Townshend's criticisms, if taken seriously, would eviscerate any distinction between short and long-run. One can only conclude that Townshend was severely lacking in basic economics training. Why Keynes took him seriously is a mystery. Perhaps it was because Keynes did not wish to embarrass his former pupil, a pupil Keynes respected intellectually.

Townshend totally ignores Keynes' discussions on pages 67–69 of the GT of the very points that he thinks he is raising in his letter to Keynes!

"Now in the modern theory of value it has been a usual practice to equate the short-period supply price to the marginal factor cost alone. It is obvious, however, that this is only legitimate, if marginal user cost is zero or if supply price is specially defined so as to be net of marginal user cost, just as I have defined (p. 24 above) 'proceeds' and 'aggregate supply price' as being net of aggregate user cost". (Keynes, GT, p. 67).

And,

"This set of definitions also has the advantage that we can equate the marginal proceeds (or income) to the marginal factor cost; and thus arrive at the same sort of propositions relating marginal proceeds thus defined to marginal factor costs as have been stated by those economists who, by ignoring user cost or assuming it to be zero, have equated supply price to marginal factor costs. (Keynes, GT, p. 55).

Fifth, Townshend states "I cannot [distinguish] between realized results and expectations" (Keynes, 1973, p. 243). He then goes into a discussion of applied cost accounting – bookkeeping. Of course,

$Y = C = I = PO$ is the actual current result while $D = D_1 + D_2 = pO$ is the expected result. The optimal result occurs when $Y = D(= Z)$ at $e_e = e_o = 0$. These functions are theoretical functions used to exemplify a theoretical argument incorporating profit and price expectations as explicit variables. The discussion of expectations in the GT is not linked to "an actuality of bookkeeping" (Keynes, 1973, p. 243). On page 209 of the GT, Keynes defined capital $P$ to represent the aggregate actual current realized price level. Unfortunately he also used capital $P$ in Chapter 20 to represent expected profit. However, this is not relevant to Townshend's problem. To understand Keynes' technical analysis, a necessary condition is that D and Y are recognized as being different functions.

Sixth, Townshend has completely confused theoretical terms like price and cost with cost accounting-bookkeeping operations. The GT is a book on economic theory. It has absolutely nothing to do with accounting practices in England in 1936.

Patinkin's reliance on the comments of an economically illiterate accountant would be astonishing were it not for the fact that a host of other economists have cited from these letters of correspondence between Keynes and Townshend.

### 3. THE MATHEMATICAL ANALYSIS ON PAGES 55–56 OF THE GT, INCLUDING FOOTNOTE 2

Keynes states:

"...we can equate the marginal proceeds (or Income) to marginal factor cost; and thus arrive at the same sort of propositions relating marginal proceeds thus defined to marginal factor costs as have been stated by those economists who, by ignoring user cost or assuming it to be zero, have equated supply price to marginal factor cost". (Keynes, p. 55).

In his footnote 2, Keynes states:

"For example, let us take $Z_w = \emptyset(N)$ as the aggregate supply function.... Then, since the proceeds of the marginal product is equal to the marginal factor – cost at every point on the aggregate supply curve, we have

$$\Delta N = \Delta A_w - \Delta U_w = \Delta Z_w = \Delta \emptyset(N) \qquad (1)$$

That is to say $\emptyset'(N)=1...$" (Keynes, p. 55).

However, Keynes then states that this result only holds subject to certain restrictions, i.e.,

> "Provided that factor cost bears a *constant* ratio to wage cost. This means that, if wages are *constant* and *other factor costs* are a *constant proportion of the wage bill*, the aggregate supply function is linear with a slope given by the reciprocal of the money wage." (Keynes, p. 56; underscore added).

It follows that in this footnote Keynes is analyzing the constant returns to labor case. We now present Keynes' analysis. First, divide (1) by $\Delta N$. We obtain

$$1 = \Delta A_w/\Delta N - \Delta U_w/\Delta N = \Delta Z_w/\Delta N = \Delta\emptyset(N)/\Delta N.$$

Next, replace "$\Delta$" by "$d$". We obtain

$$1 = dA_w/dN - dU_w/dN = dZ_w/dN = d\emptyset(N)/dN.$$

In this last paragraph above, on page 55, Keynes states that marginal user cost will be ignored or set equal to zero. We then obtain

$$1 = dA_w/dN = dZ_w/dN = d\emptyset(N)/dN.$$

However, $dA_w/dN$ is the expected marginal proceeds, revenue, income, or effective demand, and is identical to $dD_w/dN$. See Chapter 20 of the GT, pages 280–283. Substituting $D_w$ for $A_w$, we get

$$1 = dD_w/dN = dZ_w/dN = d\emptyset(N)/dN.$$

On page 283 of the *GT*, $D_w$ is defined as being equal to $p_w 0$. On page 44, Z is defined as equaling the expected return, or proceeds, which will induce a level of employment $N_r$, where $r$ = a firm or industry. Next, sum over all $r$ firms and/or industries to obtain the aggregate supply function (a.s.f.)$Z = \emptyset(N)$, where $Z = pO = D = P - wN$ or $Z = P + wN = \emptyset(N) = D = pO = f(N)$ for every expected price, p, that maximizes expected profit, $P$. Then $Z = pO = \emptyset(N)$. Now divide through by w, the money wage, to obtain

$$Z = p_w O = \emptyset(N), \tag{2}$$

where $p$ = expected price, $w$ = a uniform money wage, and $O = \psi(N)$ is an aggregate production function. On page 44, Keynes formally defines the production function $O = \psi(N)$. Substituting this into (2), we obtain

$$Z_w = p_w \psi(N) = \emptyset(N).$$

Thus, $D_w = Z_w$ occurs *only* at expected optimums. The set of all expected optimums, given p, forms the a.s.c., distinct from the a.s.f. Now,

$p_w = 1/(w/p) = 1/\psi'(N)$, where $\psi'(N)$ equals the marginal product of labor. Substituting into (3), we obtain

$$Z_w = \psi(N)/\psi'(N) = \emptyset(N). \tag{4}$$

Under what condition will $\emptyset'(N) = 1 = dZ_w/dN$? Differentiating (4), we obtain

$$dZ_w/dN = d\emptyset(N)/dN = \emptyset'(N) = [\psi'(N) \cdot \psi'(N) - \psi(N) \cdot \psi''(N)]/[\psi'(N)^2].$$

Simplifying, we obtain

$$dZ_w/dN = \emptyset'(N) = 1 - [[\psi(N)\psi''(N)]/[\psi'(N)]^2].$$

$\emptyset'(N)$ can equal 1 if and only if $\psi'(N) = 1$, which requires $\psi''(N) = O$.

Under constant returns to labor, "factor cost bears a *constant* ratio to wage cost". (Keynes, p. 55). "This means that if wages are *constant* and other factor costs are a *constant proportion of the wage bill*, then the aggregate supply function is linear with a slope given by the reciprocal of the money wage". (Keynes, p. 58; underscore added). The only other factor in Keynes' wagebill would be the *salaries* of the managers, entrepreneurs or supervisors, which on page 41 of the GT he defines to be part of the total wage cost, $E = wN$.

For Keynes to have made an error here would have required him to state that $\emptyset'(N) > 1$, the case of diminishing returns. Now let us go on to Chapter 20 of the GT, where Keynes spends seven pages, 280–286, dealing with the inverse of the a.s.f., which he called the employment function, e.f. The inverse function rule states that if the first derivatives of both the a.s.f. and e.f. are positive, a unique inverse exists and both functions are monotonically increasing. Mathematical results derived for the a.s.f. must hold for the e.f. and vice-versa. The e.f., aggregated over all r firms or industries, is

$$N = F(D_w)$$

or

$$N = F(D_w = Z_w),$$

since $D_w$, effective demand, proceeds or income is always a point on a a.s.f. and the aggregate supply curve, so that $D_w = Z_w$ always occurs at an expected maximum. The only difference between this analysis and the Chapter 4 through Chapter 6 analysis in the GT is that Keynes substituted the production function $O = \emptyset(N)$ for $O = \psi(N)$. In Chapter 20, Keynes does *not* use $Z_w = \emptyset(N)$ to denote the a.s.f.

I repeat the result below:

$$dD_w/dN = [\emptyset'(N) \cdot \emptyset'(N) - \emptyset(N)\emptyset''(N)]/[\emptyset'(N)^2] = 1 - [\emptyset(N)\emptyset''(N)/[\emptyset'(N)]^2$$

Only if $\emptyset'(N) = 1$, which requires $\emptyset''(N) = 0$, can $dZ_w/dN = 1$, which is the constant returns case.

There is an alternative way of deriving Keynes' result. Since expected $P$ (profit) = expected TR (total revenue) − $TC$ (total cost), where $TR = pO = D$ and $TC = wN$, then $P = pO - wN$ or, in wage units $P_w = p_wO - N$ or $p_wO = P_w + N$. Now $Z_w = p_wO = \emptyset(N)$, where we are using ch. 4 notation, so $O = \psi(N)$ and $p_w = 1/\psi'(N)$. We obtain

$$p_wO = Z_w = \emptyset(N) = \psi(N)/\psi'(N) = P_w + N.$$

By definition, if $\psi'(N) = O$, then $P_w = O$. You are left with

$$Z_w = \emptyset(N) = N.$$

Then $dZ_w/dN = d\emptyset(N)/dN = 1$ or, as Keynes' says, "that is to say $\emptyset'(N) = 1$". Patinkin was unable to derive this result from Keynes' analysis due to his overlooking Chapter 20 of the GT.

Finally, we present Pigou's practically identical analysis which holds in *both* his one-sector model of pages 102–103 of Pigou, 1933 and his two-sector model of pages 92–93. Pigou defines his production function as $O = F(X)$. $X$ would stand for aggregate employment. To obtain Keynes' results from Chapter 20 from Pigou's analysis, just substitute $O = \emptyset(N)$ for $O = F(X)$. Then

$X = \emptyset(X) = p_wO = F(X)/F'(X) = K_w + X$ is identical to Keynes' e.f., except for notation, which is

$N = F(D_w = Z_w) = F(P_wO) = F(\emptyset(N)/\emptyset'(N)) = F(P_w + N)$, where $K$ is Pigou's notation for economic profit (surplus). Thus,

"$\Delta X \emptyset'(X) = \Delta X$, so that $\emptyset'(X) = 1$". (Pigou, p. 92). This is identical to Keynes' statement that

"$1 = \Delta N/\Delta N = \Delta Z_w/\Delta N = \Delta \emptyset(N)/\Delta N$, that is to say $\emptyset'(N) = 1$". (Keynes, p. 55).

Since Keynes' $Z_w$, or $Z_w = \emptyset(N)$, is identical to Pigou's $\emptyset(X)$ for his one-sector model, then the constant returns case requires that $\emptyset'(N) = \emptyset'(X) = 1$, which requires $\psi'(N) = 1$ and $\psi''(N) = O$ while for Pigou $F'(X) = 1$ and $F''(X) = O$.

## 4. CONCLUSIONS

Patinkin's belief that Keynes confused "marginal and average" or confused the "total variable cost curve with the aggregate supply function", which by definition includes profits, is not borne out.

Second, Patinkin's reliance on the very misleading claims of Joan Robinson and Richard Kahn probably made it impossible for him to catch the mistake in his analysis, i.e., of a variable factor other than labor. What he was hearing from Joan Robinson and Richard Kahn served to convince him that Keynes had made a number of errors in the GT. The full impact that Kahn and Robinson have had over the last 50 years in misleading the economics profession by means of their private correspondence can only be gauged if a full and complete examination of these private sources is made available for study in the future.

Finally, Townshend's correspondence with Keynes seems to have diverted the economics profession away from the careful reading of Chapter 20 of the GT that was required in order to be able to understand Keynes' technical arguments. For instance, G.L. Shackle's often stated belief that Townshend understood Keynes better than Keynes is exactly the type of attitude that led Patinkin to his incorrect interpretation of the GT.

## REFERENCES

Brady, M.E. (1989). A restatement of Keynes' theory of effective demand based on the microeconomic foundations in Chapter 20 of the *General Theory*. (Unpublished manuscript).

Brady, M.E. (1990). "The mathematical development of Keynes' aggregate supply function in the General Theory", History of Political Economy, Spring, 1990, pp. 167–172.

Brady, M.E. (1990). A comparison-contrast of the mathematical analysis in A.C. Pigou's *Theory of Unemployment* and J.M. Keynes' *General Theory*. (Unpublished manuscript).

Brady, M.E. (1994). "Keynes, Pigou, and the Supply side of the General Theory", History of Economics Review, Winter, 1994, pp. 34–46.

Brady, M.E. (1995). "A Study of J.M. Keynes' Marshallian-Pigouvian Elasticity Approach in Chapters 20 and 21 of the General Theory", History of Economics Review, Summer, 1995, pp. 55-71.

Brady, M.E. (1996). "A Comparison-Contrast of J.M. Keynes' Mathematical Modeling Approach in the General Theory with Some of His General Theory Interpreters, Especially J.E. Meade", History of Economics Review, Winter-Summer, 1996, pp. 129-158.

Keynes, J.M. (1973). The General Theory and After: Preparation. Vol. 13 of the CWJMK, ed. by D. Moggridge. Macmillan, London.

Keynes, J.M. (1973). The General Theory and After: Defense. Vol. 14 of the CWJMK, ed by D. Moggridge. Macmillan, London.

Keynes, J.M. (1964). The General Theory of Employment, Interest and Money. Harcourt, Brace and World, New York.

Leijonhufvud, A. (1968). Keynesian Economics and the Economics of Keynes. Oxford University Press, Oxford, England.

Leijonhufvud, A. (1981). Information and Coordination. Oxford University Press, Oxford, England.

Patinkin, D. (1976). Keynes' Monetary Thought: A study of its development. Duke University Press, Durham, N.C.

Patinkin, D. (1977). "The aggregate supply function: A correction". History of Political Economy, Spring 1977, pp. 156-159.

Patinkin, D. (1978). "Keynes' aggregate supply function: A plea for common sense". History of Political Economy, Winter 1978, pp. 577-596.

Patinkin, D. (1979). "A study of Keynes' Theory of Effective Demand". Economic Inquiry, April 1979, pp. 155-176.

Patinkin, D. (1980). "New material in the development of Keynes' monetary thought". History of Political Economy, Spring 1980, pp. 1-28.

Patinkin, D. (1982). "A critique of Keynes' theory of effective demand". In D. Patinkin, Anticipation of the General Theory? Basil Blackwell, Oxford.

Patinkin, D. (1989). "Keynes and the Keynesian Cross: A further note". History of Political Economy, Fall 1989, pp. 537-544.

Patinkin, D. (1993). "On the Chronology of the General Theory". Economic Journal, May 1993, pp. 647-663.

Pigou, A.C. (1933). The Theory of Unemployment. Macmillan, England.

Roberts, D.L. (1978). "Patinkin, Keynes, and aggregate supply and demand analysis". History of Political Economy, Winter 1978, pp. 549-576.

Skidelsky, R. (1992). John Maynard Keynes. Vol. 11, Macmillan, England.

**NOTES**

In an earlier draft of the GT, Keynes (1973, p. 452), in discussing constant returns to labor, states that this "would indicate that the employment function tends to approximate to a straight line drawn at a constant angle, which on the basis of the figures I have seen would be in the neighborhood of 45°, between the axes of the quantity of employment and the effective demand measured in wage units, since there seems to be a nearly constant ratio $(D/E)$ between $\Delta D$ and $\Delta N_w$, i.e., between $\Delta D_w$ and $\Delta N''$, where $D = pO$ and $E = wN$.

Of course, this discussion is identical to the GT result (1936, p. 283) that $dD_w/dN = 1$. In footnote 2 on pages 55–56 of the GT, given that $D_w = Z_w = \emptyset(N)$ at an expected optimum, if $\emptyset'(N) = 1$, as Keynes states, we have another way of specifying constant returns, where Keynes' production function was expressed in the notation $O = \psi(N)$. Later, in his draft copy, Keynes provides yet another way (1973, p. 509) of expressing this, since "$p_{wr}\emptyset'_r(N_r)=$ the marginal product of labor = the wage unit = 1." Summing over all $r$ firms and industries, of which there are two, consumption goods and investment (capital) goods, we get $p_w\emptyset'(N)=1$, where Keynes now expresses his production function in a different notation, as $O = \emptyset(N)$. This is identical to Patinkin's "correction" of Keynes' alleged error (Patinkin, 1982, p. 145).

Two additional ways of saying the same thing were likewise provided by Keynes. "If $\emptyset''(N_r) = O$, i.e., that the marginal productivity of labor is constant." (Keynes, 1973, p. 509). Likewise, "the condition $e_{or} = 1$ means that $\emptyset''(N_r) = O$, i.e., that there are constant returns in response                                                                          to increased employment". (Keynes, 1964, p. 284).

Yet, even after five decades, one can regularly find published claims that Keynes' analysis is in error, incomplete, and/or problematic. For an example, see any paper published by Patinkin on Keynes between 1975 and 1989.

Finally, these drafts are the same drafts Keynes sent to Hawtrey, Robertson, R. Kahn and J. Robinson, etc. Unfortunately, none of these economists were able to understand Keynes' technical, analytic mathematical results. The problem is with the reader, not with Keynes' formal presentation, which is correct. Keynes, however, is also partially responsible, due to his very bad correspondence habit of refusing to point out mathematical errors or misspecifications on the part of his correspondents when he could easily have done so in just a few lines.

# CHAPTER - 15

# NEOLIBERALISM AND GLOBALISATION – JUSTIFYING POLICIES OF REDISTRIBUTION

*Kunibert Raffer*

## ABSTRACT

Economic policies are shaped by neoliberal ideas and characterized by a pronounced anti-Keynesian bias.

Arguments for globalisation, deregulation and liberalisation basically rest on the assertion that allowing market forces to operate more freely globalisation and deregulation would ultimately benefit everyone. Neoclassical economics is cited to support this claim, although even a quick look at this theory shows that present neoliberal policies cannot be logically justified by it. Quite on the contrary, this theory justifies government intervention much more readily than neoliberalism, but it is wrongly used to justify redistributive policies in favour of capital owners and the rich. Many present policies were already predicted by M. Kalecki in suprising detail as an anti-Keynesian or anti-full-employment strategy as early as 1943. Globalisation, which is the result of deliberate policies and treaties, and deregulation are tools to justify the one-sided opening of Southern economies in a way that would never be acceptable to Northern governments, and to roll back social achievements and real wages in the North. Globalisation and undue liberalisation caused the Asian crash of 1997 creating the opportunity to buy Asian firms and assets quite cheaply. The WTO system and multilateral treaties, such as NAFTA or the Multilateral Agreement on Investment (MAI) presently negotiated within the OECD, will lock-in present policies, reducing future governments' options to change them and preventing the return of Keynesianism. To do so, democracy eagerly preached to aid recipients has to be rolled back.

## 1. INTRODUCTION

Present economic policies are strongly shaped by the global victory of neoliberalism. Allowing market forces to operate more freely globalisation and deregulation are claimed to benefit everyone ultimately. In any case, there seems to be no alternative. Renato Ruggiero, Director General of the World Trade Organisation (WTO) for instance expresses this view: 'Only a free global market and a free global trading system can cope with the global challenges of our time'. (WTO 1996a, p. 11) Although mass unemployment is one of those challenges, John M. Keynes's view that government intervention can be necessary to cope with market failures is summarily rejected nowadays. Anti-Keynesian policies have gained the upper hand.

This evolution was predicted by Kalecki (1971, pp. 138f) as early as in 1943, when he analysed the political limits of Keynesian policies:

> 'The assumption that a Government will maintain full employment in a capitalist economy if it only knows how to do it is fallacious. In this connection the misgivings of big business about maintainance of full employment are of paramount importance. This attitude was shown clearly in the great depression in the thirties ... the maintenance of full employment would cause social and political changes which would give a new impetus to the opposition of the business leaders. Indeed, under a regime of permanent full employment, 'the sack' would cease to play a role as a disciplinary measure. The social position of the boss would be undermined and the self assurance and class consciousness of the working class would grow'.

Powerful pressure by big business and rentiers – presumably disagreeing that their disappearance is a great advantage (Keynes 1967, p. 376) – would prevent governments from pursuing full employment policies. Even higher profits under a regime of full employment would not change their view, Kalecki argued. This lobby, Kalecki (1971, p. 144) wrote,

> 'would probably find more than one economist to declare that the situation is manifestly unsound. The pressure of all these forces, and in particular of big business would most probably induce the Government to the orthodox policy of cutting down the budget deficit'.

In line with Kalecki's reasoning, a ›historically long period of full employment brought about by Keynesian politics was experienced in Industrialized Countries (ICs), which was finally stopped by an anti-Keynesian revolution justified by the necessity to fight inflation. Naturally, the arguments of the 1930s will not do after Keynes. Here, globalisation comes in handy. It has been widely used to justify neoliberal economic policies, to argue for real wage reductions and to push through anti-labour legislation in ICs, and to justify policies favouring capital owners. Usually the impression is conveyed that globalisation

just fell from heaven. If anyone is responsible for it at all – the culprits
are Southern Countries (SCs). Their exports are often said to force ICs
to become 'leaner' and more competitive, forcing ICs to reduce the gap
in living standards so that they can compete with low wage countries.

Globalisation is not a new phenomenon. According to Oman (1996,
p. 6): 'the last 100 years alone have witnessed three distinct periods or
"waves". While resembling earlier phases of globalisation and building
on them the present wave also differs crucially. Oman's first wave
occurred between 1870 and 1914, when a powerful surge of colonialism
swept over Africa and Asia, while considerable technological changes
occurred in the 'leading' economies. But one can trace globalisation
back to the Spanish and Portuguese, the conquest of America, the genocide of its people, transatlantic slave trade and its effects on the industrial revolution or the destruction of Indian textile production by the
British (Raffer 1987, p. 134ff). Great contemporary scientists – such as
Adam Smith, Johann Gottlieb Fichte, John Stuart Mill, or G.W.F. Hegel
– defended slavery, brutal force and robbery, even outright genocide
(ibid., pp. 15ff).

Oman's (1996) second wave occurs under the Bretton Woods system:
Western European integration started, tariffs on manufactures were lowered
considerably and foreign direct investment by transnational enterprises grew
spectacularly. He characterises the present wave of globalisation by sweep-
ing policy changes such as deregulation, privatisation and liberalisation, new
techniques and the innovation that accompanies their spread, altered dynamics of interfirm competition, and financial globalisation. Like his first
wave, which carved the whole world up into influence spheres, present globalisation is accompanied by regionalisation. Fears were voiced that regional
blocs might hamper globalisation by fragmenting world trade into more or
less open trading blocs.

Regionalisation is ambivalent. It can be a handmaiden to liberalisation and globalisation, a role increasingly emphasised recently. Oman
(1996) differentiates between 'degenerate regionalism' and its 'good'
form reinforcing globalisation by enhancing competition and productivity, weakening rent-seekers and regional special interest groups. The
WTO (1996a, p. 11) favours 'open regionalism', defined as the elimination of internal barriers to trade on the same timetable as the lowering of
barriers towards non-members of regional trading blocs. Regional trading groups have to contribute to ensuring 'that at the end of the process

both regional and multilateral approaches will have contributed to full liberalisation in a free global market'. This form of regional integration is a means to prepare economies for the global market. Again, this is not totally new. Economic integration was justified as a step towards greater openness in the 1950s and 1960s. But the uncompromising enthusiasm about full liberalisation and 'free markets' is a result of the political changes during the 1980s.

Arguments for globalisation – as well as for deregulation and liberalisation – basically rest on the assertion that free markets are best for everybody. The economic textbook market used as a justification as well as the strategies the IMF and the IBRD force on debtor countries know no losers. Under textbook assumptions everybody is better of. Free trade is, so to say, the best welfare policy.

This paper argues that this presently wide spread view is wrong. Both winners and losers exist in real life, a fact recognised by good textbooks under headings such as 'optimal tariff', or Stolper-Samuelson Theorem. To do economic theory justice it is appropriate to clarify briefly that the enthusiasm for liberalising trade preached by so many economists, the IMF, and the IBRD, and readily parroted by politicians when it suits them cannot be justified by neoclassical theory, which is apparently abused to hide other motives.

After showing with the brevity necessary because of limits of space that neoliberal policies do not follow from neoclassical theory, neoliberal policies and arguments, particularly globalisation, are analysed on the basis of Kalecki's reasoning. Globalisation is human made and serves certain interests, influencing the distribution of resources. This suggests that liberalisation is applied selectively – it actually is, as will be shown below. Presently ruling policies produce winners and losers. Among the latter are SCs in general, particularly the poor in the South, but also the majority of the North's population.

## 2. GLOBALISATION, LIBERALISATION AND NEOCLASSICAL THEORY

One quick look at a microeconomics textbook will show that the results of the perfectly competitive market cannot be approximated by eliminating some but not all market imperfections. Reducing only the number of imperfections, liberalising trade partially, might as well make things worse. Unless one assumes that a global, perfectly competitive market can be established, good introductory textbooks warn (e.g. Nicholson 1992, p. 521), liberalisation may deteriorate a country's economic position. Furthermore, while models work quite well under 2 countries/2 products/2 factors assumptions they cannot be generalised in a meaningful way.

Caveats, critical statements or theoretical findings at odds with the liberalisation dogma have usually been brushed aside to be eagerly 'forgotten', even though the very founders of present trade theory themselves warned of its applicability to real life. Bertil Ohlin (1967, pp. 308f) stated outspokenly:

> The obstinate conservatism with which the classical comparative cost thinking has been retained in theory as something more than a pedagogical introduction – or a model for the treatment of a few special problems – is evidence that, even today, there is in many quarters an insufficient understanding of this fundamental fact.
>
> It follows that not only the comparative cost model but also the factor proportions model can only be applied in special cases and used as a general introduction to illuminate the character of trade in some essential aspects ...
>
> It is characteristic of the *developing countries* that a good many factors do not exist at all and that the quality of others differs from factors in the industrialized countries. This means that a simple method of analysis – such as the factor proportions model – which does not take this into account is to some extent unrealistic'.

Eli Heckscher (1950, p. 275; stress added) explicitly found his theory *in full accordance with List's point of view, since his criticism of the "school" was directed only at the dynamic factors* – a view fully shared by List (1920, pp. 234f). Nevertheless the 'Heckscher-Ohlin Theory' is used to advocate unrestricted liberalisation and to 'disprove' List's infant industry protection argument.

The IBRD-economist H.B. Chenery (1961, p. 23) concluded that the static concept of comparative advantages creates conflicts between trade theory and growth theory so that two important bodies of orthodoxy cannot be reconciled: 'There are a number of contradictions between the implications of trade theory and growth theory. To make these theories consistent, it is necessary to discard' some assumptions, such as the crucial condition of constant returns. While the theorem of comparative advantages, the main argument of those advising unconditional liberalisation, is irrefutably correct *within* its assumptions, constant returns are necessary to guarantee an unequivocally positive outcome. If, *ceteris paribus*, this absolutely unrealistic restriction is dropped trade may be to the disadvantage of a country specialising according to the theorem. Pareto (1927, pp. 507ff) already argued that Ricardo's example was a possible, but not at all a necessary result of trade.

Graham (1923) showed that, if one country specialises on a product with increasing returns to scale, such as watches, while the other produces a good subject to decreasing returns, e.g. corn, but all other assumptions of the Ricardian case hold, global output might **decrease**. The country specialising in the product with diminishing returns will find itself in a less favourable position than before. In Graham's case country B specialising on corn, a product with increasing unit costs, loses by trade. Graham showed convincingly that it can be disadvantageous for a country to specialise on goods with increasing unit costs **despite** or rather **because** of specialisation according to the theorem of comparative advantages if unit costs depend on output.

The last textbook discussing Graham in an attempt to disprove him was apparently Viner (1937). But instead of destroying the case Viner elaborated it even better than its author. Using Viner's figures Table 1 presents the effects of Graham's assumptions. The increases in production resulting from the well known textbook (Ricardo/Torrens) constant average cost assumption are not reproduced here. Viner apparently chose his figures to illustrate Graham's point clearly.

'Global' GNP was reduced by specialisation whatever theoretically possible price might be used to measure it. Average and marginal costs (or productivities) are no longer identical in Graham's case. Determining prices in competitive markets marginal costs are decisive for specialisation. This poses no problem at all, because the theorem of comparative costs applies at the margin as well (cf. Graham, 1923; Viner, 1937, p. 471). Logical accuracy demands the addition of an assumption neither Graham nor Viner mention. The relations of productivities at the margin are identical to the relations of the averages at all stages in Table 1. This assumption simplifies the presentation of their numerical example conveniently, but it is not a necessary condition for Graham's case. As long as the two vectors of marginal productivities are linearly independent a limbo allowing relative gains for both sides exists at the margin. A and B will go on specialising on watches and corn respectively as long as $a_w/a_c > b_w/b_c$, where a and b are A's and B's marginal productivities in w(atches) and c(orn) (Raffer, 1994).

Table 1.
*Graham's Case (as presented by Viner)*

Basic Assumptions: Countries **A** and **B** both have 400 Units of (homogeneous) Labour (LU); both produce Corn and Watches initially, then specialising according to comparative advantages; the international price (ð net barter terms of trade, NBToT) remains at $4C = 3.5W$ (or: Pintl = 0.875)

| Starting Point: | | A | B |
|---|---|---|---|
| production per LU (ð productivity) | C | 4 | 4 |
| W 4 3 | W | 4 | 3 |

$P_b = 0.75$ $(4C = 3W) \leq$ Pintl $= 0.875 \leq P_a = 1$

Ricardian limbo = difference between domestic prices $P_a$ and $P_b$

**Graham's Case:**

| | | Specialisation (II) | | Specialisation (III) | |
|---|---|---|---|---|---|
| | | A | B | | A | B |
| Productivity: | C | 4.5 | 3.5 | C | 5 | 0.5 |
| | W | 4.5 | 2 | W | 5 | 0.25 |

0.571 < Pintl = 0.875 < 1    0.5 < Pintl = 0.875 < 1

**Changes in total production:**

| | Specialisation II | | | Specialisation | | | III Total Special. | | |
|---|---|---|---|---|---|---|---|---|---|
| | A | B | Diff.[*] | A | B | Diff.[*] | A | B | Diff.[*] |
| C | 450 | 1050 | −100 | 5 | 199.5 | −1395.5 | 0 | 200 | −1400 |
| (LU) | (100) | (300) | | (1) | (399) | | | (400) | |
| W | 1350 | 200 | +150 | 1995 | 0.25 | +595.25 | 2000 | 0 | +600 |
| (LU) | (300) | (100) | | (399) | (1) | | (400) | | |

[*] Difference to production in specialisation I

In Viner's example the Ricardian limbo widens substantially from [1, 0.75] to [1, 0.5] putting B more and more at a disadvantage. While the industrial country enjoys increased productivity, the raw material exporting country gets less and less productive – underdevelopment starts developing. The minimum international price at which B still 'gains' from trade (in the sense of static comparative advantages) can fall below the initial limbo interval. The widening of the Ricardian limbo means that international prices initially unacceptable to B become 'advantageous'. NBToT can fall below the initial lower threshold of the limbo, which allows the industrial country to depress the NBToTs of its trading partner more easily without providing A any incentive to pass its own productivity gains onto B via lower prices.

After attempts to disprove this so-called Graham Paradox had failed, textbooks stopped telling students about it. Approaches discussing disadvantages of foreign trade are apparently as popular with the free trade school today as Galileo's findings that the earth turned around the sun were with the Inquisition – they are treated accordingly.

In general, references to Graham are rare, and do not refer to the Paradox. In recent literature only Helpman (1984) described Graham's case briefly and correctly. After establishing sufficient conditions for a country to gain from trade Helpman showed how losses from free trade may occur, quoting the case of nationally increasing returns specifically as a confirmation of 'Graham's argument that a country may lose from trade' (*ibid.*, p. 346). Helpman's model, though, goes even beyond Graham's case, which rests on the more restrictive assumption of a combination of increasing and decreasing returns.

Raffer (1994) showed that Graham's case provides a theoretical corroboration of the Prebisch-Singer-Thesis (PST) of secularly falling NBToT, which rocked the boat of professional complacency by exposing an apparent contradiction between economic theory and practical outcome. If international markets and trade behaved according to academic models NBToT would have had to improve for SCs. As productivity has grown faster in ICs, global income relations (double factoral terms of trade, DFToT) can only remain constant if NBTOT move against the North, distributing the fruits of technical progress equally, as both Prebisch and Singer have argued (cf. Raffer & Singer 1996, pp. 31f). In this case it really would not matter on what product a country specialises. If trade is expected to narrow wage differences, as the factor price equalisation theorem suggests, NBToT would have to increase even more in favour of the South. At constant NBToT however DFToT deteriorate, which means global disparities in factor incomes increase. The world market disadvantages some participants. In parentheses it might be added that combining Graham's Paradox and the Prebisch-Singer-Thesis with the non-Marxist theory of Unequal Exchange, which uses neoclassical tools such as substutability or the lack of it (Raffer, 1987), a logically consistent explanation of disadvantaging trade emerges (Raffer, 1994).

Briefly put, textbook theory does not justify free-traders but makes a clear logical case for judicious intervention. Nevertheless the creed that the comparative advantages theorem and the Heckscher-Ohlin Theory can be applied to reality, even that actual trade mirrors these models rank high among the sacred cows of orthodoxy unwilling to accept unwelcome logic. Balassa's (1965) concept of 'Revealed Comparative Advantages' is a prime example of how uncritical mainstream economists can become vis-a-vis their own ideology . An export concentration index, which has nothing to do with the theorem at all, is named in a way to imply that all countries export according to their comparative advantages. If England specialised on wine in Ricardo's example and Portugal on cloth Balassa's index would readily reveal 'comparative advantages' in wine for England and in cloth for Portugal. Whatever a country specialises on, it cannot but 'reveal' its 'comparative advantages', even against the logic of the theorem itself. Liberalisation is always right by definition, and Balassa's name for an empirically useful index of export concentration is the final triumph of ideology over reason – a result unthinkable in sciences such as physics or chemistry.

After having shown – although quite briefly – that presently pursued policies do not derive from neoclassical trade theory as claimed by neoliberals the question arises what effects present neoliberal policies actually have.

### 3. EFFECTS ON THE SOUTH

Globalisation and neoliberalism are used to open Southern economies to Northen interests. Present policies are tailored to suit the wishes of ICs and to increase profit possibilities of their transnational firms. Ruling neoliberal ideas are generally inimical to government activities everywhere, but they are applied more rigorously to SCs. Substituting government activities by private initiative is hailed as the panacea, even in sectors such as infrastructure, where government responsibility remained unchallenged over decades.

## a) Aid and Financial Flows

One example is the trend toward substituting official development aid by private investments. In 1996 the OECD (1996, p. 58) announced the end of state-led development: 'With the shift to market-based economic strategies, these issues matter much more than they did when there was a common assumption that development would be state-led'. The role of official finance is formulated quite succinctly: it 'helps to seed and reinforce' (*ibid.*, p. 55) expanding private flows from abroad. Aid is seen as a handmaiden to private profit interests. State-led development seems to be substituted by state-subsidised private business. In many SCs privatisation means selling to foreigners due to a lack of locals able to buy. In contrast to the lack of coherence too often found with aid politics, where viable projects have frequently been destroyed by decisions of the same donors in other areas such as trade (cf. Raffer & Singer, 1996), the thrust of privatisation and liberalisation is quite coherent.

Reducing official aid combines naturally with privatisation and liberalisation, as well as with present austerity policies in practically all ICs. Combining budget cuts – for instance to comply with the Maastricht criteria – with substantial tax cuts in favour of the rich (including top politicians themselves) makes it necessary to look for savings wherever possible. Criticising aid and the rather opaque nature of political conditionality may be useful tools to justify aid cuts. Furthermore, aid has apparently lost importance after the Cold War.

The highly uncritical enthusiasm about private flows was first shown in the early 1990s. Increases in private (including highly volatile, speculative) flows to the South, were heralded as the end of the debt crisis, even though a close look at the IBRD's own data did not show that the debt overhang had been overcome in Latin America, nor did it justify the vindication of successful adjustment policies (Raffer, 1996b). Put in a nutshell: the heralded end of the debt crisis in Latin America was basically due to the toleration of extremely large non-payments, or breaches of contract. If creditors had accepted much lower, let alone similar arrears in 1982, be it in percentages of long term debts or in current dollars, there would have been no debt crisis. Steeply growing current account deficits for Latin America did not suggest a recovery either

– Mexico's balance of payments deficit had started to explode, nearly doubling every year between 1990 and 1992.

Enthusiasm was briefly dampened by the Mexican crash in 1994–95 and its $50 billion rescue package necessary to bail out private capital. This single case of socialising private losses nearly equalled the $59 billion all OECD countries spent on ODA in 1994. But immune to mere facts ruling ideology recovered quickly.

Enthusiasm about private flows was not new, but past experience has not dampened optimism about private financial flows in the 1990s. During the 1970s, when commercial banks flooded the South with easy money, Northern governments, International Financial Institutions (IFIs), most notably the IMF or the IBRD, and private banks were equally enthusiastic about the increasing amount of private loans to the South. Both IMF and IBRD strongly urged SCs to borrow in international financial markets, OECD governments congratulated commercial banks on the 'successful recycling' of money. The result, the debt crisis, is still with us, felt paricularly strongly by the poorest. Commercial banks relied on being bailed out by OECD governments and IFIs, which happened after 1982, although they had to take losses eventually.

In contrast to the private lending spree of the 1970s, which was the result of private initiative by commercial banks lending via unregulated xenomarkets, private capital movements of the 1990s were massively supported, possibly even brought about by OECD governments. The improvement in SC access to international capital markets has been supported by regulatory changes, the relaxing of quality guidelines for bond issues and the lowering of the minimum credit rating from A to BBB. Changes in regulation regarding equities occurred, making private placement in general more attractive. These regulatory changes, and a trend toward explicitly rating SC-borrowers at least partially triggered by them, allowed institutional investors to place money there. International treaties, such as the Final Act of the Uruguay Round and so-called structural adjustment have opened the South for foreign investment. In many countries inflows of foreign direct investment are to a considerable part due to privatisation, which means the selling of public companies, and therefore singular, irreproducible events. Once those state enterprises finding takers are sold, inflows cease and repatriation of profits soon becomes the preponderant balance of payments effect.

Fears are justified that the pattern of private profits and socialized losses will become institutionalised. Recalling the Mexican fiasco of 1994–5 and the problems of sustainability and stability of large global financial market intermediated resource flows the OECD (1996, p. 57) identifies systemic risks requiring 'the provision of a much larger officially provided safety net'. Less diplomatic and elegant language might simply speak of the prospect of officially subsidised speculation, whose losses are covered by governments, possibly even from donors' aid budgets. In contrast to aid catastrophic private failures are interpreted as the manifest need for even more taxpayer's money, as recent events in Asia have proved. The US Savings & Loans deregulation, which cost US taxpayers well over $100 billion, shows that public money is also available to clean up the results of neoliberal policies within ICs – in contrast to money for the poor.

### b) The Force of Globalised Capital Markets

Liberalised global capital markets have increased volatility and risk of debtor economies. While Mexico liberalised its capital account and dismantled most of its previous controls on capital movements before 1994, countries such as Brazil, Chile and Colombia have attempted to discourage short-term capital inflows by taxes of various kinds on foreign borrowing and portfolio foreign investment, or reserve requirements. The Republic of Korea had traditionally maintained strict capital controls, which have been liberalised recently in preparation of the country's OECD-membership. In the past authorities were able 'to prevent excessive speculative foreign exchange trading' (Park 1996, p. 216). Although Korea had fared quite well under the old system the author justified the recent liberalisation of the capital account with 'the inefficiency of these regulations and ... the worldwide trend towards economic liberalization' (ibid., p. 193) – meanwhile his country has become as efficiently liberalised as Mexico was at the end of 1994.

The Asian crash of 1997 was basically triggered by unduely quick globalisation, or – more politely put – problems of transition. The Thailand Department of Export Promotion and the Industrial Authority of Thailand acknowledged this in costly three-page advertisments (e.g. in Time magazine, 24 November 1997) placed to reassure investors:

'Simply put, the winds of change blew in too quickly, catching Thailand offguard. A lack of mature systems and safeguards for control meant trouble for an economy that had neither time nor macroeconomic managerial experience to adjust. Such are the pitfalls of the development cycle in today's rush to modernization and prosperity ... we have realized that transition from poverty to prosperity must be made in a deliberate manner, with controls and vigilance to prevent over-ambition and over-zealous borrowing'.

Liberalising private lending – in the wording of the Thai auhtorities: 'a runaway financial sector' – while banks and investors were still subject to obligations of the old and that far successful system was likely to create problems of compatibility, particularly so as debts incurred had rather short maturities. This is not to deny problems, such as investements in real estate, large corporate debts or the effects of exchange rates pegged to the US dollar. But government intervention and regulation would have been necessary to allow smooth transition and to avoid the crash.

Like in the case of Mexico the bail-out of international investors followed immediately. Although debts were incurred by private Asian companies the governments of the borrowing countries were taken to task – someone had to pay for the bail-out and as private buisness can go bankrupt governments have to guarantee that investors will get paid. The lending spree has made the 'tigers' lose their claws. These economies now have to open for foreign investment and reduce public spending, although this did not create the problem. Their assets are sold at highly reduced prices – the successful 'tiger' model is likely to be dead.

Privatisation used to differ strongly between Asia and Latin America. Between 1988 and 1992 privatisation proceeds amounted to slightly more than $40 billion in Latin America and to $7.5 billion in East Asia (IBRD 1994, p. 105). The share of foreigners was 56 per cent and 2 per cent respectively – in East Asia 98 per cent of assets remained under domestic control. The present crisis is likely to change this radically.

A very abrupt change regarding opinion on these countries can be observed. Until very recently hailed as models of successful development, dubbed the 'Asian miracle', and wrongly used as proofs for the neoliberal ideology, their system is no described as deplorably inefficient and flawed. They are made change their past policies fundamentally and totally. This begs the question how and why past success was achieved.

In contrast to their own advice both the IMF and the IBRD would never dream of changing their Articles of Agreement to lend themselves to private business without government guarantees nor of forgoing their preferred creditor status – in short: of accepting any risks of a market environment. Particularly eager to preach the neoliberal gospel and fiercely advocating the advantages of market mechanisms to everyone else they insist that they themselves must be protected against the market, remaining totally exempt from any form of financial accountability, apparently because they could not function under more market based conditions. The proposal to make them financially accountable for their own actions and liable to damage compensation in the way private consultants have always been (Raffer & Singer, 1996, pp. 206ff) is anathema to the Bretton Woods institutions.

### c) Lop-Sided Liberalisation of Trade

Claiming that economic theory would suggest opening one's country to the world market as invariably the optimal policy most SCs have been forced to globalise their economies by the IMF and the IBRD. Under the heading 'structural adjustment' all debtor economies were forced to privatise, liberalise and welcome foreign capital. SCs have to liberalise in a way OECD governments would never dream of applying in their own countries.

While pressing for liberalisation and opening of SC-markets, ICs keep their own markets selectively protected against Southern exports. The OECD (1992, p. 37) states with utmost clarity that SCs face higher tariffs and more non-tariff barriers, which cost them more than all development aid received. In addition, entry into export-oriented industries most accessible to SCs is retarded. The OECD does not fail to point out that while ICs have encouraged SC-diversification, IC-trade-policies often obstruct it by tariff escalation, suddenly imposed new trade barriers, antidumping actions and other selective trade restricting provisions, when SC exports start to take off successfully. This was done although the effects of increased exports of manufactures if all SCs 'had experienced the same rapid growth rate of exports as did the Republic of Korea from 1980 to 1988' would have been negligible. SCs 'would have supplied 3.7 per cent of manufactured goods in all industrial country markets by 1988, instead of the 3.1 per cent they achieved' (ibid., p. 46). Comparing these policies with the 'Trade Pledge' by OECD governments, a declaration on the need to refrain from protectionism (Raffer & Singer, 1996, p. 37), shows great inconsistencies, unless one assumes that free-marketeering is simply a tool used to gain advantages for the more powerful.

The outcome of the Uruguay Round is a clear and recent example, how ICs are able to preserve their interests against those of SCs, keeping the latters' potential advantages quite limited (Raffer, 1996a). While able to retain high protection in agriculture and integrating textiles and clothing, ICs managed to restrict or outlaw protection which would be in the interest of SCs. The development path of the successful Asian 'tigers', the only historically successful examples of late development until these governments changed their policy recently, is now virtually closed off to other SCs. Promising options are gone.

The new WTO framework denies SCs important policy options to protect nascent industries along the lines indicated by List and Heckscher. Its rules on patents favour the North, up to the point of facilitating the theft of traditional knowledge in SCs. Furthermore the North is about to establish its technological grip so firmly that promising alternative techniques are likely to be frozen, simply because the costs of changing become prohibitively high, a problem known as QWERTYnomics (cf. Raffer, 1996a).

One may talk of two forms of liberalisation – one for the South, the other for the North. The term 'structural adjustment' illustrates that well. 'Adjustment' or 'Structural Adjustment' are expressions now monopolised by the IMF and the IBRD, to describe their specific macroeconomic ideas – sometimes called the Washington Consensus – prescribed to debtor countries in the South. Initially, though, they were used to describe the adjustment of ICs to increasing imports of textiles and clothing from the South. This invites a comparison between the quick and ruthless adjustment on which IFIs insist in the case of indebted SCs with the smooth and slow adjustment of ICs.

The Multi-Fibre Arrangement (MFA) is a prime illustration of double standards. Protectionism in this sector dates back to 1935, when the US negotiated the first 'voluntary' export quota system on textiles with Japan, considering tariffs up to 60 per cent insufficient. In 1961 the Short Term Cotton Textile Arrangement was negotiated under GATT auspices at the request of the US, even though it was a clear breach of the GATT's own principles. The Long Term Arrangement Regarding International Trade in Cotton Textiles followed in 1962. It was repalced by MFA I at the request of ICs, because the use of synthetic fibres not yet covered had increased perceptibly, and some SCs had gained progressively larger market shares. But substantially increased productivity in the textile industry reducing sectoral employment in the North was another important reason (IBRD 1987, pp. 136). Thus labour saving effects of technical progress within ICs much larger than job losses due to North-South trade were shifted onto SCs, as many studies corroborate (v. Raffer, 1987, pp. 225ff). Officially ICs 'needed' protection to adjust to Southern exports. Although a clear contradiction to the very aim and essence of GATT – liberalising trade in manufactures – the Textiles Surveillance Body was established by GATT to supervise the implementation of the MFA and to arbitrate disputes. Openly condoning the MFA and breaking its own rules, the GATT sided with ICs.

At the beginning of the Uruguay Round the thought surfaced to legalise the MFA within the new framework. In comparison one may call the agreed phasing out after 10 more years a 'success' of SCs, although there is no convincing evidence that the MFA will actually be discontinued this time as agreed. Even if this should happen, this would mean that ICs will have enjoyed 'necessary, temporary' protection in one small part of their economies for up to about seven decades – while SCs are required to open their economies much more radically and quickly. ICs claim they cannot adjust to less restricted trade as quickly as they want and, helped by the IMF and the IBRD, make SCs adjust theirs. Krugman (1994) cites demands that all North–South trade be regulated after the model of protectionism and textiles and apparel.

The first phase of 'liberalisation' under the WTO regime of Textiles and Clothing covered – with one[!] exception – only products that had not been subject to restrictions before. It was therefore commercially useless to exporters. Both the EU and the US have already expessed the view that political and economic difficulties would not allow them to liberalise without a quid pro quo from Southern exporters. While OECD countries have been busily adjusting one small part of their economies for decades without feeling yet able to expose this sector to the world market, they and IFIs controlled by them have forced SCs and Countries in Transition to adjust their whole economies at much greater speed, making aid and development finance conditional on implementing those 'reforms'. Debtors are forced to open their economies immediately, without escape clauses or the breathing space considered so necessary by ICs in the case of textiles and clothing.

Reducing their income opportunities this policy makes Southern exporters more dependent on aid and loans.

Comparing structural adjustment with both its own experience and that of these successful 'tiger' economies, Japan began to doubt the policies the IBRD and the IMF were forcing on debtor countries. In contrast to the strong anti-government bias and laisser-faire ideology of structural adjustment programmes the 'miracle' in North East Asia was achieved with substantial government intervention and within the framework of a wider industrial policy. Basically exactly the opposite of what debtor countries are forced to do was done. Japanese aid has always been characterised by strong state involvement. Both theoretically and with regard to practical success this approach is diametrically opposed to the ideology of state minimalism presently preached by the IBRD and other multilaterals. Speaking up on behalf of SCs – and indeed of the poorest people most severely affected by structural adjustment – Japan differed from all other donor governments, but was unable to change present IFI policies (cf. Raffer & Singer, 1996, pp. 114ff)

The WTO – with the mandate to co-operate with the Bretton Woods institutions – has strengthened the grip of neoliberalism. Trade Policy Reviews offer a possibility of co-operation to embed the Washington Consensus firmly in SCs: 'a virtual global consensus on the fundamentals of trade policy reinforces economic an political liberalization and lessens the risk of reversion to the old ways.' (WTO 1996b, p. 6) But all the arguments about the benefits of liberalisation and free global markets carry suprisingly little weight when directed at ICs themselves, not only in the case of textiles.

The WTO's dispute settlement mechanism shows that not all countries need be treated equally. The probability of success ('fruitfuilness') is explicitly established by treaty as the guiding principle of WTO dispute settlement, more important than enforcing the rule of law with impartiality. These mechanisms will hardly realise the advantages SCs hoped for, such as efficient legal relief against violations of their rights under the treaties and protection of the legitimate interests of smaller players. The EU's complaint against the US Helms-Burton Act (officially called 'Cuban Liberty and Democratic Solidarity Act') illustrates the WTO's limits. The US threatened that 'the WTO panel process would not lead to a resolution of the dispute, instead it would pose serious risks for the new organization.' (WTO 1996b, p. 2) Following US 'advice' to 'explore other avenues' (*ibid.*) the EC requested the panel to suspend its work in April 1997. Two complaints by Korea against US anti-dumping actions were not followed recently. The Dispute Settlement Body 'deferred consideration as the United States indicated it was not in a position to agree to both requests' (WTO 1997, p. 4) – no doubt an easy way to deal with complaints not open to all members.

## 4. THE ROLE OF GLOBALISATION IN THE NORTH

Globalisation is used by politicians in the North as the main argument why substantial policy changes are unavoidable. Workers have to agree to lower wages to become more competitive in the new global market. Increased international competition and higher capital mobility are said to foce politicians to adopt 'sensible' policies, such as reducing the welfare state. Unhindered international capital movements are praised as a means to keep governments in the North and the South 'prudent'. Deregulation and liberalisation in the communication sector or with public utilities result in substantial rate reductions for large firms in Western Europe, while rates for households and small units remain relatively higher. While cross-subsidisation for social purposes is criticised, cross-subsidies are welcome in such cases.

'Growing inequality ... and a threat of exclusion faced by many people' are 'further effects of globalisation'. (Oman, 1996, p. 35) It contributes to declines in real wages of many workers in the US and to a growing number of 'working poor'. Together with growing job insecurity this marks the end of the American dream for many Americans and the end of the European welfare state according to Oman. He argues that many people mistakenly blame globalisation for labour market problems, which in his view are due to the change from Taylorist mass-production to post-taylorist flexible production in ICs. He points out that globalisation does not show any significant acceleration of industrial redeployment to SCs. On the contrary, redeployment decelerated in the 1980s. This trend, foreseen already in 1980 by some authors (v. Raffer, 1987, pp. 237ff), is due to new technologies and to new forms of organising production, such as JIT (Just In Time), which greatly enhance the benefits of physical proximity.

Flexible production, the new way of organising production, also tends to put SCs at disadvantage: 'comparative advantage in low-skilled, labour-intensive production is of diminishing value ... in global markets, relative to skills, flexibility, proximity and other competitive assets' (Oman, 1996, p. 40). Access to OECD markets, but also infra-structural requirements or educational levels securing the 'trainability' of the work force become crucial. These are precisely sectors where the Bretton Woods institutions have forced debtor economies to cut expenditures, thus reducing their possibilities to invest in their future.

Technical progress and rationalisation in ICs, which had had more important job effects than imports from SCs during the 1970s and 1980s, have remained the main causes for job losses in ICs. These job losses – or, seen the other way round, productivity gains – have been accompanied by sluggish demand during the recent past, which makes finding new jobs quite difficult for people made redundant. Whenever productivity grows more rapidly than demand a corresponding percentage of the working become unemployed. Productivity increases, whether reached within a Taylorist or non-taylorist framework, are by definition job losses unless new demand reabsorbs those made redundant. During a period of 'jobless growth' (UNDP, 1993) this is clearly not happening. Not surprisingly labour's bargaining power has been strongly reduced, as steeply declining union membership (as percentages of the labour force) indicates (UN, 1995, p. 245).

Additional productivity gains from economic integration, regional or global, increase these losses. Easier possibilities to shift production – real or perceived – increase the bargaining power of employers, allowing them to depress real and increasingly nominal wages. Doing so employers eventually reduce their own markets. Effective demand is reduced both by lower wages and by job insecurity inducing people to spend less than they would otherwise have done. These negative effects of private actions are further compounded by present fiscal policies and anti-employee legislation reducing employees' rights.

In Europe the productivity gains of a single market, routinely quoted by politicians as favourable effects of the EU, have cost jobs. During a period of labour scarcity, such as the 1960s, this rationalising effect might have been welcome. In the period of jobless growth it aggravates the situation further. Quite predictably, Austria's accession has both led to job losses and to Austria's first austerity programme after World War II, appropriately called 'Structural Adjustment Act'. By reducing expenditures for science and education extremely strongly the government also undermined the formation of 'human capital', thus compromising the future. Basically the same policies have been pursued by other EU members. Oman's (1996, p. 37) urgent recommendation to invest in education and 'human capital' to cope with the 'knowledge-intensive nature of competition today' is not heeded.

The planned EU-enlargement towards Eastern Europe will increase unemployment and pressures on labour in the West.Countries such as the Czech Republic are conveniently close to Western markets and can be readily integrated into JIT production processes. Wage differences are much larger than those in productivity. Membership in the EU would thus both increase the credibility of threats to relocate and bring about perceptible relocations to new Eastern members. Inequality and job insecurity would thus grow, while effective demand is likely to shrink further in relation to potential output. Fiscal cuts made necessary by transfer payments to the East are likely to compound contractive effects.

While SCs have been forced to adopt neoliberal policies, this is done voluntarily by IC governments. Under the cloak of the new European currency those pre-Keynesian policies responsible for the economic crisis of the 1930s are relegitimated: budgetary cuts and the dismantling of social standards are now justified by the convergence criteria. The necessity of the Maastricht criteria is shown by the fact that Belgium and Luxembourg have had the same currency for decades, although one country fulfils them and the other does not. Germany's failure to meet these criteria did not lead to perceptible devaluations of the Mark, which casts doubts on whether these criteria are necessary for a hard currency. The catchword 'Maastricht' has become a generally accepted reason to commit the errors of the 1930s all over again plus a few new ones. In contrast to then the rich have received large tax cuts, which in turn have aggravated fiscal deficits and reduced effective demand, redistributing income to groups with a lower marginal propensity to consume. At the CDU party convention in October 1996 the German Chancellor announced plans to cut taxes for the rich further, in spite of Maastricht and the heavy financial burden of reunification. Globalisation is always quoted as a factor forcing governments to adopt such policies. It is conveniently forgotten that it is itself the result of deliberate policies, decisions, and international treaties by the same governments, which use it as an excuse for policies in favour of the rich, including politicians themselves.

Present policies of IC-governments strongly reduce government influence by cutting budgets for interventions, dismantling instruments to do so, and by international treaties, such as the Maastricht Treaty, the Final Act of the Uruguay Round, or the North American Free Trade Agreement (NAFTA). NAFTA provides for investor-to-state dispute resolution, which exempts firms from national jurisdiction. It confers on them the right to sue governments for damages before an international panel of arbitrators, not at national courts, thus treating them like sovereign entities. Recently Ethyl Corporation has sued the Canadian government, arguing that it had suffered damages because Canadian legislators banned its gasoline additive as hazardous, and because its product was discussed in the Canadian parliament, thus blemishing the firm's good reputation (Center of Concern, 1997). If the $251 million lawsuit is successful this would reduce the powers of democratically elected legislators dramatically. The new Multilateral Agreement on Investment, presently negotiated under OECD auspices without much publicity, plans to confer this right to firms as well. Democracy is rolled back and the state is reduced far beyond what liberals in the 1930s considered its legitimate role.

With its Maastricht criteria and the Dublin agreement to fine members not fulfilling them in the future the European Union has locked-in present neoliberal policies, practically excluding Keynesian policies for the foreseeable future. For the first time in history an 'institutional penalty on Keynesian policies' (Raffer, 1998) was agreed on. Anti-Keynesianism was successfully institutionalised, making it next to impossible for future democratically elected governments to change economic policy in Europe, as they will be bound by EU common rules, which cannot be changed by any single country.

## 5. WINNERS OF NEOLIBERALISM AND ITS ANTI-DEMOCRACRATIC BIAS

Neoliberal policy produces winners as well. Profits soar – or in modern lingo: shareholder values increase. Understandably, lay-offs are considered good news by shareholders: as new market outlets are scarce, increased profits come mainly from cutting costs. With limited investment possibilities in real production, the amount of money available for globalised financial markets and the instability brought about by them increases too. IC-governments eager to bail-out speculators are unwilling even to consider stabilising the global financial system as their opposition to the Tobin Tax shows. This tax would run counter to present policies.

Last but not least it must be recalled that top politicians themselves are winners. Generally, they benefit from lower taxation of higher income brackets. The EU offers new and high income streams at a time when political perks are increasingly attacked on the national level in many countries. Suffice one example of members of the European Parliament (EP), who receive some $10,000 per month for expenses (flight tickets paid extra) without any other obligation than the information that the money was spent. This mere statement is a relatively new requirement hailed as a substantial improvement by the EP's president, Klaus Hänsch, on Austrian radio's Mittags journal in October 1996.

This policy of redistribution, which has changed the distribution of income and assets in all ICs considerably over recent years, is accompanied by a distinctly anti-democratic bias. So-called fast track legislation, which reduces the influence of legislators considerably, was used to negotiate NAFTA. The Mexican government suppressed an open and fair discussion on it. Austria's government behaved similarly when it had to allow a referendeum on the county's accesion to the EU. After accession the necessary laws were whipped through parliament so quickly that parliamentarians admitted publicly not having been able to read what they had voted for.

The European Parliament has neither the right to make laws nor even to propose them. Legislative powers are firmly in the hands of the administration, unelected bureaucrats and ministers, who decide in absolute secrecy. Neither discussions, nor who was for or against is made known. This reduces the influence people in any European country can wield substantially. It allows a much stronger dissociation of politics from the interests of the electorate at large to favour small groups than democratic institutions would ever allow. National parliaments are overruled by administratively made legal norms. One article in the Maastricht Treaty would have sufficed to confer full legislative power to the EP. Even national veto rights could easily have been incorporated, if that should be desired, by demanding a minimum percentage of yesvotes within any member country's EP-members in addition to the total vote. To simplify things this second 'national' voting, it could be made contingent on demand by at least one EP-member.

European regionalisation has a very strong anti-democratic bias, which allows it to accommodate the interests of small, rich lobbies much better than democratic structures would. On the other hand EU-governments busily rolling back democracy in their own countries demand SCs at least as keenly to strengthen democracy, when giving aid. This political conditionality includes that freely elected parliaments should be given full parliamentary powers, something which donors are eagerly undoing themselves. Naturally, arrangements such as the expenses of EP-members would be considered incompatible with 'good governance' in any aid receiving country.

## 6. CONCLUSION

Present neoliberal polices cannot be justified by neoclassical economics as improving welfare for all. This theory is wrongly used to justify re-distributive policies in favour of capital owners and the rich. Globalisation is a catchword used to justify the one-sided opening of SCs and to roll back social achievements and real wages in the North. It is a useful tool for implementing the policies foreseen by Kalecki.

### REFERENCES

Balassa, Bela (1965). 'Trade Liberalisation and "Revealed" Comparative Advantages', *Manchester School of Economic and Social Studies*, vol. 33, pp. 99ff

Chenery H.B. (1961). 'Comparative Advantage and Development Policy', *American Economic Review*, vol. 51, pp. 18ff

Center of Concern (1997). 'Corporate Lawsuit Against Canadian Government', Center of Concern, Washington DC, June 6

Graham, Frank (1923) 'Some Aspects of Protection Further Considered', *Quarterly Journal of Economics*, vol. 37, pp. 193ff

Heckscher, Eli (1950). 'The Effect of Foreign Trade on the Distribution of Income', in: H. Ellis & L. Metzler (eds): *Readings in the Theory of International Trade*, Allen & Unwin, London, pp. 272ff (orig. in: *Ekonomisk Tidskrift*, vol. XXI, 1919)

Helpman, Elhanan (1984). 'Increasing Returns, Imperfect Markets, and Trade Theory', in: R.W. Jones & P.B. Kenen (eds), *Handbook of International Economics*, vol. I, North Holland, Amsterdam etc., pp. 326ff

IBRD (1987). *World Development Report* 1987, Oxford UP, Oxford etc

IBRD (1994). *World Development Report* 1994, Oxford UP, Oxford etc

Kalecki, Michal (1971). 'Political Aspects of Full Employment' in: M. Kalecki, *Selected Essays on the Dynamics of the Capitalist Economy*, 1933–1970; Cambridge, Cambridge UP, pp. 138ff (Paper first published in 1943)

Keynes, John Maynard (1967). *The General Theory of Employment, Interest and Money*, London & Basingstoke, Macmillan

208

Krugman, Paul (1994). 'Does Third World Growth Hurt First World Prosperity?' *Harvard Business Review*, July-August, pp. 113ff

List, Friedrich (1920). *Das nationale System der politischen Ökonomie*, G. Fischer, Jena (3rd ed., first publ. in 1841)

Nicholson, Walter (1992). *Microeconomic Theory, Basic Principles and Extensions*, 5th ed., Dryden, Forth Worth etc.

OECD (1992). *Development Co-operation, Efforts and Policies of the Members of the Development Assistance Committee*, 1992 Report, OECD, Paris

OECD (1992). *Development Co-operation, Efforts and Policies of the Members of the Development Assistance Committee*, 1995 Report, OECD, Paris

Ohlin, Bertil (1967). *Interregional and International Trade*, Havard UP, Cambridge (Mass) (first publ. in 1933)

Oman, Charles (1996). *The Policy Challenges of Globalisation and Regionalisation*, OECD, Paris

Pareto, Vilfredo (1927). *Manuel d'économie politique*, 2nd ed., Giard, Paris

Park, Yung Chul (1996). 'The Republic of Korea's Experience with Managing Foreign Capital Flows', in: M. ul Haq, I. Kaul & I. Grunberg (eds) *The Tobin Tax, Coping with Financial Volatility*, Oxford University Press, New York & Oxford, pp. 193ff

Raffer, Kunibert (1987). *Unequal Exchange and the Evolution of the World System, Reconsidering the Impact of Trade on North-South Relations*, Macmillan, London & Basingstoke

Raffer, Kunibert (1994). 'Disadvantaging Comparative Advantages: The Problem of Decreasing Returns to Scale' in: Renee Prendergast and Frances Stewart (eds) *Market Forces and World Development*, Macmillan, London & Basingstoke, pp. 75ff

Raffer, Kunibert (1996a). 'The Uruguay Round: Tilting Trade Rules Further in Favour of the North', in: G. K"hler, Ch. Gore, U.-P. Reich & T. Ziesemer (eds) *Questioning Development, Essays in the Theory, Policies and Practice of Development Interventions*, Metropolis, Marburg, pp. 329ff

Raffer, Kunibert (1996b). 'Is the Debt Crisis Largely Over? – A Critical Look at the Data of International Financial Institutions', in R.M. Auty, John Toye (eds) *Challenging the Orthodoxies*, Macmillan: London & Basingstoke, pp. 23ff [Paper presented at the Annual Conference of the Development Studies Association, Lancaster, September 1994]

Raffer, Kunibert (1998). 'Is a revival of Keynesian ideas likely? Some comments on chapters by Sir Hans Singer and G.M. Meier', in: Soumitra Sharma (ed) *John Maynard Keynes*: Keynesianism into the 21st Century, Edward Elgar, Cheltenham (forthcoming)

Raffer, Kunibert & H.W. Singer (1996). *The Foreign Aid Business, Economic Assistance and Development Co-operation*, E.Elgar, Cheltenham [paperback: 1997]

UN (1995). *World Economic and Social Survey 1995*, UN, New York

UNCTAD (1995). *Preliminary Analysis of Opportunities and Challenges Resulting from the Uruguay Round Agreement on Textiles and Clothing*, (6 October 1995) UN, Geneva (UNCTAD/ITD/17)

UNDP (1993). *Human Development Report*, Oxford UP, Oxford etc.

Viner, Jacob (1937) Studies in the Theory of International Trade, Allen & Unwin, London

WTO (1996a). *WTO-Focus no.11*, June-July 1996

WTO (1996b). *WTO Focus no.14*, December 1996

WTO (1997). *WTO Focus no.25*, December 1997

# J.M. KEYNES'S BAD HABIT: A CRITIQUE OF HIS CORRESPONDENCE STYLE BASED ON THE HICKS-KEYNES EXCHANGE OVER THE GENERAL THEORY IN 1936-37

*Michael Emmett Brady*

### ABSTRACT

Over the course of his lifetime, Keynes developed the very bad habit, in his correspondence, of not correcting, or even mentioning, the technical errors/mistakes made by his correspondents. Keynes would only actively defend the ideas that he had put forth in his A Treatise on Probability, A Treatise on Money and General Theory. This approach of Keynes usually led to the belief that Keynes' analysis was only intuitive. Later generations of economists then incorrectly concluded that Keynes' technical apparatus was defective. This is illustrated in the Hicks Keynes correspondence of 1936-1937.

### INTRODUCTION

During his lifetime, Keynes developed the bad habit of not defending any of the technical analysis that supported his theoretical conclusions, in the Treatise on Probability, Treatise on Money, or the General Theory (GT), in any of his correspondence, except the Keynes-Robertson exchange on pp. 512-515 of Vol. 13 of the Collected Writings of John Maynard Keynes (CWJMK). Thus, some part of the blame for the subsequent misconstrual of his economic theories must rest with Keynes himself. His refusal to provide some basic technical hints to those he was corresponding which led his conrrespondents to believe that they had correctly interpreted Keynes's work as being intuitive in nature.

In his letter of 31 August, 1936, Keynes writes his initial response to Hicks:

"I should say that my theory provides for the supply of consumption goods and of goods in general having,, or being capable of having, some elasticity, whereas the classical theory assumes that the supply of output as a whole is wholly inelastic; increase in one direction being necessarily offset by a decrease in another. If I were writing again, I should indeed feel disposed to define full employment as being reached at the same moment at which the supply of output in general becomes inelastic. It is perfectly true that a great part of my theory ceases to be required when the supply of output as a whole is inelastic". (CWJMK, Vol. 14, p.71).

While this is certainly correct, Keynes needed to add the following, that "$Y = D = Z$ at $e_0 = e_0 = 0$ maximizes expected profits, potential output and employment. There is no involuntary unemployment. Thus, my theory merges with the neoclassical as long as the economy is on the boundary of its Production Possibilities Frontier (PPF)".

This small, technical, addition would have alerted Hicks that he did not yet have a complete grasp of Keynes's' formal argument. In his letter to Keynes of 2 September, 1936, Hicks clearly reveals to Keynes that he does not yet grasp Keynes's underlying technical analysis:

"On the other hand, I do not want to give up my substantial point, that output may have reached a short-period maximum, even when there are a considerable number of unemployed specialised to the investment goods industries. But I take it you would now accept this and redefine full employment to cover this case". (CWJMK, Vol. 14, p. 72).

Keynes replied:

"Thanks for your letter. 1. I agree with your point that output may have reached a short-period maximum even when there are a considerable number of unemployed specialised in skill or locality, who are not worth their minimum terms in the employment which an increase of effective demand would make available. I ought to have emphasised and explained this, but it does not, I think, require a formally new definition of full employment. The definition I gave in my previous letter is formally equivalent, I think, with that which I gave in my book". (CWJMK, Vol. 14, pp. 74-75).

Keynes needs to have added the following. "My General Theory definition dealt with the purely theoretical world of perfect, or pure, competition. If labor is not homogeneous or there are imperfect labor markets, then, of course, your case is relevant for applied public policy.

However, my condition, $Y = D = Z$ at $e_o = e_o = 0$, defines full employment and is both valid and sound. See my chapters 20 and 21 for the mathematical details".

In this reply of 16 October, 1936, Hicks' letter clearly demonstrated to Keynes that he had no understanding of the technical way Keynes had integrated expectations into the $D$, $Z$, $Y$ model of the GT, since Lindahl's approach had absolutely nothing to do with Keynes's approach.

"Of your three definitions of income, the second and third correspond exactly, I think, to the conceptions of Lindahl which I have been using in my own thinking for the last couple years. Thus

|   | Keynes | Lindahl |
|---|--------|---------|
| A | Income | - |
| B | Net Income | Income ex ante |
| C | Net income _+ windfalls | Income ex post |

I think there is an exact correspondence, so that there I feel quite at home.

But your Income A is a different matter, and while I think I grasp the definition. I cannot see that it is a useful concept.

For you say (1) that A is what the entrepreneur maximises; but since the difference between A and B is involuntary, i.e., it is a constant for him, he can just as well be thought of as maximising B.

(2) You seem to regard A as less 'ambiguous' than B.

I suppose this means less subjective. But is it? Both depend upon the entrepreneur's expectations, since the optimum maintenance (if no output is produced) will depend upon anticipated obsolescence (for example). User cost seems to be just as 'ambiguous' as net income.

If I might put my whole feeling about this in the form of a suggestion; what I should like to see happen to this part of your book is a scrapping of Income A as a concept, its place being taken by a positive investigation of the relations between net income and output. I feel this would be ever so much clearer". (CWJMK, Vol. 14, pp.77-78)

Hicks then adds the following final sentence:

"I shall be most interested to know if you disagree - with this or much of the rest of this stuff". (CWJMK, Vol. 14 p. 79) The stage is now set. Keynes now knows for certain that Hicks has no grasp either of the formal, technical elasticity analysis of the GT or of the modeling of the Theory of Effective Demand. Keynes needed to explicitly go over the definitions of Y, D and Z, as well as the elasticity analysis, as it applies to Y on pp. 114-126 of the GT, and as it applies to D on pp. 282-286 and pp.304-306 of the GT. If Keynes lacked the physical strength to do this, due to his poor health, he still needed to briefly write "see pp. 114-126, pp. 282-286, and pp. 304-306". Instead, Keynes, after waiting 6 (!) moths, writes the following:

"I found it very interesting and really have next to nothing to say by way of criticism". (CWJMK, Vol. 14, p. 70)

A page later, Keynes writes

"At one time I tried the equations, as you have done, with in all of them. The objection to this is that it over emphasises current income. In the case of the inducement to invest, expected income for the period of the investment is the relevant variable. This I have attempted to take account of in the definition of the marginal efficiency of capital. As soon as the prospective yields have been determined, account has been implicitly taken of income, actual and expected. But, whilst it may be true that entrepreneurs are over-influenced by present income, far too much stress is laid on this psychological influence, if present income si brought into such prominence. It is, of course, all a matter of degree. My own feeling is that present income has a predominant effect in determining liquidity preference and saving which it does not possess in its influence over the "inducement to invest". (CWJMK), Vol. 14, pp. 80-81)

Keynes's reply, while correct, does nothing to anchor his discussion to the technical analysis underlying it. The "My own feeling..." part of Keynes's reply could have led Hicks to conclude, wrongly, that Keynes had no formal model in the GT supporting his conclusions and that those conclusions were completely "intuitive" in nature. This is confirmed in the 9 April, 1937 letter of Hicks:

"Thank you very much for your letter about my *Econometrica* paper (which will be appearing in the April number). I had hardly hoped that you would be so much in agreement with it; but I am delighted to find that you are". (CWJMK, p.81)

Hicks now provides Keynes with overwhelming evidence that he does not fully understand the technical analysis underlying the theory of Effective Demand:

"Your other points I agree with mostly; except that I remain impenitent about including income in the marginal efficiency of capital equation. Of course I agree that it is expected income that logically matter; but the influence of current events on expectations (admittedly a loose and unreliable connection) seems to me potentially so important, that I feel much happier if it is put in and marked unreliable, than if it is merely talked about, and not impressed on the reader's mind by being put into the formula, which he will take down in his notes". (CWJMK, p. 82)

and

"over a short period (short enough to neglect interest charges) a person's receipts minus expenditure must equal net lending plus increment in demand for money. (I mean this as no more than a reflection of the two-sidedness of transactions.) It is thus an identity, and it remains an identity when it is aggregated for all persons and firms. Consequently, if we are seeking to determine (a) price, supposed for simplicity to move together, (b) the rate of interest, we have three demand and supply equations to determine them (those for 'goods and services', loans, money) one of which follows from the other two. Thus two of the equations, as you would say, are operative equations; one is a check equation, and distribute the operative equations among prices and interest as we choose. Thus there are six possible alternative 'theories'; but if they are correctly stated, they all mean the same thing, and are all equally right.

I. Prices determined by effective demand and supply for goods and services; interest by the demand for money; saving and investment a check equation.

II. Prices determined by the quantity of money; interest by saving and investment; effective demand the check equation.

And so on; of course I don't deny that some of these theories would be easier to state accurately than others". (CWJMK, p. 82)

Keynes, in this letter of 11 April 1937, finally tells Hicks, in the weakest[1] way possible, that he does not understand Keynes's theory of expectations, Effective Demand, liquidity preference, or marginal efficiency of capital.

"I do not really understand how you mean interest to be determined by saving and investment under II, near the bottom of your second page... I am there accusing you of agreeing with the Swedes in this matter. If this is a calumny, and your theory is really quite different, forgive me". (CWJMK, p. 83)

What could Keynes have said here to get Hick's attention? How about this: "I. Is a general theory applicable to all situations. II. Is a special theory which only holds on the boundary of the PPF when $e_0=e_0=0$". They" all mean the same thing, and are all equally right" only if $e_0 = e_0 = 0$.

The conclusion this author reaches is that Keynes, in his lifetime, made no technical defense of the formal analysis underlying his GT. What Keynes did was to defend the new ideas of effective demand, liquidity preference, and marginal efficiency of capital. These intuitive defenses had no impact and led to multiple, widespread misinterpretations of the GT, which continue to this very day. However, Keynes's approach is what one could have predicted, given his extremely poor *technical* defences of both the *Treatise on Probability* and *Treatise on Money*.

---

[1] Keynes took exactly the same correspondence approach with Harrod as he took with Hicks. Harrod writes on 24 August, 1936

The enclosed is what I propose to say about you to the Econometricians on Sept. 25. I should be very glad to hear if you think are any misrepresentations". (CWJMK, p. 83)

## Keynes responded to 30 August, 1936:

"I like your paper (may I keep the copy you sent me?) more than I can say. I have found it instructive and illuminating, and I really have no criticisms. I think that you have re-orientated the argument beautifully. I also agree with your hints at the end about future dynamic theory."(CWJMK, p. 84)

## But

"2. You don't mentioned *effective* demand or, more precisely, the demand schedule for output as a whole, except in so far as it is implicit in the multiplier". (CWJMK, Vol. 14, p.85)

## and

"3. You do not show how in conditions of full employment, which I should now like to define as the limiting case in the supply of output schedule ceases to be elastic, my theory merges in the orthodox theory". (CWJMK, Vol. 14, p.86)

Keynes needs to add, "Here is how I did it. The neoclassical theory holds when $D = Z = Y$ at $e_0 = e_0 = 0$. This requires that MPC +MPI= I. My theory includes this has a special case and covers all other possibilities, i.e., $Y < D = Z$ at $e_0$ or $e_0 > 0$. You only obtain *relative* maxima and not the *global* maxima of the neoclassical special case".

Harrod's response of 3 September, 1936 is the same as Hicks':

"I am delighted that you approve of the form into which I have case your theories". (CWJMK, Vol. 14, p.86)

## RFERENCES

Keynes, J.M., 1973, The Collected Writings of John Maynard Keynes (CWJMK), Vol. 13 and 14, London; Macmillan.

CHAPTER - 17

# SIR JOHN HICKS'S CONTRIBUTION IN THE FIELD OF INCOME DISTRIBUTION, PROFIT DETERMINATION AND DIFFERENTIATED BEHAVIOUR OF ECONOMIC CLASSES

## Mauro Baranzini

### ABSTRACT

In this paper we try to assess the relevance of Sir John Hicks's contribution in the field of income distribution and profit determination, with particular reference to the controversy that raged between the two Cambridges (UK vs. Mass. USA) in the Sixties, with Joan Robinson, Nicholas Kaldor and Luigi Pasinetti on one side, and James Meade, Franco Modigliani and Paul Samuelson on the other. We show that Hicks's work on *Capital and Growth* (published in 1965) opened up new ways of looking at the whole issue, in particular by introducing the hypothesis of a differentiated interest rate, or rate of growth of capital stock. Hicks's theory, moreover, provides a general background against which the issue of overlapping generations may be suitably viewed. In sum, Hicks's contribution has pioneered numerous new lines of research in theoretical economics decades before these were pursued.

## I. INTRODUCTION

When, at the beginning of Michaelmas Term 1971, I arrived in Oxford as a Lord Florey Graduate Student of The Queen's College (unaware that I would end up spending the next fifteen years there), I was surprised by the relatively little regard paid to Sir John Hicks's work in most of Oxford's official circles. One might say that, on the whole, during the long and prolific period which followed his retirement in 1965, Sir John was held in much higher esteem by foreign scholars and students visiting Oxford. Even the award of the Nobel Prize in 1972 did little to re-establish his prominence among Oxford economists, who were being chosen for high-ranking appointments at a relatively young age and on the basis of an often limited number of highly mathematical papers in equally technical economic journals. Alas, the time of *system builders* (the phrase was coined by Geoffrey Harcourt, 1997, p. 1572) was drawing to an end. As Sir John once wrote:

> During the years since 1965, while I have been writing my later books, I have been a retired professor; but I have been allowed to continue to work at Oxford, at All Souls College. Though I have useful discussions with colleagues at Oxford, I have not been a member of a group, as I was in early days at LSE. Those who have worked closest with me have been visitors to Oxford, and post-graduate students, who themselves come and go. For though in Oxford our first degree students are mainly British, most of our post-graduate students come from abroad. When they have done their two or three years, they go back to places, often very distant places, from which they have come. Such contact as one can then maintain with them must be largely by correspondence – unless one can go and see them at their homes or places of work. I have indeed done a good deal of that. It has so happened that a considerable number of economics post-graduates, and of other economists who have visited Oxford, have come from Italy. And it is not so far from England to Italy as it is to places further afield. I have explained the importance of my knowledge of Italian (which is still, I fear, little more than a reading knowledge) in the beginnings of my economics. It has been a great thing for me that I have again been able to use it in the contacts with Italian economists which I have been able to develop during the last twenty years. We [Hicks means his wife Ursula and himself] now feel that a year which does not contain a visit to Italy is a year in which there is something missing. (Hicks, 1983, pp. 363–4)

Nevertheless, Sir John ran an important seminar at All Souls, during which he would expound various parts of his latest work, which reached a *crescendo* during his retirement period – his *Risorgimento* as he once put it (Hicks, p. 362). It is interesting to note how from the age of sixty – he retired at the age at 61 with the intention of devoting all his time to research, a decision he sometimes regretted because in those days pensions were not index-linked – he advanced in his vast research programme, or indeed in his *system building* (as Geoffrey Harcourt would call it):

> The first thing I had to do, in resuming my former work, was to bring myself up-to-date with what others had being doing, and I knew that I could not understand what others had been doing unless I could restate it in my own terms. I did two exercises of that kind, which took a great deal of time. But I do not feel that these things are fully my own work; they are just 'translations'. Nevertheless,

with these behind me, I could go on. I could start to build on the work I had done in the Thirties, but I could do so in my own way. I could take those parts of Keynes's system which I wanted, and could reject those which I did not want. I then found myself led, only incidentally to formal models, but chiefly to new analytical concepts, which may have some power to improve understanding of what has happened in the world, and what is happening.

Since in those days my own field of interest was economic growth, I was attracted, long before coming to Oxford, by his *Capital and Growth*, first published in 1965. It may be of some importance to recall what Sir John wrote in the Preface to this work:

> Though I have been influenced, in many ways, by the 'growth models' that swarm in economic literature, I have allowed myself to make less reference to the work of contemporaries than the reader may well feel that he would have preferred. The field is vast; and I am well aware that my knowledge of it is only a sample. Now, as I write this Preface, but after the body of the book has gone to the printer, there comes into my hand the 'Survey' by Hahn and Matthews (Economic Journal, December, 1964). If I had had this earlier (but it would have to have been much earlier) I might have made an attempt to give further references. As it is, I must leave the reader – with their help – to fill the gap for himself.

This attitude was typical of Sir John, since he always wrote his contributions to economic analysis with absolute independence of what was being published in the field of economics. Such an independence of mind is one of the reasons why his analysis is particularly path-breaking, for he never allowed himself to be distracted by futile controversies or dead-end research lines. In this paper I would like to consider a number of ways in which this proved to be true.

### II. THE HARROD-DOMAR 'KNIFE-EDGE' AND THE POSSIBLE SOLUTIONS OF THE 'DILEMMA'

One first important point concerns the way in which a system may remain in a situation of steady-state, i.e. where all variables grow at the same rate and where relationships between economic variables do not change; which will not, for example, require a change in the institutional set-up, or even better where the institutional set-up does not require a modification of the relationships between the economic variables. It is undoubtedly a very interesting illustration of the process of economic growth, which allows for a thorough analysis of the way in which economic growth may take place in a neutral way. As it has been pointed out many times (see, for instance, Pasinetti, 1974, Ch. VI; and Hahn and Matthews, 1964) the Harrod-Domar equilibrium condition is

$$g(w) = s/v \qquad\qquad (1)$$

where $s$ is the aggregate saving ratio of the system, $g(w)$ the warranted rate of growth of the system (which may additionally include 'labour saving' technical progress) and $v$ is the capital/output ratio. If these three variables are all constant, then it is unlikely that such condition may be satisfied. Hence, in order to have a model in which the possibility of steady growth is assured, it is necessary to relax one or more of the assumptions. This can be obtained by assuming:

1. Flexibility of $v$, the capital/output ratio (also referred to as the technology assumption);
2. Flexibility of $s$ (saving assumption);
3. Flexibility of $g(w)$ (labour-market and/or labour-supply assumption).

The above cases may, of course, be combined in various ways as, for instance, in Samuelson and Modigliani's (1966a, b) model, where 1 and 2 apply simultaneously. Solution 1 was adopted by the neo-classical or marginalist school:

> Instead of there being fixed coefficients in production, there may exist a production function offering a continuum of alternative techniques, each involving different capital-labour ratios;...The consequence is that the capital-output ratio $v$ is adjustable, instead of being fixed, and this provides a way in which $s/v$ and $n$ [the rate of growth of the system] may be brought into equality (Hahn and Matthews, 1964, p. 785)

But of course this solution of the Harrod-Domar dilemma was merely the beginning, for if, on the one hand, it was necessary to provide a device ensuring equilibrium growth, on the other hand, it was necessary to define income distribution exhaustively. Hence, in order to make income distribution determinate, several restrictive assumptions were added, so that in time neo-classical economists ended up with a model incorporating a "well-behaved" constant-returns-to-scale aggregate production function, perfect substitutability between labour and capital, profit-maximising behaviour, perfect competition in the labour and capital markets – all within a single-commodity framework. In this way, whenever Euler's Theorem applies, both shares are simultaneously determined, and no residual, by definition, can exist. However, as the Two-Cambridges (U.K. vs. Mass., USA) controversies on capital theory and on the re-switching of techniques has shown, 'lower interest rates may bring lower steady-state consumption and lower capital-output ratios, and the transition to such lower interest rates can involve denial of diminishing returns' (Samuelson, 1966a, p. 583). Such a statement from a leading representative of the marginalist school would seem to imply that the whole production-function approach is to be reconsidered with great care.

### III. THE SECOND ANSWER TO THE HARROD-DOMAR DILEMMA, I.E. THE ASSUMPTION OF FLEXIBLE AGGREGATE SAVING RATIO

The second answer to the Harrod-Domar dilemma, i. e. the assumption of a flexible aggregate saving ratio was primarily adopted by the neo-Keynesian or Cambridge School of economic analysis. Of course, there are many ways in which one may lend flexibility to the average propensity to save $(s)$ ; but the hypothesis of a two-class society (namely wage-earners and profits-earners; or consumers and entrepreneurs, or workers and capitalists – each with different constant average and marginal propensities to save) has played the greatest role. In this way there always exists a distribution of income between the two classes, which produces precisely that saving ratio that will equal the value $n(K/Y)$ – where $n$ is the rate of growth and $K/Y$ is the capital/output ratio – , thus satisfying the Harrod-Domar equilibrium condition.

The reasons for this approach may be found in the following considerations that have emerged with the elaboration of successive 'generations' of post-Keynesian models of profit determination and income distribution:

1. The assumption of a uniform rate of saving for the whole economic system ignores all possible differences in saving- and consumption-behaviour among different classes of income recipients, or categories of income, or even different sectors of the economy.
2. The problem of savings aggregation might give rise to particular and unknown difficulties, so that it may be safer to consider it in a disaggregated way, as the post-Keynesian model precisely does.
3. Thirdly, this assumption also receives empirical support from the observed high rates of saving out of corporate profits and lower rates out of labour income. See, for instance, Burmeister and Taubman (1969), Kaldor (1966), and Murfin (1980); on this point see also Baranzini (1991, p. 50, footnote 3).

220

4. The nature itself of the savings differs from class to class (see, for instance, Horioka and Watanabe, 1997). Kregel (1973, ch. 11) justifies the distinction not so much on grounds of class position, as on grounds of different forms of income; for instance between 'quasi-contractual incomes' (e.g. wages, fixed interest, and rent) and 'residual incomes' (e.g. corporate profits). It is worth noting that for Kaldor (1961, pp. 194–5) residual incomes are much more uncertain than contractual incomes, and they are subject to fluctuations.

5. Finally, it may be argued (as Kaldor, 1961, p. 194–5 has done) that the need to generate internal funding in order to carry out active investment requires a high propensity to save out of profits. This requirement will be even stronger in a life-cycle model on a steady-state growth path, where the capitalists' saving ratio has to allow for (a) life-cycle wealth accumulation and (b) gradual accumulation of inter-generational assets in order to let the capitalists' wealth stock grow at the same rate as that of the population.

On this point Sir John initially states that:

> The simplest thing which has gone wrong is that we have carried the assumption of saving proportional to total income over from the Harrod-type theory (where it belongs) to the present theory, where it is much less at home. As soon as we make a distinction between factor shares (as in the Harrod-type theory we did not have to do), the question must arise: will not the saving-income proportion be affected by income distribution? (Hicks, 1965, p. 145)

At this point Sir John reflects upon two kinds of savings differentiation to be found in the literature:

> It may be affected in a 'classical' manner – that a lower rate of profit makes people less willing to save; in a Growth Equilibrium (which is quite different from Keynes's theory) that is by no means to be ruled out. But it is quite sufficient (as Kaldor has taught us) to introduce a *direct* effect of income distribution on saving. We may call it 'a different propensity to save out of profits and out of wages'; or, since we do not have to go into detail about who does the saving, we may simply make saving proportional to some weighted average of profits and wages, not simply to their sum.

And indeed flexibility in the propensity to save may be conceived in several different ways, as illustrated in Baranzini (1990a). We may note that, in more general terms, certain groups of people or consumers' units, share a common behaviour, such as a high propensity to consume and a low propensity to save; or a high propensity to endow their children with human capital and/or financial assets; or a high propensity to reinvest in the productive process; or again, in the case of pensioners, a very low income with a fairly high propensity to consume. There are, however, various parameters by which classes may be identified, aiming in particular at socio-economic phenomena. Among these we may consider:

1. different endowments (human and physical capital in particular);
2. different sources of income, or predominance of a given type of income (from labour, capital, land, etc.);
3. different propensities to consume and to save (average and/or marginal);
4. the predominance of 'life-cycle' or 'inter-generational' capital stock owned, which may be associated with different age-groups or indeed with other ways of considering different socio-economic behaviour;
5. different propensities to leave a bequest to the next generation (under the form of human capital or education, physical or financial capital, and/or social contacts);
6. different bargaining positions, which may lead to different economic rewards, e.g. income and/or wealth. This aspect is also related to the existence of residuals in certain functional theories of income distribution, where factors are not paid according to, say, their marginal productivity, but according to their particular role in the productive process.

Sir John picks up Nicholar Kaldor's proposition (1956, 1957) as an extreme case, and states that:

> The extreme case of Kaldor's assumption would make saving proportional to profits only. [It has been maintained by L. Pasinetti that this is the only assumption that we are entitled to make in a growth equilibrium model. If the model is considered as a long-period distribution theory there is much to be said for this view. But it does not seem to me that this is the only way of regarding it; it is not the aspect with which I am here principally concerned.] This is a very convenient assumption, which simplifies things considerably, so that – purely in order to exhibit the properties of the model – it is one that I shall largely use. (Hicks, 1965, p. 146)

It is important to stress that Sir John retains the 'Kaldorian' saving function as the more interesting one, since he indirectly confirms the approach of the classical and post-Keynesian economists, according to whom the distribution of income between factors of production depends uniquely on the capitalist's propensity to save and not on that of the other groups. (However, distribution of income, as well as wealth, among classes will be a function of all parameters of the model, including the propensities to save and to consume.) It is worth noting that the classical economists had also postulated a very high propensity to save on the part of the capitalist or entrepreneurial class, and a zero propensity to save on the part of the workers' classes. As a matter of fact, the latter had a wage-rate equal to the 'natural wage-rate', the rate for which, according to Pasinetti, 'besides allowing workers to live, induces them to perpetuate themselves "without either increase or diminution"'.

Hicks goes on to specify that by using Kaldor's saving assumption:

> I do not mean to imply that 'saving out of wages' is practically unimportant. But the complications which it introduces are not matters of principle; they obscure our vision if we insist on taking them into account all the time. If we make saving a fixed proportion s(1) of *profits*, the saving equation is much simplified. For we then have (...) so that [where r stands for 'profits rate']
>
> $$g = s(1)r$$
>
> a relation that is becoming well known. (Hicks, 1965, p. 146)

It is at this point that Sir John develops the rest of the model that he had formulated earlier on. Let us follow the development of his argument:

> The whole structure of the model is then vastly simplified. For many purposes there are just two equations that we have to hang on to – this *saving equation* and the *wage equation*, which (if we now allow ourselves to take the consumption good - corn - as our standard of value) may be written
>
> $$1/w = b + (rab)/(1 - ra)$$
>
> (We still need other equations for particular purposes, but the general working of the system emerges sufficiently from these two equations alone.)
> If the real wage (w) is given, the rate of profit is determined from the wage equation, and the rate of growth is then determined from the saving equation. The higher the real wage, the lower the rate of profit, and the lower (therefore) the rate of growth.

This result may be compared with the outcome of the Sraffian and the general post-Keynesian model. While in Sraffa's model the distribution of income is determined (and this is just one possibility, as Sraffa points out) by the exogenously given rate of interest (determined by the monetary policy of the Central Bank), in the Kaldor-Pasinetti's model the share of wages in national income is the residual and equal to $W/Y = 1-(P/Y) = 1 - (P/K).(K/Y) = 1 - (1/s(c)).(K/Y)$. The latter result means that the share of wages in national income is negatively associated with the share of profits as well as with the capital/output ratio. In other words, all other things being equal, the higher the level of the system's capitalisation, the lower the equilibrium of the share of wages in the economic system. Again there exists an inverse relationship between the share of wages in national income and the equilibrium rate of profits of the system. Moreover, since in post-Keynesian models postulating a class of 'pure' capitalists (whose income is derived mainly from assets or capital) the profit rate is equal to $1/s(c)$, it is clear that the share of wages in national income is positively associated with the capitalist class's propensity to save. Alternatively, this means that an increase in the entrepreneurial class's propensity to consume reflects itself positively on the share of profits in national income. (This reminds us of Kalecki's statement according to which capitalists earn what they consume.)

But let us follow Hicks's argument further:

> If it is the rate of growth that is given, the same two equations work the other way round. The rate of profit (which is consistent with this rate of growth) is then determined by the savings equation, and the rate of real wage from the wage equation. The lower the rate of growth, the lower the rate of profit, and the higher the real wage. (Hicks, 1965, p. 146–7)

It is interesting to note that the causality chain may be reversed in the following way. Consider, for instance, the Cambridge equation $P/K = n/s(c)$; which may be rewritten as $n = (P/K)s(c)$. Suppose now that the rate of profits is a direct result, for instance, of the system's need to generate a given amount of profits or of the monetary policy of the Central Bank. In this case, the equilibrium rate of growth of the system may be determined by the rate of profits multiplied by the propensity to save of the capitalist class. Both parameters have a positive effect on the equilibrium rate of growth, which may include technical progress and the growth rate of the system's labour force. This is mainly due to the fact that once either wages or profits is given, the second becomes a residual. It is also true that one of the main purposes of this kind of analysis is to define the kind of income distribution between wages and profits, or indeed among socio-economic classes, which guarantees that ex-post savings are equal to ex-ante full-employment investment (as it is determined by the entrepreneur). For this reason it is more logical to take $n$ and $s(c)$ as given, and to consider the rate of profits as well as the share of wages in national income as endogenous variable.

But let us see how Sir John brings his analysis to a close:

> The rate of growth is always less than the rate of profit (with $s(1)$ smaller than unity). The lowest growth that is consistent with equilibrium depends on the lowest profit that is acceptable; if the profit rate can fall to zero, the growth rate can fall to zero. The maximum possible growth rate is $s(1)x$ [multiplied by] the maximum possible profit rate; this, as we have seen, is limited by the technique and the limit (which must be presumed to exist) below which wages cannot fall. To compare these limits with the $g(1)$ and $g(2)$ at which we arrived under the other assumption about saving it is not very meaningful; but there should certainly be more room, under the new assumption, at the lower end – and it is possible to argue, in a similar way, that there should be more room at the upper end (of the range of growth rates) also.

Hence Hicks considers the possibility of a differentiated rate of growth of the system, i.e. of a rate of growth of the consumption sector and of the capital sector. If we suppose that capitalists consume an irrelevant fraction of their total capital income and that workers have a much higher propensity to consume than the other classes, then this different propensity to grow may be transferred from the productive sector to the socio-economic classes, characterised by different behaviour. Alternatively, one may posit that the same rate of growth may be obtained by assuming a different rate of interest or profits for the two classes. (This may be inferred from the relation $g = s(1)r$ obtained by Hicks above, which is the so-called Cambridge equation.) More generally, the distinction by classes may be rather wider than originally thought; and some reasons for their distinction, which may apply to various aspects of their economic behaviour, have already been considered above. However, the hypothesis according to which classes can be differentiated on the basis of their behaviour or of the way in which they confront economic rules is quite revealing. This is due to the fact that on the one hand, a steady-state model (like this one) requires that all variables grow at the same rate; while on the other hand the presence of different classes may explain different economic parameters.

### IV. THE HYPOTHESIS OF A DIFFERENTIATED INTEREST RATE EARNED BY CLASSES ON THEIR SAVINGS

But what are the reasons for justifying a different rate of return on investment for the two classes? Several reasons may be put forward in support of a differentiated interest rate in a two- o multi-class model.

Property rights are fundamental determinants of distribution in post-Keynesian, as well as classical and neo-Ricardian, theories where the production process implicitly or explicitly requires some form of co-operation from individuals empowered to 'withdraw' (or at least 'condition') certain essential inputs. As in most classical theories, social classes remain crucial for post-Keynesian theories, and their distinctive feature is given by saving-, consumption-, and investment-behaviour. In more sophisticated theories (such as Pasinetti's as well as Baranzini's, 1991) the assumption of 'separate appropriation' of each production factor is no longer as drastic as in other models, although it hovers in the background, even if the income – or indeed wealth – of certain classes is made up by different types of income or, respectively, by accumulated wealth. For instance, in Pasinetti's (1962, 74, 89, and so on) models, workers' income is made up of wages and interests on accumulated savings. As a matter of fact interest on accumulated savings may be linked only indirectly to the profit rate, as in the case of deposit and savings accounts which have a predetermined rate of interest (which is not necessarily linked to the overall rate of profits of the economy). Of course, in a general sense in post-Keynesian theories different rates of saving are associated with different economic and social classes. And the distribution of savings among classes will be such as to yield an overall saving equal to the desired level of full employment. In this way, a differentiated interest rate may further redistribute income among the classes of the system: for this reason its analysis represents a key element in the determination of the overall equilibrium interest rate.

Considering specific points we might say that:

1. First, historically and in most developed as well as underdeveloped countries, the interest rate has been considerably lower than the average profit rate, except for some periods characterised by recession or high inflation. In general a ratio of 2:3 is more likely to reflect the world's realities than a ratio of 1:1. This observation implies one of two things: either the economy is not on an equilibrium growth path and there is no evident hope of ever achieving such a path, or it becomes necessary to incorporate a different hypothesis into the model. Such a hypothesis will have to take into account the observed difference between the rate of interest on normal life-cycle savings and the overall profit rate.

2. Secondly, one might argue that the act of saving and the act of investing are two distinct operations. They refer, in fact, to two distinct acts of appropriation: one is closely connected with the wage-rate and only indirectly with the average profit rate of the economy; the latter, on the contrary, is more directly connected with capital and its profit rate. One might also say that saving is essentially passive, while investment is active. Not surprisingly, a higher remuneration is normally attached to (active) investment.

3. Thirdly, a different way of looking at the same phenomenon is to postulate that there is a risk factor associated with the act of investing. This risk should be reflected in the differential between rate of interest on risk-free savings and overall profit rate.

4. Finally, it may be said that to be profitable investment must be larger than a certain minimum. The wage earners, taken individually, may not be able to exploit the profit opportunities of large investments. Accordingly, their saving is likely to carry a smaller reward. This, of course, does not mean that we would have to introduce the argument of increasing returns to scale on savings. One may simply maintain that the interest rate is not necessarily identical to the profit rate. It should however be stressed that in this context by interest rate we mean the rate at which the workers place their savings in the hand of the entrepreneurial class (or in the hands of the state in a socialist country).

These points were originally expounded in Balestra and Baranzini (1971, pp. 242–4), where the hypothesis of a differentiated interest rate was for the first time explicitly considered. Hence the hypothesis of a different rate of return on capital for the study of the stead-state growth of the system, and as it may be inferred from Sir John Hicks's analysis appears quite interesting indeed.

### V. THE GENERALISATION OF THE CLASS DIFFERENCES IN A STEADY-STATE GROWTH MODEL À LA HICKS AND À LA CAMBRIDGE SCHOOL

The above argument relating to a different rate of capital growth of the two classes, or relating to a different rate of return on their savings, may indeed open up new horizons in the field of steady-state growth analysis. In particular, the idea of a different endowment of classes may be put forward: the entrepreneurial class which owns mainly inter-generational (as well as human capital) capital, and the workers' class which owns mainly life-cycle savings (as well as human capital). Alternatively, we might consider the case in which both classes own inter-generational capital, but are characterised by a different propensity to endow the next generation. This is not a completely new assumption. We know, in fact, that the entrepreneurial class has a higher propensity to save than the other classes (in particular the workers). We know, on the other hand, that one of the motives behind the savings is to endow the next generation with a physical or financial capital stock. (cf. Horioka and Watanabe, 1997). Hence a higher propensity to save will almost inevitably imply a higher willingness to transmit physical or financial capital to the next generation.

The point about these various working hypotheses is that in a steady-state situation the capital stock of all classes present in the system must grow at the same overall rate. Secondly, the assumption of a long-term horizon may be associated with the presence in the model of different generations, either overlapping or clearly separated from one another. Sir John has never been explicit on this point, though in many of his works the indirect reference to various generations is obvious.

A model of wealth distribution and accumulation has been considered in Baranzini (1991a, chapters 5–7), which includes all the elements quoted above. The results obtained are interesting since, within an original framework, the micro-economic pure exchange model (or utility-maximisation model, also following Hicks, 1965, ch. 21) is in turn encompassed by the post-Keynesian framework to define a more flexible approach to income and wealth distribution. An analysis of this kind elicits two main conclusions:

1. In a life-cycle model where the transmission of inter-generational financial assets is a prerogative of the entrepreneurial class, the equilibrium rate of interest depends on the behavioural parameters of the capitalist class; it doesn't depend on those of other classes or of technology. The fact that the equilibrium rate of interest is independent of technological factors (i.e. of the capital/output ratio) is particularly relevant, and seems to reinforce the solution which was put forward by the Cambridge School and by Sir John Hicks.

2. When both classes are allowed to pass on inter-generational assets (excluding education) to their children, then, in order to have a steady-state path, capitalists must have a much stronger will to be-

queath capital to their children than the other classes. It is only in such a situation that all classes will hold a positive share of the total capital stock. The results obtained lead us to ask the following question: 'Can this analytical result be reconciled with economic reality and common sense?' To a certain extent the answer is positive, since (a) the workers' class, by definition, derives a high proportion of its income from human capital stock, so that it may be inclined to discount its inter-generational bequest at a rate lower than the average (on this point see Flemming, 1969); and (b) it is not unrealistic to posit a situation where, in general, low-income families give higher priority to life-cycle consumption and consequently a lower one to the inter-generational capital stock. On the other hand, those classes that derive a high proportion of their income from inter-generational wealth (and the remaining part from life-cycle savings) in a long-term perspective are bound to give weight to the accumulation of such wealth, by discounting it at a rate higher than average. This different approach to the inter-generational bequest notwithstanding, as we have shown in this chapter, there exists a real possibility of a balanced growth of the system, where each class maintains a constant relative economic strength and a constant share of the capital stock. Clearly, the system may well leave such a path: this would happen if the capitalists were to show a too low propensity to pass on bequests to their children, thereby diminishing their strength; similarly a much stronger desire on the part of the workers to transmit inter-generational wealth would eventually achieve the same result.

## VI. THE GENESIS OF SOCIO-ECONOMIC CLASSES

The arguments developed above lead us to another important issue which is to be found in the background of long-run analysis, i.e. that of the formation, persistence, and dispersion of socio-economic classes at large. This issue is present in most of Sir John Hicks's works on economic growth, especially in his *Capital and Growth,* but which hasn't so far been taken up by the vast literature in this field. There exist a number of elements that are continuously at work in the determination of the progressive concentration or dispersion of wealth, which is at the very basis of the strength of a socio-economic class in the long run.

Various factors account for the dispersion of wealth. Some of them tend to level off life-cycle savings; while others may reduce the relevance of inter-generational assets in total wealth. Their impact on the formation or dispersion of classes is however the same, and may even be hard to identify once the process has been set in motion. Among these factors we may quote: (1) the fiscal policies of redistribution; (2) a drop in the value of holdings; (3) gradual using up of savings; (4) transfers in the donor's lifetime; and (5) dispersion at death. Among the factors contributing to the process of wealth concentration, we might mention instead: (1) a differentiated propensity to save, according to the level of income; (2) different age-cohorts, which account for a different values of life-cycle savings; (3) a higher return for large capital stocks; (4) a low number of children inheriting the inter-generational capital stock; (5) an unequal distribution of bequests and (6) selective mating which tends to concentrate more and more wealth in the hands of a given socio-economic class.

Let us here dwell on a final point, concerning fiscal policies of redistribution (see, for a recent development in this area, Teixeira, Suguhara, and Baranzini, 1998). This is an instrument of economic policy whose role has become increasingly used in recent decades. Atkinson and Stiglitz (1980, p. 63) indicate a variety of taxes on capital and/or return on capital which may be considered in this framework: (a) taxes on interest income, either at the same rate as other income - like labour – or at a differential rate (for instance the U.K. investment income surcharge); (b) taxes on (short-term or long-term) capital gains; (c) wealth taxes on the net value of assets owned (with special provisions that reduce the effective rate – like special treatment of housing, or life insurance and pensions, as well as certain tax-exempt bonds); and (d) special taxes, for example those on houses, land, etc. The latter are labelled as 'property taxes' in the US, 'rates' and later 'council tax' in the U.K., and 'tassa sulla casa' in Italy. In certain cases the policies on redistribution and/or taxation have been successful in stopping or slowing down the progressive concentration of wealth. Such was the explicit goal of the Labour Manifesto drafted in the U.K. in the late Sixties and early Seventies. As a matter of fact it was aimed at limiting at about half a million pounds the personal wealth which may be inherited or accumulated in other ways by a single individual.

Many economists have given particular attention to the relevance of all direct and indirect taxes on the process of wealth accumulation, and their conclusions have often been ambiguous. Nonetheless it seems clear that wealth taxes and estate duties have led to a lower concentration of wealth than one would otherwise have expected.

We may say that the conditions in which a class is born, consolidates itself or even vanishes (the latter is the case of 'below-the-average' fertility or 'low propensity to endow the next generation), are multiple, and can only be studied in the framework of a fairly complicated model. The traverse successfully studied by Sir John Hicks is surely a good starting point; however more work is needed in this direction. The recent works in the field of institutional change and structural analysis may also be of help in framing the whole issue.

## VII. CONCLUSION

In this paper we have focused on Sir John Hicks's contribution in the field of income distribution, profit determination, and class differentiation. This contribution must also been judged against all of his work. A number of analytical results obtained in Hicks's *Capital and Growth* confirm the validity of his approach, which was developed more or less at the same time as that of the neo-classical economists, James E. Meade, Paul A. Samuelson, Franco Modigliani, or that of the post-Keynesians, Nicholas Kaldor, Joan V. Robinson, and Luigi L. Pasinetti. But a number of implications drawn from other parts of Hicks's volume on capital and growth may be inferred from, and successfully integrated into, steady-state growth theory. For instance, the hypothesis of a differentiated rate of growth of the capital stock of the two classes is particularly appealing in this context, or indeed other forms of differentiation between classes. This might sound strongly anti-neoclassical; but this is also one of the reasons why Hicks's analysis may be considered anti-conventional, hence 'original' and stimulating. There is a lot to learn, a lot to be gained by re-reading Hicks, especially in connection with issues of long-term non-proportional growth. This is in fact a particularly demanding field of enquiry, but one which facilitates the analysis of trends, which in turn makes it possible to verify the conditions necessary for the creation or disappearance of nuclei of economic groups.

# REFERENCE

Ando, A. and Modigliani, F. (1963) 'The Life-Cycle Hypothesis of Saving: Aggregate Implications and Tests', *American Economic Review*, pp. 55–84.

Arestis, P. and Skouras, T. (eds) *Post-Keynesian Economic Theory*, Wheatsheaf Books, Brighton; M. E. Sharpe, Inc., Armonk, New York.

Atkinson, A. B. (1975) *The Economics of Inequality*, Oxford University Press, Oxford.

Atkinson, A. B. and Harrison, A. J. (1978) *Distribution of Personal Wealth in Britain*, Cambridge University Press, Cambridge.

Atsumi, H. (1960) 'Mr Kaldor's Theory of Income Distribution', *The Review of Economic Studies*, pp. 109–18.

Balestra, P. and Baranzini, M. (1971) 'Some Optimal Aspects in A Two-Class Growth Model with a Differentiated Interest Rate', *Kyklos*, 33, pp. 240–56.

Baranzini, M. (1975) 'The Pasinetti and Anti-Pasinetti Theorems', *Oxford Economic Papers*, 27, pp. 470–3.

Baranzini, M. (ed.) (1982) *Advances in Economic Theory*, Basil Blackwell, Oxford and New York.

Baranzini, M. (1991a) *A Theory of Wealth Distribution and Accumulation*, Clarendon Press, Oxford.

Baranzini, M. (1991b) 'The Pasinetti and Anti-Pasinetti Theorems: A Reply to K. Miyazaki and P. A. Samuelson', *Oxford Economic Papers*, 43, pp. 195–8.

Baranzini, M. (1995) 'Distribution, Accumulation and Institutions', in A. Heertje (ed.) *The Makers of Modern Economics*, Vol. II, Edward Elgar, Aldershot (U.K.) and Brookfield, Vermont.

Baranzini, M. and Scazzieri, R. (eds) (1986) *Foundations of Economics: Structures of Inquiry and Economic Theory*, Basil Blackwell, Oxford and New York.

Baranzini, M. and Scazzieri, R. (eds) 1990) *The Economic Theory of Structure and Change*, Cambridge University Press, Cambridge.

Bliss, C. J. (1975) *Capital Theory and the Distribution of Income*, North-Holland, Amsterdam and Oxford.

Bortis, H. (1976) 'On the Determination of the Level of Employment in a Growing Economy', *Revue Suisse d'Economie Politique et de Statistique*', pp. 67–93.

Bortis, H. (1978) 'Die "Renaissance" klassischer Ideen in der theoretischen Volkswirtschaftslehre', in P. Caroni, B. Dafflon, and G. Enderle (eds), *Nur Oekonomie ist keine Oekonomie*, Paul Haupt, Berne and Stuttgart, pp. 49–78.

Bortis, H. (1982) 'Dr. Wood on Profits and Growth: A Note', in M. Baranzini (ed.) (1982), *op. cit.*, pp. 262–70.

Bortis, H. (1984) 'Employment in A Capitalist Economy', *The Journal of Post-Keynesian Economics*, pp. 590–604.

Bortis, H. (1990) 'Structure and Change Within the Circular Theory of Production', in M. Baranzini and R. Scazzieri (eds), *op. cit.*, pp. 64–92.

Bortis, H. (1997) *Institutions, Behaviour and Economic Theory (A Contribution to Classical/Keynesian Political Economy)*, Cambridge University Press, Cambridge.

Britto, R. (1973) 'Some Recent Developments in the Theory of Economic Growth: An Interpretation', *The Journal of Economic Literature*, pp. 1343–66.

232

Buiter, W. H. (1997) 'Generational Accounts, Aggregate Saving and Intergenerational Distribution', *Economica*, 64, pp. 605–26.

Burmeister, E., and Taubmann, T. (1969) 'Labour and Non-Labour Income Saving Propensities', *Canadian Journal of Economics*, pp. 78–89.

Craven, J. (1979) *The Distribution of the Product*, Allen & Unwin, London.

Flemming, J. S. (1969) 'The Utility of Wealth and Utility of Windfalls', *The Review of Economic Studies*, pp. 55–66.

Flemming, J. S. (1971) 'Portfolio Choice and Taxation in Continuous Time', mimeo, Nuffield College, Oxford.

Flemming, J. S. (1974) 'Portfolio Choice and Liquidity Preference; A Continuous-Time Treatment', in H. Johnson and A. Nobay (eds) *Issues in Monetary Economics*, Oxford University Press, Oxford, pp. 137–50.

Hahn, F. H. and Matthews, R. C. O. (1964) 'The Theory of Economic Growth: A Survey', *The Economic Journal*, 74, pp. 779–902.

Hamouda, O. F. and Harcourt, G. C. (1984) 'On the Notion of Short-Run and Long-Run: Marshall, Ricardo

Hamouda, O. F. and Harcourt, G. C. (1988) 'Post Keynesianism: From Criticism to Coherence?', *Bulletin of Economic Research*, pp. 1–33.

Harcourt, G. C. (1969) 'Some Cambridge Controversies in the Theory of Capital', *Journal of Economic Literature*, pp. 369–405.

Harcourt, G. C. (1972) *Some Cambridge Controversies in the Theory of Capital*, Cambridge University Press, Cambridge.

Harcourt, G. C. (1973) 'The Rate of Profits in Equilibrium Models: A Review Article', *Journal of Political Economy*, pp. 1261–77.

Harcourt, G. C. (1976) 'The Cambridge Controversies: Old Ways and New Horizons – or Dead End?', *Oxford Economic Papers*, pp. 25–65.

Harcourt, G. C. (1977) *The Microeconomic Foundations of Macroeconomics*, Macmillan, London.

Harcourt, G. C. and Laing, N. F. (eds) (1971) *Capital and Growth: Selected Readings*, Penguin, Harmondsworth.

Harcourt, G. C. (1997) Review of L. L. Pasinetti and R. M. Solow (eds), *Economic Growth and the Structure of Long-Term Development: Proceedings of the IEA Conference held in Varenna, Italy, The Economic Journal*, 107, pp. 1572–5.

Harris, D. J. (1978) *Capital Accumulation and Income Distribution*, Stanford University Press, Stanford; Routledge & Kegan Paul, London.

Harrod, R. F. (1936) *The Trade Cycle: An Essay*, Clarendon Press, Oxford.

Harrod, R. F. (1939) 'An Essay in Dynamic Theory', *The Economic Journal*, 49, pp. 14–33.

Harrod, R. F. (1048) *Towards a Dynamic Economics*, Macmillan, London.

Hicks, J. (1932) *The Theory of Wages*, Macmillan, London.

Hicks, J. (1939) *Value and Capital. An Inquiry into Some Fundamental Principles of Economic Theory*, Clarendon Press, Oxford.

Hicks, J. (1965) *Capital and Growth*, Oxford University Press, Oxford.

Hicks, J. (1970) 'A Neo-Austrian Growth Theory', *The Economic Journal*, 80, pp. 257–81.

Hicks, J. (1969) *A Theory of Economic History*, Clarendon Press, Oxford.

Hicks, J. (1973) *Capital and Time. A Neo-Austrian Theory*, Clarendon Press, Oxford.

Hicks, J. (1974) *The Crisis in Keynesian Economics,* Basil Blackwell, Oxford.

Hicks, J. (1975) 'The Scope and Status of Welfare Economics', *Oxford Economic Papers,* 27, pp. 307–26.

Hicks, J. (1976) '"Revolutions" in Economics', in *Method and Appraisal in Economics,* ed. S. J. Latsis, Cambridge University Press, Cambridge, pp. 207–18.

Hicks, J. (1977) *Economic Perspectives,* Clarendon Press, Oxford.

Hicks, J. (1979) *Causality in Economics,* Basil Blackwell, Oxford.

Hicks, J. (1983) *Classics and Moderns; Collected Essays on Economic Theory,* Vol. III, Ch. 31, *The Formation of an Economist,* Basil Blackwell, Oxford and New York, pp. 355–64.

Hicks, J. (1985) *Methods of Dynamic Economics,* Oxford University Press, Oxford.

Hicks, J. (1986) 'Is Economics a Science?' in M. Baranzini and R. Scazzieri (eds) *Foundations of Economics: Structures of Inquiry and Economic Theory,* Basil Blackwell, Oxford and New York, pp. 91–101.

Hicks, J. (1988) 'Introductory Remarks', given at the International Economic Association Conference *'Value and Capital Fifty Years Later',* mimeo, University of Bologna.

Kahn, R. F. (1959) 'Exercises in the Analysis of Growth', *Oxford Economic Papers,* pp. 143–56.

Kahn, R. F. (1972) 'Selected Essays on Employment and Growth', Cambridge University Press, Cambridge.

Kahn, R.F. (1984) *The Making of Keynes' General Theory,* Cambridge University Press, Cambridge.

Kaldor, N. (1956) 'Alternative Theories of Distribution', *The Review of Economic Studies,* pp. 83–100.

Kaldor, N. (1957) 'A Model of Economic Growth', *The Economic Journal,* 67, pp. 591–624.

Kaldor, N. (1961) 'Capital Accumulation and Economic Growth', in F. A. Lutz and D. C. Hague (eds), *The Theory of Capital,* Macmillan, London, pp. 177–222.

Kaldor, N. (1966) 'Marginal Productivity and the Macro-Economic Theories of Distribution', *Review of Economic Studies,* pp. 309–19.

Kaldor, N. and Mirrlees, J. A. (1962) 'A New Model of Economic Growth', *The Review of Economic Studies,* pp. 174–92.

Kessler D. and Masson, A. (eds) (1988) *Modelling the Accumulation and Distribution of Wealth,* Clarendon Press, Oxford.

Kessler, D. and Masson, A. (1988) 'Introduction', in D. Kessler and A. Masson (eds), op. cit., pp. 1–18.

Kotlikoff, L. J. and Summers, L. H. (1988) 'The Contribution of Intergenerational Transfers to Total Wealth: A Reply', in D. Kessler and A. Masson (eds), op. cit., pp. 53–67.

Kregel, J. A. (1973) *The Reconstruction of Political Economy: An Introduction to Post-Keynesian Economics,* Macmillan, London.

Meade, J. E. (1963) 'The Rate of Profits in a Growing Economy', *The Economic Journal,* 73, pp. 665–74.

Meade, J. E. (1964) *Efficiency, Equality and the Ownership of Property,* Allen & Unwin, London, p. 239.

234

Modigliani, F. (1988) 'Measuring the Contribution of Intergenerational Transfers to Total Wealth: Conceptual Issues and Empirical Findings', in D. Kessler and A. Masson (eds), op. cit., pp. 21–52.

Murfin, A. J. (1980) 'Saving Propensities from Wage and Non-Wage Income', *Warwick Economic Research Papers*, No. 174, Dept. of Economics, University of Warwick, Coventry.

Pasinetti, L. L. (1962) 'The Rate of Profit and Income Distribution in Relation to the Rate of Economic Growth', *The Review of Economic Studies*, pp. 267–79.

Pasinetti, L. L. (1974) *Growth and Income Distribution. Essays in Economic Theory*, Cambridge University Press, Cambridge.

Pasinetti, L. L. (1993) *Structural Economic Dynamics. A Theory of the Economic Consequences of Human Learning*, Cambridge University Press, Cambridge.

Robinson, J. V. (1956) *The Accumulation of Capital*, Macmillan, London.

Robinson, J. V. (1962) *Essays in the Theory of Economic Growth*, Macmillan, London.

Robinson, J. V. (1966) 'Comment on Samuelson and Modigliani', *The Review of Economic Studies*, pp. 307–8.

Samuelson, P. A. (1966a) 'A Summing Up', *Quarterly Journal of Economics*, pp. 568–83.

Samuelson, P. A. and Modigliani, F. (1966b) 'The Pasinetti Paradox in Neo-Classical and More General Models', *The Review of Economic Studies*, pp. 269–301.

Samuelson, P. A. and Modigliani, F. (1966c) 'Reply to Pasinetti and Robinson', *The Review of Economic Studies*, pp. 321–30.

Scazzieri. R. (1993a) *A Theory of Production (Tasks, Processes and Technical Practices)*, Clarendon Press, Oxford; Oxford University Press, New York.

Scazzieri, R. (1993b) 'Actions, Processes and Economic Theory', in A. Heertje (ed.), *The Makers of Modern Economics*, Vol. I, Harvester Wheatsheaf, London and New York.

Scott, M. F. (1989) *A New View of Economic Growth*, Oxford University Press, Oxford and New York.

Teixeira, J. R. (1991) 'The Kaldor-Pasinetti Process Reconsidered', *Metroeconomica*, 42(3), pp. 257–67.

Teixeira, J. R. and J. T. Araùjo (1991) 'A Note on Dalziel's Model of Long-Run Distributive Equilibrium', *Journal of Post-Keynesian Economics*, 14(1), pp. 117–20.

Teixeira, J. R., Suguhara, R. N., and Baranzini, M. (1998) 'The Micro-Foundations of the Kaldor-Pasinetti Growth Model With Taxation on Intergenerational Bequest', mimeo, University of Lugano.

Vaughan, R. (1988) 'Distributional Aspects of the Life-Cycle Theory of Saving', in D.Kessler and A. Masson (eds), op. cit., pp. 193–235.

Walsh, V. and Gram, H. (1980), *Classical and Neoclassical Theories of General Equilibrium*, Oxford University Press, Oxford and New York.

Wolff, E. N. (1988) 'Life-Cycle Savings and the Individual Distribution of Wealth by Class', in D. Kessler and A. Masson (eds), op. cit., pp. 261–80.

# CHAPTER - 18

# THE BIRTH OF KARL POPPER'S OPEN SOCIETY: A PERSONAL REMINISCENCE

## Colin Simkin

### ABSTRACT

The author, a friend of Karl Popper as well as of John Hicks, offers insights into the genesis of The Open Society with which he was associated in its first three years' of writing. In 1937, Popper, a 35-year old Austraian School teacher, took up an appointment as lecturer in philosophy at Canterbury University College in New Zealand, which I joined in 1939. He spent eight years there during which he wrote two major books, *The Poverty of Historicism* and *The Open Society* and Its Enemies. Both were written under severe difficulties in regard to time, resources and teaching conditions. The Poverty began as a considerable revision and extension of an address given to Hayek's seminar at the London School of Economics, and The *Open Society* began as marginal notes on the history of historicism. But it developed into a much larger book which Popper regarded as his war work, constituting a strong condemnation of all forms of totalitarianism and giving strong justifications for tolerant and open minded democracy. The difficulties in writing these great works were followed by difficulties in finding publishers for them. But eventually Hayek had The *Poverty* published as three articles in *Economica*, and helped in getting Routledge to publish the two-volume *Open Society*. He was so impressed by both works that put Popper's name forward for a vacant Readership in Logic and Scientific Method at the LSE, an appointment which Popper took up in 1945. When he arrived there, Popper soon found that he had been lifted from relative obscurity in a small university, remote from Europe, to considerable fame in a leading intellectual centre, a fame which increased with further important publications and numerous honorific awards.

## 1. INTRODUCTION

In my previous paper, I expressed my great indebtedness to John Hicks, but also acknowledged a similar indebtedness to Karl Popper; both were my mentors and friends. To my regret, I do not thing they ever met, partly because Hicks was based in Oxford and Popper in Penn then Kenley and, after he took up residence in Penn, Popper seldom moved from it except to do one day a week's work at the LSE or to pay visits to other countries. Those who wishes to see him in England had to visit him at Penn or Kenley.

Their views on methodology were incompatiable. Popper was a famous specialist in scientific method, holding to a basic thesis, formulated in the 1930s, that scientific theories were bold conjectures about factual relations, not logically derivable from factual observation but could be falsified by such observation. Hicks did not become seriously interested in scientific method until the 1974, when he attended a conference on the micro-foundations of macro-economics, and then moved to a position that was the opposite of Popper's. He did write that 'theory gives no right to pronounce on practical problems unless one has been through the labour, so often the formidable labour, of mastering the relevant facts'. But as Marc Blaug[1] correctly wrote in a caustic critique of Hicks' views, as expressed in *Causality in Economics* (1979) and in his essay, A Discipline not a Science, Hicks 'decisively parted company with all varieties of empiricism, Popperianis,, falsifiability, or call it what you will, in economics'[2]. And, Blaug concluded, 'it is impossible to extract any coherent methodology of economics from the writings of Hicks'[3].

Both men wrote very famous books, Hicks *Value and Capital*[4], a major contribution to economics, and Popper *The Open Society*, a major contribution to political thought which still commands wide attention.[5] I had nothing to do with the writing of *Value and Capital*, but something to do with the writing of *The Open Society*, and devote this essay to some account of its genesis.

---

[1] Chapter 7 in *The Popperian Legacy in Economics*, edited by Neil de Marhi, Cambridge University Press, 1988.

[2] Op. Cit. P. 183.

[3] Idem. P. 194.

[4] He wrote much later: 'they gave me a Nobel Prize for my work on "general equilibrium and welfare economics"... work which has become part of the standard literature. But it was done a long time ago, and it is with mixed feelings that I find myself honoured for that work, which I myself felt myself to have outgrown'. *Economic Perspectives*, 1977, p.v. Oxford University Press, 1977.

[5] It has done that recently because of the impressive efforts of George Soros, a former pupil and leading financier, to spread its message through the foundation of the Central European University and in other ways, such as financing the publication of *The Open Society* in Russia and other former communist countries.

The Birth of Karl Popper's Open Society: a Personal Reminiscence
Two remarkable things about The Open Society are that this great work of scholarship was produced under very unfavourable circumstances for research, and that there was considerable difficulty in getting it published.

In 1937 Dr Karl Popper, a 35-year old Austrian refugee, joined the small Department that taught Philosophy and Psychology in Canterbury University College, Christchurch, a constituent college of the then federal University of New Zealand. He was given a heavy teaching burden as the only philosopher, and it was made more onerous by continual harassment from the psychologist who was Head of the Department. For economic reasons Popper also undertook some teaching for the local Workers' Educational Association, and he was in demand for addresses to student and other societies. Much of his teaching was evening work in the days when the constituent colleges catered largely for part-time students. There was, of course, nothing in the way of research grants for staff who were not natural scientists, and very little for those who were. Nor did he have any secretarial assistance from the College; the typing of his many drafts and letters was all done by his exceptionally cooperating wife, Hennie. The Head of his Department even went so far as to make him buy paper used for non-teaching purposes. There was no effective authority to whom appeal could be made; the governing body of Canterbury University College (as I was myself warned soon after taking up an appointment there) seemed to regard time spent on research as time filched from the primary job of teaching.[1] It was not until Popper left New Zealand, and partly through his efforts[2], that its universities recognized research as a normal facet of their teachers' work.

Popper was also handicapped by a paucity of both library resources[3] and intellectual contacts. He had been unable to bring more than a few of his own books to New Zealand, and the College library was very small, particularly deficient in non-English books (beyond literary works for the language departments)[4]. The few other professional philosophers were all in distant colleges, the nearest and most valuable being John Findlay, then a professor in Dunedin, 200 miles away, with whom he developed a warm friendship. He also corresponded with Henry Forder, the Professor of Mathematics in far away Auckland, who was interested in modern logic. But he quickly attracted the friendship of some of Canterbury's natural scientists[5] and that meant much to him as he tells in Unended Quest, his intellectual autobiography.

They could not, of course, help him with political philosophy, and there were then no departments of politics in the University of New Zealand. He had come to Christchurch with the material of an address which he gave, in 1936, to Hayek's seminar at the London School of Economics, and which was to become his *Poverty of Historicism*. Soon after arrival he began to shape this material into an article, and discussed it with Harold Larsen, a temporary lecturer in the Department of Economics, but Larsen left for London late in 1938.

Early in the following year I came to Christchurch as the only lecturer in economics, and very soon was visited by Karl Popper who charmingly introduced himself and asked for help such as Larsen had given him. As he put it, his English was bad and he was ignorant of the social sciences, so that he needed help from someone like me. I felt confident about assisting him with the English language, but less confident that a 24-year old lecturer of quite limited experience could render the same service with the social sciences.

As it quickly turned out, my confidence in regard to English was misplaced. Karl's command of the language was, naturally, then imperfect so that my pencil made many rapid changes to what he put before me. But, as he also tells in Unended Quest his first book (*Die beiden Grundprobleme der Erkenntnistheorie*) had been most critically read by Robert Lammer who had insisted that everything be made crystal clear, a lesson which Karl took permanently to heart and which he applied to my corrections. I had to justify all of them and was often in difficulty when confronted by Fowler's Modern English Usage, which was then Karl's main recreational reading - along with stories about Dr Dolittle6. I had also, of course, like almost everyone else beyond Vienna's philosophical circles, no initial understanding of the methodological ideas which Karl had recently published in *Der Logik der Forschung* and which he was now trying to apply to social science.

I had unwittingly begun an informal post-graduate course in which, besides arguing with him about English, I learnt something about epistemology, natural science, probability and mathematics in return for a little help in regard to economics. More than that, our close friendship led to discussions over a wide range of subjects, with wonderful insights into the political conditions and intellectual life of postwar Austria and its neighbours. In his inimitable way, he stimulated my mind and widened its horizon. I have always been most grateful to him for that, and also for much personal kindness.

Work on the Poverty article was soon upset by the outbreak of war. I remember our sense of despair for Europe when listening together to a BBC report of Paul Reynaud's final appeal to the United States as France was succumbing to Hitler's guns, tanks and planes. Karl had already told me that he felt the still far from completed article was too abstract for wide appreciation, and that he would embark on a companion article to be called 'Marginal Notes on the History of Historicism'. He now regarded both these articles as his war work, and four years of most intense labour went into writing them. But much higher priority was given to the second which became *The Open Society* and *Its Enemies* although this title was not adopted until shortly before publication.

Karl increased not only his own research effort but also his demands on my own time, somewhat to the resentment of the girl I had married within three months of my appointment to Canterbury University College, although our two wives also became warm friends. He now, however, had help from Henry Broadhead, the scholarly lecturer in Classics, with that half of the book which is devoted to Plato and in which authoritative translations and interpretations of this revered philosopher are sharply challenged. Apart from linguistic help, and giving Karl opportunity (which he always needed) to clarify his ideas by talking about them, my own contribution was mainly to the chapters on Marx. Like Karl, I had delved into Marxist literature during radical student days, and he seized upon my copy of Emile Burns's *Handbook of Marxism*. Our collaboration ceased in May 1942 when I entered the Royal New Zealand Air Force and was soon posted overseas. But it was not long before Margaret Dalziel, a new lecturer in English, came to help him put both The Open Society and The Poverty of Historicism into final shape.

I returned to Christchurch in May 1944 to spend there what were to be my last fifteen months in the RNZAF and so resumed personal contact with Karl, although necessarily a much more limited one than before. He told me that both *The Poverty* and *The Open Society* had been accepted for publication, but only after a most frustrating period. Mind, the leading journal of philosophy in Britain, had rejected the *Poverty* as being insufficiently philosophical. This had grown so long that, when eventually accepted by Economica, it had to be published as three articles. *The Open Society* had been sent to a friend in the United States in the hope of arranging quick publication in a country which was much less affected by wartime shortages of paper than was Britain. His friend consulted other friends, and they felt so dubious about the book that they asked a well-known scholar for an evaluation. It was so unfavourable that they did not submit the book to a publisher. Karl was very upset; all this had cost him months of delay in finding a publisher, and unfavourable opinions are discouraging. He fully realized that, over and above wartime difficulties in publishing books, his own risked rejection because of its severe criticisms of Plato, Hegel, Marx, historicism, socialism and much of sociology, - all more influential then than they have now become.

But the clouds of despair began to break when, by chance, he was given the address of a family friend, Ernst Gombrich, the art historian, who was then working for the BBC in Reading. Gombrich had responded at once to Karl's appeal for help in finding a publisher for *The Open Society*, although it took many more months before one was found. In April 1943, Karl had sent Gombrich a list of possible publishers, in order of preference, together with many suggestion about how they should be approached. At the same time he had written to both Hayek and Susan Stebbing, asking them to assist Gombrich in this task, and soon after wrote in a similar vein to Herman Levy; he had met all three during the time he spent in England before going to New Zealand. Towards the end of this year he also sent to Hayek the three parts of the *Poverty*, asking for help in getting them published also. Hayek was greatly impressed by both the book and the articles, so much so that, as Karl told me in confidence, Hayek had raised the possibility of Karl coming to the LSE as a Reader.

By this time he had become so dissatisfied with his own academic conditions in Christchurch that he was anxious to escape from them; a return to the intellectual life of Europe, a congenial institution, and a much better salary were very inviting[7]. But he realized that Hayek's prospect was quite uncertain and would, in any case, involve considerable delay. He also felt that his chances would be much improved if he could add the book and the articles to his list of publications, and that made him desperate to have them published as soon as possible.

Before long Hayek expressed willingness to publish the articles in *Economica*, which he then edited, provided that they could be somewhat reduced. It was not until a full year after my return to Christchurch that Karl had the satisfaction of seeing the first of them published, after a good deal of further work in satisfying Hayek's reasonable requirements and in making his own improvements. Meanwhile the joint efforts of Gombrich and Hayek to find a publisher for The Open Society were not succeeding. Cambridge University Press had turned it down, and unsuccessful approaches were then made consecutively to other English publishers. Early in 1944 Hayek tried Routledge where Herbert Reade found the book very impressive and sent a contract to Karl in May[8].

That was an enormous relief, but Karl now began to send many corrections and additions for the ever patient Gombrich to make in the text, and to urge Reade that the book be published quickly. Gombrich also had a good deal to do in regard to Karl's application for the LSE Readership which had now been advertised.

The strain of all this, on top of a heavy teaching load and continued harassment, had undermined his health. He was doing with very little sleep as he spent most of his nights getting the last part of the Poverty and some of The Open Society into final shape. His blood pressure became very low, so that his doctor put him on to a variety of tablets and injections. On medical advice he also took two short holidays in the Southern Alps towards the end of 1944, and felt better for them. The improvement, however, was temporary as before long he was suffering from a burnt back, toothache, colds and sore throats. Nevertheless he went, at the invitation of John Eccles, the physiologist, to give most successful lectures on scientific methodology at the Otago Medical School, and was urged to apply for the Chair of Philosophy which his friend Findlay was vacating in order to return to South Africa. It was not unattractive to him, and he might have gone to Otago but for a cable from Hayek telling of his appointment to the LSE, a post which he definitely preferred. (He had already declined an invitation from the University of Sydney owing to some fuss about the appointment of an enemy alien.)

After signing his contract with the LSE, in May 1945, Karl set about what proved to be a tiresome business of getting exit permits and nationalization from New Zealand, entry permits into England, and shipping passages. It was not until late November that he and Hennie sailed from Auckland. I saw them just before they left as I had come to be interviewed for the local Chair of Economics[9] and recall that Karl was taking, for reading on the voyage, The Theory of Games and Economic Behaviour which had just appeared from the pens of von Neumann and Morgenstern. Such was his idea of relaxation.

Within a few months of their arrival in London the final article of the *Poverty* appeared in *Economica* and the *Open Society* came into the bookshops. After eight years of comparative obscurity in a small and distant university college, Karl became almost immediately famous in a great intellectual centre, where he stayed for the rest of his salaried career.

Hayek's *The Road to Serfdom* had appeared a little earlier than The Open Society, and both attracted wide attention for their complementary and striking exposures of the intellectual roots of totalitarianism and the dangers of its various manifestations. Some attention was also given to Karl's methodological ideas as explained in the Poverty articles, but it was not until another fifteen years that they became fully available to English readers with the publication of *The Logic of Scientific Discovery*, the translation and extension of his 1934 *Logik der Forschung*.

It and the Postscript, completed in 1956 but not published until it appeared in 1982-1983 as three volumes edited by William Bartley - *Realism and the Aim of Science, Quantum Theory and the Schism in Physics*, and *The Open Universe* -, are Karl's towering intellectual achievements, although he has since written much else of prime interest, more especially in connection with his important ideas of 'evolutionary epistemology' and a 'propensity theory' of probabilities. But, after leaving New Zealand, he wrote little about the problems of the social sciences, and although some of his terms came to be widely used by economic theorists, they seldom interpreted them properly or realized their import. Nor did the Logic have a better reception from philosophers, especially in English speaking countries, mainly perhaps because of their absorptions with various forms of logical positivism, linguistic analysis, Marxism or, more vulgarly, with trendy social issues.

Karl's main influence has been on natural scientists and on thinking People outside universities, especially in Continental Europe. The Royal Society has elected him to a fellowship, and similar honours have come from foreign academies of science. His books have sold widely, and gone through many editions and translations. He has, moreover, received two royal honours, many honorary doctorates and three other prestigious international awards[10]. No other philosopher, living or dead, has had so much public recognition yet such professional neglect. The Open Society is the most popular of all his books; up to 1984 it has gone through five editions, and the last edition through six reprints. In 1989 a sixth edition appeared. Philosophers themselves have praised it highly, - Russell, Ryle and Berlin among them. The reason for its success may well be that it gives much more than a thorough exposure of the fallacies of historicism and collectivism - it gives the soundest case for a liberalism that is suffused with both rational and humane values. But it should be read together with the Poverty because, as this account shows, in spite of the Poverty's less lively style and narrower range, both are aspects of the same analysis.

That, too, is the case with the Logic and its Postscript. In this sense, Karl has written only two books, both master works, as the others[11] can be regarded as collections of important essays. For all of them, the main assistance Karl had was given by his remarkable wife, and especially during the difficult times for the first three - the *Logik, The Open Society,* and *The Poverty.* Times so difficult, and the tasks so great, that I regard these books as a triumph of spirit as well as a triumph of mind.

## NOTES

1    It was predominantly a lay body and although there was a kindly and scholarly Rector, James Hight, who was sympathetic to Popper, there was also a powerful Registrar, who had little personal contact with the academics and much influence with the Council.

2    The official history states: 'Popper's most significant   achievement at the College was to force the research door open. ... the movement he fathered was to become an irresistible force in the postwar years'. W.J. Gardner, E.T. Beardsley and T.E. Carter, *History of the University of Canterbury,* pp 264-65.

3    He was also handicapped by poor accommodation as his 'study' was a small room in a ramshackle wooden building above a carpenter's shop where a buzz-saw was often in operation.

4    In 1934 the College library had only 15,000 books and a budget of ú340. As a further indication of the very limited resources of university libraries in New Zealand at this time I may mention that, when I became Head of the Department of Economics at Auckland University College in 1946, my allocation for books was a mere ú25 a year.

5    The main ones were Hugh Parton, a physical chemist, Robin Allen, a geologist and next-door neighbour, Frederick White, a physicist, and George Roth, a radiologist.    They all became enthusiastic converts to his views about the methodology of the natural sciences, which he expounded in a number of voluntary addresses.    Parton and Allen, in particular, joined him in a fight to have the local universities recognize the place of research.

6    Karl had a strong sympathy with children and liked good stories for them. I don't think he missed seeing, during his time in Christchurch, any talkie of Deanna Durbin, an appealing child star who appeared in singing roles.

7    In spite of personal austerity the Popper's had difficulty in keeping their expenditure within their income. They had a heavy mortgage, Karl had taken out an expensive insurance policy in order to protect Hennie in the event of his death, and he contributed something towards the care of an ill sister by the Swiss Red Cross.

8    Karl and Hennie celebrated this good news by going to a local beach and indulging themselves with ice creams. He has a very sweet tooth, evidenced also by his liking for chocolate, upon which he often lunched. Sometimes he came to our nearby flat between afternoon and evening lectures, refusing offers of food beyond chocolate or other cake.

9    I got it largely because Karl had represented my merits to his influential friend Forder, who persuaded those responsible for making the appointment to take me seriously.

10    The Danish Sonning Prize, the Alexis de Tocqueville Prize, the Catalan Prize and the Kyoto Prize to mention only some of the sixteen honours, awards and medals that were conferred on him..

11    Except for *The Self and Its Brain*, a joint work with John Eccles.

# CHAPTER - 19

# MR. HICKS AND THE CLASSICS

*Michel Rossier*

## ABSTRACT

In this article, "The Unification of Macro-Economics", Hicks established a very tight link between Keynes and the Pre-Classics, Smith being the last man of this group. Keynes and Smith would have the same "method", which does not make of the prices-mechanism the corner-stone of all economic problems. Both would also build macro-models of the same nature, in which the economy is viewed as a set of monetary aggregates, and in which the multiplier plays a central part. At first sight, Hicks' parallel is a bit puzzling for two reasons at least. First, Smith is commonly considered as the founder of the classical school, more economics, because he would have been the first to focuse on the prices-mechanism. Second, Smith is generally regarded as a radical critic of mercantilists, while Keynes defended them. Nevertheless, Hicks' ideas are very suggestive and can be developed in many directions.

## 1. INTRODUCTION

In his last article, entitled "The Unification of Macroeconomics", and submitted to *The Economic Journal* just before his death, Hicks seems to burn what he has previously cherished, namely the neoclassical synthesis between Keynes and Walras (Hicks, 1990). He defends the Keynesian approach against the neoclassical universalism. He states that the era during which the neoclassical method rises and consolidates its position is a kind of parenthesis which opens after Smith and closes just before Keynes; and he says perhaps too rashly that this parenthesis was a *"Dark Age"* for macroeconomics (Hicks, 1990, p. 534).

In the first section, we shall expose the main features of the Hicksian synthesis of the Classics and Keynes, and indicate why it is different from the other attempts of the same nature. In the second section, we shall show what results from the Hicksian quest of a Classical multiplier. In the third section, we shall see how the Ricardian treatment of fixed capital may be viewed as embodying the premices of the continuation theory that Hicks was looking forward, in so far as it could be the unifying framework for Smith's and Keynes' macroeconomics.

### I. KEYNES' AND CLASSICS' PLUTOLOGY

Hicks sets a parallel between Smith and Keynes that must be surprising for most economists. They generally admit that everything opposes these two authors. The former is a liberal, who founded the real approach to fight the mercantilism; the latter is an interventionist, who revived the monetary approach of this ancient school. Much work has alrady be done to demonstrate that this dichotomy was mostly a caricature and that Smith's thought was indeed far more complex (Pack, 1991). But Hicks wants to go further than this. He tries to prove that the two authors deeply agree on a conceptual level.

Smith and Keynes would partake the same "method", which means in Hicks' language that their models would have the same analytical genes (Hicks, 1965, p. 28). They would belong to the same macroeconomic family, which is specified as follows: *"The methode is to take the table of social accounts as it is in a particular period (year), enquire into the propensities and policies (of the period) which have made it what it is, and ask how it would have been changed if these had been different"* (Hicks, 1990, p. 536). The macro family would contrast with the neoclassical one, whose basic principle is that the sole economic problem is the problem of price mechanism, in the sense that all other economic problems could be reduced to it (Hicks, 1990, p. 536).

To the members of this second family, Hicks declares *"to have some hard things to say"* (Hicks, 1990, p. 536). Their models would not be of no utility: they would be well adapted to micro questions. But they would not be convenient for dealing with macro ones (Hicks, 1990, p. 536). Hicks defines nowhere what he really means by micro and macro. Nevertheless, without bending to much his thought, one can identify micro to what he names *"catallatics"*, i.e. the science if exchange

(Hicks, 1976, p. 10), and macro to what he baptises *"plutology"* (Hicks, 1976, p. 13), i.e., the science of wealth. This latter science has for purpose to answer the following questions: *"what the social product of a nation is, what is meant by its being large or small; what is meant by its growing"* (Hicks, 1976, p. 7). Even when this science wonders about distribution, it is to know what its effects on the amount of wealth are. In brief, the macroeconomics is, in the first place, preoccupied by the level of activity.

This article is not so surprising, because one can find its main ideas in works dating from the very beginning of Hicks' carreer: the accounting as the mean of defining economic magnitudes, the relation between past and future as the core of the conception of the capital and of the period, the importance of the relationship between statics and dynamics...[1] Inventorying and analysing the occurences of these themes in Hicks' numerous books and articles would certainly lead to the conclusion that his very last paper is far to be the outgoing of a old man brain. But it is not such an explanation of Hicks' theoretical life coherency that we are going to dedicate ourselves here. Our starting point will be the parallel Smith-Keynes. In fact, once accepted that there are certain convergences between the two authors, one can detect or guess the existence of many others. But, before carrying on with this quest of analogies, it is necessary to map out and, in some cases, to solve out difficulties encountered by the Hicksian interpretation of the Classics.

The parallel between Smith and Keynes breaks apparently apart the Classical school. On one hand, it presents Smith as the achievement of an intellectual movement, beginning with the Mercantilists, involving Physiocracy, and finishing with *The Wealth of Nations*. On the other hand, it tends to sketch Ricardo[2] as a double faced character who stands with one foot in Smith's world and one foot in the Dark Age. But this is

---

[1] To be convinced that Hicks had continuously these themes in mind, one needs only to read the introduction to *The Social Framework* (Hicks, 1942), that he would have prefered to entitle *"The Social Accounts"* (Hicks, 1979, p. 360). In this work, he insists on the link that tights policy and political economy together (Hicks, 1942, p. 1). And he defines economics as the conjunction of a social accounting and a theory of value (Hicks, 1942, pp. 194–195). Here we must precise what sens Hicks gives to the expression "theory of value": *"It is of the first importance to emphasise that the primary purpose of that theory of value is not to explain prices, that is to say, to explain working of markets; its primary purpose is to identify the values which are needed for the weighting of the social product"* (Hicks, 1976, p. 8).

[2] Of whom Hicks says not much in his article.

too much at variance with what Hicks said in his previous works, where he maintained the unity of Classical school. All its members concentrated on the accumulation of capital, and thus on the tranferring of capital from a period to another; but, while Smith was more interested in its global quantitative aspects, Ricardo rather studied its qualitative aspects, related to the changing structure of capital.

The 1990 paper outlines a yet unknow portrait of the Classical synthesis. Indeed, Hicks reproduces some of the traditionnal arguments used by the neo-Ricardian school[3] to sustain the compatibility between Keynes and the Classics. Those arguments are of three kinds: 1) the treatment of time; 2) the structural decomposition of society into distinct groups of interest; 3) the search for causal relations, as opposed to simultanous solutions to a set of equations. The first point is the only one considered by Hicks, who insists that Keynes and the Classics have in common a notion of period in a strong sense, that is to say a way of identifying the present, in respect with a past and a future.

Beyond such methodological considerations, it is necessary to give the Classical synthesis an analytical content. At this point, difficulties are arising from at least three distinctions: 1) between the Classical theory of accumulation, in the long run, and the Keynesian theory of employment, built for the short run; 2) between the Keynesian thesis that macroeconomics has a distinctive task, that cannot be fulfilled by the theory of prices, consisting in dealing with the level of activity of the economic system as a whole, and the Classical view (more especially held by Ricardo and Mill) that this question doesn't claim a specific apparatus, but can be treated within value theory; 3) between the "realistic" approach (of the production) by the Classics, and the "nominalist" approach (or circulatory) advocated by Keynes. Hicks ignored this latter point, but, on the two formers, he offers an original contribution. As we shall see, its main interest is to make irrelevant the distinction between short and long run analyses for discussing the viability of a Classical synthesis, and so to go aside from the theoretical road on which one has been engaged since Harrod's pionneering work.

The question in debate here is to know whether it is sensible to study the long run evolution of the economy (its "trend") independantly of the short run adjustments, and whether the long period model thus obtained

---

[3]Presented in Arena (1982), Pasinetti (1972) or Robinson (1972).

includes or not some sorts of adjustment ignored by the short period analysis, and of higher quality. The long term, as an empirical reality, necessarily exists, but does it imply that long period analysis represents a specific scope for economic theory ?

Marshall and Ricardo clearly answered positively to both questions. So did post-war theorists of growth, either neo-Classical or Cambridgians. Pasinetti and the neo-Ricardian school stand firmly on this position too. The monetarist schools also adopt this view, as well as all theoricians of the monetary cycles' theory, from Wicksell to Fisher, Hayek included[4], whose conception of economic fluctuations rests upon a distinction between a short run (or temporary) monetary equilibrium and a "real" long run equilibrium. Keynes and Kalecki are undoubtedly those who most decidedly answered negatively.[5] Smith is not explicit on the matter, but seemingly stands on their side[6], as well as Walras does.[7] A third attitude is to leave no room for anything else than a long run equilibrium, corresponding to a situation of full coordination of plans, as it is the case with Arrow-Debreu's inter-temporal general equilibrium. Some authors have an incertain attitude, among them Hicks, as well as Marx[8] and Kaldor[9]. But his 1990 paper, along with his concept of temporary equilibrium[10] locate him very near of Keynes and Kalecki, as do a good part of his writings on growth (at least all he wrote on the "traverse").

---

[4]At least in *Prices and production* (1931). But the "old Hayek" (after 1941) clearly refuses the existence of any "final position of equilibrium" that could be deduced from any initial position, to put forward the notion of "tendency to equilibrium".

[5]According to Kalecki, "*in fact, the long run trend is but a slowly changing component of chain of short periods situations; it has no independant entity*" (1968, p. 165).

As regards Keynes, he asserts that his theory of interest remains "*substantially unchanged*" on the long run, and that the only thing that could justify to elaborate a distinct model of the "long period" would be the case in which we consider a static economy, which a constant state of expectations, where the notion of a "*final position of equilibrium*" could eventually make sense. See Keynes (1932; 1936b).

[6]See Rosier 1992.

[7]Some evidence is given in Tutin 1994.

[8]Who balanced between the "tendancial laws of motion of capitalism" and the reproduction analysis of how capital is renewed from period to period. Kalecki is a typical marxist of the "second type".

[9]Depending on which Kaldor we consider: the "Keynesian" Kaldor of instability, or the "Ricardian" Kaldor of the models of growth and distribution.

[10]Himself never tried to demonstrate any convergence of temporary equilibriums towards an Arrow-Debreu inter-temporal equilibrium.

## II. THE CLASSICAL MULTIPLIER

Three texts are milestones of the evolution of Hicks' attitude towards Smith. In Chapter IV of *Capital and Growth*[11], Smith's model is considered as static (Hicks, 1965, p. 42), and essentially anti-Keynesian (Hicks, 1965, p. 41). In Chapter II of Volume III of his *Collected Essays*, entitled "The Social Accounting of Classical Models", it is not static any longer (Hicks, 1983, p. 24), but it remains, nonetheless, anti-Keynesian (Hicks, 1983, p. 30). In the end, in the article "The Unification of Macroeconomics", Hicks thinks that this model is dynamic (Hicks, 1990, p. 532), and puts on Smith's shoulders the gawn of Keynes' great precursor (Hicks, 1990, p. 528).

In the text of 1965, Hicks aims at restoring what he names the *"primitive growth model"* which is contained by the Book II of *The Wealth of Nations* (Smith, 1776). The assumptions of this model are: 1) the whole capital is circulating, and entirely used to pay wages; 2) capital and product are entirely made of corn; 3) a period is the length of time which elapses between two crops, i.e. an agricultural year starting with the transferring of the previous crop, and ending a new crop; 4) the crop may be employed either to sustain agricultural workers or unproductive people.

With these assumptions, the model is summed up into the following formula:

$$X_t = (p_t/w_t)K_t = k_t(q_t/w_t)X_{t-1} \tag{1}$$

where $X_t$ is the volume of the crop, $k_t$ the proportion of productive uses, $q_t$ the productivity per head of agricultural workers, et $w_t$ the wages in corn given to a worker at period $t$.

This primitive model would be static, not in the sense that $q_t$, $k_t$ et $w_t$ are constant, but because these parameters depend exclusively on the

---

[11]It is his first book in which he has an analytical interest in classical economics, that will never cease afterwards. 1965 may thus be considered as the "frontier" between a (young) purely neo-classical Hicks, and a "late Hicks", who rediscovered classical economists at the same time he became more and more critical with the "neo-classical synthesis" to which he contributed 20 years before. This return to the Classics takes its roots in the defense of the "fundist" conception of capital, against the "realist" (or neo-classical) conception. See Hicks (1974).

circumstances of the period and not at all on those of past and future periods (Hicks, 1965, p. 42). This independance would be due to the fact that capital and product are formed of only one good (Hicks, 1965, p. 41). Thus, Hicks argues that, if Smith had admitted that the output of a period transferred to the next could have been composed of *"corn and chickens"*, then he would have been naturally lead to ask himself what could explain the structure of this output, and therefore to take into account the expectations made on the next period (Hicks, 1965, p. 40).

The homogeneity of product and capital would be also responsible for two big defects of Smith's primitive model. Fisrt, this assumption would be the cause of Smith ignoring the gap between savings and investment (Hicks, 1965, p. 41). Second, it would be also at the origin of the dichotomy (Hicks, 1965, p. 42). All that makes Smith appear as the anti-Keynesian *par excellence* in the text of 1965:

> "It is generally recognised (Keynes himself recognized) that in the age of Adam Smith there was an 'anti-Keynesian Revolution'; that it was this period that the 'Classical' doctrine of savings and investment (using 'Classical' in Keynes' sens) took shape. But it does not seem to be so generally appreciated that the main agent of the 'Revolution' was Adam Smith himself" (Hicks, 1965, p. 41)[12].

In the text of 1983, Smith becomes the last of a series of economists who have the same accounting approach: Petty, Cantillon, Quesnay. About Petty, Hicks contents himself to note that his *Political Arithmetic* marks the birth of this approach (Hicks, 1983, p. 17)

According to Hicks, Cantillon would have transformed Petty's ideas in a true analytical framework. The economy is divided into two sectors of activity: agriculture and town; each of those two employes labour, respectively $L$ et $L^*$; and each produces a single good, in particular the agriculture produces corn. The agents of this economy are three classes. Two are agricultural: the country men and the landlords. The last one is urban: the craftsmen. These three classes have the same type of consumption behaviour: they spend a constant proportion of their revenue in buying corn, respectively a, b and c.

---

[12]*"Keynes himself"*? In his "Notes on mercantilism", to which Hicks refers above, Keynes is much more cautious: *"Even Adam Smith was extremely moderate in his attitude to usury laws. For he was well aware that individual savings may be absorbed either by investments or by debts, in that there is no security that they will find an outlet in the former."* (Keynes, 1936, p. 352)

If w is the wages in corn and $q$ the productivity per head of the producers of corn, then total rent $(R)$ is equal to:

$$R = qL - wL$$

Agricultural revenue has therefore two components: wages and rents. In contrast, urban revenue is wholly formed of wages.

Thence, Hicks builds an accounting table which put together the basic relationships of Cantillon's model (Hicks, 1983, p. 20). And he derives an *"equation of consistency"* from the point of view of the agricultural sector:

Demand to agriculture= $awL + b(q - w)L + cwL*$
Revenue of agriculture= $wL + (q - w)L = qL$

or:

$$awL + b(q - w)L + cwL* = qL \qquad (2)$$

or else:

$$(1 - a)wL + (1 - b)(q - w)L = cwL* \qquad (3)$$

This last equation is regarded as expressing the equilibrium of town's balance of payments: the member on the right corresponding to town's importations of corn, and the one on the left to the amount of town's exportation, measured in corn.

Quesnay would have translated Cantillon's analytical framework in explicit accounting terms (Hicks, 1983, p. 21), and drawn a multiplier of the Keynesian type from the equation of the balance of payments (Hicks, 1983, p. 22). If one supposes that the demand for handicraft goods by the country classes increases, that is to say, that the amount of town's exportation rises, then the member on the right in equation (3) will also rise: $cwL*$. But, $c$ being less than one ($c < 1$), this implies that $wL*$ will grow still more. And, $w$ being constant because of labour supply elasticicity[13], the growth of town's revenu will pull up its employment level.

At this stage, Hicks wonders: *"Why did not this append with Adam Smith? We shall see"* (Hicks, 1983, p. 22). The reason Hicks invokes is the temporal structure of Smith's model. As his predecessors, he has two

---

[13]*"The reason why we must be at the level in normal conditions (...) is that the supply of common labour is perfectly elastic at that wage. Men multiply like mice in a barn if they have unlimited means of subsistence' as he [Cantillon] puts it himself"* (Hicks, 1983, p. 19).

sectors, the one productive and the other unproductive. But his productive sector is larger, since it covers all the agricultural and industrial activities, which take time and require some capital made of goods in process. On the contrary, the second sector gather service activities of which *"the labour perishes in the very instant of its performance'"*[14], and, in consequence, have no capital of goods in process (Hicks, 1983, p. 23). Thence, a period cannot be the time that elapses between two crops any longer (Hicks, 1983, p. 25).

Anyway, Hicks believes that there are two distinct models in Smith. The *"first model"* is still based on the agricultural period, and its formula is identical to the formula (1) of the primitive model of 1965. But, this time, Hicks derives it otherwise. He gets it from Cantillon's equation (2) by stating some simplifying assumptions[15] and by introducing time subscripts in order to distinguish the dates when the product is created and when it is used.

However, this first model would not be Smith's complete model. In the *"second model"*, the period is not the agricultural one, and what is conveyed from a period to another cannot be finished goods ready to consume. The transfer consists in goods in process which collaborate in a period to producing new goods consumed in the same period. So consumption goods are now produced and used in the same time (Hicks, 1983, p. 25).

Therefrom, Hicks proposes an accounting table which differs from Cantillon's one, since a portion of the revenu is now saved. This portion is associated with the increase of the stock of goods in process. The formula of the second model is:

$$K_{t+1} = K_t + q_t L_t - C_t \tag{4}$$

where $K_t$ is the stock of goods in process, $q_t L_t$ the production and $C_t$ the consumption of period $t$ (Hicks, 1983, p. 25).

Hicks underlines a difference between the first and the second models that Smith would have overlooked. In the first one, the whole product comes back into the hands of the producers of corn, so that the savers and the investors would be the very same persons. On the contrary, in the second one, it would not be the case any more. Part of the

---

[14]It is one of the three definitions of productive labour in *The Wealth of Nations*

[15]The consumption behaviours are supposed to be such that $a = 1$ and $b = 0$ (Hicks, 1983, p. 24).

savings could be held by the productive labourers and the unproductive people. The problem of transmission of savings to capitalists is then raised. Smith would not have seen this problem because he "*was not of 'normal' importance*" in his time (Hicks, 1983, p. 27).

It is this so-called distinct feature of the first model, wrongly applied to the second one, which would essentially oppose Smith to Keynes. In fact, Hicks is totally mistaken. First, the question of savings transmission may already be formulated in the first model. It is true that the price of the whole product falls into the producers' purses, but this price is used, for instance, to pay rents to the landlords who may save a part of them. Second, it is absolutely false that Smith never worried about savings transmission; he made it the central matter of Chapter IV of Book II of *The Wealth of Nations*[16].

In the conclusion of his text of 1983, Hicks enounces what is, according to him, the real demarcation line: on one side, Cantillon and the Physiocrats; on the other, Smith and Ricardo. The same demarcation line would have divided political economy in the thirties: Keynes playing Cantillon's and Quesnay's role; Hayek playing Smith's role. In this sketch, Keynes is obviously the goody and Hayek the bady. Yet, under their own mask, the one has some shortcomings and the other some virtues. Keynes, after Cantillon and Quesnay, would have neglected the temporal nature of production: inputs come before outputs. That is why the "*Smith-Hayek*" objection to the multiplier theory is meaningfull: the consumption goods necessary to increase the number of workers with constant real wages cannot be produced by the new workers. Such an increase needs beforehand "*an increase of the wage-fund*" (Hicks, 1983, p. 30).

In the text of 1990, Hicks gives quite an other image of Smith. He becomes the most eminent predecessor of Keynes (Hicks, 1990, p. 528). Hicks does not think any more of him as the problematic ending of a line Petty-Cantillon-Quesnay, but rather as its achievement. Concerning the three first authors, Hicks repeats almost word for word what he wrote in 1983. But, concerning Smith, he adds important points. Some of them get him closer to Keynes, some other seems apparently to push him away from Keynes.

---

[16]See note 12 above.

As to the accounting period, Hicks explains that Smith conceived it as having a past and a future, because the phenomenons he tried to elucidate belong to growth theory (Hicks, 1990, p. 532). From this statement, which sounds a bit queer when recalling what Hicks said in his 1965 paper, he concludes straightway that Smith agrees with Keynes on the conception of the period (Hicks, 1990, p. 532). No sign here of the themes that before seperate the two authors; no sign of the structure of capital and of the expectations as in the text of 1965; no sign of transmission of savings as in the text of 1983.

Hicks emphasises a quite different topic: its length. For Keynes, it must be sufficiently long so that certains decisions can developp all their consequences (Hicks, 1990, p. 532). No doubt, the decisions and the consequences, which are here at stake, are related to the process of multiplication. In contrast, Smith would have an infinitesimal period, because he defines unproductive labour as any labour whose output perishes at the very moment it is created (Hicks, 1990, p. 532). In reality, this infinitesimal period is a mere illusion generated by a pure rhetoric trick, i.e., the confusion of *"instant"* and *"period"*. Anyway Hicks does not think it very essential, since, afterwards, he argues as if the Smithian period had a finite length.

As to savings, Hicks indicates briefly the distinction between the first and the second Smithian models, but he discusses mainly the former. Again Hicks points to a quite different error which Smith would have committed. He would not have been able to see all what can be done during a period with the corn produced before. He would have consider only three uses of it: 1) feeding productive workers; 2) answering the needs of landlords; 3) sustaining unproductive workers. But there would be an other use: corn grown in the period before may be stored all over a period to be transferred to the next. Hicks compares this fourth use to Smithian parsimony and says that, if Smith had taken it into account, he would have been less dogmatic about the positive effect of parsimony on growth (Hicks, 1990, p. 533).

First of all, one has to remark that Hicks' critic is partly irrelevant. According to Hicks himself, the main characteristic of Smith's second model is that the stock carried from a period to another is made of goods in process. And it is quite clear that the corn which would be hoarded all over a period may be indentified to goods in process. So this use is integretated by the formula (4) of the second model.

Moreover "*it seems useful to show that the exception [the fourth use] could have been allowed for within*" the first model (Hicks, 1990, p. 533). The model without hoarding may be stated as follows:

$$K_{t+1} = (1 + s)[K_t - C_t] \qquad (5)$$

where $K_t$ is the stock inherited from preceding period, $C_t$ the unproductive consumption, and $s$ the rate of surplus. Now if one notes $H_t$ the amount of corn hoarded, the formula becomes:

$$K_{t+1} = (1 + s)[K_t - (C_t + H_t)] + H_t \qquad (6)$$

As Hicks underlines it, $H_t$ is "*unproductive*" (first $H_t$ in the formula), "*but not consumption*" (second $H_t$ in the formula) (Hicks, 1900, p. 533). And $H_t$ has of course a negative effect on growth, that appears when rewritting (6) as below:

$$K_{t+1} = (1 + s)[K_t - C_t] - sH_t$$

So the effect of the level of total parsimony $(K_t - C_t)$ may be counterbalanced by the effect of its structure, that is, its partition into productive $[K_t - (C_t + H_t)]$ and unproductive parsimony $(H_t)$:

$$K_t - C_t = [K_t - (C_t + H_t)] + H_t$$

Hicks could have registered the importance of the structure of savings among the elements corroborating his idea that Smith and Keynes are near parents. But he regards the parsimony from an other angle to make it play an other part in his undertaking: what is hoarded by unproductive parsimony may eventually be dishoarded. In 1983, he explained that Keynes' answer to the Smith-Hayek objection was probably to suppose that the extra goods needed for sustaining the new workers were taken out of stocks previously accumulated (Hicks, 1983, p. 31). In 1990, Hicks repeats the Hayek objection[17]. But, this time, Smith is placed on Keynes' side: "*in the case of closed economy, of which both Smith and Keynes were of course in the first place thinking, the reserves will have to real reserves*" (Hicks, 1990, p. 533). Hicks conceiving unproductive parsimony as storing goods for future consumption, it becomes the mean to guarantee stable real wages and therefore the effects of the multiplier. "*So Smith was not not so wrong in his statement about Parsimony, so*

---

[17]Notice that it is not any longer Smith's one.

*long as it is qualified by the possibility of drawing on reserves*" (Hicks, 1990, p. 535).

Hicks' argumentation is obviously looser in 1990 than in 1983. Though, the texts of both dates have in common the same intuition which is expressed in the same question: "*Why did Smith not have a multiplier?*", stated at the same stage of the reasoning, i.e. when leaving Quesnay for Smith (Hicks, 1983, p. 22; 1990, p. 531). In 1983, Hicks says that there can be no multiplier at all, because of the Hayekian spirit that pervades Smith's model. In 1990, Hicks is far less categorical. He does not find a multiplier in *The Wealth of Nations*, but yet he claims that Smith had at least enounced the condition for setting at work such a multiplier.

We are going to show that Hicks' intuition is a good one: there is indeed something like a Smithian multiplier. Keynes' multiplier theory is founded on two accounting relationships:

– a global equation

$$\text{Total Income} = \text{Global Demand} \qquad (6)$$

– and a division of global demand based on a classification of activities, based itself on accounting considerations[18]:

$$\text{Global Demand} = \text{Consumption} + \text{Investment} \qquad (7)$$

It adds to them a behavioural propensity which determines consumption:

$$\text{Consumption} = c \text{ Total Income} \qquad (8)$$

where c is the propensity to consume. From (6), (7) and (8), one deduces:

$$\text{Total Income} = [1/(1-c)] \text{ Investment}$$

Then one only needs that investment be autonomous to get a multiplication effect.

Let us see whether there is such relation in Smith. As Hicks underlines it, he does also look at things from an accounting point of view:

$$\text{Total Income} = \text{Global demand} \qquad (6)$$

---

[18]Investment, as bying, is registered among assets of balance-sheets and, as sale, in profits and losses accounts, while consumption appears only in profits and losses accounts.

He also divides global demand (D), but according to the sectorial division: agriculture (Da); manufacture (Dm), so that:

$$D = Da + Dm \qquad (7')$$

He still admits that the structure of global demand (d) defined as:

$$d = Dm/D \quad \text{and} \quad 1 - d = Da/D \qquad (8')$$

is determined by the saving and consumption behaviours of three classes of people, behaviours which are described by propensities (Rosier, 1987, p. 183-184). From (6), (7') and (8'), one deduces:

$$\text{Total Income} = [1/(1 - d)]Da$$

Finally, Smith supposes that the amount of corn demanded (*Da*) in period *t* is fixed by the quantity of corn produced at period *t* − 1, because *"as men, like all other animals, naturally multiply in proportion to the means of their subsistence, food is always, more or less, in demand"* (Smith, 1776, p. 162). Thus Da of a period appears as an exogenous magnitude in this period.

If things are so simple, why did Hicks not see them? It is true that he aimed at reconstructing Smith's model (Hicks, 1965), but he concentrated too much his attention on growth, so he missed the reproduction aspect, more precisely, Chapter XI of Book I of *The Wealth of Nations*. Unfortunately, it is this chapter that furnishes conclusive elements allowing to bring out a Smithian multiplier (Smith, 1776, 180–182). In particular, Hicks applied a wrong sectorial division (unproductive/productive) under which he tried in vain to subsume the effective one (manufacture/agriculture). But if he was so eager about his division that is because he thougth it more in agreement with Keynes' division (consumption/investissement). Thus, paradoxically, it migth be Hicks' desire to establish a stronger analogy than the one detected with Quesnay that impedes Hicks to discover the close family link which unites Smith and Keynes[19]

To conclude that section, let us note that a divergence between Smith and Keynes subsists as to the exogeneity of corn demand for the former and of investment demand for the latter. In Smith, the exogeinity is

---

[19]By the way, let us remark that Smith's multiplier is effectively more alike Keyne's one than Quesnay's one. The first and the second ones act on total income, while the third one acts on the activity level of one of the two sectors, i.e. the town.

caused *"backward looking"*, by the nutritional qualities of the quantity of corn produced in $t - 1$ and transferred to $t + 1$. In Keynes, the exogeinity is caused *"forward looking"*, by the expectations formed about the periods to come. It is on purpose that we use the expressions *"backward looking"* and *"forward looking"*; they are the ones that Hicks does use himself in order to distinguish the two great conceptions for evaluating the amount of capital (Hicks, 1973). These very two ways of looking at economic process must be put together to get a period with a past and a future.

### III. CAPITAL, STRUCTURE AND EMPLOYMENT

Of course, Hicks doesn't appeal to Ricardo about effective demand. In defense of Say's law, Ricardo constantly maintains - against Malthus - that any form of spending is as good as another, so that a demand of any kind can always be a substitute for any other, in order to prevent a partial desequilibrium to degenerate into a "general glut". Thus, something like a pure "level-effect" is properly unconceivable.[20] Because he doesn't aim at putting the concept of effective demand into the framework of a long period model, in which no magnitude is "exogenous", as neo-Ricardians usually do, Hicks can extract from the Ricardian theory of accumulation some elements that can fit the Keynesian approach. His Ricardo is not the one of the laws of distribution and the stationary state analysis, but the one of the "traverse", i.e. of technical change and unemployment. He appears in Hicks (1990 only in connection with the *"continuation theory"*, to which *"Ricardo (...) did attend, in the difficult chapter on machinery which he added to the last edition of his book"* (Hicks 1990, p. 537). In this field, *"Keynesians have not (...) done much"*, and *"perhaps that is why their doctrine has got the reputation of being short-sighted"* (1990, p. 537). Even if *"it will make no difference to the accounts of the current period"*, Hicks regards this question of *"what is the form in which (capital) leaves it terminal stock"* (1990, p. 537) as of the utmost importance so far as the dynamic path of the economy is concerned. The structure of capital does have consequences upon the temporal profiles of activity and employment.

---

[20]According to his famous answer to Malthus: *"No law can be laid down respecting quantity, but a tolerably correct one can be laid down respecting proportion."* (Ricardo 1820, p. 278)

Hence, Hicks brings out two points. First, Keynes himself was fully aware of the matter. As Hicks notes it: *"We meet it in a chapter in the General Theory, which notoriously has not passed into Keynesian tradition, the chapter on user cost"* (Hicks, 1990, p. 537). Second, Ricardo's chapter "On machinery" gives an accurate treatment of the way in which the reproduction (or formation) of fixed capital will influence the current level of employment. Ricardo can thus complete the Keynesian theory of effective demand, in a way that deserved few attention from the neo-Ricardians. What is initially a pure "proportionnal" effect then becomes a "level" effetc. The change of proportions between fixed and circulating capital (or between different types of fixed capital as well) has an impact on the dimension of the economy, because they have no expression in the current set of relative prices, so that there is no market adjustment able to respond to any modification of them. Dimension depends upon the structure of capital and its variations through time.

Hicks' interest in Ricardo's machinery effect is rather ancient. Three of his books attest it: *Capital and Growth* (1965), *A Theory of Economic History* (1969) and *Capital and Time* (1973), this latter being for a large part (2 chapters) devoted to it. It is pretty easy to give an account of Hicks' progression from one book to another, for he explained it himself in *Economic Perspectives* (1977). In *A Theory of Economic History*, Hicks' concern is the impact of industrialization on the labour market; more precisely, the matter is to understand why real wages of workers have so slowly and so lately followed the path given by the trend of capital accumulation. One of the possible answers is the machinery effect, exposed by Hicks through a numerical example. A further and more sophisticated treatment is proposed in *Capital and Time*. Despite *"the demonstration (...) given there (...) can be claimed to be quite rigorous"*, it *"is not all that is required"* (1977-a, p. 185), so that Hicks refines once again the argument in his *Economic Perspectives* (1977-b). Three points have to be cleared up, in respect with this matter: 1) Hick's interpretation of Ricardo's machinery effect; 2) the relevance of the austrian method for explaining it; 3) the relationship it can have with a Keynesian theory of employment "in the long run". We shall limit ourselves to the arithmetical example given in the appendix of (1969), and its commentary in (1977b).

The likelihood of Ricardo's hypothesis can be established from a comparison of the conditions of production between two processes, corresponding to two distinct types of "machine", each of them being of the same length (2 periods), and made of a "construction" stage (where the machine is built) and an "utilization" stage (where the final product is produced with the machine). Each process can be described by 2 technical coefficients, corresponding to the quantity of labour at each of the 2 stages necessary for producing one unit of the final product. The new technique induces both a change in the cost of the product, and a change in the proportion between direct and indirect labour.

With subscipts indicating the technics (1 steming for the initial technique, and 2 for the new one), and exponents the stages, and if $L_1^U$ and $L_2^U$, $L_1^1$ and $L_2^1$ are the quantities of labour respectively used for construction (stage 0) and utilization (stage 1) in each of the processes, the 2 techniques are described by the following coefficients:

$c_1 = L10 / X1$ and $u_1 = L11 / X1$ for technique I
and $c_2 = L20 / X2$ and $u_2 = L21 / X2$ for technique II

Technique II is introduced only if it is more profitable than technique I, which does have to mean that its average labour-cost is smaller, given that the real wage is the same for all producers. Three cases may correspond to such a situation:

1) $c_1 > c_2$ and $u_1 > u_2$

In this case, there is no obstacle to an immediate expansion of production, because the change of technique requires no transfer of labour.

2) $c_1 \leq c_2$ and $u_1 > u_2$

a) The new technique saves direct labour (at the utilization stage), but is more costly in indirect labour (necessary for constructing the new machine). It can nevertheless be more profitable if the direct labour spared is greater than the indirect labour added. In this case a Ricardo effect must occur.[21] If the construction coefficient has raised ($c_2 > c_1$), the introduction of technique II requires a transfer of labour from stage 1 to

---

[21]The third case, in which $u_1 < u_2$, but the difference is more than compensated by c1>c2, doesn't produce a machinery effect, because the new machine has first to be put in production, so that the transfer required from the construction stage to the utilization stage is made possible by the very construction of the new machine.

stage 0, which is not feasable immediately (in period 1). If there was initially (in period 0) full employment, this transfer implies a reduction of production at the ultimate stage, that will be compensated for only through time, as Hicks illustrates with a numerical example in A *Theory of Economic History*.

b) If the construction coefficient remains unchanged, there will be no fall in final output, and the rise will come earlier, because a transfer becomes possible as far as period 2, and the new machine can be put in production in period 1.

So, a rapid process of industrialization, caracterized by a mecanization of production, may be limited by a lack of savings, which can be solved only by a fall in the production of consumption goods, and then in real wages. Hicks shows that this conclusion can hardly be sustained by the standard neo-classical mode of reasoning, which leaves unclear the notion of *"strongly labour-saving invention"*. But the machinery effect can easily be interpreted in Hayekian terms, with the austrian conception of capital, as Hicks did it in his *Capital and Time*.

For him, such a reading of Ricardo is not only possible, but even necessary.[22] The reason for that is not the virtual character of prices introduced in the other approach (known as the Sraffa/Von Neumann method). *"The true justification (...) is different"*. It rests on the claim for a dynamic analysis of the transition process (the "traverse") as soon as *"we leave the steady state"*, or the stationary state of the Classics, and allow for innovation and changes in the industrial structure. In such a context, Hicks sees a decisive advantage for the Austrian method, who *"deal much better than its rivals with the basic economic effects of what is surely the most important kind of innovation, that which takes the form of new methods for making the same final product"*, and thus *"involve the introduction of (...) new sorts of "machines", and of the intermediate products. It is here undesirable that these goods should be physically specified, since there is no way of establishing a physical relation between the capital goods that are required in the one technique and those that are required in the other. The only relation that can be established runs in terms of costs, and of capacity to produce*

---

[22]Considering the course of his own thought, this corresponds to a return of the "old Hicks" to his ancient love; indeed, some of his first grea *t* articles were written, under Robbins' sollicitation, to solve the *"inner mystery"* (Hicks 1967) involved in the cyclical process described by Hayek in *Prices and production* (Hicks (1931) and Hicks (1933)).

*final output; and this is precisely what is preserved in an Austrian theory"* (1977b, p. 193). This is both what Ricardo had in mind in his chapter "On Machinery", and what is dealt with in *Capital and Time*, in a model in which capital goods as such do not appear.

In such a framework, even if a smooth convergence to a new equilibrium position is ensured - as it is in the standard case of *Capital and Time* - *"there is the possibility that technical progress may have drastic, and possibly unacceptable, effects on distribution - the Ricardo machinery effect"* (Ibid., p. 194). In a more general way, the time-shape of the normal productive processes can oppose serious obstacles to the convergence towards a new position of full employment equilibrium.[23] Those obstacles are serious enough to think that convergence may either never occur or, if it does, only after a considerable interval of time, so that *"before that time had elapsed, something else (some new exogenous shock) would have occured"*. Hence, Hicks *"began to lose interest in convergence"*, and became more and more concerned with *"the short-run and medium-run effects of an innovation"* (Ibid., p. 195), for which the austrian method is best fitted. Then, if short-run effects are indeed *"of the first importance"*, one cannot avoid to ask wether it is reasonable to take as a starting point a state of affairs, the steady state equilibrium, that no one can assure *"it would ever be reached"* at any time by any real capitalist economy.

At this point of the argument, Hicks has bridged the gap between growth theory and Keynesian employment theory. His final rejection of the steady state analysis is nothing else than Keynes' denial of interest for the study of *"final positions of equilibrium in a static world"*.[24] And the traverse analysis looks much like a multiperiodic analysis of *"moving equilibriums"*, that Keynes aimed to reach, beyond the scope of short-run analysis, to which the *General Theory* is confined.

There is a threshold, Hicks did not go through: the family of models within which such an approach can be implemented looks very alike the Classical models of reproduction. If Hicks had not neglicted the reproduction face of Smith, he could have got further in his "Classical synthesis".

---

[23]One of them - not the most realistic - being signaled by Hayek in *Prices and production*, due to the lenghtening of the processes (which corresponds to the addition of a third stage -1 in the above example).

[24]See note 5 above.

As far as Ricardo is concerned, Hicks misses a deeper reconciliation with Keynes, because he expresses the machinery effect in terms of declining real wages, where Ricardo speaks of job loss. The common point is that, in both presentations, there is less "funds" left for paying labour. But in one case, the effect has a Hayekian look, and in the other a Keynesian flavour. Keeping the Ricardian glasses, we can rectify the unfair error Keynes committed when he supposed that there could be no unemployment of labour if there was full employment of capital, as assumed by Ricardo, according to Say's law.[25] The Classical notion of "overpopulation" is not a "Classical" notion of unemployment, in the (pigovian) sense used by Keynes.

Ricardian unemployment is not linked with an "excess" in real wages. In the course of events resulting from the situation described by Hicks, the adjustment variable can be the level of employment, so that the resorbtion of excess workers is made possible by the rise of profits (and not the fall of wages), which allows a rise in the accumulation rate. The technical progress which provokes unemployment is the same cause that also leads to further restauration of employment.[26] And the question remains of knowing if the final effet on employment will be positive or negative. Ricardo was very cautious on this point, but rather pessimistic on the whole: at least, he thought that the level of employment could be lowered for an indefinite duration, if not definitely.[27] Hicks shows that the capacity to produce final goods, and the effective supply of final goods, will be raised at the end. But he says nothing of the final level of employment, which must depend upon the way profits are spent.

In the context of contemporary Keynesian debates, this is an important point. Hence, the notion of Ricardian unemployment[28] can be presented as a response to the argument that Keynesian theory ignores unemployment due to "supply-side effect". This technological unemployment is a supply-side effect that doesn't invalide the principle of effective demand. Hence, it can be seen as a notion of unvolontary un-

---

[25]In that sense, his reading of Ricardo on machinery is much better than Morishima's (1989) one, who dosen't accept (just like Keynes) that there could be at the same time full utilization of capital and under employment of labour.

[26]A mechanism of "reserve army" can be added to this process. But they are two distinct mecanisms.

[27]For Ricardo, only "a portion of the people thrown out of work in the first instance, would be subsequently employed" (1821, p. 390).

[28]Which could be labeled "marxian unemployment" as well.

employment, that can be reduced by a rise in the accumulation rate, and not by a fall in wages. According to those properties, it can stand for a "Keynesian long run unemployment"[29] A full development of this idea seems to require a restatement of the model, in terms of employment capacity (rather than production capacity), using Keynes-Smith measure of units (the wage unity).[30] At least, it is necessary to consider the working of the classical labour market[31], which is a traditionnal source of difficulties for neo-classical economists.[32]

Thus, the use of the austrian theory of capital for interpreting Ricardo could lead to a reconciliation between Hayek ... and Keynes ! This is another subject of perplexity. Hicks approves Hayek when he criticizes Keynes for being only interested in the net revenue. Nevetheless he does not follow him to think that considering gross investment and gross product leads to invalidate the keynesian theory of current employment (i.e. for a given stock of fixed capital). He shows that the austrian theory doesn't stand for the use made by Hayek. The "Hayekian case", of which Hicks had already argued (see "The Hayek Story" (1967)) that it couldn't sustain a theory of the downswing, is an extreme situation, in which the construction coefficient raises, but also the number of stages. By the way, he gives a reply to Hayek's objection to the multiplier, that consisted in suspending its effectivity to the prior disposal of a sufficient stock of original factors and goods in process. But his reply is somewhat ambiguous, for the obstacle opposed by technological change is identified as a lack of savings.[33] In the case of an

---

[29]From an historical point of view, we can wonder whether Ricardian unemployment could not offer part of the explanation of european mass unemployment since the end of the seventies. That would mean that, after a period of decline in the relative price of capital goods, from 1945 to 1975, europeans economies entered a period of rise in that relative price. At least at the light of the French experience, this is not a very bold hypothesis.

[30]That has always been a popint of disagreement between Hicks and Keynes, the former arguing that the choice of the numéraire is indifferent, while the other maintained that it does has an importance. This explains why Hicks doesn't pay any attention to the question of the choice of unit in Smith's.

[31]The question of wage fixity is adressed by Hicks in a paper written with Samuel Hollander (1977), but in the context of a long period equilibrium model, which is inadequate for the present discussion.

[32]Goodwin (1967) and Rebeyrol (1986) have proposed a model that respect the classical notion of natural wage, and offers a mechanism of gravitation.

[33]This interpretation is confirmed in "Hayek story" (1967).

opened economy, it can be interpreted as a need for external finance. But what for the case of a closed economy, or of the world economy as a whole ? It seems to be too much Ricardian for being fully Keynesian ...

## CONCLUSION: THE LAST HICKS AND THE PREVIOUS ONES

The "reunification" of Keynesian macroeconomics with Classical theory advocated by Hicks in his last paper is not a totally new suggestion, even if its very concised form in the 1990 article gives it a very provocative form, and seems to put it in contradiction with the general stream of his work.

As we tried to show it from the analysis of two authors (Smith and Ricardo) and two themes (the multiplier and the structure of capital), it is announced a number of times in his former writings, especially those of the "old Hicks" of 1965 and after[34], and correspond to permanent preoccupations.

Being stated without any reference to general equilibrium theory, this project nevertheless represent a rupture both with some former works (such as *Value and capital*) usually considered as the most representative of Hicks' contribution to economic theory, and with the usual interpretation of Keynes in mainstream economics. The Hicksian synthesis contrasts with the neo-classical synthesis, to which the "young Hicks" initially contributed, along with Hansen, Samuelson, and others. It neither suggests to integrate Keynes within the walrasian paradigm, nor discuss of the relation between the two in terms of their relative degree of generality. In contrast with the actual "new Keynesian" intents, it doesn't aim either to bridge the gap between micro and macroeconomics.

The consistency of such a project is nothing but self-evident. Further theorizing has to be accomplished before it can stand by its own. Hicks opens a new territory, but doesn't picture the whole landscape. In other texts (*Crisis in Keynesian economics* (1975) or the *Market theory of Money* (1989)), the "old Hicks" give some indications of what it could be. They suggest that, besides the austrian-Ricardian model of capital

---

[34]Corresponding to the publication of *Capital and Growth*, of which Hicks said (Hicks, 1979) it was his first book of economic theory after a long period of work on questions of applied economics, related to development, and can thus be considered as the beginning of his second carreer as a theorist.

assets, one should elaborate a model of passifs. The notion of debt-economy, if it is seen as a theoretical notion[35], gives such an opening.

Moreover, Hicks tends to understate the gap between the Mercantislists and Smith, as well as between Smith and Ricardo. This might be due to his conviction that *"monetary disorders may (...) be superimposed upon other disorders, but (that) the other disorders are more fundamental"* (1973, p. 134). We are reaching here the limits of the possible "unity" between Keynes and the "Great Classicals". As Hicks himself points out, *"there is much more to be done"*, in order *"to continue with the continuation (theory)"* (1990, p. 538). Since his death, his *"call to others"* for further developments hasn't been much echoed. In sharp contrast with what happened with earlier of his contributions in other fields of economic theory (or other doctrinal orientations), it did not *"become a pivotal element in the litterature, and has (not) led to a major redirection of research in the area"*[36]

Answering to Hicks' call would imply further works in two directions. The interpretation of the Keynesian theory of investment as a theory of capital reproduction is at present a mere intuititon, and should be established in a formal model. As regards the Classics, the monetary dimension of reproduction should be entirely built up.[37]

## REFERENCES

Arena, R., 1982, "Réflexions sur la compatibilité des approches ricardienne et keynésienne du fonctionnement de l'activité économique", *Economie Appliquée*, Tome XXXV, N°3

Goodwin, R., 1967, "A Growth Cycle", in FEINSTEIN, *Socialism, capitalism and economic growth*, Cambridge, Cambridge University Press.

Harrod Roy, 1973, *Dynamic Economics*, London, McMillan.

Hayek, Friedrich, 1929, *Prices and production*,

Hicks, J.R., 1931, "Uncertainty and Profit", *Collected Essays on Economic Theory*, Vol. II, Oxford, Basil Blackwell, 1986.

Hicks, J.R., 1933, "Equilibrium and the Cycle", *Collected Essays on Economic Theory*, Vol. II, Oxford, Basil Blackwell, 1986.

---

[35]As Hicks noticed, this notion was not very successfull, at least in the anglo-american world. But it became quite famous and common in France, where it was interpreted most often as an empirical notion.

[36]William Baumol reviewing Hicks in *The Swedish Journal of Economics*, December 1972.

[37]For explanatory work in this direction see Catherine Martin (1993), who develops a very original interpretation of Ricardo, grounded on a concept of monetary demand.

Hicks, J.R., 1937, "Mr Keynes and the "Classics": A Suggested Interpretation", *Collected Essays on Economic Theory*, Vol. II, Oxford, Basil Blackwell, 1986.

Hicks, J.R., 1939, *Value and Capital*, Oxford, At the Clarendon Press, 1974.

Hicks, J.R., 1942, *The Social Framework*, Oxford, At the Clarendon Press, 1950.

Hicks, J.R., 1962-1982, "The Foundations of Monetary Theory", *Collected Essays on Economic Theory*, Vol. II, Oxford, Basil Blackwell, 1986.

Hicks, J.R., 1965, *Capital and Growth*, Oxford, Oxford University Press.

Hicks, J.R., 1967, "The Hayek Story", *Critical Essays in Monetary Theory*, Oxford, Oxford University Press.

Hicks, J.R., 1969, *A Theory of Economic History*, Oxford, Oxford University Press.

Hicks, J.R., 1973, *Capital and Time: A Neo-Austrian Theory*, London, Oxford University Press.

Hicks, J.R., 1974, "Capital controversies: ancient and moderns", *American Economic Review*, May, Reprinted in (1977-a), pp. 149-165

Hicks, J.R., 1974, *Crisis in Keynesian Economics*, Oxford, Basil Blackwell.

Hicks, J.R., 1976, "'Revolutions' in Economics", *Collected Essays on Economic Theory*, Vol. III, Oxford, Basil Blackwell, 1986.

Hicks, J.R., 1977-a, *Economic Perspectives*, Oxford, Clarendon Press.

Hicks, J.R., 1977-b, "Explanations and revisions", in (1977-a), pp. 177-195

Hicks, J.R. and HOLLANDER S., 1977, "Ricardo and the moderns", *Collected Essays on Economic Theory*, Vol. III, Oxford, Basil Blackwell, 1986.

Hicks, J.R., 1979, "The Formation of an Economist", *Collected Essays on Economic Theory*, Vol. III, Oxford, Basil Blackwell, 1986.

Hicks, J.R., 1980, "IS-LM - An Explanation", *Collected Essays on Economic Theory*, Vol. II, Oxford, Basil Blackwell, 1986.

Hicks, J.R., 1982, "Introductory: LSE and the Robbins Circle", *Collected Essays on Economic Theory*, Vol. II, Oxford, Basil Blackwell, 1986

Hicks, J.R., 1989, *A market theory of money*, Oxford, Clarendon Press

Hicks, J.R., 1990, "The Unification of Macroeconomics", *The Economic Journal*, June, pp. 528-538.

Kalecki, M., 1968, "Trend and the Business Cycle", *Selected Essays on the Dynamics of the Capitalist Economy*, Cambridge University Press, 1971

Keynes, J.M., 1932, "Fragment", *Collected Writings*, Volume 29, Macmillan, 1979, pp. 54-57

Keynes, J.M., 1936-a, *General Theory of Employment, Money and Interest*, The Collected Writings of John Maynard Keynes, Royal Economic Society, Mac Millan, Vol. VII.

Keynes, J.M., 1936-b, "Letter to Henderson", Collected Writings, Vol. 29, 1979, pp. 221-224.

Martin, C., 1993, *Demande et formation des prix monétaires: Une réinterprétation de Ricardo*, Thèse, Université de Paris 1.

Pack, S., 1991, "Règlementation, intervention et impôt régressif dans la *Richesse des Nations*", *Cahiers d'économie politique*, n°9.

Pasinetti, L., 1974, "From Classical to Keynesian Economic Dynamics", in *Growth and Income Distribution*, Cambridge University Press

Rebeyrol, A., 1987, "Gravitation et marché du travail: un essai d'interprétation", *Economie et sociétés*, Série HPE, "Oeconomia", n°7

Ricardo, D., 1820, "A letter to Malthus", *The Works and Correspondence of David Ricardo*, Cambridge, Cambridge University Press, Vol. VIII, 1952.

Ricardo, D., 1821, *On the Principles of Political Economy and Taxation, The Works and Correspondence of David Ricardo*, P. Sraffa Ediotor, Cambridge University Press, Vol. 1, 1951

Robinson, J., 1972, "Keynes and Ricardo", *Journal of Post-Keynesian Economics*.

Rosier, M., 1987, "Le modèle de reproduction et d'accumulation de Smith", *Recherches économiques de Louvain*, vol. 53, n°2.

Rosier, M., 1992, "Déviations temporaires et permanentes des prix de marché dans *La Richesse des Nations*", *Cahiers d'économie politique*, n°20–21.

Smith, A., 1776, *The Wealth of Nations*, The Glasgow Edition of the Works and Correspondence of Adam Smith, Indianapolis, Liberty Classics, 1981.

Tutin, C., 1993, "Synthèse ricardienne, illusion keynésienne ? - Un commentaire", *Cahiers d'Economie Politique*, n°22.

Tutin, C., 1994, "Les extensions du modèle de l'échange, ou les limites du syncrétisme", Communication aux Journées détudes *"Existence de l'équilibre général concurrentiel"*, CAESAR/Université de Paris X Nanterre, 6-7 octobre 1994

CHAPTER - 20

# "NEO AUSTRIAN PROCESS(ES)"

*Jean-Luc Gaffard, Lionello F. Punzo and
Mario Amendola*

## ABSTRACT

The Neo-Austrian approach is a conceptual means to describe an economy, but
it also implies a dynamics in which production processes are the key actors.
This paper tries to clarify this twofold aspect of the Neo-Austrian approach, in
particular focusing on its formalised dynamics vis-a-vis the standard formalism
deployed in economics, of Frisch's and Goodwin's descent.

We will discuss the analytical nature of a Neo-Austrian process and define a
dynamics of production processes, so as to provide a background to evaluate it
against well known formal techniques of Economic Dynamics. In particular, we
will re-examine the issue: what are the requisites of a formal mathematical
model to be a faithful representation of Neo-Austrian dynamics. As it will turn
up clearly, the Neo-Austrian approach does not fit very well into any of the
standard classifications, e.g. it is neither a long run (like growth) nor a short run
theory (in the sense of business cycle theories). Its particular strategy to tackle
the complexity that necessarily arises in economic dynamics will be dealt with.
After discussing the evolution of the Neo-Austrian model from the Hicksian
original analysis of the Traverse to its more modern versions, we will present it
as the analytical framework which, following again Hicks's intuition, makes it
possible to realise the unification of macroeconomics. Finally, the use of Neo-
Austrian models as 'heuristic tools' to provide light for policy interventions will
be contrasted with the 'predictive' role of standard formal dynamic models.

## 1. INTRODUCTION

The Neo-Austrian approach originates from J.R. Hicks (1970, 1973). It
is a conceptual means to describe an economy, but it also implies a dy-

namics in which production processes are the key actors. This paper tries to clarify this twofold aspect of the Neo-Austrian approach, in particular focusing on its formalised dynamics vis-a-vis the standard formalism deployed in economics, of Frisch's and Goodwin's descent.

In section 2 we will discuss the analytical nature of a Neo-Austrian process and define a dynamics of production processes, so as to provide a background to evaluate it against well known formal techniques of Economic Dynamics. In particular, we will re-examine the issue: what are the requisites of a formal mathematical model to be a faithful representation of Neo-Austrian dynamics. As it will turn up clearly, the Neo-Austrian approach does not fit very well into any of the standard classifications, e.g. it is neither a long run (like growth) nor a short run theory (in the sense of business cycle theories) (section 3). Its particular strategy to tackle the complexity that necessarily arises in economic dynamics will be dealt with in section 4. After discussing the evolution of the Neo-Austrian model from the Hicksian original analysis of the Traverse to its more modern versions (section 5), we will present it as the analytical framework which, following again Hicks's intuition, makes it possible to realise the unification of macroeconomics (section 6). Finally (section 7), the use of Neo-Austrian models as 'heuristic tools' to provide light for policy interventions will be contrasted with the 'predictive' role of standard formal dynamic models.

## 2. DYNAMIC ISSUES AND DYNAMIC METHODS

The definition of Dynamic Economics is a matter of controversy. Economic models are often considered to be dynamic when they employ dynamic methods. Steady-growth has been reckoned a dynamic method; the introduction of non linearities is said to lead to dynamic models; the use of dynamic optimisation appears as a significant advance in the field of dynamic economics. We maintain instead that dynamic analysis, in economics, depends on dealing with issues which are in the nature of dynamic problems, rather than referring to supposedly dynamic methods.

What is a dynamic problem? As stressed by Hicks[1] it has to do with change: but change cannot be reduced to a steady state, that is, to a

---

[1]"Dynamic theory is the analysis of the processes by which they [certain key variables] change" (Hicks, 1985, p. 2).

static equilibrium continuously blown up by multiplication by a scalar. Change implies a structural modification which can only be brought about through a process in real irreversible time. Innovation (which follows what Hicks names an 'impulse') is the foremost example of change. Therefore, what matters is that, when change does take place, the previously existing productive structure is disturbed and its way of functioning is affected. This puts the economy out of equilibrium, and as a result a problem of intertemporal complementarity of production arises which calls for co-ordination over time of economic activity to render the process of change undertaken viable.

Dynamic analysis essentially comes down to the analysis of restructuring processes. Viability is the main problem associated with these processes, and interaction, complementarity and co-ordination over time are the relevant issues for viability.

This different perspective affects both the modelling of the process involved and the kind of analysis to be carried on. In the first place commodities are no longer defined with reference to a date, a place and a state of nature, as in general equilibrium models, but in terms of production processes of which they are the outcome, each with its specific time profile. A different interpretation of the terms 'exogenous' and 'endogenous' follows (Amendola and Gaffard, 1998). In any model there are variables as well as parameters: the parameters (given magnitudes and coefficients) reflect the existing constraints. Exogenous, in the standard analysis, are the constraints which exist outside and above the economy and which determine its behaviour. Within this framework endogenizing means that something which was treated as a parameter in the above sense is being made the explicit outcome of some behaviour specified in the model: the form of the behaviour function, and its coefficients, become now the exogenous constraints.

Once it is recognised that the time over which change takes place is a continuing and irreversible process shaping the very change "it is impossible to assume the constancy of anything over time...The only truly exogenous factor is whatever exists at a given moment of time, as a heritage of the past..." (Kaldor, 1985, p. 61). In the analysis of a process of change "we thus, have to consider as a parameter, and hence as exogenous, not some given element chosen beforehand in reason of its nature or characteristics, but whatever, at a given moment of time, is inherited from the past. What appears as a parameter at a given moment of time is therefore itself the result of processes which have taken place within the economy, processes during which everything - including resources and the environment, as well as technology – undergoes a transformation and hence is made endogenous to the change undergone by the economy. Thus, while the standard approach focuses on the right place to draw the line between what should be taken as exogenous and what should be considered instead as endogenous in economic modelling – a line that moves according to what we want to be explained by the model – out of equilibrium ..... the question is no longer that of drawing a line here or there but rather one of time perspective adopted. Everything can be considered as given at a certain moment of time, while everything becomes endogenous over time." (Amendola and Gaffard, 1998, p.33).

Furthermore, "if a system has no lags, so that every thing is determined contemporaneously, it cannot (endogenously) engender a process' (Hicks 1967, p. 207). In the Hicksian Traverse, and, more generally, in any process of change which takes place out of equilibrium, production and decision lags are essential ingredients of dynamics.

## 3. MODELS OF ECONOMIC DYNAMICS

To put the Neo-Austrian approach in the right analytical perspective , we need to revert to a piece of history of economic analysis. Historically, formal theories of economic dynamics were born relatively recently out of the empirical observation (a primitive stylised fact) that, although the then existing theories predicted equilibrium states to prevail, this 'fact' could not be readily ascertained in actual time series. Modern economic dynamics, in other words, was created to provide the explanation of why economies were never visibly close to the equilibrium theoretically defined on the basis of general equilibrium theories dominating up to the middle of the century. Thus, it was the failure of equilibrium theories, in the narrow sense of general equilibrium (GE) theory, that generated the efforts to build modern-style models of economic dynamics. Given these conceptual origins, they remained trapped in a dichotomy: some of them attempted to incorporate and so preserve the notion of (the isolated) equilibrium and developed it further into growth dynamics. On the other side, there were those that boldly attempted a disequilibrium interpretation of observed fluctuations in the levels of economic activity. This generated in particular theories of the business cycles. In this way we obtained the 'division of labour' between growth theories, essentially extensions of GE equilibrium theories, and theories of oscillations, or of off-equilibrium dynamics.

Until very recently, this separation has been preserved. To this dichotomy corresponded a further distinction between, broadly speaking, 'exogenous' and 'endogenous' theories. Growth dynamics would then be treated as (if) entirely determined by structural, slowly changing factors or *fundamentals:* in other words it was given an exogenous explanation. Fluctuations, on the other hand, were seen as the joint result of the system in-built (propagation) mechanisms and exogenous impulses. Hence, they were assigned a partially endogenous interpretation. It is clear from the above that the archetypes we are considering, are Solow-type of growth theory and Frisch's type of impulse-propagation oscillatory mechanism (that has been often referred to as the 'econometric model'[2]).

The above mentioned division of labour implied complementarity between the two specialised theories of dynamics. A natural, but often little perceived, shortcoming of this train of thought is that observed fluctuations are referred to (i.e: 'they become fluctuations around') equilibrium paths, the growth paths, which, though they are un-observed in the actual dynamics, can be mathematically defined to the required level of precision independently of the actual time series' record. They become 'tendencies' which are not extracted from actual histories; they are derived from elsewhere, from independent knowledge of the law(s) governing the evolution of the *fundamentals.*

This shows again that, once the notion of equilibrium is used, its pre-eminence tends to dwarf all disequilibrium dynamics. Most of actual or observed dynamics becomes then *conceptualised,* in fact, in the narrow space allocated to deviation dynamics, deviation being measured as distance from posited equilibrium path(s)[3]. It is known that these theories cannot account for the *persistence* of off-equilibrium dynamics, except by assuming a systematic shock-releasing process to re-initialise deviations whenever needed[4].

---

[2]Once we interpret the initial impulse as a stochastic disturbance, of course.

[3]This explains the prevalence of the stochastic interpretation in the theory of business oscillations, as it represents the shortest route to explain actual behaviours as deviation from equilibrium.

[4]The obvious alternative is Goodwin's theory of the business cycle which, to be en-

The Neo-Austrian approach is not readily classifiable within either one of the sides of the above, historical 'theoretical divide'. In Hicks's original dynamics, something called an impulse or a shock does play a role, and from this point of view one can classify it as an exogenous theory. But in subsequent developments of the theory, once the dynamics has flared up, the model focuses on endogenous mechanisms.

What is the role of shocks in Neo-Austrian dynamics, then? As it will be argued, it is to generate out-of-equilibrium dynamics but in a sense that is not allowed by simple linear dynamics.

The role assigned to shocks is in fact twofold: first, to initialise a dynamics leading off a postulated initial equilibrium. This is a purely notional role, and has the same function as an initial disturbance ·in a controlled experiment. The other, and more important, function is 'to keep alive' the dynamics off the original unique equilibrium behaviour. The shocks, in other words, are needed to create *evolution paths* along the history of the economy, *which did not exist before*. More importantly, they are to do so in a non pre-defined sequence. It is the latter connotation that might justify their being treated as shocks, but they really are innovations, as this term is understood in economics.

Two aspects call our attention hereafter: i) shocks shift equilibria in a non-predictable way and ii) they are there to explain persistence in out-of equilibrium behaviour itself.

### 4. COMPLEX DYNAMICS, NEO-AUSTRIAN STYLE

How does a Neo-Austrian model deals with out-of-equilibrium dynamics?.

It is sometimes useful to think of the design of an economic system as a mathematical description of its internal structure, a network of functional relations between component parts. The associated dynamics is the outward manifestation of properties of such a structure/design *plus*, in general, the effects of its interaction with an external dynamical environment (stochastic or otherwise, depending on the frontier chosen for the system description). While we can 'see' the system dynamics, we cannot say the same of the internal structure: this is one of the dimen-

---

dogenistic, had to be non-linear.

sions of dynamic complexity, the functional relationship between the two is itself an unknown.

There are two basic strategies to handle dynamic complexity: i) to simplify dynamics while preserving a rich system internal structure; or, alternatively, ii) to preserve dynamic complex and simplify the economy's internal structure. There is in fact a finite limit to our capabilities to handle both issues at the same time, and thus there is a trade off in modelling, between complexity at one (e.g. design) or the other (hence, outcomes) levels (Goodwin and Punzo 1987; Punzo, 1995).

The Neo-Austrian model opts for the former strategy and it is in good company: GE models seem to rely pretty much upon the same strategy. Some recent theories of endogenous oscillations and economic chaos are produced by the latter strategy[5].

But, compare Neo-Austrian models with standard GE models, and in particular with linear production models. They share the property of having an articulated internal design. Their difference can be formulated in terms of parallel versus sequential structures, due to the principle with which 'economies' are assembled out of their model components. The 'simplified' dynamics that either one generates, reflects the properties of the corresponding architecture.

In GE, and in von Neumann input-output (IO) family of GE models[6], the various components of the economy, whether production processes or households, can be run only simultaneously, in other words *in parallel* but, if run, they are interconnected by an intricate network of links of forward and backward (and of course feedback) types. This web of relations makes an 'economy': if realised, the virtual web gets transformed into a theoretically actual structure. This can only happen in equilibrium. 'Theoretically' is here emphasised for that a web satisfies certain equilibrium conditions and describes a model economy, *does not* (necessarily) imply that it be the realised or observed economy. However, if in any of the realisable webs, individual productive processes cannot be

---

[5] Not all empirically based theories of oscillations are explicit about their stand on this issue. One instance in point is the 'real business cycle' theory.

[6] What follows applies to all computational models derived from General Equilibrium analytical structures. The whole argument in the text assumes that we are dealing with computational (re)formulations of theoretical models. The reference to the von Neumann and IO family is made to contrast their assimilation with the Neo-Austrian model, a hasty conclusion that can be found in the original review paper by Burmeister (1974).

run independently of the other processes in the same web. It is this, the particular form which horizontal complementarities take in this approach: in the model economies of GE analysis, complexity is attached to the coherence within the given economic structure if realised, it may or may not receive a super-imposed dynamics of a changing structure.

In Neo-Austrian economies, design complexity arises from treating a population of production processes articulating in time and it is reflected into the properties of the evolution of the population structure. Complementarities are vertical, in the sense that they are over time. This has two immediate consequences. On the one hand, the very distinction between the two forms of dynamics, adjustment dynamics and structural change, becomes blurred and operationally unimportant; and structural change becomes the focus as a result of this.

The other major consequence is that Neo-Austrian models naturally 'go macro'. One can see this in the following way. If macroeconomics is about a whole economy (as it is conventionally, after the Keynesian tradition), its generalisation would look at populations of economies. Traditionally, this means doing International Economics. The one reason for resorting to this generalisation, however, is that from a macroeconomic or aggregate description, there is no way to recover a unique micro (or 'meso') description of the same economy. There are many compatible descriptions; if one is lucky, there is only a well identified class of them to discover. Thus, one can only hope to find 'laws' or simply regularities, stylised facts and the like, by comparing across countries and/or histories, rather than doing experiments with different parameter values in some set of axiomatically posited microfunctions.

Hicks's trick in founding the Neo-Austrian approach is to employ just such idea both to describe a single economy and explore some of its scenarios of evolution. To really understand the approach, one needs to think of a typical Neo-Austrian process as representing by itself, virtually, a whole economy. Thus, we get the notion of a population of (self-contained) economies, each economy being a process dynamically de-coupled of all other processes. In a typical Neo-Austrian style economy one meets several processes which are different just because they are differently dated and because their time profiles are different. A Neo-Austrian economy is therefore far distant from the model economies of General Equilibrium theories. In the latter things do not change if not exogenously, and if they do so, they do it in leaps and bounds, in a totally discontinuous fashion. The Neo-Austrian out-of-equilibrium dynamics is one peculiar account of irregular behaviour comparable to the accounts produced by non-linear theories. Let us now consider this account.

## 5. FROM TRAVERSE TO FULL OUT-OF-EQUILIBRIUM DYNAMICS

Let us see how the Neo-Austrian approach, from the original analysis of the Traverse (the transition from an old to a new technique), has evolved into a proper dynamic method. The starting point is the consideration of production as a fully vertically integrated process, which contemplates only one primary resource, labour, and retains the vital distinction between construction and utilisation, but almost nothing else. This is enough both to exhibit explicitly the phase of construction of productive capacity by bringing it inside the production process, and to focus on the intertemporal complementarity of this process. The appearance of problems of intertemporal complementarity is in fact the main consequence of the shock represented by the adoption of a different technique; and again the intertemporal complementarity of the production process the main link of the sequence of periods along which the barter economy dealt with by Hicks (1970, 1973) - an economy in which a homogeneous commodity appears both as input and output - is made to move from the previous technique to the new one by means of the mechanism provided by the assumption of Full Performance. This implies that all the output not absorbed by consumption out of wages paid to workers engaged on existing production processes (whether still in the construction or already in the utilisation phase) or by consumption of other kinds, is in fact used to start new production processes. The rate of starts, thus made endogenous, sketches out the path followed by the economy – a fully predetermined path leading to a new equilibrium state univocally defined by the characteristics of the new technique – once the value of the parameters of the model are given. Full Performance, on the other hand, also implies flow equilibrium in each period, both in the sense that final output is totally absorbed by existing demand and in the sense that investment is equal to ex ante saving. Thus the existing productive structure is smoothly transmuted into the one adapted to the new technique as resources are gradually freed and invested into the building of the latter. In this context there is no decision process and there are no disequilibrium co-ordination problems; Full Performance allows to dispense with them and with the imbalances which could otherwise arise from the strictly ad hoc, arbitrary saving function corresponding to the hypothesis of a constant, exogenously determined 'take out' (consumption out of profits). However, Full Performance only concerns final output; there is nothing of the sort on the labour market. This makes it possible to make the bold step forward that is represented by the analysis of the Traverse: to bring to light "what happens on the way" (Hicks, 1973, p. 10), in particular to employment, as the result of taking explicitly into account the time structure of production in an out-of-equilibrium context. The simple consideration of the distinction 'between investment at cost and investment of output capacity" (Hicks, 1973, p. 98), which can be appreciated when there is a breaking of the intertemporal complementarity of production, allows important analytical insights: of paramount importance is the demonstration of Ricardo's 'machinery effect' – the appearance of a transitory unemployment associated with changes in technology[7] – a highly controversial issue in the history of economic thought.

In this analysis Hicks is resorting to an 'analytical escamotage': breaking down a complicated (in principle highly non-linear) dynamics into a set of segmented or local models that can take on a linear formulation. They illustrate the simplified dynamics associated with the complex system design, that was indicated as one of the strategies available in section 4 above. Formally, they describe a traverse path between two-well defined steady states. This technical idea has re-emerged in econometric literature recently; for the records, this same idea was exploited already in Hicks' classic *A Contribution to the theory of the trade cycle.*

Another simplification is the treatment of the Traverse as a (monotonic) asymptotically stable path leading from the old to the new equilibrium. By contrast, it is long run dynamics that follows an irregular path. The latter is the global dynamics of the model, which the Traverse exercise has segmented into a set of exemplary local dynamics.

To be able to deal with such global dynamics requires modifying the extreme hypotheses (in particular, Full Performance,) which make it possible to sketch out the Traverse itself as a predetermined trajectory to a given point of arrival. Removal of these assumptions, and explicit consideration of a decision process, allows to realise that the appearance

---

[7]The above mentioned hypothesis of a constant take out, together with a fix wage assumption, is made on purpose to let unemployment appear as the result of the breaking of the intertemporal complementarity of production.

of problems of intertemporal complementarity of production also implies problems of co-ordination of economic activity (Amendola and Gaffard 1998). As the result of the interaction of the intertemporal complementarities of the production process and of the decision process the evolution of the economy becomes the expression of a thoroughly sequential process which cannot be charted beforehand unless we ourselves travel with it. The global dynamics of the model we expect to be anything but regular, so that we cannot look for steady states, growth paths, or even oscillations (relatively) easily decomposable into their principal modes. Neo-Austrian dynamics is a way of handling complex dynamics by simplifications, and shares the themes at the core of theories of complex dynamics. In other words, the Neo-Austrian model becomes relevant if and only when it leads to some interesting dynamics, meaning dynamics that cannot be resolved into some simple law. It becomes really interesting when it leads to computational experiments as the means to analyse its implications.

R. Day discerns 'two fundamentally distinct characterisations of economic dynamics, both descendant of classical and neo-classical economics: one of adapt*ed* equilibrium dynamics and one of adapt*ive* evolutionary dynamics" (1993, p. 21). The property of adaptive, evolutionary approach is to focus "on the characterisation of the way economies work out of equilibrium" and to explicitly represent "their capacity to change structure, i.e., to evolve or self organise" (ibid.). Many difficulties and problems are inherent to such an approach. Neo-Austrian dynamics, which is based upon a clear characterisation of production and decision processes, provides a solution to "the problem of generating out-of-equilibrium dynamics and of characterising economic evolution itself using disequilibrium theory" (ibid.).

## 6 TOWARDS A UNIFICATION OF MACROECONOMICS

The task implicitly devoted to a Neo-Austrian model by Hicks is to explore some essential macroeconomic issues. In his last paper he tried "to show that the teaching of Keynes and that of the Great Classics can be made compatible, so that it can be available to us as a coherent system of thought " (1990, p. 536).

As a matter of fact, as already mentioned, Neo-Austrian analysis is a theory of the economic process as a whole i.e. a macroanalysis. But it differs from the Keynesian macroanalysis insofar as it does not rely upon the restrictive assumption which consists in considering the technique of production and the capital equipment as given in the short run. This assumption has been criticised by J.A. Schumpeter who observed "that the restrictive assumption in question excludes the very essence of capitalist reality, all the phenomena and problems of which – including the short run phenomena – hinge upon the incessant creation of new and novel equipment, and that, because of this, a model framed upon this restrictive assumption has next to no application to questions of practical diagnosis, prognosis, and, above all, economic policy unless reinforced by extraneous considerations" (Schumpeter, 1954, p. 280n). Neo-Austrian theory, because it brings into light both the intertemporal complementarity of production processes and the intertemporal co-ordination of decision processes, provides a framework in which it becomes possible to show how "all the phenomena and problems hinge upon the incessant creation of new and novel capital equipment ".

The interaction between short and long period is at the heart of this creation, and it can be captured by sketching out both an intra and an interperiod sequence, where the one depends on, and at the same time determines, the other. To do so it is necessary in the first place to figure out a different relation between parameters and variables (between exogenous and endogenous magnitudes) with respect to standard analytical models - that is, as already stressed in section 2 above, a relation based on the time perspective under which we look at economic magnitudes rather than on any specific character of these magnitudes. This different relation reflects a change in analytical focus of the model considered - no longer aimed at singling out growth factors but at analysing processes of change. This goes along with a different structure of the model itself and a different use to which it can be put .

The effective link between short and long period in such a sequential model are the state variables, which at each given moment represent the existing constraints but are themselves the result of what has been happening along the sequence of periods which has led to the present state of the economy. "Thus to-day's decisions, taken on the basis of to-day's constraints, go to modify the constraints that will affect tomorrow's decisions - and so on in the sequence 'constraints-decisions-constraints' "(Amendola and Gaffard, 1988, p. 49). This intertemporal complementarity of the decision process - characterised out of equilibrium by a lag in the transmission of information – interacting with the intertemporal complementarity of a production process characterised by a construction lag, determines how the economy evolves sequentially over time.

Within the sequential context, output, prices and wages determination mechanisms carry over and most likely amplify the imbalances in the structure of productive capacity (first of all the one between construction and utilisation) which result from the original breaking up of the functioning of the economy due to the attempt to carry out a qualitative change. This stirs an out- of-equilibrium process that causes fluctuations in output and prices, and hence in available financial resources and in investment, which make productive activity less and less consistent over time and hence undermine the viability of the path followed by the economy; so that the viability of this path becomes the crucial analytical problem

Fluctuations are then the typical way in which the evolution of the economy takes place, and hence they no longer appear as deviations from a predetermined trend[8].

### 7. WHICH USE FOR THE MODEL

The Neo-Austrian approach is neither stochastic nor deterministic. We have seen that 'shock' is a linguistic device to focus upon a special time span or a short run that highlights the moment when structural change is undertaken. The shock starts up the out-of-equilibrium process through which the change takes place. The latter is a break in a routine, an innovation.

The Neo-Austrian model is not designed 'to predict' in the sense for which formal economic dynamics was created. Classical Macrodynamics, as a set of deterministic theories of both growth and oscillations, focused upon the investigation of the long run behaviours of an economy cast in the formal language of dynamical system theory. Accordingly, 'well behaved systems' were – defined to be – those that exhibited a finite number of attractors, so that, depending perhaps upon initial conditions belonging to one or the other of the various associated

---

[8]We have to mention that in the modern neo-classical macrodynamic theory, which also lays claim to a unification of macroeconomics, the distinction between the short run and the long run vanishes and macroeconomic time series are described as random walks, rather than as fluctuations or deviations from deterministic trends

basins, the model could predict future or emulate past history of an economy more or less precisely, though most often only qualitatively. This is because classical dynamics and Macrodynamics were both build around the analysis of state attractors and attractors are the predictors of the systematic dynamic behaviours, whether point-equilibria or closed curves of self-sustaining oscillations.

All other dynamical systems, and in particular those without well identified attractors, were not to be handled, for they could not be accommodated within a certain philosophy. Such systems can only be dealt with numerically – with numerical experiments. Until not long ago, they were treated as 'anomalies'.

The Neo-Austrian model accepts such anomaly, in this sense. To characterise its dynamics in contrast to classical macrodynamics, it may be useful to think in the following terms. In the classical approach, dynamics is classified into disequilibrium dynamics, that is, the set of transient dynamical behaviours, and long run attractors, that are locally unique dynamical behaviours. With the neo-Austrian model, instead, we look for qualitative features of the out-of-equilibrium path which is not a transition path (because, once the very specific assumptions of the analysis of the Traverse have been relaxed, there is no attractor) but a process which builds up step by step. This is because, once the very specific assumptions of the analysis of the Traverse have been relaxed, there is no attractor. In relation to this process we do not (and probably cannot) derive anything similar to the invariant laws implicitly governing long run dynamics that are sought by the classical approach. Our intellectual scenarios are derived by construction, rather than by mathematical properties of well defined solution paths. As a matter of fact, Neo Austrian models with complex structures generate complex dynamics. "Time series" which are generated by running numerical experiments with such models are however artificial. Therefore, it is useful and sometimes necessary to select some key variables in order to draw phase diagrams and obtain thus information more amenable to interpretation. The choice of particular phase diagrams is determined by their being consistent with the aim of producing a comprehensive view of the system evolution. Within such phase diagrams, different regimes can be identified, corresponding to delimited regions in the phase space in use. Changes of regimes may be interpreted as signs of the emergence of viability issues.

Thus the model cannot predict states, it is inherently a purely quali-tative formal model of dynamics. Its 'predictions' therefore can only be qualitative, if they can emerge at all. What is the use of such models, then?

An economy travelling on an equilibrium path (be it a steady state or not) is fully adjusted. Rational expectations prevent the agents of this economy from making errors that would be 'fossilised' in the capital equipment or in the human capital. This is the reason why given proper-ties of 'technical' functions (production and utility functions) and given initial conditions, including the information structure, are sufficient for determining the trajectories followed by this economy. On the contrary, an economy which is not fully adjusted travels on an out-of-equilibrium path. Its evolution depends not only on 'fundamentals', but also and mainly on behaviour mechanisms which reveal how the market informa-tion is treated step by step. Cumulative changes far away a notional equilibrium characterize possible paths as well as travels near such equilibrium. The essence of Neo-Austrian models is to consider such an economy. They cannot describe complete trajectories. They only allow to explore medium run sequences which derive from certain impulses and certain behaviours adopted in reaction to market disequilibria.

The neo-Austrian analysis puts (at least, implicitly) the emphasis on interdependence as do general equilibrium models. However, in general equilibrium models interdependence is instantaneously obtained as the result of establishing an equilibrium system of prices (whatever the in-formation structure that the prices themselves express) which represent the only interdependence link. In this perspective the temporal order of decisions does not matter by definition. Contemporaneous causality is used, alone. As Hicks put it, " a 'Walrasian' model of growth equilib-rium (...) has the defect (...) that it is clumsy in dealing with the order in which events occur, that it pays less than due respect to sequence in time ' (Hicks, 1970, p. 257).

The interdependence that Neo-Austrian models do take into account, instead, is interdependence along the out-of-equilibrium, path. This takes the form of feedback mechanisms over time. Different types of disequilibria can follow from this and interact with each other sequen-tially. As we have seen, Hicks focuses on one of them: the Ricardo ma-chinery effect. Now, in principle, different evolution paths of the economy may be associated with any kind of original shock (impulse).

Neo-Austrian or sequential models are heuristic tools that make it possible to explore them. What Neo-Austrian analysis is after is not mimicking reality, though. Rather it attempts to unveil sequential causality relations which represent the backbone of processes of economic change. Unlike in the equilibrium approach these processes are not already totally sketched out by the 'fundamentals' of the economy but are rather the outcome of what happens on the way; and this may change according to the decisions taken and the policies followed sequentially.

The main point to be stressed, here, is that different kinds of interventions - aimed at regulating the working of the existing dynamic mechanisms (prices, wages and output determination systems as affected by the control variables of the economy), or at providing other compensating mechanisms - are required to interact dynamically in order to correct both the bias in construction and/or that in utilisation resulting from the shock which has originally affected the economy, thus reestablishing the consistency over time of productive activity and making the evolution of the economy viable. This mix of interventions, on the other hand, cannot be made once and for all but must be continuously modified as the interventions are interventions over time that have to deal with a process affected by perturbations which take on different shape and intensity in time. "Such viability creating mechanisms are the analogue of equilibrium 'existence' proofs, but in the out-of-equilibrium setting. They are required to guarantee the existence of a continuing 'solution' to the system in terms of feasible actions for all its constituent model components" (Day, 1993, p. 39). This is the different way in which the concept of 'solution' must be intended when referred to an out-of-equilibrium process (It is evident that this has very little to do with the analytical solution which defines a steady state or, more generally, an intertemporal equilibrium). It calls for a monitoring of the process itself to bring into light its salient moments: which can only be obtained by means of numerical experiments, that is, by simulations that, under certain conditions allow to unveil what happens 'along the way'. As Day put it, model simulation "can never yield general inferences from a given system of assumptions but can yield specific inferences of great variety and interest" (Day, 1975, p. 29).

Thus the Neo-Austrian model appears as a heuristic device to throw light on the crucial links which characterise the sequential development of a process of structural change, so as to help to single out the inter-

286

ventions that, moment after moment, make it possible to render this process viable.

## REFERENCES

Amendola, M. and J-L Gaffard (1988): *The Innovative Choice: an economic analysis of the dynamics of technology*, Oxford, Basil Blackwell.
— (1998): *Out of Equilibrium*, Oxford, Clarendon Press.
Burmeister E. (1974): 'Synthesizing the Neo-Austrian and Alternative Approaches to Capital Theory: a Survey', *Journal of Economic Literature*, 413–56.
Day, R.H. (1975): "Adaptive Processes and Economic Theory", in R.Day and T.Groves eds. *Adaptive Economic Models*, New York: Academic Press.
— (1993): "Non-linear Dynamics and Economics. A Historian' Perspective". In Day R. and Ping Chen eds. *Non-linear Dynamics and Evolutionary Economics*, Oxford: Oxford University Press.
Goodwin, R.M., and L. F. Punzo (1987*): The Dynamics of a Capitalist Society. A Multisectoral Approach*, Cambridge, Polity Press.
Hicks, J.R. (1951): *A Contribution to the theory of the trade cycle*, Oxford: Clarendon Press.
— (1970): "A Neo-Austrian Growth Theory", *The Economic Journal* 80, 257–79.
— (1973): *Capital and Time*, Oxford: Clarendon Press.
— (1985*): Methods of Dynamic Economics*, Oxford: Clarendon Press.
— (1990): "The Unification of Macroeconomics", *The Economic Journal* 100, 528–38.
Kaldor, N. (1985): *Economics without Equilibrium*, New York: M.E.Sharpe Inc.
Punzo, L. F. (1995), "Some Complex Dynamics for a Multisectoral Model of the Economy", *Revue Economique*, 46, 1541–1560.
Schumpeter, J.A. (1954): *History of Economic Analysis*, London, Allen & Unwin.
Solow, R.M. (1992): "Siena Lectures on Endogenous Growth Theory", Collana del Dipartimento di Economia Politica, Università degli studi di Siena.

# CHAPTER - 21

# CULTURE AND ECONOMIC GROWTH: THE STATE AND GLOBALIZATION[1]

## Keith Griffin

### ABSTRACT

The essay begins by challenging the widely held view that there is an inherent conflict between equity and growth. The state, it is argued, can introduce policies that simultaneously reduce gender, social and ethnic inequalities while accelerating economic growth and human development. Indeed a greater concern for equity is essential because the modern state is inescapably a pluralist and multicultural institution. Pluralism, in turn, should be seen as a public good that confers benefits on society as a whole. That is, pluralism and the cultural interchange that accompanies it result in greater diversity which then leads to increased creativity and innovation. This occurs at both the country and global levels. Indeed globalization does not result in a single global culture. On the contrary, globalization leads to new permutations of cultures and greater diversity. This greater global diversity is a source of dynamism, creativity and increased well being, but rules of the game must be created and enforced to ensure that cultural interpenetration is a two way street rather than a path to domination.

## 1. INTRODUCTION

Sir John Hicks not only was a great economist, he was also a remarkably wide ranging economist. He wrote before the age of specialization and made substantial contributions to many branches of economics. Among

[1] I am grateful to Steven Helfand, Azizur Rahman Khan, Prasanta Pattanaik and Jan Nederveen Pieterse for helpful comments on an earlier version of this essay. This paper is a much shortened version of my "Culture, Human Development and Economic Growth," UNRISD-UNESCO *Occasional Papers on Culture and Development*, No. 3, 1997. This version was presented at a conference on Global Futures at the Institute of Social Studies in The Hague in October 1997.

his relatively neglected works is a little gem entitled *A Theory of Economic History* (Oxford University Press, 1969). This is a small book in which he brings his formidable erudition to bear on the deep causes of economic change, including the role of global interchange between peoples of different cultures. This essay in his memory is written in the spirit of *A Theory of Economic History*, and in particular of Chapter IV of that book, "City States and Colonies".

It is commonly argued in economics that growth and human betterment can best be achieved by the accumulation of physical capital, that attempts to reduce inequality are likely to reduce economic efficiency and the rate of growth, that government can contribute most by doing least, and that culture has little or nothing to do with improving the material well being of people or promoting human development. All four of these propositions have recently been challenged anew and this essay should be seen as part of that challenge, albeit a small part. In addition to challenging ancient orthodoxies, however, I wish to look forward and consider briefly the policy implications of the revisionist views and the outline of a possible alternative future.

### INEQUALITY AND GROWTH REVISITED

There is a long tradition in economic thought that postulates a conflict between efficiency and equity, growth and equality. Indeed this conflict sometimes is described as the "great trade-off."[2] The conflict has its origins, depending on the author, in the historical role of the capitalist class, in the importance for investment of a high share of profits in national income[3] or in the propensity of the rich to save a higher proportion of their income than the poor.[4] Whatever the precise formulation, the conclusion inevitably reached is that any attempt by the government to reduce inequality in the distribution of income is highly likely to impair efficiency in the allocation of resources or lower the rate of growth, and probably both.

---

[2]Arthur Okun, *Equality and Efficiency: The Big Tradeoff*, Washington, D.C.: Brookings Institution, 1975.

[3]Nicholas Kaldor, "Capital Accumulation and Economic Growth," in Nicholas Kaldor, ed., *Further Essays on Economic Theory*, New York: Holmes and Meier, 1978.

[4]Mahbub ul Haq, *The Strategy of Economic Planning*, Karachi: Oxford University Press, 1963.

The human development perspective challenges these propositions and casts a different light on these issues.[5] For example, one implication of the human development approach is that the more equal is the distribution of income, the easier it is for the fruits of growth to be transformed into human development. It is equally plausible that under some circumstances, the greater is the degree of equality, the faster is likely to be the rate of growth. Why might this be the case?

First, the perpetuation of inequality can be costly. Severe inequality produces resentment, discontent and unruliness, even rebellion. Containment of unruliness, suppression of discontent requires resources in the form of expenditure on the police and armed forces, the judiciary, prisons and the penal system – resources that could otherwise be used to promote economic expansion. In extreme cases inequality can make a society ungovernable and cause serious disruption of the economy.

Second, even in less extreme cases, inequality can undermine the legitimacy of the political regime. Inequality, and the avarice and ruthlessness that often are required to sustain it, weakens the rule of law, severs the bonds of trust that enable a society to function properly and destroys the social solidarity necessary for an "imagined community" to operate as an effective state.[6] Moreover modern technology has destroyed the monopoly of the state over the means of violence. Crime, terrorism and insurgent movements have become banal; violence has become democratized; the victims of injustice have explosive means to vent their anger. And all of this can lower the rate of economic growth. One need look no further than Africa, the Middle East or American ghettos for evidence.

The other side of this coin is that measures to reduce inequality can simultaneously contribute to faster growth. For example, third, there is much evidence that small farms are more efficient than either large collective farms of the Soviet type or the capitalist latifundia one finds in

---

[5]For statements of the human development approach see Amartya Sen, "Development as Capability Expansion," in Keith Griffin and John Knight, eds., *Human Development and the International Development Strategy for the 1990's*, London: Macmillan, 1990 and United Nations Development Programme, *Human Development Report 1990*, New York: Oxford University Press, 1990, Ch. 1.

[6]The phrase "imagined communities" is borrowed from B. Anderson, *Imagined Communities: Reflections on the Origin and Spread of Nationalism*, London: Verso, 1983.

Latin America and elsewhere.[7] A redistributive land reform and the creation of a small peasant farming system can produce performances as good as if not better than those of other agricultural systems. The experience of such places as China and South Korea is instructive.

Fourth, what is true of small farms is equally true of small and medium industrial and commercial enterprises. An egalitarian industrial structure, as Taiwan vividly demonstrates, can conquer world markets.[8] Large enterprises do not in general enjoy competitive superiority – the importance of economies of scale is much exaggerated – and often in developing countries large enterprises depend on the state for protection from foreign producers, for subsidized bank credit, for tax favours and for guaranteed sales to the public sector under state procurement policies. Industrial policy thus often encourages both inequality and inefficiency. Small enterprises in contrast often face numerous official barriers, the removal of which would reduce inequality while encouraging faster growth.

Fifth, investment in education, particularly at the primary and secondary levels, is a highly effective way to reduce inequality in the distribution of income. It is also, as is becoming widely recognized, an effective way to stimulate growth. Even if one remains an unreconstructed advocate of growth and is unpersuaded by arguments that human development is the ultimate objective, there is a strong case for supporting large public and private expenditure on education. There probably is no easier way to combine equality and rapid growth. The whole of East Asia is testimony to the veracity of this proposition.[9]

A final example of the falsity of the great trade-off is the liberation of women. Equal treatment of women would release the talent, energy, creativity and imagination of half the population. As it is, women already do more than half the world's work, but they have little control over resources (and often over their own bodies); they have restricted opportunities for education, employment and participation in political

---

[7]See, for example, Albert Berry and William Cline, *Agrarian Structure and Productivity in Developing Countries*, Baltimore: Johns Hopkins University Press, 1979 and Keith Griffin, *The Political Economy of Agrarian Change*, London: Macmillan, 1974.

[8]John Fei, Gustav Ranis and Shirley Kuo, *Growth with Equity: The Taiwan Case*, Oxford: Oxford University Press, 1979.

[9]See, for instance, Nancy Birdsall, David Ross and Richard Sabot, "Inequality and Growth Reconsidered: Lessons from East Asia," *World Bank Economic Review*, Vol. 9, Nov. 3, September 1995.

life; they are engaged in sectors such as the household economy which are severely undercapitalized compared to other sectors, and which therefore condemn them to low productivity labour and low returns on their effort; and they are denied opportunities for advancement.[10] The subjugation of women produces inequality, inefficiency and a slower rate of growth than would otherwise be possible. The removal of discrimination, in contrast, would reduce inequality and promote growth, while of course raising the level of human development.

The old conflict between equality and growth thus turns out to be a shibboleth. Under some circumstances greater equality actually can accelerate economic growth and greater equality almost certainly would contribute to human development. Thus intervention by the state to reduce inequalities in opportunities, income and wealth, if properly designed and implemented, can have very beneficial consequences.

### CULTURE AND THE STATE

Although in principle the state can introduce policies to reduce inequality, increase the pace of economic growth and enhance human development, in practice states often are weak or use such power as they have to benefit particular classes, groups or factions in society rather than the population as a whole. This can occur in both democratic and authoritarian states as the experiences, respectively, of Brazil and the Sudan attest. There are many possible reasons for this, but one neglected explanation –and possibly an important one – has to do with the role of culture.

Defining culture broadly, as is most appropriate in this context, as "ways of life" helps to highlight several notable features of the contemporary world. First, there are of course a great many ways of life that one can observe. Some ways of life are geographically restricted whereas some cultures cover a large terrain. Indeed there are more ways of life, i.e. more cultures, than there are states. One obvious implication of this is that cultures and states do not coincide; the jurisdiction of territorial states does not "map" the space occupied by distinct cultures. There is a disunity of coverage and this lack of coincidence creates a possibility of conflicting allegiances, divided loyalties and contested claims for primacy of affection.

---

[10]A great deal of evidence is assembled in UNDP, *Human Development Report 1995*, New York: Oxford University Press, 1995.

Second, the cultures that one observes today are almost always older than any existing state. In fact the contemporary state is a relatively recent institutional innovation, dating roughly from 18th century Europe, and the majority of actual states were created in the 20th century after the disintegration of the worldwide imperial system. Most cultures antedate the emergence of the state system and the nationalism and patriotism associated with it. This does not imply that cultures are necessarily ancient, traditional or static, much less that they are timeless. On the contrary, cultures should be seen as changing, dynamic, fluid, in a constant state of flux. Thus cultures, paradoxically, are simultaneously young and old; they represent distinctive ways of life yet they are influenced by other cultures with which they come into contact.

Third, cultures often are transnational phenomena. Geographically, cultures frequently transcend the boundaries of territorial states. This obviously is true of Arab culture in the Middle East, of many African cultures divided by arbitrary boundaries during the colonial period, of "Western" culture, of Kurdish culture in Turkey, Syria, Iraq and Iran, of Chinese culture in East and Southeast Asia, and so on. Cultures thus pose, or are perceived to pose, both an external challenge to some states and a risk, perhaps only a latent risk, of internal subversion. States often respond to these threats, real or imaginary, either by suppressing transnational cultural minorities (e.g. the suppression of the Kurdish minority by the Turkish state) or by half-hearted obeisance to ideals of transnational economic and political union (as in the various, and unsuccessful, pan-Arab, pan-African and pan-Latin American movements). Only in western Europe, with the formation of the European Community, have strong supranational institutions been created within a relatively homogeneous cultural space.

Fourth, virtually all states include within their boundaries a multiplicity of cultures. Indeed the term "nation state" is a misnomer. Modern states include a large number of national groups, ethnicities, "tribes", languages and religions, i.e., ways of life. The modern state is irreversibly a multi-cultural institution. Pluralism is a fact of life of the contemporary world, a fact which has yet to be properly digested by analysts and policy makers alike. Some states (Israel, Pakistan, Iran) behave as if they contained a homogeneous population of uniform religious belief; few states (Switzerland is an obvious exception) have constructed institutions which explicitly take into account the linguistic, religious and ethnic diversity of citizens.

Many states have made attempts, of varying degrees of effort and success, to reduce discrimination against minority groups, to integrate those of different "race" into the mainstream and to assimilate the foreign-born, the indigenous population and other minorities into the dominant society. Diversity, pluralism and multi-culturalism within states, however, raise issues which go beyond assimilation, integration, affirmative action, anti-discrimination and the like. They raise questions of access to resources and institutions, participation in the wider life of the polity and society, as well as issues of fairness and equity. Cultural diversity raises the questions of how best to protect the interests and rights of minorities, how to avoid the tyranny of the majority, and how best to secure adequate representation of minorities in decision making institutions.

How one approaches these questions depends in part on how one views the role of multi-culturalism within states. At one end of the spectrum of opinion are those who view pluralism as a disadvantage. Diversity is a source of conflict; it often leads to violence and bloodshed; it results in political instability; and it makes it hard for people to get along together in their daily life. Multi-culturalism is something that must be contained or managed, preferably by making "them" as much like "us" as possible. Far from contributing to economic growth and human development, cultural diversity is an obstacle that in one way or another must be overcome or got around.

At the other end of the spectrum are those who regard cultural diversity not as a liability but as an asset. Different ways of life, different ways of looking at the world, different ways of thinking are indeed challenging and a source of dissonance and tension that can lead to conflict and violence. But those challenges and tensions are also a source of creativity (in all its forms) and it is creativity (not capital in any of its forms) which is the fountainhead of economic growth and human development. That is, it is new knowledge, new technology and new institutional arrangements which are the ultimate sources of growth and development[11] and it is a plausible hypothesis that cultural diversity acts

---

[11]This idea is nicely captured in Joseph Schumpeter's statement that "add successively as many mail coaches as you please, you will never get a railway thereby." (Jo-

as a stimulus to innovative activities of all sorts. That is, one can view cultures as "experiments" which are sources of knowledge. The more experiments humanity conducts, i.e. the greater is cultural diversity, the more knowledgeable and innovative we are likely to be.

It has long been recognized that minorities often are highly innovative in business and account for a disproportionate number of entrepreneurs. Think of the Chinese in southeast Asia, the Lebanese in west Africa, the Indians in east Africa and the Quakers in the United Kingdom. The claim being made here, however, is more general, namely, that pluralism contributes to creativity in all fields of endeavour. If this is true, then over the very long run multi-cultural states have more potential than states with a relatively homogeneous population. A potential for human and material progress does not of course imply that the potential inevitably will be realized. The translation of potential into actual achievement depends on whether in a particular time and place the advantages of pluralism can be brought into play and the disadvantages minimized. At any given moment some culturally homogeneous societies (e.g. Japan, South Korea) may appear on balance to be less divisive and more dynamic than some pluralist societies, but given a longer time horizon, pluralism is likely to be more advantageous than homogeneity.

### GLOBALIZATION AND CULTURAL INTERCHANGE

Cultural diversity is of course much greater at the global than at the country level. It might have been possible once upon a time to imagine cultures as being separated from one another – with room to breathe and to develop independently – but technological change in transport and communications has for centuries been dissolving time and space, breaking down the barriers which surround even the most isolated cultures. This process has accelerated dramatically in the last fifty years and is part of a wider tendency toward globalization. One consequence of globalization is that cultures are coming into increasingly close contact with one another. The Chinese culture rubs against the Indian culture. The Indian culture rubs against the European culture. The European culture rubs against African cultures, and so on.[12]

---

seph A. Schumpeter, *The Theory of Economic Development*, Cambridge: Harvard University Press, 1959, p. 64, n.1.)

[12]Indeed it can be argued that European culture was constituted historically by non-European (namely Asian and African) influences and is a product of cultural mixing that

The "rubbing" of cultures is not a question of physical proximity and, indeed, strictly speaking cultures do not have fixed boundaries. They interpenetrate and for this reason cultures are not homogeneous; they are, rather, hybrids.[13] It is thus particular cultural attributes that rub against one another and not one particular reified culture (much less a singular national or state culture) that rubs against another.

Be that as it may, this "rubbing" has been going on for a long time and before considering the implications for the contemporary world, it is worth glancing back at history. It would be fatuous to claim that technological change and the cultural interchange that follows it have been universally beneficial. Development has been uneven and, more important, the impact of cultural interchange has often been asymmetrical, some groups and cultures losing absolutely, not just relatively. Central Asia, for instance, long occupied a strategic position on the caravan trade routes connecting China with the eastern Mediterranean and Europe. Its cities of Samarkand, Bukhara and Khiva (now in Uzbekistan) were centres of economic, political and cultural activity where the arts and architecture, the natural sciences and mathematics and theology flourished. Beginning in the 15th century, the development of transoceanic transport, however, made overland transport through Central Asia unprofitable and the region fell into a steep decline. The maritime regions of Asia were brought into closer contact with Europe while parts of the interior of Asia became increasingly isolated.

Closer contact, however, has been a mixed blessing. Whether one considers the explosive conquests of Islam beginning in the 7th century, which from the epicentre in Arabia covered the whole of the Middle East, all of North Africa and the Iberian peninsula in Europe, or the westward migration of the Mongol "hordes" of the 13th century, which ended at the Danube River and the outskirts of Budapest, or the unrelenting expansion of Western Europe from the 15th century onwards to virtually every corner of the globe, cultural interchange often seems more like a one way street than a dual carriageway highway. Cultural

---

goes back at least to ancient Egypt. See, for example, Jan Nederveen Pieterse, "Unpacking the West: How European is Europe?", in Ali Rattansi and Sallie Westwood, eds., *Racism, Modernity and Identity: On the Western Front*, Cambridge: Polity Press, 1994.

[13]See Jan Nederveen Pieterse, "Globalisation as Hybridisation," *International Sociology*, Vol. 9, No. 2, June 1994.

contact often has been a by-product of military encounters and has been associated with violence, pillage, war, enslavement, conquest, colonialism and imperialism.[14] It has led to the introduction of alien diseases to those who had no natural resistance to them and in some cases to the decimation of indigenous populations. It has helped to spread racism;[15] occasionally it has resulted in genocide; more often it has led to the destruction of pre-existing social structures and the system of beliefs that sustained them.[16] Historically, globalization often had a fatal impact.[17]

Yet there is another side to the story: cultural contact was indeed a mixed blessing. The initial effects of cultures rubbing against one another may well be accurately described by the phrase "a fatal impact",[18] but the longer term effects were more positive. Contacts between cultures led to a myriad of exchanges and adaptations that were of benefit to all parties. Consider foodstuffs and primary commodities. Latin America gave us maize, potatoes, the tomato and natural rubber; Ethiopia and Yemen gave us coffee; China gave us tea and noodles (which the Italians transformed into pasta), and so on. The world's pharmacopoeia similarly draws on botanical products from many different regions. The same is true of our domesticated animals.

Early Chinese science led the world and in the field of technology China gave us paper, porcelain (or fine "china"), the compass, gunpowder and much else.[19] The Arabs gave us our system of numerals. The Central Asians gave us algebra and taught us how to measure the motions of the heavens. India gave us Buddhism, the Arabian peninsula Islam and Palestine Christianity. Mutual influences in art and architec-

---

[14]Hartmut Elsenhans, *Development and Underdevelopment: The History, Economics and Politics of North-South Relations,* New Delhi: Sage Publications, 1991.

[15]For an analysis of how scientific and technological achievement became a measure of the value of a civilization in the 18th century, justifying the right to "civilize" inferior "races" and to dominate the world, see Michael Adas, *Machines as the Measure of Men,* Ithaca: Cornell University Press, 1989.

[16]For a study of how this continues today in the Amazon, see Norman Lewis, *The Missionaries,* London: Secker and Warburg, 1988.

[17]The phrase is borrowed from Alan Moorehead, *The Fatal Impact: An Account of the Invasion of the South Pacific, 1767–1840,* London: Hamish Hamilton, 1966.

[18]The impact effects of European expansion and the "development of underdevelopment" are discussed in Keith Griffin, *Underdevelopment in Spanish America,* London: Allen and Unwin, 1969, Ch.1 and Andre Gunder Frank, "The Development of Underdevelopment," *Monthly Review,* Vol. 18, No. 4, September 1966.

[19]See the multi-volume study by Joseph Needham, *Science and Civilisation in China,* Cambridge: Cambridge University Press, various years.

ture, music and dance, crafts and household technology are too numerous to recount. All our cultures have been immeasurably enriched by contact with others.

Similar processes can be observed today. Indeed, whatever may have been the case in the past, today no culture, no society is completely closed.[20] The questions revolve around the degree of openness and the terms on which a culture interacts with other cultures. That is, whether the relationship is one of subordination, domination and exploitation or one of equality, mutual respect and beneficial exchange. The difference today is that globalization has made cultural interchange more frequent than in the past, deeper and more rapid. Some have speculated that we are witnessing the emergence of a "global culture" and submerging local cultures under an irresistible tide of Western influence. Culture worldwide is becoming more homogeneous: coca-cola, blue jeans and North American popular music rule the roost. Local dialects and entire languages are disappearing by the hundreds, local cuisines are being replaced by Western-style fast foods, traditional ways of life are being abandoned in favour of pale images of the American way of life.

While there is some truth to this, cultural interchange in the modern world is a two-way exchange. Capital, technology and even labour circulate globally. Science is universal and accessible to all to a greater degree than ever before. Ideas, information and knowledge are transmitted much more rapidly and more widely than in the past. The result is an increase in diversity: greater heterogeneity, not greater homogeneity. This evidently is true at any given location, as more and more ways of life learn to coexist, and it also is true globally, as cultural interpenetration multiplies the number of permutations and in the process creates new ways of life, new cultures. This increased diversity, in turn, has led to an acceleration in creativity and innovation. There has been an explosive growth of knowledge and technology in the last fifty years and this

---

[20]In the late 1960s to the early 1980s some analysts advocated policies of semi-autarky and "delinking" underdeveloped countries from the global economy. (See, for instance, Samir Amin, "Crisis, Nationalism and Socialism," in S. Amin, G. Arrighi, A.G. Frank and I. Wallerstein, eds., *Dynamics of Global Crisis*, New York: Monthly Review Press, 1982.) It is obvious today, however, that neither involuntary delinking (as in Iraq and North Korea) nor voluntary delinking (as in Mayanmar and Pol Pot's Cambodia) are promising avenues for economic growth or human development. (See Jan Nederveen Pieterse, "Delinking or Globalisation?", *Economic and Political Weekly*, 29 January 1994.)

has greatly contributed to the rapid advances in human development that have occurred and to the rapid economic growth we have enjoyed, a pace of growth worldwide that is unprecedented in human history. Cultural interchange has indeed been a mixed blessing, but the positive contribution of interchange has been extraordinarily large.

### THE INTRINSIC AND INSTRUMENTAL VALUES OF CULTURE

Culture (or the communal aspect of life) is analogous to human development (which focuses on the individual) in that culture is valued in itself and also as a means to obtain other things which are desired or valued. That is, culture possesses both intrinsic and instrumental value. The intrinsic value of culture has long been recognized and is reflected in many ways: in concerns to preserve cultural heritage, to respect our traditions and the preceding generations who passed them on to us, to record spoken languages before they disappear, to conserve, restore and maintain historical monuments, art objects and ancient artifacts. Culture as our way of life is something most of us treasure and wish to preserve in a recognizable form; it contributes to our sense of self or who we are and to our sense of satisfaction or well being.

In addition, however, culture as a means is becoming widely recognized. Increasingly the instrumental value of culture is being used by leaders in various areas of life to achieve economic, social and political purposes. This includes the appeal to tradition to forge new alliances based on ethnicity or nationality, sometimes with the objective of creating new, culturally homogeneous states, as with the Serbs in Bosnia. It also includes the revival of religious and other traditions in an attempt to re-establish an old order, to re-create a "golden age" and to impose ancient, fundamental values on a society regarded as immoral and godless. The Christian, Jewish, Islamic and Hindu "fundamentalist" movements can be interpreted in this way.

Thus culture has been used in places for sectarian and reactionary purposes and as a weapon to preserve or create a particular way of life. These uses of culture reflect "a politics of nostalgia."[21] These uses of culture, however, are only part of the global picture. As argued above, globalization has led to an intensification of cultural interchange and

---

[21]Jan Nederveen Pieterse, "The Cultural Turn in Development: Questions of Power, "*European Journal of Development Research*," Vol. 7, No. 1, 1995, p. 185.

this, in turn, is transforming local cultures without necessarily producing cultural uniformity. For example, culture is being used to create new forms of expression: English is becoming the *lingua franca*, yet spoken English is evolving in different directions in different regions of the world and taking on a separate identity while at the same time, the number of people who are bi-lingual or multi-lingual is increasing rapidly. Similarly, cultural interchange has led to new ways of communicating (e.g. via the fax and internet), new types of music, new ways of doing business (the transnational corporation), new forms of political organization (e.g. the European community), new channels of international crime and even new ways of finding a spouse (e.g. by advertizing in the international media). This burst of cultural creativity or cultural vitality, although uneven across space, is very widespread and indeed is reshaping the world, simultaneously creating elements of a "global culture" while strengthening many features of "local culture" or, better still, "popular culture".

One can think of culture as the glue that binds people together and enables them to interact. But cultures may not be equally successful in enabling people to live well, in peace and harmony, and to exercise their creativity. A culture of peace and harmony, for instance, is something that must be created, not just taken for granted. Genocide, ethnic cleansing, civil conflict, repression of minorities, domestic violence -- today as in the past, nationally and internationally -- are a reproach to our political cultures. Far too many people on this planet experience violence as an undesired aspect of their "way of life". Indeed, for many, violence or the threat of violence have become routine, a commonplace.

Yet at another level the glue provided by culture makes human development and economic growth possible. At this more profound level, culture is the most valuable instrument of all. Culture gives people a sense of identity and helps to define one's place in the world. It provides a degree of psychological security by enclosing each person within symbolically visible cultural boundaries. It fosters trust and cooperation within the group and thereby facilitates collective agreements, working together and market exchange. It makes people's behaviour and reactions more predictable than otherwise and this, too, facilitates cooperation, exchange and economic transactions in general. It inhibits (or at least contains) interpersonal, interkinship and intercommunity conflict while at times accentuating conflict with those of other cultures, particularly when "the other" is sharply defined or differentiated.

Globalization is bringing cultures into increasingly close and frequent contact with one another. This "rubbing" produces friction and the possibility of conflict,[22] which in turn require further cultural adaptation and institutional innovation. But cultural contact also leads to cultural exchange, to mutually profitable borrowing and lending, and to cultural adaptation. These, in turn, result in cultural vitality for all concerned, in aesthetic, scientific and technological creativity and in economic expansion. Indeed it is quite possible that cultural exchange is one of the roots, perhaps the principal root, of global dynamism and the ultimate source of human creativity, human development and economic growth.

If one adopts a culture-centred rather than a state-centred view of the world, things look rather different. Culture seen from a global perspective can be regarded as human "software".[23] This is a global asset which in principle is accessible to all, although in practice some groups have much greater ease of access than others. Access to this "software" takes place when cultures interpenetrate, an historical process that goes back as far as one can see. Today, however, cultural interpenetration is more frequent, more rapid and more pervasive than ever before. This aspect of globalization ultimately may be more significant than other features of the process that receive so much attention, namely, the rapid growth of international trade, the investments by transnational corporations, the huge flows of financial capital, the migration of labour and the political and institutional transformations occurring at supra-national levels. The reason cultural interpenetration is so important is that it implies cultural exchange and this, in turn, implies diversity, heterogeneity and a breaking down of mental and conceptual boundaries. That is, cultural exchange can be understood as "a translocal learning process"[24] which stimulates creativity and is the fountainhead of material progress and human development.

---

[22]Samuel Huntington has argued that in future the "principal conflicts of global politics" will be dominated by the clash of civilizations or cultures. See Samuel P. Huntington, "The Clash of Civilizations?", *Foreign Affairs*, Vol. 72, No. 3, Summer 1993.

[23]See T. Banuri, "Modernization and its Discontents: A Cultural Perspective on Theories of Development," in F. Appfel Marglin and Stephen A. Marglin, eds., *Dominating Knowledge*, Oxford: Clarendon Press, 1990.

[24]Jan Nederveen Pieterse, "Globalisation as Hybridisation," *loc. cit.*, p. 177.

## AN ALTERNATIVE FUTURE

A reassessment of the four propositions with which we began has implications for an alternative future. This alternative future could be constructed around the nexus of equality, growth, human development and culture. I have argued that for any given increase in output, the greater is the degree of equality in the distribution of income and wealth, the greater will be the increase in the average level of human development. That is, the impact of growth on human development depends in part on the distribution of income. At the same time, however, the greater is the degree of equality, the faster is likely to be the rate of growth of output. That is, the direction of causality runs from equality to growth, and not just the other way round. There are thus good reasons to give greater prominence to policies to reduce inequality than has been common in recent policy debates.

Technical change in the armaments industry has led to the democratization of violence. The state no longer has a monopoly of the instruments of warfare or the means to control the civilian population and hence its ability to maintain law and order has been eroded. Recognition of this fact will result eventually in greater recognition by the state that it must seek to reduce the justifications or pretexts for violence adduced by those who oppose the established order. If the state increasingly is unable to control the supply of the instruments of violence, it will have little alternative but to diminish the desire for violence. This implies the creation of a "culture of peace", nationally and internationally, based on respect for human rights, participation in political life and a celebration of cultural diversity and pluralism. Equality in this sense is likely to be high on future global agendas.

Greater public expenditure on education (especially at the primary and secondary levels), and greater investment in human capital in general, would almost certainly result in a reduction in inequality and, simultaneously, in an acceleration of the rate of growth of incomes and output. The denigration of the welfare state, so fashionable today, has gone much too far and an alternative future consistent with the arguments of this paper is bound to include a prominent role for public expenditure on human development.

The liberation of women – and specifically the provision of greater educational opportunities for girls, the creation of opportunities for paid employment by women, the removal of discrimination and barriers to occupational mobility, the provision of greater access to credit, and the equal treatment of women by the legal system, including inheritance laws--evidently would do much to redress pervasive inequalities. By releasing the talents, energy and creativity of half the population, greater equality for women also would stimulate economic growth.

These changes require action by the state. No desirable alternative future can be based on a withering of the state. The contemporary state, however, requires considerable adaptation. The point of departure is recognition that modern states are inescapably pluralist and multicultural institutions, and this implies that the legitimacy of states in future will have to rest on the foundation of wide participation in political, social and economic institutions; unhampered access to resources by those who can use them productively; fairness and equity in all spheres of life, including for instance, language policy in multilingual societies; and constitutional or other mechanisms to ensure that the rights of minorities are protected.

The reconstruction of the state on a multicultural foundation would reflect not only the reality of pluralism as a social fact of life but also recognition that pluralism is a collective asset, a public good which can yield benefits to all. Cultural heterogeneity is a source of creativity and dynamism and arguably the ultimate source of economic growth and human betterment. Openness to ideas and to alternative ways of life, to the "other" and to "them", is a more secure and more fruitful foundation for future states than an attempt to construct a community around a homogeneous "nation", at least in the long run. Indeed the aspiration to create "nation-states" is little more than a will-o'-the-wisp.

Just as one must recognize that states contain a multiplicity of cultures, so too one must recognize that individual cultures often cross state boundaries. This fact of cultural geography rarely is reflected in our political institutions. In future, however, we may well see the growth of supranational institutions which embrace transnational cultures and which provide a layer of organization somewhere between the state and the global level. Seen in this light, the European Community may be a harbinger of things to come. The Association of South-East Asian Nations (ASEAN) may be another.

Globalization in the realm of culture is however a very powerful force, no less powerful than economic globalization. Moreover, cultural interchange globally is as valuable as commercial interchange, and ultimately perhaps more valuable. The interpenetration of cultures at the global level that we are now witnessing will not in my judgment lead to a "world culture" but rather to the creation of new hybrids, new permutations and greater diversity. That is, globalization will spawn new cultures, and these new cultures – like the old ones – will be a source of dynamism, creativity and increased well being. We must use our imagination however to ensure that cultural interpenetration is genuinely a two way street, i.e., that exchange rather than domination characterizes cultural globalization.

Rules of the game will have to be established and enforced, e.g., concerning trade in valuable cultural artifacts, the preservation of treasured sites and monuments, the recording of languages threatened with extinction, and the use by transnational media of the airwaves and space (part of our global commons) for transmission of cultural material. Some progress has been made already, but we have a long way to go.[25] If cultural interpenetration is to be a two way street, then the rules of the game must be based on principles of equality and mutual respect which, in turn, reflect widespread recognition that cultural interchange is mutually advantageous.

---

[25]See the report of the World Commission on Culture and Development, *Our Creative Diversity*, Paris: UNESCO, 1995.

# CHAPTER - 22

# FINANCING OF GOVERNMENT EXPENDITURE AND THE EFFICACY OF IS-LM

*Surajit Sinha*

## ABSTRACT

Since Hicks' publication of Mr. Keynes and the "Classics", the IS-LM framework has remained a very useful tool with the macroeconomists. Keynes' revolutionary contribution in General Theory brought the role of government to the forefront of the economic thinking. This paper finds that the IS-LM framework has very few shortcomings to deal with alternative methods of financing government expenditure, but with a caveat: there is atleast one oversimplified assumption on which it has been constructed.

## 1. INTRODUCTION

Sir John Hicks in his seminal paper Mr. Keynes and the "Classics"; A Suggested Interpretation, outlined the IS-LM framework which is still popular with the macroeconomists. Hicks constructed it to compare the classical model with some of Keynes' contributions in General Theory. The most important difference between these two models is regarding the effectiveness of fiscal and monetary policies. These two policies are totally ineffective in the classical model, whereas both are effective in Keynes atleast in the short run. These results are due to their respective labour market assumptions. The classical model assumes flexible money wage and price. These assumptions keep the economy fully employed at all times. Consequently, the supply curve becomes a vertical line at full employment output.

[304]

The Keynesian labour market on the other hand, assumes a rigid money wage level in the short run, as a result the labour market remains under fully employed, and the supply curve becomes an upward sloping curve. The supply curve will turn vertical once the surplus labour is exhausted due to rise in prices. The Keynesians prefer to assume that the workers have money illusion in order to delay this possibility.

It will be easy now to appreciate why demand management policies are ineffective in the classical model in terms of their influence on output and employment, but effective in the Keynesian model atleast in the short run. These results follow from the IS-LM framework.[1]

The discussion in the rest of this paper will centre around the efficacy of the IS-LM framework concerning different financing methods that are used to fund government expenditure. The role of government acquired considerable significance after the publication of Keynes' General Theory. For a long time it was thought that sufficient government participation in the economy alone could recover an economy from any recession, although it might cost her some inflation. The current trend however is to reduce the scale of government activities. Still, governments the world over are required to spend in certain key sectors of the economy.

## 2. THE CLASSICAL MODEL

The classical seldom spoke about the role of government in the economy. The only policy variable they considered in their model was money supply which can be affected solely by printing new currency and putting them into circulation from a helicopter.[2] However, textbooks often prefer to include all three policy variables commonly mentioned in the Keynesian model, viz. government expenditure, income tax and money supply, in their discussion of the classical model. See, for instance Turnovsky (1982).

Let us assume that the economy is fully employed and that output is supply – determined. Therefore, the following two demand-side equations are sufficient to represent the classical model:

---

[1]The interested reader can verify these results from any textbook, such as Turnovsky (1982).

[2]This method is often referred to as 'helicopter money' or as 'mann from heaven'. Deficit financing is similar to this method except that the new currency is put into circulation through government spending.

$$Y = C - \overline{T} + I(r) + \overline{G} \tag{1}$$

$$\frac{\overline{M}}{P} = hY \tag{2}$$

where

$$Y = Y^f, \quad I_r = \frac{dI}{dr} < 0 \text{ and } 0 < h < 1 \tag{3}$$

$Y$ is output or real income. $C$ is residual consumption. $I(r)$ is the investment function where $r$ is the real rate of interest. $\overline{T}$ and $\overline{G}$ are respectively, lump sum tax and government expenditure, exogenously determined by the government.[3] $\overline{M}$ is the exogenous supply of money and $P$ is the price level. $hY$ is the transaction demand for money where $h$ is the coefficient of transaction demand. $Y^f$ is full employment output.

Eq. (1) is the goods market clearing condition. It can be rewritten as

$$S + \overline{T} = I(r) + \overline{G} \tag{4}$$

where $S = Y - C$ is savings. In the classical model

$$S = S(r, Y), \text{ where } S_r, S_y > 0 \tag{5}$$

Therefore, Eq. (4) becomes

$$S(r, Y) + \overline{T} = I(r) + \overline{G} \tag{6}$$

Eq. (6) can be drawn in the $Y - r$ plane as an IS curve. The slope of this curve will be

$$\frac{dr}{dy} = \frac{S_y}{I_r - S_r} < 0 \tag{7}$$

Similarly, the money market clearing condition in Eq. (2) can also be drawn in the $Y - r$ plane as a vertical LM curve at full employment output

$$Y^f \left[ = \frac{\overline{M}}{hP_0} \right].$$

Price $P_0$ is determined by this equation.

---

[3]Lump sum tax is assumed for simplicity's sake. A proportional tax system will not alter any of the results of this section.

Since Eq. (1) solves for $r$, the two equations are therefore independent of each other.

Now, consider three possible methods of financing government expenditure in the classical model. First, consider the possibility that an additional amount of $\overline{G}$ is bond-financed. Suppose government sells bonds to the public, and commercial and other banks. This will divert the savings of the economy to the government, thereby reducing the availability of funds for the private investors. As a result, the banks will be compelled to raise the rate of interest in order to increase the supply of savings on the one hand, and reduce private demand for loans, on the other.

Eq. (8) below confirms this line of reasoning. By totally differentiating Eq. (6) given that $dY = d\overline{T} = 0$, we get

$$\frac{dr}{d\overline{G}} = \frac{1}{S_r - I_r} > 0 \qquad (8)$$

Next, consider the possibility that government expenditure is deficit-financed. Suppose government sells treasury bills to the central bank against new currency to fund $d\overline{G}$. Since the IS curve will shift upwards again, the interest rate will rise. Contrary to the first case, money supply in the economy will also increase, but price rise will eventually restore the initial supply of real balance $\overline{M}/P$. This is the quantity theory of money.

Is there any logical explanation of this interest rate effect? Since under this method government no longer competes with the private investors for funds from the economy, there is not logical reason behind the rise in $r$ that the IS-LM framework indicates.

Finally, it follows from Eq. (6) that a balanced budget increase in government expenditure (i.e. $d\overline{G} = d\overline{T}$) will not affect either savings or investment, hence $r$ will remain unaffected. In other words, the IS curve will remain unaffected by this policy, therefore there is no reason why $r$ should change. The additional $\overline{T}$ will come out of $C$, and the new government goods will replace the consumer goods that are no longer produced because of the reduction in consumption demand owing to the additional $\overline{T}$ that is collected by the government.

### 3. THE KEYNESIAN MODEL

Consider a fixed price IS-LM framework for Keyne's model where the supply function is horizontal for simplicity's sake. The following two equations represent the IS and LM functions, respectively:

$$Y = c(Y - \overline{T}) + I(r) + \overline{G} \qquad (9)$$

$$\frac{\overline{M}}{\overline{P}} = hY + L(r) \qquad (10)$$

where

$$0 < c < 1 \text{ and } L_r < 0 \qquad (11)$$

$c$ is the marginal propensity to consume and $L(r)$ is the speculative demand for money. The rest of the variables and parameters have their earlier definitions and restrictions. The IS and LM curves can be drawn in $Y - r$ plane. The IS will be a downward sloping line as before, but the LM curve will be upward sloping in this case. Eq. 9 and 10 form a simulaneous equation system where $Y$ and $r$ will be simultaneously determined.

First, consider the possibility that government expenditure is bond-financed. Government sells bonds to the rest of the economy which will lower their price in the economy. If we assume the usual inverse relationship between the price of securities and the interest rate, then $r$ will rise[4] One can also argue that since banks will now have less funds for the private investors, they will be compelled to raise the interest rate. Moreover, output increase will increase the transaction demand for money, which will reduce the demand for bonds and other securities.[5] This will exert further downward pressure on security prices.

The IS-LM framework confirms this conclusion. If we totally differentiate Eq. (9) and (10) while holding $\overline{M}$ constant, we find

$$\frac{dr}{d\overline{G}} = -\frac{1}{(1-c)(Lr/h) + I_r} > 0 \qquad (12)$$

---

[4] We are assuming that the supply of shares remains unaffected throughout this discussion.

[5] $dy/d\overline{G} > 0$ can be easily verified from Eq. (9) and (10).

Let us now turn our attention to the deficit financing case. Government asks the central bank to print new currency against treasury bills in order to fund its additional expenditure. One obvious consequence of this policy will be increased availability of money and income in the economy. Logically, the economy will save more and at the same time invest more in the security market and also in physical capital. The former type of investment is expected to lower the interest rate, while the latter may even raise it. In addition, the increase in the transaction demand for money may also contribute to the rise in $r$. Therefore, the net effect seems uncertain.

If we totally differentiate Eqs. (9) and (10) given that $dG = dM / P$ and $dT = 0$, we find

$$\frac{dr}{d\overline{G}} = \frac{s-h}{sL_r + hI_r} \gtreqless 0 \text{ depending upon whether } s \lesseqgtr h \tag{13}$$

$s = 1 - c$ is the marginal propensity to save. Eq. 13 suggests that the direction of change in $r$ will depend upon the relative strengths of the marginal propensity to save and the coefficient of transaction demand for money. When $s < h$, economic agents will have to release funds from the securities market to fulfill their transaction needs. Moreover, increased investment demand relative to savings will contribute to the rise in $r$. In other words, a high propensity to consume in the economy will have a tendency to raise $r$.

On the other hand, when the marginal propensity to save is relatively greater than the transaction demand coefficient, the demand for securities will increase, consequently $r$ will fall. The interested reader is requested to probe into the third possibility where the interest rate remains unaffected when $s = h$. impact on the rate of interest: whether the direction of change in the interest rate or a situation of no change, seems logical according to economic reasoning. The few important findings are as follows:

(i) The IS-LM framework does well even for the classical model although they were seldom interested in the role of the government in the economy. However, it is somewhat disturbing that the deficit financing case did poorly, particularly when the classics (and later, the monetarists) considered 'helicopter money' as the only method of affecting the supply of money in the economy.

(ii) As expected the IS-LM framework does very well for the Keynesian model. It even provides more insight into the deficit financing case than one might expect of it. However, the author finds it difficult to interpret in two cases under deficit financing:

(a) When taxes are lump sum, if $s = h$ the interest rate doesn't change; and

(b) When taxes are proportional, there is no reason for $r$ to fall as $t$ increases.

These findings highlight the fact that there are only a few shortcomings of this tool in macroeconomics. However, a comprehensive examination could distort some of the simplicities of the results mentioned above. What seems no so logical to this author is how changes in the demand for investment goods will still keep the capital stock of the economy unchanged even in the short run. The supply curves mentioned in the beginning of this paper crucially depend upon a given amount of physical capital.

If one allows them to get affected in the course of changing $r$, supply shifts will be inevitable. In that case, significant changes will follow if the IS-LM framework is used. For instance, one will not be able to conclude anymore that fiscal measures do not affect output and employment. Instead, the rise in $r$ when $\overline{G}$ is bond-financed will reduce full employment output, hence prices will rise. The model will then tend to become unstable because LM will also shift backwards, which will raise $r$ further, causing more reductions in the capital stock of the economy, and so on. Therefore, despite Hicks' phenomenal contribution, the IS-LM framework may be based on some very simplified assumptions and may be containing a few unrealistic results.

## REFERENCES

J. Hicks, Mr. Keynes and the "Classics"; A Suggested Interpretation, *Econometrica*, Vol. 5, April 1937, pp. 147–159.

J. M. Keynes, The General Theory of Employment Interest and Money, Macmillan & Co., London, 1957.

S. Sinha, Keynes and Pigou on Classical Theory, this journal, Vol. 5(2), 1996, pp. 105–110.

S. J. Turnovsky, Macroeconomic Analysis and Stabilization Policy, S. Chand & Company, New Deli, 1982.

# CHAPTER - 23

# HICKS' APPROACH TO ECONOMIC THEORY

*R.S. Dhananjayan and N. Sasikaladevi*

### ABSTRACT

Economic theories propounded by Hicks always sought to comprehend the economic phenomena in their operational setting. Though, economists know a lot of economics, rarely very few like Sir. John Hicks succeed to comprehend them in a theoretical framework. The passage of time and changes in the institutional net work, compel economic theories to be constantly improved, revised and reformulated. Despite astonishingly wide range of Hicks' contributions to the economic discipline, we do not have 'Hicksian Economics' in the same tradition of 'Ricardian or Marxian or Keynesian Economics'. In his life long voyage in the wavy sea of economics, one thing that distinguishes him and his economic theories is the 'unique method' that he developed. It is the 'Hicksian Method'. To Hicks, economic theories should address the ever changing objective conditions of economic realities, so that they illuminate a part of the detail. But, he warns a theory which illuminates a right thing at a given point of time, may illuminate wrong things at another time. On the question of the theory of history, Hicks seemed to position himself nearer to Marx. Rejection of economic theories, unlike in natural sciences occurs not because they are being 'falsified' or 'proved wrong', but more so because they have become 'inappropriate' to handle the phenomena under the given empirical realities. This, to him is the source of 'Revolutions in Economics'. Hicks emphasised that theories must be practically useful and should be a servant of applied economics.

## 1. INTRODUCTION

Hicks' contribution to economics has been well designed to enrich the theoretical base. In the formulation of theories, his approach sought to comprehend the economic phenomena in their operational setting. The logical strength of the theories were derived from the unique tools he

[311]

employed to deal with the real world spectrum of economic activities. Economists know a lot in economics, but, rarely very few like Sir. John Hicks succeed to comprehend them in a theoretical framework. In all such domains of economics where Hicks' intellect evolved newer amplifications viz. the demand theory, modern welfare economics, theory of general equilibrium, theory of trade cycle, growth theory and monetary theory, the fellow economists were struck by the profundity of his analytical strength and originality to make them practically relevant.

He was always alert in his clairvoyant curiosity to recognise that in economics as compared to other disciplines, due to passage of time and changes in the institutional network, theories needed constant improvements, revisions and reformulations. Perhaps, this was the driving force as to why his interest and focus never remained fixed on one filed of enquiry. He responded in his own inimitable and unique style by conjuring new theories in several branches of economics which in his judgment needed practically useful alternatives. His theories were not pure mental constructs dealing with abstract relationships between events. But, they were rays of powerful intellectual wisdom aimed at illuminating the phenomena at work in real world conditions. Despite astonishingly wide range of contributions to the discipline of economics, we do not have 'Hicksian Economics' in the same tradition as 'Ricardian or Marxian or Keynesian Economics'.

However, an ardent student of Hicks carefully going through the contributions in its depths and heights, will discover that all his economic theories at the core had a unique method much fundamentally different from his contemporaries. This method is the 'Hicksian Method' [1]. He toiled not only on the general design of theories, but went into much finer details to bring the abstract discussions and descriptions of the economic phenomena into a coherent analytical system. By this, he was able to relate the causality between events more apparently discernible in a logical framework. His life long voyage in the wavy sea of turbulent economic upheavals, led him to discover that economics is more a 'discipline' than a 'science'. It is in this discipline, Hicks became the master craftsman. His methodology gave him the power to scale newer heights and tread fresh frontiers in the subject matter of economics.

## HICKS ON REVOLUTIONS IN ECONOMICS

The process by which advancements take place in the sphere of human knowledge has been the subject matter of the philosophy of science. While every progress in the scientific knowledge is welcome, resentments are often voiced when obstacles tend to stagnate scientific advancements. Scientific revolutions result in paradigmatic shifts in the hard core of the laws and theories in scientific disciplines. There are sharp differences among philosophers of science as to whether the progress is evolutionary in a historical time frame or discrete with powerful interceptions of sudden jumps of a revolutionary nature taking the progress to advance by leaps and bounds. In either case, the progress in science takes place when one system of thought embedded in a paradigm gives place to another.

Hicks wrote a paper on 'Revolutions in Economics', in memory of Imre Lakatos. Though the paper was not presented in the conference held at Mafplion in Greece, was written later and was published in the second volume of the conference proceedings viz., Method and Appraisal in Economics, which was edited by Spiro Latsis. It is in this article that Hicks has made quite explicit the methodology, he felt appropriate to deal with the subject matter of economics. Hicks observed that 'economics is more like art or philosophy than science, in the use that it can make of its own history' [2].

He drew a distinction between how a natural scientist works in his discipline and how an economist's position differed from it. 'when a natural scientist has come to the frontier of knowledge, and is ready for new explorations', Hicks commented that, 'he is unlikely to have much to gain from a contemplation of the path by which his predecessors have come to the place where he now stands'. But, Hicks was convinced that the position of economists are different. Hicks asserted that 'we cannot escape in the same way from our past. We may pretend to escape; but the past crowds on us all the same. Keynes and his contemporaries echo Ricardo and Malthus, Marx and Marshall are still alive. Some of us are inclined to be ashamed of this traditionalism, but when it is properly understood it is no cause for embarrassment; it is the consequence of what we are doing or trying to do'. Hicks' perception of the methodology of economics vis-à-vis other faculties of human knowledge draws very succinct but a powerful distinction.

It was made quite apparent in his words that 'facts which we study are not permanent, or repeatable, like the facts of natural sciences; they change incessantly and change with out repetition. Considered as individual events, they are often events of great interest. Every business has a history of its own, every consumer has a history of his own. We are trying to detect general patterns amid the mass of absorbing detail; shapes that repeat among the details that do not repeat. We can only do this if we select something less than the detail which is presented to us. In order to analyse, we must simplify and cut down'. In this context economic theories are rays of light, which illuminate a part of the whole, leaving the rest into the dark. Hicks, by interfacing this nature of economic theories with the ever changing objective conditions of economic realities warns, that it is the changing world that we are studying, hence a theory which illuminates the right thing now i.e. at a given point of time may illuminate wrong things at another time. Therefore, there can be no economic theory which will do everything for us at all time that we want to do.

It is this recognition of historical specificity of economic theories which has drawn Hicks close to Marx, who always held historical dialectics as a method of analysis while he wrote on the theory of history. 'My theory of history', wrote Hicks, 'will be good deal nearer to the kind of thing that was attempted by Marx, who did take from his economics some general ideas, which he applied to history, so that the pattern he saw in history had some extra-historical support. That is much more the kind of thing I want to try to do' [3].

There is however a tendency among economists to be obsessed with the utility of theories which are useful now, forgetting that it would be unwise to have nothing to deal with a condition which will be different tomorrow. When we have theories which are more useful to comprehend the general behavioural pattern of a chosen phenomenon today, we can be justified to reject the earlier one. But, there is a sharp distinction in this between economics and other disciplines in science. Our rejection of theories are not based on the fact that they are either 'falsified' or 'proved wrong', but more so because they have become inappropriate to handle the phenomenon under the existing empirical realities. This is the reason why 'revolutions' in economics have taken place. On the nature of revolutions, Hicks distinguishes between 'large' and 'small' ones. The Keynesian revolution is an obvious example of a big-revolution. There are no more than two or three other, which could be convincingly compared to it. If we start from the classical economics we can find the gravity slowly but steadily having drifted from the emphasis of costs of production theory of value of Smith, towards the labour theory of value of Ricardo. Hicks recognises this transition as a minor revolution. But, as the time went on, the significance of land and rent problems became less acute in England making the Ricardian schema less relevant. The dawn of Industrial Revolution created the need for another revolution to provide a new focus for economic theory. Thus, the time was set for another revolution in economics. In this context, Hicks considers two revolutions having taken place at the same time. The one was from Karl Marx and the other from Jevons, Walras and Menger. Between these two revolutions economics was divided and stood at cross roads.

Viewed from the central focus of the classical political economy, the distinguishing feature of the Marxian revolution was the fact that it shifted the gravity to distribution as the focal domain of the system. In other words, instead of tracing the causality from production to distribution, it was reversed and the system was examined from distribution to production and to other economic moments. The other revolution which tookplace is better known to students of economics as the 'Marginal' revolution, which in the opinion of Hicks was a theoretical novelty by which it took economics from the base of production and distribution, to a new base viz. exchange. It also tried to integrate exchange with social welfare. On the course of things that followed with the success of marginal approach, Hicks very cautiously observed, that though 'marginal utility' had its difficulties (difficulties of which we in our time have become increasingly aware), it was becoming easier to think of 'individuals' having given wants, or given utility functions, than to swallow the homogeneous 'wealth' of the old political economy. It was easier to think of the economic system as a system of interrelated markets or as an adjustment of means to ends, than to keep up the fiction of the social product any longer. It provided a new way of taking up the economic problem; not just a theory, but a new approach which was capable of much development. The reason for the success is the availability of the statistical material on which it can rely upon.

In summing up the article, Hicks makes his purpose distinctively clear when he observes, 'what we want, in economics, are theories which will be useful', and went on to qualify it further by adding, 'practically useful'. Another aspect of economic theory also was outlined by Hicks. In an indirect reference to the historic specificity rather an universally valid theory, Hicks makes the following property to be very important. Economic theories, one should not forget must have application to history, not to the history of thought but to economic history. Hence, theories are needed not only for application to the present but also for the interpretation of the past. Elaborating this further, Hicks goes on to observe that 'we should not analyse nineteenth century history in terms of nineteenth century theories; for our knowledge of the facts of that time is different from that of contemporaries and the question that we ask are different from that of those that contemporaries asked'.

## CONCLUDING REMARKS

From the preceeding discussions it is obvious that Hicks' concern for economic theories was on their practical usefulness. However, it cannot be concluded that Hicks had tremendous faith in econometric models, since with the econometric tools one can develop theoretical models that could be applied to empirical situations. On this question Hick's position needs careful understanding. Hicks in his essay on 'The Formation of an Economist', wrote that 'I have felt little sympathy with the theory for theory's sake(view), which has been the characteristic of one strand of American economics; nor with the idealisation of the free market, which has been the characteristic of another; and I have little faith in econometrics, on which they have so largely relied to make their contact with reality'.[4]. Hicks has always held (as he wrote in the Preface to Value and Capital) that theory should be the 'servant of applied economics', but he was aware that theory gives one no right to pronounce on practical problems, unless he through the labour, formidable labour, has mastered the relevant facts.[5].

## REFERENCES

1. Helm, D. (1984). *The Economics of John Hicks*, Basil Blackwell Publishers Limited, Oxford.
2. Hicks, J.R. (1976). "Revolutions in Economics", in Latsis, S. (ed.), *Method and Appraisal in Economics*, Cambridge University Press, Cambridge.
3. Hicks, J.R. (1969). *A Throery of Economic History*, Oxford University Press, Oxford.
4. Hicks, J.R. (1988). "The Formation of an Economist", in Kregel, J.A. (ed.), *Recollections of Eminent Economists*, Vol. I, Macmillan Press, London.
5. Hicks, J.R. (1939). *Value and Capital*, Oxford University Press, Oxford.

# CHAPTER - 24

# IN MEMORIAM: JOHN HICKS

## *Axel Lejonhufvud*

### ABSTRACT

The Sienna International Summer Workshop were initiated in 1986 and John Hicks attended the first two workshops and he was intending to attend the third also. The proceedings of the first two workshops have been published. In the 1989 workshop, I attended where, instead of listening to the presentation of Hicks, I had to present a momorium containing the saga of life of Hicks and Ursula and to some extent, the main events in Hicks's writings in economics.

John Hicks hoped that be would be with us tonight. In April 1989, he wrote me as follows:

"I should very much like to come. . . if I were in a state to do so. But I am not in as good condition as I was last year, and so I am not at all sure that I shall be fit to do so. But I will come if only for a day or two if I can".

With every passing year, he got physically more frail. But his spirit never weakened. This is how the letter continues:

"I would have plenty to offer to you. For the book of which you have seen something will. . . at that point be just appearing. It will be called A MARKET THEORY OF MONEY. I could pick out one of the later chapters, which you will not have seen, such as the one on The International Economy, or that on what is bad about Inflation, for instance. But I have also a piece which I have only just now finished writing. . .I am at the moment calling it 'The Unification of Macroeconomics'.

Not bad for a celebration of my 85th birthday".

[317]

In the last few years, John was heard on more than one occasion to say ; "I am dying from the feet up". It was a rueful joke but with a little note of pride that his mind was unimpaired. I have a second letter, dated on the day he died, which shows that, to the very last, his intellectual appetite was what it had always been. In this letter, he mentions a paper "which I received yesterday and have been reading greedily". _ I treasure that last word "greedily".

\* \* \* \* \*

To non-academics, the course of John Hicks' life must look outwardly uneventful . . . and steady progression up the academic ladder, a career of ever growing distinction:

    Scholarship to Clifton, 1917
    Balliol College, Oxford, 1922–25
        M. Lit, 1926
    Lecturer, LSE 1926–35 (nine years!)
    Fellow, Concills and Caius, Cambridge (1938)
        Liked to remember being interviewed by Figou and Keynes for position
    Javons Chair of Pol, Econ., Manchester, 1938–45
    Fellow, Nuffield College, 1946–52 (one of the founders)
    Drunmond Chair of pol. Econ., All Souls, 1952–65
        Emeritus Fellow, All Souls, 1965–89

    crowned by the Nobel Memorial Prize in 1972.

A summary of his private life adds much warmth but little excitement to this picture. The great event is his marriage to Ursula Webb in 1935. He was very fortunate in his marriage. They shared a broad range of interests and enthusiasms, and always seemed to enjoy each others' company. Travel was one of their shared enthusiasms – particularly, of course, travel to Italy. They always went together and the demand for Ursula's Expertise in public finance took them to some corners of the globe that John might not otherwise have seen. Ursula possessed a straightforward competence in most things practical that John often lacked. She drove the car, even in latter years when after several operations her hips gave her constant pain. "Sir John was a _deplorable_ driver", she once declared with a shudder at some fifty-year old memory.

\* \* \* \* \* \*

If John Hicks' life seems "outwardly uneventful", as I have suggested, that is largely because he willed it to be a life of scholarship and learning – and because he was far, far better than most of us, who profess the same ideal, in not allowing himself to be distracted from it.

When a book or paper caught his interest, he might read it "greedily", as he said in that letter, but you could hardly find another use for that word in connection with John and Ursula Hicks. Material possessions were not to distract them from the life they valued. As everyone here knows, John gave his Nobel Prize money to the LSE library. He phrased it as a gift of gratitude to that institution but it was also a declaration of his dedication to a life of strictly limited material ambitions.

He retired from the Drummond Chair (and its emoluments) early – at about the age of 60 in order to be able to concentrate on his work. More than half of his life's output belongs to the period after his retirement.

At home, in Porch House, Blockley, the daily routine was a disciplined one. Visitors learned the schedule. In his seventies and eighties, John would devote the morning hours to writing; these hours were invaluable – he was not to be interrupted; after lunch, he and Ursula would spend some time with visitors – in the garden (British weather at all permitting); a brief rest, with the balance of the afternoon devoted to reading; then drinks and talk – good talk – in the evening. with this regimen, he maintained an amazing productivity into old age.

It is this dedication, this determination so to arrange his life that distractions were kept to a minimum, that makes his achievements understandable. I will not enumerate the titles of the works that constitute John Hicks' achievements. In present company, we will take that as read. But allow me a coupe of reflections on it.

(i) He has, of course, been enormously, amazingly influential. His ideas have seeped into the ways economists think and work to the point where the very familiarity of many Hicksian ideas make it difficult for us rightly to assess the contribution.

Yet, it is *parts* of his work that has had this influence – and some of it has not had quite the influence that he originally intended or would later have wished. Hicks, more than most authors, had to experience in his lifetime how the readers wrest control of the text from the author. so, it was *part* of the "Suggestion for Simplifying Monetary Theory", *most* of "Mr. Keynes and the Classics", only the first eight chapters of *Value and Capital*, and *so on – that* went into the foundations on which post-World War II economic theory was built. The elder Hicks has produced an extensive commentary on the developments that he had a hand in, clarifying his original intentions and explaining his latter reservations. It is a pity that these writings have had as rather narrow audience for the man knew whereof he was speaking.

(ii) Economic theory to John Hicks was always more an exercise in *judgment* than in *deduction*. The economists constantly makes choices – among methods or approaches, among assumptions, and among "facts". Hicks, even 55 years ago, always discussed his choices with the reader. You always know the *reasons* for all his choices and, if you disbelieve his conclusions, it is possible to track back and find where you differ with his judgment.

(iii) Over the years he developed a style of writing that is really quite remarkable. It is clean, spare, direct with a simple conversational tone that is quite engaging – but can be in equal measure misleading, if the apparent simplicity lulls you into overlooking the depth at which he is penetrating very complex problems.

The feeling that one has in reading Hicks, particularly the elder Hicks, of participating in a conversation with him is something that is still left to us now that he is gone. We can still take him off the shelf and engage with him in *one* of the pursuits that he loved: economic theory.

I have stressed that he devoted his life to learning. By now, I may have given the false impression that he jealously economized on his time and energies so that he could do *economics* all the time. But, of course, it is the *breadth* of his interests and his knowledge, and his love and enthusiasm for poetry, for painting, for history and mathematics and for so many other things that first comes to mind when you recall John Hicks.

He used to do number theory in his head to go to sleep and keep a note-pad beside his bed for any results that would come to him at night. This was his practice for many years. Last year, during Siena Workshop II, we were eating in a grape arbor at a restaurant outside town. Several of his Sienese friends were present. I asked him whether he still did number theory. "No", he said, "I stopped doing that a couple of years ago. Now, I have this game I play with myself to go to sleep. I try to remember at least one stanza of poetry from each century from about 500 BC to the present". and he started to tell us about what centuries were the most difficult and so on. Before we left that place, we had heard John Hicks quote poetry from memory for at least a couple of hours. When reciting something he really liked, something that had touched him, his blue eyes would flash with enthusiasm – and that habitual stammer would entirely disappear.

John Hicks' achievements will stand quite independently of us. What is important is that we remember – and find occasions to recall – the kind of man he was. We will not see his like in the Economics profession again.

It is a melancholy fact that John Hicks is gone, but to have learned from him, to have known him, to have had his friendship – those are things to celebrate for as long as we are around.

# SIR JOHN R. HICKS,
# PUBLISHED WRITINGS

1928: 1. 'Wage-Fixing in the building industry', Economics, June, pp.159-67.

1930: 1. 'The early history of industrial conciliation in England', Economica, March, pp.25-39.

2. 'Edgeworth, Marshall and the inderterminateness of wages', Economic Journal, June, pp.215-31 (repr.1983a, pp.72-84).

1931: 1. 'A reply' to M.Dobb, 'A note concerning Mr.J.R.Hicks on "The inderterminateness of wages"', Economic Journal, March, pp.145-6.

2. Review of W.W.M.Amulreee: Industrial Arbitration, Economica, February, pp.105-6.

3. 'The theory of uncertainty and profit', Economica, May pp.170-89 (repr. 1982a, pp.11-27).

4. Review of W.H.Hatt: The Theory of Collective Bargaining, Economica, May, pp.244-7.

5. Review of M.T.Ranking: Arbitration Principles and the Industrial Court (An analysis of decisions 1919-1929), Economica, November, pp.480-2.

6. With W.Beveridge, 'Quotas and import boards', and 'The possibility of imperial preference', In W.Beveridge, Tariffs: The Case Examined by a committee of economists under the chairmanship of Sir William Beveridge, London: Longmans, Green, pp.210-29.

1932: 1. Marginal productivity and the principle of variation' followed by 'A reply' to Henry Schultz, Economica, February, pp.79-88 and August pp.297-300.

2. The Theory of Wages, London: Macmillan (Italian edn 1934).

3. Review of D.M.Goodfellow: A Modern Economic History of South Africa, Economic Journal, March, pp.109-11.

4. Review of D.H.Robertson: Economic Fragments, Economica, May, pp.255-6.

5. Review of C. Bresciani - Turroni: La Vicende del Marco Tedesco, Economica, August, pp.370-2.

6 Review of F.Simiand: Le Salaire, l'evolution et la monnaie, Essai de theorie experimentale du salaire, Economic Journal, September, pp.451-74.

7. Review of L. Mises and A. Spiethoff (eds), Probleme der Wertlehre, Economic Journal, September, pp.477-8.

1933: 1. Review of E.W.Taussig: Wages and Capital, Economica, February, pp.101-4.

2. 'Gleichgewicht und Konjunktur', Zeitschrift fur Nationalokonomie, June, pp.441-55, trans. As 'Equilibrium and the trade cycle', Economic Inquiry, October, pp.523-34 (repr. 1982a, pp.28-41).

3. 'A note on Mr.Kahn's paper (on elasticity of substitution)', Review of Economic Studies, Vol. 1, No.1 October, pp.78-80.

4. Review of A.E.Monroe: Value and Income, Zeitschrift fur Nationalokonomie, vol.4, pp.663-5.

5. Review of Reichenau: Die Kapitalfunktion der Kredits, Zeitschrift fur Nationalokonomie, vol.4, pp.668-9.

1934: 1. 'A reconsideration of the Theory of Value', Part I; Part II by R.G.D.Allen, Economica, February and May, pp.52-76 and 196-219 (repr. 1981, pp.5-29 and 30-55; and in Helm, 1984a, pp.25-48).

2. Review of K.S.Isles: Wages Policy and the Price Level, Economic Journal, September, pp.473-75.

3. 'A note on the elasticity of supply', Review of Economic Studies, 2(1) October, pp.31-7 (repr. 1983a, pp.237-45).

4. 'Leon Walras', Econometrica, October, pp.338-48. (repr. 1983a, pp.86-95)

5. Review of G. Myrdal: Monetary Equilibrium, in F.A.Hayek (ed.), Beitrage zur Geletheorie, and Economica, November (repr. 1982a, pp.42-5).

6. Review of F.A.Hayek (ed.), Beitriage zur Geldtheorie, Economica, November, pp.479-86.

7. Review of P.H.Wicksteed: Common sense of Political Economy (repr.), Economica, August, pp.351-4.

1935.: 1. 'Annual survey of economic theory: the Theory of Monopoly' Econometrica, January, pp.1-20 (repr. 1983a, pp.132-52).

2. 'A suggestion for simplifying the Theory of Money', Economica, February, pp.1-19 (repr. 1967, pp.61-82; 1982a, pp.46-63; and in Helm, 1984a, pp.168-85).

3. Review of C.E.Ross: Dynamic Economics, Economic Journal, June, pp.336-7.

4. Review of H. von Stackelberg: Marktform und Gleichgewicht, Economic Journal, June, pp. 334-6.

5. Review of S.M. de Bernardi (ed.), De l'utilite et de sa mesure par Jules Dupuit: Ecrits choisis et republies (Turin repr.), Economica, August, pp.341-2 (repr. 1983a, pp.329-30).

6. 'Wages and interest: the dynamic problem', Economic Journal, September, pp.456-68 (repr. 1963b, pp.268-85 and 1982a, pp.67-79).

1936: 1. Review of A.C.Pigou: The Economics of Stationary States, Economic Journal, March, pp.329-30).

2. 'Mr Keynes's Theory of Employment', Economic Journal, June, pp.238-53 (repr.1982a, pp.84-99).

3. 'Distribution and economic progress: a revised version', Review of Economic Studies, 4(1) October, pp.1-12 (repr. 1963b, pp.286-303).

4. 'Economic theory and the social sciences', contribution to a symposium on the Social Sciences, Institute of Sociology.

1937: 1. 'Mr Keynes and the "classics"', Econometrica, April, pp.147-59 (repr.1967, pp.126-42; 1982a, pp.101-15; and in Helm, 1984a, pp.186-99).

2. La Theorie mathematique de la valeur en regime de libre concurrence, trans. G. Lutfalla, Paris: Hermann.

1939: 1. Value and Capital, Oxford: Clarendon Press (other edns: Spanish (Mexican) 1945; Japanese, 1950; French, 1956; Hindi, 1971; Polish, 1975; Urdu, 1975; Hungarian, 1978).

2. (with Ursula Hicks), 'Public finance in the national income', Review of Economic Studies 6(2), February, pp.147-55.

3. Review of R.G.D.Allen: Mathematical Analysis for Economists, Economica, February, pp.92-4.

4. Review of A.G.Pool: Wage Policy in Relation to Industrial Fluctuation, Economica, May, pp.233-5.

5. 'Mr Hawtrey on bank rate' and 'The long-term rate of interest', followed by 'A reply' to Hawtrey, Manchester School of Economic and Social Studies, vol. X, pp.21-39 and pp.152-5 (repr. Of Mr Hawtrey ....,' 1982a, pp.116-26).

6. 'The foundations of welfare economics', Economic Journal, December, pp.696-712 (repr.1981, pp.59-77, and in Helm, 1984a, pp. 126-43).

1940: 1. 'The valuation of the social income', Economica, May, pp.105-24 (repr.1981).

2. 'A comment' on O. Lange's 'Complementarity and interrelations of shifts in demand,', Review of Economic Studies, 8(1), pp.64-5 (repr. In Wood and Woods, 1989, vol.1, pp.42-4).

1941: 1. (with ursula Hicks and L. Roastas) Taxation of War Wealth, Oxofrd: Clarendon Press (2nd edn, 1942).

2. 'Rehabilitation of consumer's surplus', Review of Economic Studies, 8(2) February, pp.108-16 (repr. 1981, pp.101-13).

3. 'Saving and the rate of interest in war time', Manchester School of Economics and Social Studies, April, pp. 21-7.

4. 'Education in economics', Manchester Statistical Society.

1942: 1. The Social Framework: An Introduction to Economics, Oxford: Clarendon Press (other edns: Swedish, 1945; Spanish (Mexican), 1950; Greek (pirated), 1955; Portuguese, 1956; German, 1962, Sinhalese'Tamil, 1964).

2. 'The monetary theory of D.H. Robertson', Economica, February, pp. 53-7 (extracts repr. 1982a, cf. pp.127-31).

3. 'Maintaining, capital intact: a further suggestion', Economica, May, pp. 174-9.

4. 'Consumers' surplus and index numbers', Review of Economic Studies, 9(2) Summer, pp.126-37 (cf. 1981, pp.114-32).

5. Review of Davis: The Theory of Econometrics, Economic Journal, December, pp.350-2.

6. 'The budget White Paper of 1942', Journal of the Institute of Bankers.

1943: 1. (with Ursula Hicks) Standards of Local Expenditure, Cambridge: Cambridge University Press (National Institute of Economic and Social Research, Occasional Papers).

2. 'History of economic doctrine', Review of C. Rist: History of Monetary and Credit Theory, Economic History Review, 13, pp.111-15 (repr. 1982a, pp. 132-9).

3. (with Ursula Hicks) 'The Beveridge Plan and local government finance', Review of Economic Studies, 11(1) Winter, pp.1-19.

4. 'The four consumer's surpluses', Review of Economic Studies, (11(1) Winter, pp.31-40 (repr. 1981, pp.114-32).

1944: 1. 'The inter-relations of shifts in demand: commen', a discussion with D.H.Robertson and O. lange, Review of Economic Studies, 12(1) (31), pp.71-8 (repr. In Wood and Woods, vol.1, pp.97-101).

2. (with Ursula Hicks and C.E.V. Leser) Valuation for Rating, Cambridge: Cambridge University Press (National Institute of Economic and Social Research Occasional Papers).

1945: 1. (with Ursula Hicks) "the Incidence of Local Rates in Great Britain, Cambridge: Cambridge University Press (National Institute of Economic and Social Research Occasional Papers).

2. 'Recent contributions to general equilibrium economics', Economica, November, pp.235-42.

3. 'La theorie de Keynes apres neuf ans', Revue d'economie politique, 55, pp. 1-11.

4. Review of A.C.Pigou: Lapses from Full Employment, Economic Journal, December, pp.398-401 (repr. 1982a,, pp.140-3).

5. The Social Framework of the American Economy (adapted by A.G.Hart) New York: Oxford University Press.

6. 'The generalized theory of consumer's surplus', Review of Economic Studies, 13(2)(34), pp.68-74 (cf.1981, pp.114-32).

7. Value and capital, 2nd edn, Oxford: Clarendon Press.

1947: 1. 'World recovery after war: a theoretical analysis', Economic Journal, June, pp.151-64 (repr. 1959a, pp.3-19 and 1982a, pp.148-61).

2. 'Full employment in a period of reconstruction', Nationalokonomisk Tidsskrift, 85, pp.165ff. (repr. 1982a, pp.162-72).

3. 'The empty economy', Lloyds Bank Review, July, pp. 1-13.

1948: 1. 'The valuation of the social income: a comment on Professor Kuznets' Reflections', Economica, August, pp.163-72 (extracts repr. 1981, pp.98-9).

2. Review of F. Sewell Bray: Precision and Design in Accountancy, Economic Journal, December, pp.562-4.

3. 'L'economie de bien-etre et la theorie des surplus du consommateur' and 'Quelques applications de la theorie des surplus du consommateur', Economie appliquee, January-March, pp. 432-46 and 447-57.

4. The Problem of Budgetary Reform, Oxford: Oxford University Press (Apanish edn, 1957).

1949: 1. "Devaluation and world trade', Three Banks Review, December, pp.3-23 (repr. 1959a, pp.20-39).

2. 'Les courbes d'indifference collective', Revue d'economie politique, 59, pp. 578-84.

3. 'Mr.Harrod's dynamic theory', Economica, May, pp.106-21 (repr. 1982a, pp.174-92).

1950 1. A Contribution to the Theory of the Trade Cycle, Oxford: Clarendon Press (other edns: Italian, 1951; Spanish, 1954; Japanese, 1954).

2. Articles on 'Value', 'Demand', 'Interest', 'Wages' and 'Rent', Chamber's Encyclopaedia.

3. Part II of Report of Commission on Revenue Allocation, Nigeria, pp. 45-56 (repr. 1959a, pp.216-36).

1951 1. "A critical note on the definition of related goods: a comment on Mr Ichimura's definition' Review of Economic Studies, 18(3)(47), pp.184-7.

2. 'Free trade and modern economics', Manchester Statistical Society, March (repr. 1959a, pp.40-65).

3. Review of C.Menger: Principles of Economics (trans. J. Dingwall and B. Hoselitz), Economic Journal, December, pp.852-3 (repr. 1983a, pp.333-4).

1952: 1. Social Framework, 2nd edn, Oxford: Clarendon Press.

2. Review of T. Scitovsky: Welfare and Competition, American Economic Review, September, pp.609-14 (repr. 1982a, pp. 155-62).

3. 'Contribution to a symposium on monetary policy and the crisis: comments', Bulletin of Oxford University Institute of Statistics, April-May, pp.157-9 and August, pp.268-72.

1953:  1.  Inaugural lecture: 'Long-run dollar problem', Oxford Economic papers, June, pp.117-35 (extract repr. 1959a pp.66-84; revd version 1983a, pp.207-16).

2.  'A note on a point in Value and capital (a reply to M. Morishima)', Review of Economic Studies, 21(3)(56), pp.218-21 (repr. In wood and Woods, 1989, vol. 1, pp.164-8).

1954:  1.  'The process of imperfect competition', Oxford Economics Papers, February, pp.41-54 (repr. 1983a, pp.163-78).

2.  'Robbins on Robertson on utility', Economica, May, pp.154-7.

3.  Review of Myrdal: The Political Element in the Development of Economic History (trans. P. Streeten), Economic Journal. December, pp. 793-6 (repr. 1983a, pp.343-6).

1955:  1.  (with Ursula Hicks) Report on Finance and Taxation in Jamaica, Kingston, Jamaica, Government Printer.

2.  'Economic foundations of wage policy', Economic Journal, September, pp.389-404 (repr. 1959a, pp. 85-104 and 1982a, pp.194-209, 210-13).

3.  The Social Framework of the American Economy, 2nd edn, (adapted by A.G.Hart and J.W.Ford), New York: Oxford University Press.

1956:  1.  A Revision of Demand Theory, Oxford: Clarendon Press (other edns: Spanish (Mexican), 1958; Japanese, 1958).

2.  'The instability of wages', Three Banks Review, September, pp.3-19 (repr. 1959a).

3.  'Methods of dynamic analysis' in Twenty-five Economic Essays in English, German and Scandinavian Languages in honor of Erik Lindahl. Stockholm: Edonomisk Tidschrift, (repr. With addendum 1982a, pp.219-35 and in Helm, 1984a, pp.200-15).

1957:  1.  'A rehabilitation of "Classical economics", Review of D. Patinkin: Money, Interest and Prices: an Integration of Monetary and Value Theory, Economic Journal, 67, pp.278-89 (repr. 1967, pp.143-54 as 'The classics again').

2.  'National economic development in the international setting', and 'Development under population pressure', in Bulletin. the Central Bank of Ceylon (repr. 1959a, pp.161-95 (revd version) and pp.196-215).

1958:  1.  'The measurement of real income', Oxford Economic Papers. June. pp.125-62 (repr. 1981, pp.142-88 and in Helm, 1984a, pp.57-95).

2.  'Future of the rate of interest', Manchester Statistical Society, March  (revd version, 1967, pp.83-102).

3.  'A world inflation', The Irish Banks Review, September (repr. 1959a, pp.121-51).

1959:  1.  Essays in World Economics (including 'A Manifesto [on welfarism]' (repr. 1981, pp.135-41); 'Unimproved value rating (the case of East Africa)'; 'A further note on import bias' (extract repr. 1983a, pp.217-23); 'The factor-price equalization theorem'), Oxford: Clarendon Press (other edns: Japanese, 1965; Spanish, 1967).

2.  Review of H. Leibenstein: Economic Backwardness and Economic Growth, Economic Journal, June, pp.344-7.

3.  'A "Value and Capital" growth model', Review of Economic Studies, June vol.26, pp.159-73.

1960:  1.  Social Framework, 3rd edn, Oxford: Clarendon Press.

2.  'Linear theory', Economic Journal, 280(70) December, pp.671-709 (repr 1966 in Surveys of Economic Theory, Vol.III, American Economic Association, London: Macmillan and in 1983a, pp.246-91).

3.  'Thought on the Theory of Capital: the Corfu Conference', Oxford Economic Papers, June, pp.123-32.

1961:  1.  'Prices and the turnpike: the story of a mare's nest', Review of economic Studies, 28 February, pp.77-88 (repr 1983a, pp.292-307).

2.  'The Nature and Basis of Economic Growth' in J.R.Hicks et al. (eds) Federalism and Economic Growth in Underdeveloped Countries, London: Allen & Unwin, pp.70-80.

3.  'The measurement of capital in relation to the measurement of other economic agregates', in F.A.Lutz and D.C.Hague (eds), The theory of Capital, Institute of Economic Affairs, London: Macmillan, pp.18-31 (repr 1981, pp. 189-203).

4.  'Pareto revealed', Review of V. pareto: Pareto's Letters to Pantaleoni, Economica, August, pp.318-22 (repr 1983a, pp.338-42).

5.  'Marshall's third rule: a further comment', Oxford Economic Papers, October, pp.262-5, (extract repr 1963b, pp.376-8).

1962:  1.  'Liquidity', Economic Journal, December, pp.787-802 (repr 1982a, pp. 238-47).

2.  'Economic theory and the evaluation of consumer's wants', Journal of Business, University of Chicago, July, pp.256-63.

3.  Review of J.E.Meade: A Neo-Classical Theory of Economic Growth, Economic Journal, 286 (72) pp.371-4.

4.  Review of A.K.Sen: Choice of Techniques: an Aspect of the Theory of Planned Economic Development, Economic Journal, June, pp.379-81.

1963:  1.  'International trade: the long view', Cairo: Central Bank of Egypt.

2.  The Theory of Wages, 2nd edn (with reprint and commentary) London: Macmillan (Spanish edn, 1973).

3. (with Ursula Hicks) "The reform of budget accounts; Bulletin of Oxford University Institute of Statistics, May, pp.119-26.

4.  Review of M. Friedman: Capitalism and Freedom, Economica, August, pp. 319-20.

5.  Review of F. Modigliani and K.J.Cohen: The Role of Anticipations and Plans in Economic Behaviour and Their use in Economic Analysis and Forecasting, Economic Journal, March, pp.99-101.

1965:  1.  Capital and Growth, Oxford: Clarendon Press (other edns: Spanish, 1967; Italian, 1971; Polish, 1982).

2.  Review of T. Scitovsky: Papers on Welfare and Growth, American Economic Review, September, pp.882-3.

3.  Review of R.G.Lipsey: An Introduction to Positive Economics, Economica, May, pp.229-31 (repr 1983a, pp.347-8).

1966:  1  Dennis Robertson: 'A Memoir' in D.H.Robertson, Essays in Money and Interest, London: Collins, pp.9-22.

2.  'After the Boom', Institute of Economic Affairs, Occasional Papers, II.

3.  'Growth and Anti-Growth', Oxford Economic Papers, November, pp.257-69.

4.  Review of J.E.Meade: The Stationary Economy, Economic Journal, June, pp.370-1.

5.  "Essays on balanced economic growth', The Oriental Economist, Tokyo.

1967:  1.  Critical Essays in Monetary Theory, Oxford: Clarendon Press (other edns: Spanish, 1971; Italian, 1971; Japanese, 1972).

1968.  1.  'Saving, investment and taxation: an international comparison', Three Banks Review, June, pp.3-21.

328

1969: 1. A Theory of Economic History, London: Clarendon Press, Oxford University Press (other edns: Swedish, 1970; Japanese, 1971; Portuguese (Brazilian), 1971; French, 1973; Norwegian, 1974; Spanish, 1974).

2. 'Autonomists, Hawtreyans and Keynesians', Journal of Money, Credit and Banking, 1(3), pp.307-17 (revd version 1977a, pp.118-33).

3. 'Direct and indirect additivity', Econometrica, April, pp.353-4 (repr 1983a, pp.308-11).

4. '"Maintaining capital intact: a further suggestion', in R.H.parker and G.C.Harcourt (eds) Readings in the Concept and Measurement of Income, pp.132-8.

5. 'The rehabilitation of consumer's surplus', in K.H.Arrow and T. Scitovsky (eds) Readings in Welfare Economics, pp.325-35.

6. 'Value and volume of capital', Indian Economic Journal, October-December, pp.161-71.

7. '"The measurement of capital - in practice', Bulletin of the International Statistical Institute, 43 (repr 1981, pp.204-17).

8. Review of B.P.Pesek and T.R.Saving: Money, Wealth and Economic Theory, Economic Journal, March, pp.129-31.

1970: 1. 'Expected Inflation', Three Banks Review, 87, pp.3-34 (extract repr 1977a, pp.108-17).

2. Review of M. Friedman: The Optimum Quantity of Money, Economic Journal, December, pp.669-72 (revd version 1982, pp.276-81).

3. 'Inflazione e interesse', Bancaria, June, pp.675-82.

4. 'Capitalism and industrialism', Tahquqat Eqtesadi (Quarterly Journal of Economic Research) Teheran, Spring, pp.1-13.

5. 'Elasticity of substitution again: substitutes and complements' Oxford Economic Papers, November, pp.289-96 (revd version 1983a, 'Elasticity of substitution reconsidered', pp.312-26.

6. 'A neo-Austrian growth theory', Economic Journal, June, pp.257-81.

1971: 1. The Social Framework, 4th edn, Oxford: Clarendon Press (other edns, Japanese, 1972; Portuguese (Brazilian), 1972).

2: 'A reply to Professor Beach "Hicks on Ricardo on machinery" Economic Journal, December, pp.922-5 (repr in Wood and Woods, 1989, vol.II, pp. 170-3).

1972: 1. '"Ricardo's theory of distribution', in M.Preston and B.Corry (eds) Essays in Honour of Lord Robbins, London: Weidenfeld & Nicolson, pp.160-7 (repr 1983a, pp.32-8).

2. (with Ursula Hicks) 'British fiscal policy', in H.Giersch (ed.) Fiscal Policy and Demand Management, Tubingen: Mohr.

1973: 1. 'The Austrian Theory of Capital and its rebirth in modern economics', in J.R.Hicks and W. Weber (eds) Carl Menger and the Austrian School of Economics, Oxford: Clarendon Press, pp.190-206, (repr 1983a, pp.96-112).

2. The mainspring of economic growth', Swedish Journal of Economics, December, pp.336-48 (repr 1977a pp.1-19).

3. '"Recollections and documents', Economica, February, pp.2-11. (repr 1977a, pp.134-48).

4. Capital and Time, a Neo-Austrian Theory, Oxford: Clarendon Press (other edns: Italian, 1973; Japanese, 1973; French, 1975; Spanish (Mexican), 1976).

5. (with H.-C.Recktenwald) 'Walras' economic system', in H.-C.Recktenwald (ed.) Political Economy: An Historical Perspective, pp.261-5.

6. 'On the measurement of capital', The Economic Science, Nagoya University, Japan.

1974: 1. 'Capital controversies: ancient and modern', American Economic Review, May, pp.307-16 (repr 1977a, pp.49-65).

2. The Crisis in Keynesian Economics, Oxford: Basil Blackwell (other edns: Italian, 1974; Spanish, 1976; Japanese, 1977; Hungarian, 1978).

3. 'Preferences and welfare', in A. Mitra (ed.) Economic Theory and Planning: Essays in Honour of A.K.Das Gupta, Calcutta: Oxford University Press, pp.3-16.

4. 'Real and monetary factors in economic fluctuations', Scottish Journal of Political Economy, 21(3), pp.205-14 (extract repr 1977a, pp.171-81 and in M.Monti (ed.) 1976, The 'New Inflation' and Monetary Policy, New York: Holmes & Meier Pub., pp.3-13).

5. 'Future and industrialims', International Affairs, April, pp.211-28 (repr 1977a, pp.20-44).

6. (with N.Nosse) The Social Framework of the Japanese Economy, Oxford: Oxford University Press.

1975: 1. "The permissive economy', in 'Crisis ' 75 ...?' Institute of Economic Affairs, Occasional Papers, 43.

2. "Pareto and the economic optimum', Rome: Accademia nazionale dei lincei.

3. ;'The scope and status of welfare economics', Oxford Economic Papers, 27(3), pp.307-26 (repr 1981, pp.218-39).

4. Annual survey of economic theory: 'The Theory of Monopoly' in E. Mansfield (ed.) Macroeconomics: Selected Readings, pp.188-205.

5. 'The quest for monetary stability', South African Journal of Economics, December, pp.405-20.

6. 'Revival of political economy: the old and the new' (a reply to Harcourt), Economic Record, September, pp.365-7.

7. 'What is wrong with monetarism?', Lloyds Bank Review, 118, pp.1-13.

1976: 1. Review of J.R.Whittaker (ed.), The Early Economic Writings of Alfred Marshall (1867-1890), Economic Journal, January, pp.367-9 (repr 1983a, pp.335-7).

2. 'Forward trading as a means of overcoming disequilibrium', in B.A.Goss and B.S.Yamey (eds) The Economics of Futures Trading Readings, New York: Wiley, pp.63-7.

3. 'The little that is right with monetarism,', Lloyds Bank Review, 121, pp.16-18.

4. 'Must stimulating demand stimulate inflation?', Economic Record, December, pp.409-22(repr 1982a, pp.301-17).

5. "'Revolutins' in Economics', in S.J.Latsis (ed.) Method and Appraisal in Economics, Cambridge: Cambridge University Press, pp.207-18 (repr 1983a, pp.3-16 and in Helm, 1984a, pp.244-56)

6. 'Some questions of time in economics', in A. Tang, F.M.Westfield and J.S.Worley (eds) Evolution, Welfare and time in Economics: Essays in Honour of Nicholas Georgescu-Roegen, Lexington, Mass: Heath Lexington Books, pp.135-51 (repr 1982a, pp.282-300 and in Helm 1984a, pp.263-80).

1977: 1. Economic Perspectives: Further Essays on Money and Growth, Oxford: Clarendon Press (other edns: Portuguese (Brazilian), 1978; Italian, 1980).

2. (with S.Hollander) 'Mr Ricardo and the moderns', Quarterly Journal of Economics, August, pp.351-69 (repr.1983a, pp.41-59).

1978: 1. Review of V.Lachmann: Capital Expectations and the Market Process, South African Journal of Economics, December, pp.400-502.

330

2. 'La funzioni della moneta internazionale', Bancaria, July, pp.661-7.

3. Review of R.D.Collison Black (ed.), Papers and correspondence of W.S.Jevons, vols. III-V, Economic Journal, June, pp.347-8 (extract repr 1983a, pp. 331-2).

1979: 1. 'The Ricardian system: a comment', Oxford Economic Papers, March, pp. 133-4.

2. 'The formation of an economist', Banca Nazionale del Lavaro Quarterly Review, September, pp.195-204 (repr 1983a, pp.355-64 and in Helm 1984a, pp .281-90).

3. 'Is interest the price of a factor of production?', in M.J.Rizzo (ed.) Time, Uncertainty and Disequilibrium, Lexington, Mass: Lexington Books (repr 1983a, pp.114-28).

4. Review of E.R.Weintraub: Microfoundations: the Compatibility of Microeconomics and Macroeconomics, Journal of Economic Literature, December, pp.1451-4 (repr 1983 a, pp.349-52).

5. 'The concept of income in relation to taxation and business management', Greek Economic Review, December, pp.1-14 (repr 1983, pp.189-203).

6. 'On Coddington's interpretation: a reply', Journal of Economic Literature, 17, pp.989-95 (repr in Wood and Woods, 1989, Vol. III, pp.208-16).

7. Causality in Economics, Oxford: Basil Blackwell and New York: Basic Books (other edns: Italian 1981; Spanish (Agrentinian), 1982).

1980: 1. 'IS-LM: An explanation', Journal of Post Keynesian Economics, Winter, pp.139-54 (repr 1982a, pp.318-31 and in Helm, 1984a, pp.216-29).

2. 'Equilibrium and and the trade cycle' (translation of 1933b 'Gleichgewicht und Konjunktur'), Economic Inquiry, October, pp.523-34 (repr 1982a, pp.28-41).

3. Review of J.Presley: Robertsonian Economics, Canadian Journal of Economics, August, pp.517-20.

1981: 1. Wealth and Welfare, Collected Essays on Economic Theory, vol. I, Oxford: Basil Blackwell (including 'Valuation of the Social Income III: the cost approach', (repr in Helm, 1984a, pp.96-121)).

1982: 1. Money, Interest and Wages, Collected Essays on Economic Theory, Vol. II, Oxford: Basil Blackwell (including 'The foundation of monetary theory, part IV, The credit economy', repr in Helm, 1984a, pp.230-9).

2. 'Limited liability: the pros and cons', in T.Orhnial (ed.) Limited Liability and the Corporation, London: Croom Hel, (repr 1983a, pp.178-88).

3. Forward to Andrew Shonfield, The Use of Public Power, Oxford: Oxford University Press.

4. 'Planning in the world depression', Man and Development,India.

1983: 1. Classics and Moderns, Collected Essays on Economic Theory, Vol.III, Oxford: Basil Blackwell.

2. "Culture as capital, supply and demand', Rome: Accademia nazionale dei lincei.

3. 'Edgeworth', in Murphy (ed.) Studies of Irish Economists.

4. 'A sceptical follower', The Economist, June, pp.21-4.

1984: 1. 'The "new causality": an explanation', Oxford Economic Papers, 36, pp. 12-15.

2. 'Is economics a science?', Interdisciplinary Science Reviews, 9(3), pp. 213-19.

3. (with S.K.Ghosh and M.Mukherjee), The Social Framework of the Indian Economy, an Introduction to Economics, India and New York: Oxford University Press.

1985: 1. Methods of Dynamic Economics, new edn of the first part of Capital and Growth, oxford: Clarendon Press.

2. 'Sraffa and Ricardo - a critical view', in G.A.Caravale (ed.) The legacy of Ricardo, Oxford: Basil Blackwell, pp.305-19.

1986: 1. 'Towards a more General Theory', Symposium on Monetary Theory, Taipei, Taiwan: The Institute of Economics, Academia Sinica, January, pp.5-19.

2. 'Loanable funds and liquidity preference', Greek Economic Review, December, pp.125-31.

3. A Revision of Demand Theory, Oxford: Oxford University Press. (Published posthumously).

1989: 1. A Market Theory of Money, Oxford: Clarendon Press.

2. 'The assumption of constant return to scale', Cambridge Journal of Economics, March, pp.9-17.

1990: 1. 'The unification of macro-economics', Economic Journal, June, pp.528-38.

1991: 1. The Status of Economics, Oxford: Basil Blackwell.

---

The published works of Sir John R. Hicks listed above as an Annexe is reproduced from Puttaswamaiah.K., from his three volume book "NOBEL ECONOMISTS - LIVES AND CONTRIBUTIONS" published in a set of three volumes in 1994. In this book, each chapter is devoted to each nobel laureate and at the end their contributions are listed yearwise. Similarly, in Volume 1, Chapter VII relates to Sir John Hicks, who received the Nobel Prize in 1972. In this chapter, the writings of Hicks are contained in pp.155-163. With permission, the list of writings contained at the end of the book, "SIR JOHN HICKS, THE ECONOMISTS ECONOMIST" by O.F.Hamouda is also made use of with a view to identify the discrepancies.

# PRESENTATION OF THE KANNADA VERSION OF 'VALUE AND CAPITAL' TO PROF. J.R. HICKS, AT MYSORE ON 7TH FEBRUARY 1979[*]

By way of introduction, I should like to say a few words regarding the great work in the theory of Economics by Prof. J.R. Hicks, the Nobel Laureate, which has been translated by me into Kannada. This publication is entitled "Maulya mathu Bandavala", Kannada translation of 'Value and Capital–An Inquiry into Some Fundamental Principles of Economic Theory'.

The book is published under the centrally sponsored scheme of production of books in regional languages at the university level. The scheme has been put into operation by the Government of India in the Ministry of Education, Department of Culture, New Delhi.

The Nobel Prize for the year 1972 was awarded to Sir. John Hicks. He had long ago emerged as a leading Oxford Economist. He was among those responsible for the resuscitation and refinement of indifference curve analysis and for the assimilation of the general equilibrium approach into economic theory. He made notable contribution to welfare economics, to consumer's surplus, to marginal productivity theory, to the classification of innovations and to growth theory. His latest studies include monetary theory and the theory of business cycles. His book "A Theory of Economic History" is a path-breaking effort to establish a logical sequence in the development of economic institutions. His work on the theory of the trade cycle has been regarded as a major contribution, described as "a beautiful theory of the cycle built up with an admirable economy of means, undoubtedly a *tour de force.*"

The famous "Hicks-Hansen" effect in interest theory is an acknowledged improvement in the Keynesian framework. The symptoms of an ailing economy are recognised as inflation, balance of payments deficits and a variety of monetary and exchange disorders. Macro-economic

---

[*]'Introduction' by Puttaswamaiah, K., Translator of *"Value and Capital"* when Kannada version was presented to Sir John Hicks.

texts and textures have led to the recomposition of the Keynesian system into sub-models. In such a conditional equilibrium the interest rate equates the demand and supply of money and clears the markets for other assets.

By his profound contribution in the field of economic theory, Professor Hicks may be said to have joined the ranks of immortals like the earlier economists Marshall and Keynes. He has a flavour of his own. His style and idiom and diction are quite uncommon among economists and this poses a challenge to the translator and interpreter in a foreign language.

Among his various books, there stands out in unity a trilogy, namely Capital and Value, Capital and Growth. Capital and Time, all of which constitute a most exhaustive study of all phases and avatars of capital as well as time. What has Karl Marx, another famous "capitalist" to say for it?

The translator who willy nilly also becomes an expounder or interpreter has a wonderfully exciting time of it. But the play of the author's mind on all the economic problems and issues, his engaging, limpid style, his unfailing charm and persuasive manner to let you into the treasures of his mind. For the translator these are like virtue being its own reward and what more does a translator want?

Having undertaken this onerous as well as exciting task of turning an English Hicks into a Kannada Hicks, I conceived my work at two levels; the first was easy enough, for I had been a Hicks follower from my undergraduate days when Professor D'souza, subsequently the Vicechancellor of the University, created a taste in me for Hicksian economics as well as Hicksian style. I have been an ardent follower of Prof. Hicks through all his books and journal contributions. My admiration for my guru, Hicks, (guru is Kannada for teacher) eventually spread also to Dr. Ursula Hicks whose devotee I became simply on the grounds that I could find some more of the Hicksian magic and I did. We are very glad to welcome her and we assure her that her writings in public finance and related subjects are much appreciated and have enabled us to improve our performance in various walks of life.

In the Preface to *Value and Capital*, after surveying the work done by his colleagues and contemporaries, Sir John says, "The one debt that I have to acknowledge which runs all through is that to my wife." He goes on to say, "She was a member of the group from which these ideas came. My '*Value and Capital*' has profited most from her 'Finance of British Government' but there is no part which has not profited from her never ending advice that the place of economic theory is to be the servant of applied economics." Personally I make bold to say that all this wholesome talk is not lost on the gracious "Economic Eves" who are present here. Usually, a professor's wife gets off with the generous tribute "But for whose silence, this book could never have been written."

When I was invited to accept the high honour of rendering into Kannada Professor Hick's monumental work on 'Value and Capital' I felt elated and slightly giddy. I said to myself, was I, Puttaswamaiah rising all at once from the level of a pedestrian economist, no doubt with an excellent academic record, now raising myself somewhere nearer the level of the Gods? There shot into my memory a quotation from Prof. Hicks which I had treasured. Comparing poets and economists, he said, "Poets, in the words of Shelley are the unacknowledged legislators of the world." Then pointing to himself he said, "how easy it is for economists to fall into the same delusion! That they do on occasion influence events is not to be denied". For himself his modesty would not permit him to take full credit for the role he has played in the development of economic thought and philosophy.

When I set forth on my adventurous journey of a translator of 'Value and Capital' which had already become a classic I found that on the theory side I could feel confident and I was well-versed already with all the abracadabra of equilibrium which is never there despite all the mathematical aids for model building.

When I summoned my assets as an over-ambitious translator I found at first that I had bitten off more than I could chew. Economic theory is hard going but thanks to my Professors I was able to feel myself at home but as translator I felt I got myself into a frightful mess. On the first night sitting in my attic I toiled putting down all the technical jargons in passable Karnataka language without doing violence to such grammar, lexicography and linguistics that I could muster.

Professor Baumol, a discerning critic says, "On re-reading the works of Professor Hicks one cannot help being struck by the extent to which his ideas have been absorbed by the current literature. Almost as soon as his works appear their contents become standard pieces of economic analysis whose source it is almost unnecessary to acknowledge". In every field in which he has worked the Hicksian contribution, he says, "has almost always become a pivotal element in the literature, and has often led to a major redirection of research in the area." As a translator-economist what was I up against!

The book has been presented already to Sir John Hicks in seven languages–so that we now have a French Hicks, an Italian Hicks, a Japanese Hicks, a Spanish Hicks, a Polish Hicks, a Urdu Hicks, a Hindi Hicks and last but not at all the least a Karnataka Hicks. We understand that a Hungarian Hicks is on the way. We have been a little slow in the race. We will be more aware next time.

The Director of the Institute of Kannada Studies and the Vice-Chancellor are responsible for making this assembly possible. I am indeed very grateful to them. I am grateful to Dr. V.K.R.V. Rao, the Chairman of the Institute for Social and Economic Change for his speech on this occasion.

Prof. D'souza who is presenting the Kannada version of the 'Value and Capital' to Prof. Hicks, in spite of his pre-occupations, has made it possible to be with us. It is difficult for me, as it has been for many a student of Prof. D'souza to sum up what we have acquired from this great teacher and architect of youthful minds and their careers. He made economics, our special subject for Hons. and for M.A., an instrument for the development of our higher faculties, a stimulus and impulse for growth, a striving after excellence and reaching out or at least attempting to do so, reaching out to the skies.

His philosophy of Buru-Sishya relationship comprehends a large number of aims and ambitions. If sometimes we found the discipline, hard going, which we never expressed in words but a few judicious, well placed yawns, yes, I must not forget Rome was not built in a day. Next day he would wary his counsel thus: Michelangelo, the greatest sculpture of antiquity used to tell his pupils—"look here you fellows, remember the more the marble wastes, the better the statue grows."

His interest in his students is life-long and that is why we wish him long life. We salute our Guru and for having blessed me on this great event in my life.

I am grateful to the Vice-Chancellor, D.V. Urs for the keen interest he took in organising this function. My gratitude is permanently carved in my heart to Prof. John Hicks, the Nobel Laureate, and to Prof. Ursula Hicks for their gracious presence in this auspicious occasion.

# INDEX

[336]

342

344

# CONTRIBUTORS

PAUL A. SAMUELSON

Institute Professor Emeritus, Department of Economics, Massachusetts Institute of Technology, Cambridge, Massachusetts, LTCB Visiting Professor of Political Economy, Japan-U.S. Center, Stern School of Business, New York University, New York, U.S.A.


COLIN SIMKIN

Emeritus Professor, University of Sydney, New South Wales. Australia.


O.F. HAMOUDA

Associate Professor of Economics, Department of Economics, Glendon College, York University, Ontario, Canada.


MICHIO MORISHIMA

Sir John Hicks Professor of Economics, London School of Economics and Political Science, London, U.K.


SYED AHMAD

McMaster University, Hamilton, Ontario, Canada.


FRANK HAHN

Churchill College, Cambridge, United Kingdom.


HARALD HAGEMANN

Institut fur Volkswirtschaftslehre, Universitat Hohenheim, Stuttgart, Germany.

[345]

JOSEPH HALEVI

Department of Economics, University of Sydney, Australia.


J.W. NEVILE

Department of Economics, School of Economics, The University of New South Wales, Sydney, Australia.


B.B. PRICE

Professor, Department of History, Glendon College, York University, Toronto, Ontario, Canada.


CARLO BENETTI

Sciences Economiques, Universite Paris, Nanterre Cedex, France.


KUNIBERT RAFFER

Department of Economics, University of Vienna, Vienna, Austria.


MAURO BARANZINI

Professor of Political Economy, University of Southern Switzerland and City of Cambridge, Bellinzona, Switzerland.


MICHAEL ROSIER

Universite de Picardie (ERSI) and CAESAR, Nogent Sur Marne, France.


CHRISTIAN TUTIN

Universite Paris – I, Pantheon-Sorbonne (Matis) and CAESAR, Paris, France

JEAN LUC GAFFARD

Professor de Sciences Economiques, Universiti de Nice-Sophia Antipolis, Valbonne.


MARIO AMENDOLA

University of Roma


LIONELLO F. PUNZO

University of Sienna


KEITH GRIFFIN

Department of Economics, University of California, River Side, U.S.A.


SURAGIT SINHA

Assistant Professor, Department of HSS, IIT Kanpur, Kanpur, India.


R.S. DHANANJAYAN

Professor of Economics, Bharathiar University, Coimbatore, Tamil Nadu, India.


N. SASIKALA DEVI

Lecturer in Economics, Guruvayurappan Institute of Management, Coimbatore, Tamil Nadu, India.


AXEL LEIJONHUFVUD

Professor, Department of Economics, UCLA, Los Angels, U.S.A.

Printed in the United States
by Baker & Taylor Publisher Services